Toronto

timeout.com/toronto

Published by Time Out Guides Ltd, a wholly owned subsidiary of Time Out Group Ltd.
Time Out and the Time Out logo are trademarks of Time Out Group Ltd.

© Time Out Group Ltd 2007
Previous editions 2003, 2005.

10 9 8 7 6 5 4 3 2 1

This edition first published in Great Britain in 2007 by Ebury Publishing
Ebury Publishing is a division of The Random House Group Ltd,
20 Vauxhall Bridge Road, London SW1V 2SA

Random House Australia Pty Limited 20 Alfred Street, Milsons Point, Sydney, New South Wales 2061, Australia
Random House New Zealand Limited 18 Poland Road, Glenfield, Auckland 10, New Zealand
Random House South Africa (Pty) Limited Isle of Houghton, Corner Boundary
Road & Carse O'Gowrie, Houghton 2198, South Africa

Random House UK Limited Reg. No. 954009

For details of distribution in the Americas, see www.timeout.com

ISBN 10: 1-84670-015-9
ISBN 13: 978184670 0156

A CIP catalogue record for this book is available from the British Library

Printed and bound by Firmengruppe APPL, aprinta druck, Wemding, Germany

The Random House Group Limited makes every effort to ensure that the papers used in our books are made from trees
that have been legally sourced from well-managed and credibly certified forests. Our paper procurement policy can be
found on www.randomhouse.co.uk.

Time Out Guides Limited
Universal House
251 Tottenham Court Road
London W1T 7AB
Tel + 44 (0)20 7813 3000
Fax + 44 (0)20 7813 6001
Email guides@timeout.com
www.timeout.com

Editorial

Editor Paul French
Deputy Editor Hugh Graham
Consultant Editor Pamela Cuthbert
Listings Editor Paul French, Pamela Cuthbert
Proofreader Sylvia Tombesi-Walton
Indexer Anna Norman

Managing Director Peter Fiennes
Financial Director Gareth Garner
Editorial Director Ruth Jarvis
Deputy Series Editor Dominic Earle
Editorial Manager Holly Pick

Design

Art Director Scott Moore
Art Editor Pinelope Kourmouzoglou
Senior Designer Josephine Spencer
Graphic Designer Henry Elphick
Junior Graphic Designer Kei Ishimaru
Digital Imaging Simon Foster
Ad Make-up Jenni Prichard

Picture Desk

Picture Editor Jael Marschner
Deputy Picture Editor Tracey Kerrigan
Picture Researcher Helen McFarland

Advertising

Sales Director Mark Phillips
International Sales Manager Fred Durman
International Sales Consultant Ross Canadé
International Sales Executive Simon Davies
Advertising Sales (Toronto) DPS Media
Advertising Assistant Kate Staddon

Marketing

Group Marketing Director John Luck
Marketing Manager Yvonne Poon
Sales and Marketing Director North America Lisa Levinson

Production

Group Production Director Mark Lamond
Production Manager Brendan McKeown
Production Coordinator Caroline Bradford

Time Out Group

Chairman Tony Elliott
Financial Director Richard Waterlow
Time Out Magazine Ltd MD David Pepper
Group General Manager/Director Nichola Coulthard
Time Out Communications Ltd MD David Pepper
Time Out International MD Cathy Runciman
Group Art Director John Oakey
Group IT Director Simon Chappell

Contributors

Introduction Paul French. **History** Hugh Graham (*Big ideas*, '*Death or Canada*' Paul French). **Toronto Today** Paul French. **Architecture** Paul French. **Literary Toronto** Paul French. **Where to Stay** Pamela Cuthbert (*Get on your glad rags* Paul French). **Sightseeing Introduction** Ruth Jarvis. **Downtown** Kim Gertler; Brent Ledger. **Midtown** Kim Gertler. **West End** Paul French. **North Toronto** Kim Gertler. **East Toronto** Paul French. **Restaurants & Cafés** Pamela Cuthbert. **Bars** Nathalie Atkinson; Paul French. **Shops & Services** Nathalie Atkinson; Pamela Cuthbert. **Festivals & Events** Paul French. **Children** Denis Seguin. **Comedy** Andrew Clark. **Film** Pamela Cuthbert. **Galleries** Paul French; Catherine Osborne. **Gay & Lesbian** Brent Ledger. **Music** Kerry Doole (*The curtain rises* Paul French). **Nightlife** Paul French; Li Robbins. **Sports & Fitness** Perry Stern (*A new game in town* Paul French). **Theatre & Dance** Kamal Al-Solaylee; Paul French. **Trips Out of Town: Getting Started** Steve Veale. **Niagara Falls & Around** Betty Zyvatkauskas; Pamela Cuthbert (*Over the edge* Jan Fuscoe). **Directory** Annette Bourdeau.

Maps JS Graphics (john@jsgraphics.co.uk). Map on page 280 reprinted by kind permission of TTC.

Photography Alys Tomlinson, except: page 12 MEPL; page 25 Getty Images; page 167 Carlos & Jason Sanchez; page 171 Reuters; page 180 Jeff Vespa/Wire Image; page 182 Toronto Special Events; page 212 NBAE/Getty Images; page 219 Hannah Levy; page 225 Scott Gilchrist/Masterfile; page 227 B. Redman/Tourism Niagara; page 229 Tourism Niagara.

The following images were provided by the featured establishments/artists: pages 18, 33, 141, 172, 211, 215, 230, 235, 241.

The Editor would like to thank Bill Bobek, Marilyn Bolton, Betsy Foster, Bruce Hutchinson, Robert Kearns, Erica Kelly, Jim Labumbard, Nisha Lewis, Roberto Martella, Emily McInnes, Christine Pearson, Jumol Royes, Lynley Swain, Sousie Tsotskos, Christina Vlahos, Christina Zeidler and all contributors to previous editions of *Time Out Toronto*, whose work forms the basis for parts of this book.

Contents

Introduction

For a big city, Toronto is an easy place to get to know. Travellers say they feel at home here, and that's because it's a homely place. Not that the people are overbearingly friendly; they're not (they are accommodating and famously polite, but seem to have inherited a hint of English reserve). It's more the scale of the place that you can warm to – big enough to be interesting, but not so big that you feel lost or intimidated. Even on a cold winter's day, it can feel welcoming; the blue skies take the edge off the seasonal blahs, and coming in from a snowstorm, the restaurants, bars and shops feel cosy. That said, the city is arguably at its best in the other three seasons: in spring the midtown streets suddenly become forests; in summer the patio bars and waterfront come alive; in autumn the leaves change colour and the air is clean and crisp.

Whatever season you come, don't expect non-stop tourist attractions. Instead, slow down and stroll through the neighbourhoods, soaking up the different cultures that make their mark on Toronto. Kensington Market is a good place to start: this bustling, bohemian neighbourhood is where successive waves of new Canadians have forged their way and given colour to the cityscape. The Annex, Chinatown, Greektown, Cabbagetown, the Beach and Yorkville are other characterful districts that are worth a ramble. For inconspicuous consumption, veer away from the mainstream towards Toronto's quirkier streets – West Queen West, the Danforth, College Street – where individuality comes across in unique shops and places to eat. To get away from it all, explore the city's wilder side in the many green oases and beaches. Or take in a festival – it seems the city can't let a month go by without throwing one, many of them among the world's best.

Sure, there are a few key tourist sights – some visitors aren't happy until they get to the top of the CN Tower; Niagara Falls is a must – but traditional sightseeing is not a forte. The city realises it's got to beef up its attractions, and many of the cultural venues are in the process of getting ambitious makeovers. A slew of star architects – Frank Gehry, Daniel Libeskind, Will Alsop and Norman Foster among them – are adding some dazzle to what has traditionally been a visually underwhelming destination.

Canadians are famously modest, self-deprecating even, but in Toronto lately there's a sense of strut and swagger in its residents. Instead of looking enviously south of the border or across the pond, they are starting to realise that Toronto is an excellent city in its own right. Now the rest of the world is finally catching on.

ABOUT TIME OUT CITY GUIDES

Time Out Toronto is one of an expanding series of travel guides produced by the people behind London and New York's successful listings magazines. Our guides are all written and updated by resident experts who have striven to provide you with all the most up-to-date information you'll need to explore the city, whether you're a local or first-time visitor.

THE LOWDOWN ON THE LISTINGS

Above all, we've tried to make this book as useful as possible. Websites, telephone numbers, transport information, opening times, admission prices and credit card details are all included in our listings. And, as far as possible, we've given details of facilities, services and events, all checked and correct at the time we went to press. However, owners and managers can change their arrangements at any time.

Before you go out of your way, we'd strongly advise you to call and check opening times, dates of exhibitions and other particulars. While every effort has been made to ensure the accuracy of the information contained in this guide, the publishers cannot accept responsibility for any errors it may contain.

PRICES AND PAYMENT

We have noted whether venues such as shops, hotels and restaurants accept credit cards or not but have only listed the major cards – American Express (**AmEx**), Diners Club (**DC**), MasterCard (**MC**) and Visa (**V**). Many businesses will also accept other cards, including Switch/Maestro or Delta, JCB, Discover and Carte Blanche. Virtually all shops, restaurants and sights will accept travellers' cheques issued by a major financial institution (such as American Express).

The prices we've supplied should be treated as guidelines, not gospel. Fluctuating exchange rates and inflation can cause charges, in shops and restaurants particularly, to change rapidly. If prices vary wildly from those we've quoted, ask whether there's a good reason. If not, go elsewhere. Then please write and let us know. We aim to give the best and most up-to-date advice, so we always want to know if you've been badly treated or overcharged.

THE LIE OF THE LAND

Toronto's geography is easy to grasp. To make it even easier, we have divided the city into areas based on local usage, but as there are no formal boundaries we have occasionally used arbitrary divisions. These areas are defined in our Sightseeing chapters and used throughout the book, both in addresses and chapter subdivisions. We've included cross streets in our addresses, so you can find your way about more easily.

These areas are also shown on the Toronto Transport & Areas map on page 279. The street maps start on page 265; on them are pinpointed the location of hotels (**❶**), restaurants (**❶**) and bars (**❶**) featured elsewhere in this guide. There is also a Subway map; *see p280.*

TELEPHONE NUMBERS

Greater Toronto has three area codes: 416, 905 and 647, 416 being the most central. To dial from anywhere within the city to anywhere else,

even within the same area code, you need to dial the code followed by the seven-digit number. To dial long-distance numbers, precede the area code with 1 (note that some 905 numbers are long distance). Numbers preceded by 1-800, 1-888, 1-877 and 1-866 can be called free of charge from Toronto (and usually the rest of Canada and the US) but incur an international charge from abroad.

Canada shares the US's international code of 1 (so calling from the US is the same as making a long-distance national call), followed by 1 and then the area code and number.

For more details of phone codes and charges, *see p256.*

ESSENTIAL INFORMATION

For all the practical information you might need – including visa and customs information, disabled access, emergency telephone numbers, websites and the lowdown on local transport – turn to the Directory chapter at the back of this guide; *see p245.*

MAPS

There's a series of fully indexed street maps, along with Southern Ontario and Toronto Overview maps, at the back of the guide, starting on page 265. Venues listed in the book that fall into the area covered have a page and grid reference to take you directly to the right square.

LET US KNOW WHAT YOU THINK

We hope you enjoy *Time Out Toronto*, and we'd like to know what you think of it. We welcome tips for places that you consider we should include in future editions and take notice of your criticism of our choices. You can email us on guides@timeout.com.

There is an online version of this book, along with guides to over 100 international cities, at **www.timeout.com**.

Amsterdam

Time Out
Travel Guides

Worldwide

All our guides are
written by a team of
local experts with a
unique and stylish
insider perspective.
We offer essential tips,
trusted advice and
honest reviews for
everything you need
to know in the city.

Over 50 destinations
available at all good
bookshops and at
timeout.com/shop

Time Out Guides

Brussels

Croatia

Istanbul

Marrakech

Paris

Athens

Bangkok

Barcelona

Beijing

Berlin

Boston

Budapest

Buenos Aires

California

Cape Town

Chicago

Copenhagen

Dubai

Dublin

Edinburgh

Florence

Havana

Hong Kong

Las Vegas

Lisbon

London

Los Angeles

Madrid

Mallorca

Miami

Milan

Mumbai & Goa

Naples

New Orleans

New York

Patagonia

Prague

Rio de Janeiro

Rome

San Francisco

Seville & Andalu...

Shanghai

Singapore

South of France

Stockholm

Sydney

Tokyo 東京

Toronto

Turin

Vancouver

Venice

Vienna

Washington, DC

Amsterdam

Athens

Bangkok

Barcelona

Beijing

Berlin

Boston

Brussels

Budapest

Buenos Aires

California

Cape Town

Chicago

Copenhagen

Croatia

Dubai

Dublin

Edinburgh

Florence

Havana

Hong Kong

Istanbul

Las Vegas

Lisbon

London

Los Angeles

Madrid

Mallorca

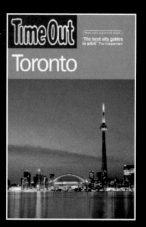

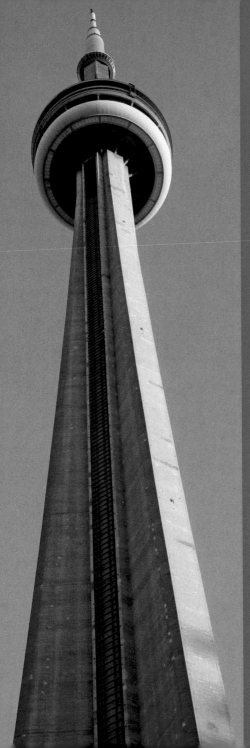

In Context

History

From backwoods to boom town, the rise and rise of Toronto.

Toronto may be considered part of the 'New World', but people have lived in this part of southern Ontario since the last Ice Age 13,000 years ago. Hunters roamed the icy wilderness pursuing mammoths, mastodons and caribou with their stone-tipped spears. By 1,000 BC, a warming climate brought vegetation and settlement to the area. Nomadic types were replaced by Toronto's first settlers: the ancestors of the Iroquois, who built villages along the lake and grew crops. By the 17th century, the Huron tribe moved in and brought the first white man to Toronto in 1615...

THE FRENCH CONNECTION
... and that man was a woodsman named Etienne Brûlé, an adventurous young Frenchman sent into the wilds by Samuel Champlain, his fur-trading boss in New France (Quebec), to befriend the Indians. Facing frequent attacks from the fierce Iroquois, the French allied themselves to a rival tribe, the Huron, who showed Toronto to Brûlé on 9 September 1615. The earliest appearance of the name 'Toronto' on French maps dates from the 1680s. For a long time it was thought that the name derived from the Huron word 'toronton', ('place of meetings'). But recent scholars say it comes from the Mohawk word 'tkaronto', meaning 'where there are trees standing in the water', a reference to the fishing weirs that natives created by driving wooden stakes into the lake.

During the 17th and 18th centuries, French and English fur traders were engaged in a frenetic expansionist rivalry, building trading posts to gain control of the rich hunting grounds around the Great Lakes. It wasn't until 1720 that the French established a permanent trading post in Toronto on the Humber River, by which time most of the Huron tribe had died from European diseases. Over the next 40 years Toronto's population consisted of a mixture of Mississauga and

Iroquois Indians, Jesuit missionaries and French fur traders who exchanged trinkets with the natives in return for pelts. To consolidate their supremacy, the French built Fort Rouillé (also known as Fort Toronto) in 1751, now the site of the Canadian National Exhibition. But in 1756 England and France went to war, and in 1759 the British took Toronto. Rather than surrender their fort, the French burned it to the ground in retreat.

While the 1763 Treaty of Paris brought an end to French rule in Toronto, the British took little interest in their new possession, leaving it undisturbed for 30 years. But when Britain lost the American Revolution in 1783, the city suddenly assumed strategic importance.

RULE BRITANNIA

After the American Revolution, thousands of United Empire loyalists fled the US to settle in British North America. To handle the massive influx, the British government created a new province in 1791: Upper Canada, to the west of Quebec, which was to have English systems of law, land tenure and politics.

The British appointed John Graves Simcoe, a decorated soldier who had fought in the American Revolution, as the province's lieutenant-governor. His mission was to carve a capital out of the wilderness, and Toronto seemed perfect from a military and naval standpoint. It had a sheltered harbour and a good 20-mile stretch of water separating it from the US. Not only that, but Lord Dorchester, the governor of British North America, had already purchased the site from the Mississauga Indians in 1787 to secure the area for British trappers. For the mighty sum of £1,700, the British gained a portion of land 22 kilometres (14 miles) across and 45 kilometres (28 miles) deep.

On 30 July 1793 Simcoe arrived from England – after a stint at Niagara – in the forest that was Toronto, with his wife Elizabeth, who fell in love with her new surroundings. One of his first acts was to change Toronto's name to York, in honour of Frederick, Duke of York, a son of King George III. Simcoe, after all, was on a mission to bring English civilisation to the New World. Moreover, he professed an 'abhorrence of Indian names'.

Next Simcoe ordered his regiment, the Queen's Rangers, to build a garrison, Fort York, to protect the settlement from a possible American invasion. He also had his men survey Yonge Street, which replaced the Indian trails to the Upper Great Lakes. Named after the then British war secretary, Sir George Yonge, the street would eventually become the world's longest, starting at the lake shore and running

1,896 kilometres (1,178 miles) to the north-west, ending at Rainy River, Minnesota. Yonge Street facilitated fur trade and allowed farmers a route to bring their goods to market. Other roads were also being laid – an orderly, ten-block grid including King, Front, George, Adelaide and Berkeley Streets – which attracted merchants and craftsmen to the area. But Simcoe's main interest in Yonge Street was strategic: it could be an escape route from marauding Americans.

'Toronto's first colonial residents shared their streets with wolves, bears and deer.'

Simcoe also ordered the construction of the first parliament buildings, which were erected in 1796. To placate grumpy colonial officials, resentful of being transferred to this marshy outpost, he granted them a series of free 100-acre 'park' lots north of Queen Street. The roads that ran between these farms were often given family names, including Finch, Sheppard, Lawrence and Eglinton. This system of land concessions resulted in Toronto's rectangular, evenly spaced layout. Despite Simcoe's generosity, the new residents were disparaging of the town, referring to it as 'Muddy York' because of its notoriously squishy streets. They were, after all, essentially living in the wilderness: packs of wolves were killing farmers' sheep, bears were attacking horses, and deer were commonly seen on the streets.

DAMN YANKEES

By 1812 York was positively civilised: it had a tailor, a baker, a brewer, a watchmaker and an apothecary to serve the population of 700. The ruling elite erected dignified mansions along King Street, and a British-style landed gentry was firmly taking shape. York's leaders were all Church of England Tories, and fiercely loyalist – they were horrified by American notions of democracy. And this anti-American sentiment was about to intensify.

On 18 June 1812 America declared war on Britain. Former president Thomas Jefferson had said that 'the capture of Canada is a mere matter of marching'. President James Madison wanted to establish a trade monopoly on all North America's natural resources. Americans were also furious at the devious British practices of kidnapping their sailors at sea and supplying arms and encouragement to hostile Indian tribes.

Within a year of declaring war, York's worst nightmare – an American invasion – became a grim reality. In April 1813, 14 ships carrying

Home sweet home office: William Lyon Mackenzie's notorious printing press. *See p15.*

1,700 American troops invaded the town, and succeeded in blowing up Fort York and burning the parliament buildings to the ground. But although Americans won the Battle of York, the US army suffered devastating losses and failed to take the rest of Canada (one of the prouder moments in the country's history). By 1814 the British had negotiated an end to the war.

BLUE BLOOD VERSUS NEW BLOOD

In retaliation for the burning of Fort York, a group of angry local soldiers stormed Washington, DC, in 1814 and set fire to the president's residence. (It was painted white soon after to cover up the charred wood, and subsequently became known as the White House.) American immigrants, who had previously been welcome additions to the town, were now banned by York's staunchly British, aristocratic leaders. Indeed, York's ruling political regime, composed mainly of lawyers, doctors, judges and Church officials, was so tight-knit, and prone to intermarriage, that it became known as the Family Compact. This elite group's stranglehold on politics would come to be resented as the population grew.

And grow the population did. In Britain the demobilisation of 400,000 soldiers following the Napoleonic Wars, coupled with a depression and the mass evictions of Scottish crofters, prompted a huge exodus to Canada. In the 20 years following the war, York's population increased from 700 to 9,250.

The old guard suffered a blow in 1834, the year the town became incorporated as a city, when a bill to readopt the name of Toronto was passed. Traditionalists were opposed to the move – York sounded more British.

REBELS WITH A CAUSE
Around this time, resentment at the Family Compact's political dominance reached fever pitch. Even Charles Dickens, who visited the city in 1842, was moved to comment on the city's Conservative bent. 'The wild and rabid Toryism of Toronto is, I speak seriously, appalling.' Leading the resistance was William Lyon Mackenzie, a Scottish firebrand who had been publishing anti-Tory rants in his own newspaper, the *Colonial Advocate*, since 1825.

Mackenzie called the ruling elite 'thieves', arguing that too much money, land and power was held by too few. The main target for his scorn was Bishop John Strachan, whom he dubbed 'the governor's jackal'. Mackenzie's bilious columns became such a worry for the Family Compact that Conservatives broke into his office and tipped his printing presses into the lake. But it was too late: Mackenzie had already amassed a devoted following of farmers, merchants and new immigrants, and in 1834 he was elected Toronto's first mayor.

Mackenzie hoped that a provincial election in 1836 would bring his party, the Reformers, to power in the province of Upper Canada. But the Tories won what was perceived to be a crooked election – one Conservative ploy was to offer free booze to anyone who voted for them – and Mackenzie called for rebellion.

On 5 December 1837, Mackenzie and 700 rebels gathered beyond the city, at what is now Yonge and Eglinton, outside Montgomery's Tavern. The plan was to march on Toronto, seize the 5,000 guns stored in City Hall, and capture the governor. But the sheriff, William B Jarvis, had been tipped off, and his militia crushed the rebellion. Mackenzie fled to America and lived there until 1849, when he was pardoned. He returned to Upper Canada and was elected to the Legislature, where he served until his death in 1858.

Despite the failure of the rebellion, a new era of more democratic government followed,

'Death or Canada'

On the multi-culti streets of Toronto, the city's immigrants have plenty of tales to tell, from hard-luck stories to rags-to-riches fairytales. The Irish always like a good yarn, but sadly, their story was not a cheerful one. Fleeing the potato famine, 38,000 Irish immigrants arrived in Toronto in the summer of 1847 – a gruesome episode in this city's history. Because many new arrivals carried typhus, they were housed in makeshift 'fever sheds' at the corner of King and John Streets, where more than 800 people perished from the infectious disease. Their journey had been desperate enough already: most had been turned away by the Americans when their boats sailed into New York City harbour. With few options open to them, the Irish immigrants' plight was summed up by a headline of the day in the *Limerick Reporter*. 'Death or Canada' (insert joke here).

Ireland Park, opened in 2007, pays moving tribute to those brave souls who made the journey to the New World. Located at the foot of Bathurst Street, not far from where the Irish landed, the small waterside memorial bears the names of those who died (and those who died trying to help them), etched in 300 tons of Kilkenny limestone. In addition, five gaunt figures are portrayed in bronze by Irish sculptor Rowan Gillespie, echoing his Dublin sculptures on the River Liffey quayside.

In 2006, excavation of the fever-shed site at King and John unearthed an array of artefacts from that grim period. The site is being redeveloped as the Festival Centre, home of the film festival. But the discovery of the artefacts underscored the absence of a museum that tells the history of Toronto – and the hardships its early citizens endured to make the journey here.

St James' Cathedral

ST. JAMES CATHEDRAL

k's first church was built here in

of public subscriptions

coinciding with another wave of immigration. In addition to the British influx, scores of freed black slaves arrived from America. Britain officially outlawed slavery in 1834, and by the 1850s blacks made up three per cent of the city's 25,000-strong population.

Another group found refuge in York – the Irish (*see p15* **'Death or Canada'**). They arrived in droves, particularly in the 1840s during the potato famine, and soon comprised a third of Toronto's population. Many were Catholic, which provoked sectarian tensions with Irish Protestants. Riots on July 12, the day of the Orangemen parades, became an annual occurrence.

While immigrants flooded the city, native Canadians disappeared from the area. Many died of European diseases, while some settled on nearby Indian reserves – such as the Six Nations Reserve near Brantford – that were established in treaties with the British throughout the period.

THE BIRTH OF A NATION

As immigrants poured in, Toronto made the transition from rural backwater to bustling industrial city. The construction of a north–south railway line to America in the 1850s, followed by a coast-to-coast national line in the 1880s, further cemented Toronto's prosperity. In addition to the existing industries – sawmills, flour mills, tanneries, furniture, wagons, soap processing, leather goods, brewing, publishing – the city became a centre for ship manufacture and a trading hub for timber imports and exports. Banks appeared everywhere, merchant empires were founded, railroad tycoons emerged, and the Toronto Stock Exchange was opened in 1852.

> ## 'In 1867, Canada gained independence from Britain, but Ottawa beat Toronto as the national capital.'

If it was an age of industry, it was also an age of leisure. In 1858 Toronto's freakish weather for once provided the city with a blessing: the creation of Toronto Island. Formerly a peninsula, the island was created when a storm destroyed the spit of land that joined it to the mainland. Taking a ferry across the harbour soon became a summertime tradition: holiday cottages went up, as did an amusement park, bicycle trails and the Royal Canadian Yacht Club.

In 1867 Canada gained independence from Britain, and Toronto was named the capital of the new province of Ontario. An accolade, sure,

but competition was hardly stiff, and locals were (and remain) more than miffed that Queen Victoria, apparently on the basis of a few paintings she'd seen, favoured Ottawa as the national capital. However, as a small compensation, Toronto finally got some decent shopping. In 1869, a young Irishman named Timothy Eaton opened a general store at the corner of Yonge and Queen. His new shop offered a revolutionary and exciting sales technique: satisfaction guaranteed or your money back. The successful shop quickly evolved into a bona fide department store, spawning a mail-order catalogue that eventually reached all corners of Canada.

During this prosperous Victorian era, Toronto's architecture also became downright glamorous. The opening of the University of Toronto in 1843 was significant for more than just academic reasons: it yielded some of the city's most ornate buildings, most notably the spectacular Romanesque University College (King's College Circle, 1856). Throughout the city, the dignified colonial town of plain Georgian buildings gave way to a new craze for neo-Gothic. Jarvis and St George streets and the neighbourhood of Rosedale became hotbeds of Romanticism in a flurry of gargoyles and turrets. The American author John Updike called these buildings 'lovingly erected brick valentines to a distant dowager queen'. Surviving examples include the Keg Mansion (515 Jarvis Street), the Flatiron building (49 Wellington Street East, 1892), the York Club (135 St George Street, 1892), the Ontario Legislature at Queen's Park (1892) and the Old City Hall (1888-99).

Some of the most striking buildings of the period were Gothic churches, such as St James' Cathedral (65 Church Street, 1850). The city's preponderance of spires, coupled with its puritanical mores, soon earned it the sobriquet 'Toronto the Good'. Anti-vice laws at various times in the city's history would include a ban on alcohol between 1916 and 1927, and Sunday bans on just about everything. Department stores drew curtains across their windows on Sundays, and public houses were closed on the Sabbath until 1971. Leopold Infeld, Einstein's collaborator, famously said that he hoped he would die on a Saturday, 'so that I won't have to spend another Sunday in Toronto' (the ban on Sunday shopping was only lifted in 1992).

The city's prissy outlook was coupled with a continued devotion to Queen and country. The Queen's Jubilee was celebrated in spectacular style in 1897, and on 25 October 1899 a massive parade sent off thousands of Toronto troops to fight in the Boer War, in a frenzy of Union Jacks and weeping mothers.

Big ideas

'Eureka' moments from Toronto's inventive past

● Though Thomas Edison is widely regarded as the inventor of the electric light bulb, Henry Woodward of Toronto should take some credit, as he sold a share in his patent to Edison, who went on to design a more practical version in 1879.

● In nearby Brantford, Ontario, Alexander Graham Bell first outlined the scientific principle that would convey the human voice over wires in 1874, two years before 'inventing' the telephone in Boston. Later that year, Bell made the first long-distance telephone call from his home in Brantford to Paris, Ontario.

● The discovery of the pancreatic hormone insulin by scientists Frederick Banting and Charles Best at the University of Toronto in 1921 is the most famous Canadian medical achievement. Insulin remains the only effective treatment for diabetes.

● Edward Rogers Sr invented the world's first alternating-current (AC) radio tube in 1925, which enabled radios to be powered by ordinary household current. The revolutionary 'battery-less' radio was the key factor in allowing the medium to go mainstream.

● Toronto scientists James Till and Ernest McCulloch first proved the existence of stem cells in the early 1960s, paving the way for research into cloning.

● With time on their hands, two journalists, Scott Abbott and Chris Haney invented Trivial Pursuit in 1981. The board game went on to sell more than 90 million copies in 17 languages.

● MAC Cosmetics, one of the world's most popular brands of make-up, was founded by Torontonians in the 1980s.

● The IMAX cinema was invented in Toronto, where the IMAX company is based. The world's first permanent IMAX cinema, opened in 1971, is located at Ontario Place.

● Film firsts: Toronto had the world's first multiplex cinema, opened in 1979. The 18-screen Cineplex Odeon Centre, now closed, was located in the Eaton Centre.

● The Canadian Opera Company invented 'surtitles', projecting the (often) translated text of an opera on a screen above the stage, and it licenses the technology to opera companies around the world.

● SkyDome (now Rogers Centre) was the world's first stadium with a retractable roof when it opened in 1989.

● The world's first fully electronic toll highway, Highway 407, opened in 1997. A camera records license plates or a radio signal detects vehicles with attached transponders; a bill is sent in the post.

● Research in Motion, based in nearby Waterloo, Ontario, invented the Blackberry, the wireless hand-held device, in 1999. The number of subscribers to this addictive piece of technology rose from two million in November 2004 to eight million by 200.

20TH-CENTURY BLUES

If the 19th century ended in a surge of imperial fervour, then Toronto's 20th century started with a blaze of a different kind. On 19 April 1904, fire broke out at a downtown tie factory on Wellington Street West, and within eight hours, 122 buildings and 20 acres of downtown had been destroyed.

While the Great Fire devastated the city on one level – 6,000 people lost their jobs and the business district was destroyed – Toronto bounced back quickly. How could it not, with the wave of immigrants flooding in? In 1894 the population was 168,000; by 1924 it had risen to 542,000, and by 1934 it was 640,000. And they weren't all British. Jews from Russia and Poland settled in Kensington Market and opened textile businesses around King and Spadina, the garment district; the Greeks worked on the railroads and made the Danforth their home. By 1921, more than 8,200 Torontonians were of Italian ancestry, many of whom built roads and bridges. The Chinese settled around Dundas Street West, opening laundries and restaurants.

'Seventy thousand Toronto men fought in World War I; 13,000 died.'

The New World wasn't all bliss. Many Irish labourers settled in Cabbagetown, an area in the east of the city named after the vegetables they grew to feed themselves. Toronto writer Hugh Garner described Cabbagetown – now a gentrified neighbourhood – as 'North America's only Anglo-Saxon slum'.

THE GREAT WAR

As is often perversely the case, war – in this case World War I – brought renewed prosperity to the city, not to mention another bout of imperial zeal. Citizens sang 'Rule Britannia' in the streets, and thousands of volunteers poured into armouries. Seventy thousand men – one seventh of the city's population – left Toronto for Europe; 13,000 died.

The city played a major role in Britain's war effort, serving as a training ground for pilots. Toronto companies manufactured aeroplanes, including the famous Flying Jennies, and explosives and munitions. Jewish textile firms made blankets, tents and uniforms. Women went to work in large numbers, in weapons factories and as volunteer Red Cross nurses. In fact, a young Amelia Earhart was a nurse in Toronto during the war, and it was here, while watching pilots at Armour Heights, that she caught the flying bug.

THE ROARING '20S

The end of the war was followed by a mini economic slump, but by 1925 Toronto was roaring, spurred along by the age of the automobile. American firms such as General Motors and Ford set up plants in and around the city to avoid a 35 per cent Canadian tariff on car imports. Not everyone was driving around in Buicks, however: the Toronto Transit Commission was founded in 1921, after the public voted to establish a publicly owned and operated mass transport system. Soon 575 electric streetcars cruised the streets.

The city was also reaping the benefits of a mining boom in Northern Ontario, triggered by the discovery there of gold, copper, nickel and silver. The price of wheat on the international market also rocketed during this period, which meant that the agricultural machinery plants of Massey-Harris flourished.

Such a wealthy city required a spectacular hotel, and in 1929 the Royal York, with its 1,600 rooms, running water and ballroom, opened. The largest hotel in the British Empire, it was built by the Canadian Pacific Railway for easy access to the similarly magnificent Union Station (1927), a Beaux Arts gem that epitomised the grandeur of the railway age. Wealth provided riches for culture seekers, who flocked to the Art Gallery of Ontario to see the striking landscape paintings of the Group of Seven, Canada's most famous painters, or view Egyptian mummies at the Royal Ontario Museum. Performers such as Al Jolson entertained the masses at the Royal Alexandra Theatre, and hometown girl Mary Pickford, the world's biggest silent-movie star, drew the hordes to Shea's Hippodrome.

THE DIRTY '30S

The good times came to an end with the stock-market crash of 1929, and by the time the Great Depression hit in 1932, there was 30 per cent unemployment in the city. Queues formed around the block for soup kitchens. Poverty lead to bigotry, with signs that read 'No Jews, Niggers or Dogs' appearing on beaches. The scorching summer of 1936 compounded the misery, with temperatures reaching 41° C (106° F), coinciding with a polio epidemic. World War II brought the city back to life. As in the previous two wars, Toronto rushed to sign up for military duty – 3,300 of its citizens would ultimately die in combat – but along with the exodus of soldiers, the city experienced its own European invasion: British children and Norwegian men. Eight thousand young Britons were shipped to Toronto to sit out the war safely, while Norway sent its airforce to the city for training. Once again the city functioned as an aviation centre, with local companies manufacturing around 3,000 airplanes, including the Mosquito bombers that some experts believe played a large part in winning the air war. And once again, women took up work in the factories, producing 100,000 machine guns. And in the tunnels of Casa Loma – the city's most eccentric architectural folly – anti-submarine weapons were developed.

'In 1920, 80 per cent of the population was of British origin. By 1960 only 50 per cent had British roots.'

Behind this industriousness lay a continued fierce loyalty to the Mother Country, which helped Canadian citizens endure rationing on alcohol, sugar, meat and tea, and frequent 'dim-outs'. In 1940, when the Toronto Squadron was shot down in the skies above London, the Toronto Symphony Orchestra played 'There'll Always Be an England' at Massey Hall.

BOOMTOWN STATS
Toronto's white-bread, Little England persona was about to receive a makeover. In 1920, 80 per cent of the city's population was of British origin. By 1960 only 50 per cent of the population could make that claim, and by the '90s, well, the UN had declared Toronto the most multicultural city on earth – Toronto had more Italians than Florence, more blacks than Kingston, Jamaica, and more Chinese than any other city in the world outside China. After the war, Canada relaxed its immigration laws, and it seemed the world came to Toronto. Russians, Yugoslavs, Poles, Hungarians and other many other Eastern Europeans poured into the city, as did Portuguese, Greeks and West Indians, followed later by further waves of immigration from India, Africa, Central and South America and Asia.

By 1953 the population of the Toronto urban area had mushroomed to 1.2 million. Disputes between the city and the suburbs were growing frequent, so a new, overarching city government was formed: the Municipality of Metropolitan Toronto, which would be comprised of the city of Toronto, plus five suburban boroughs, each with its own mayor. This new government would be responsible for major infrastructure, while the individual municipalities would still retain control over local matters. The mayor of this new super-city, Fred Gardiner, had grand visions of a great North American metropolis with major highways running through it: the first, the monstrous Gardiner Expressway,

was laid down during the '50s along the lake shore, effectively cutting off the city from the lake. The 401, a mega-highway to the north of the city, followed soon after, as did malls, and utopian, post-war suburbs, perfect for raising baby-boomers. Don Mills, built in 1952, was a modernist's dream, designed to be a self-contained suburb where the car was king. This was followed in 1964 by Yorkdale, the first giant mall in North America, in the northern suburbs.

In the city centre, developers started ripping down old Victorian and Edwardian buildings – which were seen as fading relics of colonial Toronto and the Depression – and replacing them with high-rise apartment buildings and office blocks. Between 1955 and 1975, 28,000 buildings were torn down in the city. A large post-war public-housing complex called Regent Park provided a low-density park setting for the city's underclasses. But, shielded from the streets, its inner courtyards proved a haven for criminals and the drug trade, and in 2006 the site was razed, paving the way for a 21st-century experiment in housing the poor.

THE MODERN ERA
Though the wrecking ball wreaked havoc on the city, it didn't destroy everything. Many handsome, centrally located neighbourhoods – the Annex, Rosedale and Forest Hill – survived intact. And much of the change was positive: the first subway line, consisting of 12 stations and running for 12 kilometres (7.4 miles) underneath Yonge Street, opened in 1954. This was followed by an east-west line under Bloor Street and Danforth Avenue.

Moreoever, this prosperous era yielded some stunning architecture. The Toronto-Dominion Centre (1964-9), a cluster of four black steel-and-glass skyscrapers, was hailed as the crowning glory of Mies van der Rohe, one of the gods of modernist architecture.

The New City Hall, built in 1965, was another modernist classic. Designed by Finnish architect Viljo Revell, this *Star Trek*-style spectacle – two semi-circular office towers surrounding a UFO-esque council chamber and adjoined by a public square – symbolised the birth of a more civic-spirited city. Other new gems included the gold Royal Bank Plaza (1976), the atrium-style Eaton Centre shopping mall (1977) and the Toronto Reference Library (1977).

But of all the new buildings, the CN Tower (1976) was the most important symbolically. The world's largest free-standing structure, this majestic television tower became Toronto's Big Ben or Empire State Building, lending the city an instantly recognisable skyline. 'As the tower

Casa Loma. *See p20*.

was being planned, Torontonians were starting to consider, with shy pleasure, the novel idea that their city might be attractive, even enviable,' wrote journalist Robert Fulford.

SWING, SWING, SWING

Along with this great wave of construction and immigration, the once-uptight city was at last outgrowing its starchy, Waspish image. In 1947, the people of Toronto voted to go 'wet', and the city's first cocktail bar, the Silver Rail, opened on Yonge Street, spawning a thriving bar culture. A British writer who returned to this relatively louche city in 1959 said 'it was like finding a Jaguar parked in front of a vicarage and the padre inside with a pitcher of vodka Martinis reading *Lolita*'.

By the 1960s Toronto was becoming positively hedonistic. Spliff-smoking flower children colonised Yorkville (Toronto's answer to Haight-Ashbury), playing acoustic music in coffee houses: Joni Mitchell, Neil Young and Leonard Cohen all played the circuit. In 1972 Toronto got a hip television station, Citytv, which showed blue movies in the wee hours. Around this time, strip joints and adult-movie theatres opened along downtown Yonge Street, as did bars frequented by Toronto's burgeoning gay community. Jarvis Street, once home to Toronto's wealthiest families, became the city's unofficial red-light district. It wasn't all salacious: amid the general buzz, the city became home to an increasing number of renowned writers, including Robertson Davies and Margaret Atwood. Then the Toronto International Film Festival made its debut in 1975, and the local government poured money into the theatre.

The thriving cultural scene attracted, and was strengthened by, Americans dodging the Vietnam War. Another anti-war protester with vision was Jane Jacobs, the famed urban planning critic, who in 1971 led a successful fight against the proposed Spadina Expressway, which would have destroyed several downtown neighbourhoods. This victory spurred a civic reform movement in the '70s that emphasised preservation of historic neighbourhoods, public transport and smart developments, including publicly funded projects designed to lure tourists: Ontario Place in 1971, and the Metro Zoo and Ontario Science Centre in 1974.

Tourists certainly discovered Toronto in the '70s, but so did architects, urban planners and journalists. The US media was impressed that the city had managed to avoid the mistakes of many a crime-ridden, dying American metropolis. *Time* magazine devoted a cover story to 'the world's newest great city', *Harper's* dubbed it 'the city that works'; and the actor Peter Ustinov called it 'New York run by the Swiss'. And the *National Geographic* announced that 'the drab stepsister of Montreal has become worldly, wealthy and relatively problem-free'. In fact, Toronto officially took over from Montreal as Canada's most populous city in 1976, when its population hit 2,303,206.

Regent Park. *See p20.*

Time marches on: the Gothic **Old City Hall** is dwarfed by modernist blocks. *See p17.*

A MATERIAL WORLD

The 'me decade' brought some glamour and decadence to the city. Yorkville, once beatnik central, became the city's most exclusive shopping district, its old Edwardian houses transformed into chi-chi boutiques and flashy bars. Formerly poor immigrant areas like Cabbagetown, Greektown and Little Italy were discovered, and gentrified, by yuppies: great for the restaurant scene, bad for house prices. The gay community colonised the Church & Wellesley district during the 1980s. As the population mushroomed – 65,000 new immigrants arrived in Toronto every year – a development boom ensued, in which modest suburban bungalows were demolished in favour of gigantic 'monster homes'. Architectural showpieces that were erected during the era included Roy Thomson Hall (the new home of the Toronto Symphony, 1982), and SkyDome (now called the Rogers Centre, 1989). Three ornate vaudeville theatres from the early 1900s were lovingly restored and reopened as commercial theatres: the Elgin, the Winter Garden and the Pantages (now the Canon). Toronto's cosmopolitan appeal attracted US film producers, who used Toronto as as a stand-in location for other big cities.

The conspicuous consumption and glam lifestyles of the 1980s continued apace in the '90s, but were accompanied by a loss of social conscience. The province elected its very own Margaret Thatcher in the form of the neo-conservative Ontario premier Mike Harris, who slashed funding for the city, resulting in a growing number of street people. Meanwhile, Harris courted the suburban vote by expanding highways and allowing urban sprawl to fester. The city's five boroughs were merged in 1998 into one massive, 'megacity' government, which removed self-rule from neighbourhoods and caused more cuts to public services. As the first mayor of the new Toronto, Mel Lastman proved inept and there were scandals in the administration.

A NEW DAY

Politicians don't solve problems in a vacuum – it takes a city's collective spirit to bring about change. Tossing out the old guard was vital. The deadly outbreak of SARS in 2003 was a wake-up call; the years of cutbacks in public services left the city vulnerable.

Now into his second term as mayor, David Miller is championing the importance of cities for the well-being of the nation as a whole. For years, the provincial and federal governments have been offloading costs on the city government while simultaneously reducing its power. Miller is pressuring them to open their chequebook and allow the city to regain control over its future.

Toronto Today

The winds of change are blowing through Toronto.

Toronto is the largest city in Canada, which gives the place a certain status but also makes it a target. Admittedly, it's an easy one: Toronto likes to draw attention to itself, and it is constantly seeking validation on the world stage (it seems that every cultural attraction, restaurant, shop and building is billed as 'world-class'). This boasting does not endear Toronto to the rest of Canada. To them, Toronto is the glutton at the table, self-involved and all-consuming. It's often the butt of jokes and general disdain. But the Greater Toronto Area (GTA) is unperturbed, a little smug even. And it can afford to be: it gets to throw its weight around as the economic powerhouse of the country. And it has the numbers on its side. As of spring 2007, the population of Greater Toronto is 5.9 million. It is home to one in six Canadians. And one quarter of the country's population dwells in the slightly larger area known as the Golden Horseshoe, which wraps around Lake Ontario from Niagara Falls to points east of the city.

If growth is any measure of success, the GTA certainly has a lot going for it. Another one million residents will arrive in the city over the course of the next generation. But size isn't everything: other measures cast Toronto in a favourable light as it approaches its 175th birthday in 2009. Crime is tame compared with American cities of similar size. More people are killed by cars (75 pedestrians a year, on average) than by gunfire. Indeed, the stereotypical image of being a clean and safe place sure beats the alternative. And Toronto has put the SARS debacle behind it; after the airborne terror struck in 2003, the world stopped coming. Now, as visitors start returning, Toronto is a wiser, more mature city.

Despite its relative safety and cleanliness, Toronto has cast off the sterile quality that characterised it for much of the 20th century. These days, it is famous for its polyglot composition, with 100 established foreign-tongued communities. True, as far as race relations are concerned, it is not always a bed of roses. Toronto, like other metropolises, has had scares of the home-grown terrorist variety, and American-style gun-and-gang violence is starting to creep over the border. But despite all this, Toronto is still a model of working harmony much to be admired. In fact, this multicultural dynamic is arguably the city's biggest attraction. Forget the CN Tower: the ethnically diverse neighbourhoods, enticing with their sensory overload, have become tourist destinations in their own right.

Still, old stereotypes die hard. At the risk of damning the city with faint praise, Toronto ranks among the most polite cities on the planet. In fact, it officially ranks third in the civility stakes. Then again, New York City took top honours in the poll of somewhat dubious scientific grounding, conducted by *Reader's Digest*. If you want to to test it out for yourself, bump into a Torontonian on the street; chances are they'll be the one to apologise.

GOING FOR BROKE

One thing the mayor of Toronto doesn't apologise for is the fact that the city is going broke. David Miller spends a lot of time lobbying provincial and federal governments to pick up their share of the tab and keep his municipality healthy. Years of cutbacks have left the city on the hook for more than it can muster from its own tax base. As of 2007, Toronto gained new powers to raise money but has yet to act. Councillors talk about collecting tariffs on everything from billboards to booze to bring in extra dosh, but they don't want to rile an electorate that is already feeling taxed to the max.

Despite its financial woes, Toronto is also in the midst of a cultural renaissance. Money committed a decade ago from those same federal and provincial governments,

complemented by funds from a wealthy coterie of philanthropists, has brought about spiffy new theatres, museums, music halls and galleries. This billion-dollar investment should pay dividends for years, providing new impetus for others to come to the city while giving Torontonians something new to crow about. The first purpose-built opera house in the country may not mean much to the average Joe, but for many culture vultures it means that the city has come of age.

'The mayor is on a mission to make Toronto the greenest metropolis on the planet, with energy-efficient buildings and more trees on the cards.'

Controversial architecture is also transforming the cityscape, rendering it more dynamic and challenging. Recent talking points include Will Alsop's playful Ontario College of Art and Design, Frank Gehry's striking addition to the Art Gallery of Ontario, and Daniel Libeskind's controversial revamp of the Royal Ontario Museum.

And the city is on the cusp of an even more ambitious transformation. Vast tracts of barren downtown plots are primed for development, in a bid to show off the city's greatest natural asset: Lake Ontario. The West Don Lands, East

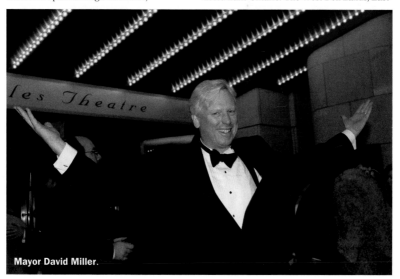

Mayor David Miller.

On the right track: the subway is being extended into the northern suburbs.

Bayfront and the Portlands will bring low-rise, mixed-income housing, more parks and greater access to the waterfront over the next ten years; the first homes will be ready in 2009. Too bad this kind of growth on the east side of town stands in stark contrast to what's rising on the west: a towering mass of market-driven condominiums approved by the previous city council, which had little regard for providing public space or even service amenities. These new developments have the look and feel of a soulless community adrift in the city.

SPRAWL AND THE CITY

Speaking of soulless communities, Toronto's satellite cities of Mississauga, Brampton, Richmond Hill, Markham and Pickering are the other side of Toronto, the nadir of North American urban sprawl. The hinterland is known as 905, a reference to the telephone area code in the city's outskirts but also a disparaging sobriquet used by downtowners to describe commuters who bought into the gas-guzzling dream of tract housing, highway commuting and strip malls. Who can blame them, though; the hunt for affordable housing is what's pushing this outward expansion.

The challenge now is to manage these duelling cities, a task that pits the mayor against his suburban counterparts in a healthy tussle to lure businesses. In terms of job creation, the suburbs are winning hands down. One symbolic divide was overcome in

the spring of 2007, when the city decided to extend the subway line out into the 'burbs. It seemed like a no-brainer, but the difficulty in getting competing jurisdictions to work together – the city and the suburbs have different transport systems – is not to be underestimated. In fact, it has led to some of the worst suburban planning in North America.

THE GREEN SCENE

Now the mayor is on a crusade to make Toronto the greenest metropolis on the continent. This means convincing people to leave their cars at home. As the downtown continues to build skyward, the city will become a lot less user-friendly for the automobile; a London-style toll to drive into the centre is being considered, but is unlikely to pass; the aforementioned subway extension, to York University and the northern suburbs beyond, is another step in the right direction. A new wind turbine at Exhibition Place (**photo** *p28*) provides power to about 250 households. More energy-efficient buildings and more trees are also on the cards. About time too: smog used to be a problem synonymous with Los Angeles, but Toronto is having to own up to its own polluting ways in order to combat the growing number of health-alert warnings in the summer, when air conditioners get juiced up, the air becomes noxious, and the city's power grid is stretched to the limit.

Issues of affordable housing and the environment provide some welcome distraction

Flight test

The Toronto Islands are a slice of tranquillity, but be warned: your peaceful summer day may be marred by the sound of propellers buzzing overhead. The arrival of upstart Porter Airlines at the City Centre airport on Hanlan's Point is either a symbol of progress or a noisy nuisance best vanquished from the shores of Lake Ontario.

It's a debate that has helped get Mayor David Miller elected and galvanised islanders and lakefront residents. Prior to his first term in office, Miller had vowed to halt Porter Airlines from using the downtown airstrip as its base, saying it ran counter to his vision of a 'clean, green waterfront'. He lost that battle, only to be re-elected in November 2006, just as the airline took to the skies.

The airline's maiden flight coincided with a flurry of publicity. Canadian-born style guru Tyler Brûlé (late of *Wallpaper** magazine) created Porter's casual-chic interiors for the Toronto-built, 70-passenger turboprop planes. He also designed the retro uniforms and stylish lounge and came up with the airline's name. The decor is just one aspect of the airline's boldness.

Since 1939 the island airport has been a playpen for recreational pilots, but its history with commercial aviation has been a failure; managed by the federal government, the airport has lost millions of dollars. Locals always campaign to have the airport turned into parkland. But Porter was undeterred.

In fact, if the airline had its way, the island would no longer be a proper island. Porter had wanted the city to build a bridge across the channel to the island, but it settled for a new ferry and terminal after Ottawa paid it $35 million (this was to settle a legal battle between the airline and the city). Now, First Nations people are laying claim to the airport land, saying it wasn't part of a historical treaty settlement. All the claims have created a highly charged atmosphere: in the past, passengers who actually fly Porter have been greeted by protesters.

The airline's sky-high ambitions to fly to large North American cities (it currently flies to Ottawa and Montreal) will likely meet with more turbulence. For those who do take a flight from the island, the views of the harbour and skyline should smooth the way.

from Toronto's loftier ambitions, for which the city has a dismal track record. Undeterred after its second failed bid to host the Olympics, the always-the-bridesmaid-never-the-bride mentality brought forth the idea to host Expo 2015. This was to be a next-best opportunity to shine. But with a deadline to step up to the plate in the autumn of 2006, Toronto stumbled again when it couldn't secure provincial approval to cover the losses the fair would incur, and so lost another shot at the brass ring. In fact, many people breathed a sigh of relief.

RISING STAR

Those more attuned to what the city has to offer know Toronto doesn't need one-off mega-events to give shape to the place. The city has come to life in recent years, with a vibrant music scene, buzzing clubs and festivals everywhere you turn. Nuit Blanche, the all-night art party launched in September 2006, was a roaring success. Doors Open, the annual architecture tour, is building awareness of the city's urban landscape.

What's more, Toronto does not have to rely on the presence of American film crews to generate buzz: the days of Hollywood North have passed. The reasons range from the rising Canadian dollar to Governor Arnold Schwarzenegger's rallying cry to the movie industry to bring film production back to California. No matter: Toronto has enough glamour of its own now. And it has spawned its fair share of global celebrities, ranging from the famous – Mrs Elton John (the singer's

partner David Furnish grew up in Scarborough, as did Mike Myers) – to the infamous (notorious newspaper baron Conrad Black).

'Developers knock down architectural treasures.'

As the city looks to the future, though, it is in danger of neglecting its past. Seduced by the allure of the new, it has destroyed much of its own history. This flies in the face of what Jane Jacobs believed. The renowned urban thinker made Toronto her home for the last 40 years of her life, and one of her core philosophies – that new ideas need old buildings – has been ignored of late. Developers can be relied upon to knock down architectural treasures to erect a condominium or, on residential streets, a slew of tasteless monstrosities. To underscore this architectural neglect, there is no museum of Toronto, nowhere to see a comprehensive account of how the city came to be.

Instead, fleeting ideas of 'rebranding' the city abound. That's the mantra heard around Toronto as the city tries to grab its share of the global limelight. And Toronto won't be able to rely on one city landmark for much longer. After a 30-year run as the world's tallest free-standing structure, the CN Tower will soon be eclipsed by Burj Dubai. Locals aren't bothered: they have developed a bit of a blind spot for the cement stick. Besides, there are more interesting things taking place closer to the ground.

Exhibition Place wind turbine. *See p26.*

New City Hall. *See p32.*

Architecture

If you build it, they will come.

A cultural renaissance requires bricks and mortar. And the embarrassment of new cultural venues – for theatre, opera, music, art and dance – is raising the curtain on architecture as well. These buildings are stealing the spotlight, but other architectural developments are also underway. New skyscrapers (the first in a decade) are in the works, a plethora of condo towers is on a relentless march onwards and upwards, and innovative, design-savvy buildings are turning heads. Soon, Toronto could be a destination for the architourist – a surprise development. The cream of the crop is showcased at the annual Doors Open Toronto (*see also p167*), where the public gets to tour buildings that are off-limits the rest of the year.

THE SHOCK OF THE NEW

In the era of the starchitect, the opening of the **Michael Lee-Chin Crystal** at the **Royal Ontario Museum** (Queen's Park; *see also p78*) in the spring of 2007 grabbed the headlines. Love it or hate it, the provocative, angular addition to the ROM by globetrotting designer Daniel Libeskind has thrust architecture to the fore. Those who have seen Libeskind's work at the Jewish Museum in Berlin, the Denver Art Museum or the Graduate Centre at London's Metropolitan University, may wonder what all the fuss is about. But adding edgy glass shards to a traditional museum has upset the purists, proving that Toronto can still be shocked by the new.

Frank Gehry's makeover of the **Art Gallery of Ontario** (317 Dundas Street West; *see p73*), set to open in 2008, takes a more muted approach. The master builder (who grew up around the corner from the AGO) is adding a billowing glass-and-titanium façade on the Dundas Street side. A titanium-clad tower will house a new contemporary-art section facing Grange Park on the south side. But the addition is less flamboyant than the Bilbao Guggenheim: Gehry wants it to fit in with the residential neighbourhood.

The Toronto architectural firm Kuwabara Payne McKenna Blumberg (KPMG) is the driving force behind a clutch of cultural buildings that are winning recognition for

Box clever: Will Alsop makes his mark with **Ontario College of Art & Design**.

their restraint and aesthetics. Through glass walls inspired by curtains, the **National Ballet School** (404 Jarvis Street; *see also p80*) offers glimpses of the rehearsal halls, where ballerinas bend and stretch at the barre above the traffic outside. The **Young Centre for the Performing Arts** (Distillery District; *see also p222*) combines industrial chic and warmth. Fashioned out of Victorian industrial buildings, it has an airy two-storey lobby that melds Douglas-fir timber and huge glass windows, kept cosy by a fireplace and lounge. KPMG's addition to the **Gardiner Museum** (*see also p78*) also reawakened a neglected gem. The sleek, angular limestone extension incorporates a light-filled third floor, with balconies off Jamie Kennedy's new restaurant. The same firm is working on the **Telus Centre** at the **Royal Conservatory of Music** (273 Bloor Street W; *see also p196*), turning a traditional music school into a multi-purpose cultural centre (due to open in autumn 2007), and the **Festival Centre**, the new home for the Toronto International Film Festival, slated to open in 2009.

Another Toronto architect, Jack Diamond, gave music and ballet lovers a permanent home with the **Four Seasons Centre for the Performing Arts** (145 Queen Street W; *see also p198* **The curtain rises**). Though critics damned the boxy building with faint praise, the intimate 2,000-seat hall is winning over performers and audiences.

One of the most visually arresting additions to the city is the vertical expansion to the **Ontario College of Art & Design** (100 McCaul Street, *see also p71*) – a black and white box that 'floats' 30 metres above street level, supported by 12 stilts in bright crayon colours. British architect Will Alsop designed this highly appropriate addition to the province's leading art school. Another Brit, Norman Foster, has provided another show-stopper with the **Leslie Dan Pharmacy Building** (144 College Street). In its atrium, the giant floating pods (they are lecture halls) come alive at night with coloured lights. Next to this is the **Terrence Donnelly Centre for Cellular and Biomolecular Research** (160 College Street), with hanging gardens, a bamboo forest in a glass podium and an inviting glass façade for what is essentially a tower of laboratories. Designed by Alliance/Behnisch Architects, it won the Royal Institute of British Architects (RIBA) International Award in 2006.

This flurry of activity bodes well for the future of architecture in the city. Once the bar is raised, it is hoped new projects will rise to the competition, and drown out the plethora of mediocrity on display. There is now an annual awards ceremony, the Pugly (www.pugly toronto.com), designed to shame developers and architects who bring uninspired work into the public realm (despite its fan club, the National Ballet School won the 2006 prize). The *Toronto*

Star asked readers to name the ugliest buildings in the city and, to its credit, it published a list that included the brutalist *Toronto Star* building at No. 1 Yonge Street.

ALL MIXED UP

Without a definitive style to call its own, Toronto's architecture embraces an eclecticism that has referenced other movements and influences as the city has come of age. Humourist Bruce McCall likened Toronto's overriding appearance to 'Early Penitentiary' style. Stone and brick were the city's literal building blocks, quarried from the local hills and kiln-baked in the Don Valley. Stalwart, unadorned homes rose in keeping with the prevailing Presbyterianism of the 19th century. For larger projects, these materials expressed the lofty aspirations of an emerging metropolis. Examples are found in the centre of town: **Old City Hall** (1888-99, 60 Queen Street W; *see also p66*) is a fanciful statement built from Credit Valley red sandstone in the Romanesque Revival style by the legendary EJ Lennox (who also designed **Casa Loma**; *see p88*). Its monumental scope allowed for flourishes such as a 90-metre (300-foot) clock tower, gargoyles and grotesques, one of which is Lennox's own

face. Despite its eminent pedigree, the building nearly met with the wrecker's ball simply because it fell out of fashion, representing the city's past. The original plan for the Eaton Centre was to have included the land where Old City Hall stands today, and the battle to preserve Lennox's building was a catalyst for the heritage movement. It's now a courthouse, and though security can be tight it's worth getting inside to admire the stained glass and the grand staircase.

Of the city's original bank towers, **Commerce Court North** (1931, 25 King Street W), a 34-storey limestone skyscraper, has the hauteur that comes from being the tallest building in the Commonwealth until 1962. Look up to see the giant heads that surround the old viewing platform. Cathedral-like doors lead into the banking hall modelled after the Baths of Caracalla in Rome, with its vaulted ceiling in blue and gilt mouldings.

Beaux Arts style is displayed magnificently at **Union Station** (1927, 65 Front Street W; *see also p65*), with the façade's imposing Doric colonnade echoed by the main hall's 22 mighty pillars. The pitched, château-like roofline is echoed across the street by the **Fairmont Royal York Hotel** (1929, 100 Front Street W;

Street talk

With a cavalcade of new cultural attractions on the horizon, urban-planning gurus are now turning their attention to public spaces; in a rush to build shiny new temples to art and music and commerce, it seems the streetscape got left behind. Much of downtown is dowdy, if not downright uninviting. Until recently, the city's response was to put out a few potted plants. Yonge-Dundas Square (2003) signalled a bold attempt to address a dearth of public meeting places. And while the controversial square is certainly an improvement over the strip of low-rise stores it replaced, the fountains and chairs do little to soften the bus terminal aesthetic, and the barrage of video-screen billboard advertising – an example of the creeping privatisation of public space – is impossible to tune out. Despite the square's location in the heart of downtown, Toronto still doesn't have a defining intersection or open space, at least not one you'd care to use, although Nathan Phillips Square is being remodelled to make it more approachable.

Small measures can help improve the public realm, and Toronto doesn't lack for

champions of the cause. The Toronto Public Space Committee (http://publicspace.ca) is made up of volunteer crusaders whose guerrilla-gardening tactics bring flowers to neglected corners. They also defend the right to put up posters, and launched the quarterly magazine *Spacing* (www.spacing.ca). Others defend the funky wooden telephone poles that still line major thoroughfares.

The city's next step is to replace the clutter of newspaper boxes, transport shelters and garbage bins with a uniform style and there are plans to beautify Bloor Street's main shopping stretch with a procession of trees. Toronto's Poet Laureate Pier Giorgio di Cicco believes more benches are the remedy to the impersonal and chilling effects the city sidewalks can have on locals and visitors alike. Even the internet is having an effect: though it may not be the most beautiful city around, Torontonians express an endless fascination with their streetscape through an inordinate number of photo blogs (toronto.photobloggers.org) dedicated to charting the city's evolution. Log on and see the streets through an artistic filter.

see also p41). Art deco's most expressive example is found in the **Design Exchange** (1937, 234 Bay Street; *see also p66)*, former home of the Toronto Stock Exchange.

The city's push to modernism came in 1957 with a design competition for the **New City Hall** (*see also p73*; **photo** *p29)*. Finnish architect Viljo Revell won the contest with his two curving towers and central oyster-shaped dome for the city council chambers. The project, completed in 1965, included a much-needed public space (named after the mayor of the day, Nathan Phillips), which symbolically reflected the city's own opening up to new ideas. The square is set to get a makeover that will include adding more greenery. The **Toronto-Dominion Centre** (1964-9, 55 King Street W; *see also p65)* heralded the international style, piercing the skyline with Ludwig Mies van der Rohe's austere twin black towers, the taller at 54 storeys; the tower is one of van der Rohe's late masterpieces. Diverting human traffic from the open plaza at street level to an underground concourse was part of the design, meant to emphasise the inhuman scale of the towers. Fostered by bank rivalries, IM Pei's 57-storey stainless-steel box of **Commerce Court West** (1968-72, 199 Bay Street; *see also p65)* rose to prominence across the street.

RESTORATION DRAMA

By the 1980s preservationists were fighting to end the destruction of old buildings, but with unintended consequences. City Hall compromised by allowing developers to incorporate bits of earlier buildings into their designs, creating a strange hybrid known as façadism. This has proved to be a hit-or-miss proposition. **Queens Quay Terminal** (1983, 207 Queens Quay W; *see also p60)* is a successful early example on the waterfront. **BCE Place** (1992, 181 Bay Street; *see also p65)* displaced an 1840s bank façade that now sits without context amid the wonderful modern atrium by Santiago Calatrava. The **Air Canada Centre** (1990, 200 Bay Street; *see also p200)* retains the charming bas-relief scenes of maple leaves and beavers from a former postal station, proof that the rampant commercialism of professional sport must bow at the altar of such iconic Canadian imagery. With **Maple Leaf Gardens** (1931, 33 Carlton Street; *see also p79)* – the revered Art Moderne hockey shrine – set to become a supermarket, façadism has perhaps gone too far, but at least the building is not being knocked down.

Successful restorations have brought some architectural gems back to life. For sheer decorative exuberance, the **Elgin & Winter Garden Theatres** (1913, 189 Yonge Street;

see also p68) are in a gold leaf, cherub-filled, faux forest class of their own. The **Carlu** (1930, 444 Yonge Street), once known as the Eaton Auditorium, is back in all its Art Moderne glory, with a distinctly nautical theme. This is the work of French designer Jacques Carlu, who devised the interiors of ocean liners *Ile de France* and *the Normandie*, favourite ships of his patron, Lady Eaton. The **Summerhill LCBO Store** (1916, 10 Scrivener Square; *see also p156)* now displays its full marble-laden attributes as a former midtown train station. Over in the east side, the **Distillery District** (1859-61, 55 Mill Street; *see also p85)* has kept the largest Victorian-era industrial complex in North America intact as boutiques, galleries and restaurants move in.

Inventive uses of landscape architecture are creeping into public spaces, transforming the notion of city parks, and infusing small parcels of land with imagination. The **Village of Yorkville Park** (1993, Cumberland Street, at Bellair Street) tantalises with its references to Canada's wilderness – granite boulders, wild grasses and water – contained in an urban setting. **HtO** (Spadina Quay; *see also p61)* adds a whimsical touch to where land meets water, and next to it, the **Toronto Music Garden** (2000, 475 Queens Quay; *see also p61)* creates a tranquil space for an intimate grass amphitheatre.

THE SKY'S THE LIMIT

Toronto's skyline continues to be dominated by new condominium towers, which are doing little to build an architectural legacy. The city's lack of vision for the waterfront allowed developers to erect a cement curtain that cuts off the pleasures of the lake to the majority. Architecture critics dine out on trashing the ghastly design of some of these buildings, and rightfully so. One of the more ambitious undertakings is **City Place**, which, when completed in 2010, will consist of 7,500 condo units in 21 towers, in the space occupied by former railway yards west of the Rogers Centre (1 Blue Jays Way; *see also p63)*, that architectural marvel with the world's first retractable roof, whose form has outlived its function (the hulking structure is now a white elephant and was sold in 2004 for a fraction of what it cost to build).

Now that the **CN Tower** (301 Front Street W; *see also p63)* is about to be eclipsed by the Burj Dubai as the world's tallest freestanding structure (after a 30-year reign), Toronto's size complex can finally be left behind. With any luck, the qualities of beauty, grace and innovation will characterise the city's new wave of architecture.

Word on the Street. *See p170.*

Literary Toronto

Toronto by the book.

Toronto is a literary town. You can see it in the poetry panels on the subway, the sold-out reading series, the smart bookshops and the array of award programmes, not to mention the **International Festival of Authors** (*see p35*) and the **Word on the Street festival** (*see p170*), which tempts hundreds of thousands of people to peruse titles under the trees of Queen's Park.

Writers find inspiration in Toronto's patchwork of cultures, languages and landscapes. Take a walk through the streets and ravines of Toronto and you may experience a sense of déjà vu. In fiction, the city's terrain plays as big a part as the characters, which is typical CanLit: big country, few people. Though wilderness is a recurring theme in Canadian literature, critics often interpret Toronto's dark, wooded ravines as symbols for a murky subconscious, rather than a back-to-nature call of the wild. Most notably, **Michael Ondaatje**, **Margaret Atwood** and **Anne Michaels** have followed their characters down paths of human discovery through the city's forests.

This tradition stems from the earliest Toronto writers: travellers and settlers such as **Anna Jameson**, **Susanna Moodie** and **Ernest Thompson Seton** all memorably captured the forbidding wilderness of 19th-century Toronto. Seton penned two classics about his youthful adventures exploring the Don Valley: *Two Little Savages* and *Wild Animals I Have Known*. Moodie wrote of the hardship of taming this savage land in *Roughing It in the Bush*, which inspired Margaret Atwood's 1970 poetry collection *The Journals of Susanna Moodie*.

The shift from books about nature to stories about people was spearheaded by **Stephen Leacock**, who moved from England to Toronto when he was a boy. Leacock grew up on Lake Simcoe, just north of Toronto, and his gently humorous *Sunshine Sketches of a Little Town* (1912) – based on local town gossip gleaned from his barber – made him a literary star at home and abroad. After his death in 1944, an annual award in his name was created to recognise the best in Canadian literary humour.

THE UNSUNG HERO

The next author of significance was **Morley Callaghan**, the first Canadian writer to use Toronto extensively in his fiction. Born in Toronto in 1903, Callaghan became one of the giants of early 20th-century Canadian literature (along with Hugh MacLennan, from Nova Scotia). He was encouraged by Ernest Hemingway, whom he met while the American did a stint reporting for the *Toronto Star*. He later joined Hemingway in Paris and hung out with other stars such as F Scott Fitzgerald and James Joyce. It was there that he knocked out Hemingway in a boxing match; his 1963 memoir, *That Summer in Paris*, documents the period. Callaghan's stories are characterised by gritty realism and themes of morality and often populated by prostitutes, criminals and social climbers. Though many reviewers criticised him for being earnest, noted American critic Edmund Wilson called him 'the most unjustly neglected novelist in the English-speaking world'. He won a Governor General's Award in 1951 for *The Loved and the Lost*. From 1951 until his death in 1990, he lived at 20 Dale Avenue in Rosedale, where he wrote *A Fine and Private Place* and *A Wild Old Man on the Road*.

ATWOOD AND BEYOND

In the 1960s, Canadian nationalism was on the rise, and the Canadian publishing scene, based in Toronto, came into its own. Small publishing houses like Anansi and Coach House fostered new talent, among them **Margaret Atwood**. Winner of both the Booker Prize (*The Blind Assassin*, 2000) and the Governor General's Award (*The Handmaid's Tale*, 1985, and *The Circle Game* for poetry in 1966), she is arguably Canada's most famous author. She lives in the Annex with her partner Graeme Gibson, and has set many of her novels in Toronto. *Life Before Man*, her 1979 tale of a tense love triangle, is a vivid portrait of 1970s Toronto that uses the Royal Ontario Museum to startling effect. The old hippy-dippy culture of the Toronto Islands provides the setting for *The Robber Bride*. Both *Lady Oracle* and *Cat's Eye* draw on middle-class life in the 1940s and '50s. The latter memorably depicts the deep, dark ravines that hold so many of Toronto's secrets and also jumps forward to the artsy scene of Queen West. In *Oryx and Crake* Atwood returns to the dystopian terrain of *The Handmaid's Tale*, a form she prefers to call speculative fiction as opposed to science fiction. Her latest novel, *The Tent*, is her most autobiographical work, based in part on one of her high-school English teachers in Toronto.

Both Callaghan and Atwood attended the University of Toronto, which has been home to a clutch of literary giants. **Northrop Frye** taught English there for more than 30 years and was one of the eminent literary critics of his day, famed for his teachings on Shakespeare and his deconstruction of the Bible in *The Great Code*. **Marshall McLuhan** was an early sage of the media age, coining the phrase 'global village' and the dictum 'the medium is the message'. The celebrated **Robertson Davies** was the master of pseudo Oxbridge Massey College. And he described the city in novels like *What's Bred in the Bone* and *The Rebel Angels*. His works contain elements of satire, magical realism and Jungian psychology, and explore themes of illusion and identity. *Fifth Business*, his 1970 novel about saints, fate and theatre, is set partly in Toronto, about which Davies could be merciless: 'I think of Toronto as a big fat rich girl who has lots of money, but no idea how to make herself attractive,' says his fictional alter ego, Samuel Marchbanks.

READING THE CITY

Other glimpses of the city can be gleaned from books such as *Lunatic Villas*, the humorous 1981 novel from **Marian Engel**. It tells the story of a depressed housewife who juggles writing a magazine column with taking care of seven children and having an affair, but Engel is better known for *Bear*, an inter-species love story that won the Governor General's Award. The city is also on display in the poetry of **Raymond Souster**, a Torontonian who spent most of his life in the High Park area and named some of his poems after different parts of the city, including 'Kensington Market' and 'Yonge Street Bar'.

Hugh Garner, a Governor General Award-winner, rose to fame in 1950 with the publication of his novel *Cabbagetown*, which paints a gritty picture of Toronto's infamous slum during the Depression. For his efforts, he later had a housing co-operative named after him in Cabbagetown. Half a century later, **Matt Cohen**'s 1997 roman à clef, *The Bookseller*, also explores the city's grimy underbelly. Called 'a literary film noir' by the *New York Times*, it depicts a bleak world of used bookshops, seedy hotels and dodgy pool halls. For his efforts, Cohen, who died in 1999, was enshrined in the streetscape: the Matt Cohen Park is at the corner of Bloor Street West and Spadina Avenue. **Timothy Findley**, a CanLit legend, depicts a dystopian Toronto in his 1993 novel *Headhunter*. In a surreal nightmare, the city is awash with AIDS and pornography and ruled by a corrupt, wealthy cabal. Perhaps the elite he depicts so scathingly was inspired by the affluent neighbourhood of Rosedale, where

Findley spent his childhood and of which he once wrote: 'Them as live in Rosedale are them as keep their shit in jars.' *Unless*, the 2004 novel from the late Pulitzer winner Carol Shields, also touches on Toronto's dark side; it's a melancholy tale about a small-town, middle-class woman whose daughter chooses to live life on the streets of the big city.

DISPARATE VOICES

The multicultural wave that hit Toronto has brought more diverse voices to the scene. For years, African-Canadian writing boiled down to one name, the Barbados-born **Austin Clarke**. But the author of *The Polished Hoe*, which won the Commonwealth Writers' Prize and the Giller Prize in 2002, set the stage for a younger generation led locally by **Dionne Brand** (*What We All Long For*), **André Alexis** (*Childhood* and children's novel *Ingrid and the Wolf*) and dub poet **Lillian Allen**.

Michael Ondaatje is probably the most famous transplanted author now living in Toronto. Born in Sri Lanka, he won the Booker Prize for *The English Patient* and before that

wrote of Toronto's monuments in a way that elevated them to mythical status. *In the Skin of a Lion* depicts Toronto in the 1920s, with star turns from the Bloor Street Viaduct, the RC Harris Filtration Plant in the Beaches and Union Station. Entering Union, a character says: 'This train station was a palace, its niches and caverns an intimate city ... They were in the belly of a whale.' Another South Asian writer, **Rohinton Mistry**, emigrated from India in 1975 and hit the motherlode with his first novel, *Such a Long Journey*, winning the Governor General's Award, the Commonwealth Writers' Prize and a shortlisting for the Booker. He continues to write about life in India in the acclaimed *A Fine Balance* and *Family Matters*.

Toronto authors whose work is rooted in Canada include **David Adams Richards**, who writes of New Brunswick and **Wayne Roberts**, who writes of Newfoundland. **Ann-Marie MacDonald** set her bestselling debut novel, *Fall on Your Knees*, in Nova Scotia (her debut is also a bestseller thanks to a plug by Oprah Winfrey). **Alice Munro**, the celebrated short-story author who has won

International Festival of Authors

Toronto may not be the world's number one travel destination, especially in October when the chill sets in. But every autumn, at the height of the book world's prize-giving season, the leading lights of literature hope to be invited to the city. Some come for the good scotch that flows during the ten-day International Festival of Authors; others seek the company of their contemporaries. 'It's one of the few places on the planet where those who have just won the Booker Prize – or come close – can get together,' says Geoffrey Taylor, the event's artistic director.

The Pulitzer and Nobel winners have always been a draw, but Taylor is taking the festival in new directions by including more first-time and non-fiction writers. He can afford to: the festival's reputation has reached such lofty heights that authors have immortalised it in their books. Mordecai Richler had a character read there and John Irving set a scene at the festival. When it started back in 1980, founder Greg Gatenby couldn't have known how big it would become. The first festival attracted only 18 authors. But Gatenby, a witty man of letters, was determined to boost Toronto's cultural standing (he later went on to write *The Literary Guide to Toronto*). And

his dream has been realised. With more than 100 authors from 20 countries in attendance each year, the word is getting out.

International Festival of Authors

Various venues at the Harbourfront Centre, Waterfront (416 973 3000/www. readings.org). Streetcar 509, 510/subway Union Station. **Date** *mid to late October.*

Listen up

Torontonians may be voracious readers but they are not content to sit at home in their armchairs. They want to see the authors up close, hear them read their works, and subject them to a barrage of (polite) questions. To that end, the city boasts a number of reading series to keep audiences sated until the biggie: the **International Festival of Authors** (*see p35*). The **Harbourfront Reading Series** and the **University of Toronto Bookstore Reading Series** are the two mainstays. The Harbourfront series (from September to June) tends to stick with literary fiction by established names (Monica Ali, Ian McEwan and Colm Toibin were recent readers) while the University of Toronto series (March-June, September-December) emphasises non-fiction (recent guests have included Edward Rutherfurd and *New Yorker* editor David Remnick). For poetry readings, head to the tree-lined bohemian enclave of Mirvish Village: the long-running Art Bar series takes place at the Victory Café every Tuesday night and specialises exclusively in poetry. The

Scream Literary Festival, which began 15 years ago as a one-night rant under the stars, has become a week-long series of poetry readings in early July. It culminates in an alfresco spectacle in the leafy surroundings of High Park.

Art Bar Poetry Series
Victory Café, 581 Markham Street, between Bloor & Lennox Streets (416 516 5787/ www.artbar.org). Subway Bathurst.

Harbourfront Reading Series
Brigantine Room, Harbourfront Centre, 235 Queen's Quay West, Waterfront (416 973 4000/www.readings.org). Streetcar 509, 510/subway Union Station. **Map** p277 E8.

Scream Literary Festival
Various locations (416 466 8862/www. thescream.ca).

University of Toronto Bookstore Reading Series
Various locations (416 640 5836/ www.uoftbookstore.com/events).

more Governor General's Awards (three) than any other writer, mastered a style dubbed southern Ontario Gothic. She has given a voice to rural Ontario through coming-of-age tales and moral dilemmas (most famously in *Lives of Girls and Women*). Following the publication in 2006 of her latest collection, *The View from Castle Rock*, Munro hinted that she may retire.

BRIGHT YOUNG THINGS
Literary magazines such as *The Walrus* act as launching pads for new writers. **Randy Boyagoda** had a short story published in the magazine, then fleshed it out in his first novel *Governor of the Northern Province*, which was shortlisted for a Giller Prize in 2006. Other journals that publish fiction and poetry include *Brick, Lichen, Taddle Creek* and the *Queen Street Quarterly*. Online literary outlets include *The Danforth Review* and www.imaginingtoronto.com. **Chester Brown** is at the forefront of graphic novels with work published by Drawn & Quarterly including *Louis Riel: A Comic-Strip Biography*.

On the edgier side of things, **Barbara Gowdy** consistently pushes the frontiers of acceptable behaviour in her fiction. *Mister Sandman* and the short-story collection *We So Seldom Look on Love* dwell in the freakish and

bizarre, exploring necrophilia and transvestism. Set in Toronto, her latest novel *Helpless* probes the psyche of a paedophile.

Other recent and rising stars include **David Bezmozgis**, whose critically acclaimed debut collection of short fiction, *Natasha and Other Stories* (2004) explores the Jewish immigrant experience; **Russell Smith**, who delves into the nightlife scene of clubs and trendy young things in *How Insensitive* and *Young Men* and skewers the cultured set in his satire *Muriella Pent*; and **Michael Redhill**, who spans Toronto's centuries in a hunt for the earliest photographs of the city in *Consolation* (2004).

The latest literary up-and-comer to score big, **Vincent Lam** has a story that is itself the stuff of good fiction. The Toronto medical student had always wanted to write. A chance encounter with Margaret Atwood on a cruise ship in the Arctic (he was the ship doctor) resulted in the kind of encouragement new writers crave. *Bloodletting & Miraculous Cures* blends short stories about Lam's medical-school training and the immigrant experience.

Many readers anxiously await the return of **Anne Michaels**. The poet's fiction debut, the Orange Prize-winning *Fugitive Pieces* (1998), was set in Poland, Greece and Toronto's ravines. It is currently being made into a film.

Where to Stay

Features

Gladstone Hotel. *See p52*.

Where to Stay

From skyscrapers to sensual boutique hotels: lie back and think of Toronto.

Something old, something new: the stately **Windsor Arms** has gone sleek. *See p43.*

When it comes to getting some shut-eye, Toronto offers variety and value, especially for those travelling with strong currencies (particularly pounds and euros). And though, in past years, the city's 35,000 rooms were characterised by a cookie-cutter sameness, things are improving. An explosion of high-end hotels is imminent, with the **Ritz-Carlton**, **Trump**, **Shangri-La** and a new **Four Seasons** all on the horizon. **The Hazelton** is first out of the five-star gate, opening in the summer of 2007. All of them are bundling their spacious suites and services with condo towers on top – a new hotel trend.

For more down-to-earth types, innovative and individual boutique properties are adding some spice to the mix. The **Cosmopolitan Toronto** (*see p50*) is going for a Zen-inspired experience, but for truly edgy accommodation, check into **The Gladstone Hotel** (*see p46* **Get on your glad rags**). Once a flophouse, the city's longest-operating hotel has had a

radical revamp: each guest room is designed by a different local artist.

For a decent cheap sleep, it's worth investigating bed and breakfasts such as the **Baldwin Village Inn** (*see p46*) or **Victoria's Mansion Guest House** (*see p50*). And for a room with a view – of the waterfront, the playing field, or the fast-growing skyline – Toronto's hotels are not short of options.

RATES, SEASONS AND GRADINGS

In this chapter we have divided our listings according to the price of the cheapest double room; **Budget** is under $100, **Moderate** $100-$169, **Expensive** $170-$289 and **Luxury** anything from $290 to your life savings; hostels are listed separately. However, hotels tend to quote wide price ranges over the phone. The rate depends on many factors, especially the season: in slow periods, a 'luxury' hotel might reduce its rates to the expensive category, and during special events like the film festival or the

Toronto Grand Prix, everyone's prices shoot through the roof. As a rule of thumb, high season runs from April to October, when deals are hard to come by. However, some corporate hotels get quiet in the summer; hit them while they're down and ask for a reduced rate. In addition, enquire about deals for students, seniors, teachers, members of Canadian Automobile Association (CAA), American Automobile Association (AA) or AA members, or any other group you belong to. Always ask about special offers or upgrades; many hotels have partnered with other attractions to offer dinner/show or spa/shopping packages, which can save you money.

Though we have specified in the listings whether a hotel offers internet access, note that some hotels charge for this service (check before you book). Also be aware that if you smoke, not all hotels will accommodate you. With tighter smoking laws in effect, some properties have chosen to ban puffing altogether. Others offer designated floors (often the lower ones without views) or specific rooms.

Note that rates listed do not include federal tax, which is six per cent (though there are ways of claiming this back; *see p253*). Unless otherwise stated, the following rates only include breakfast at B&Bs, not hotels.

BOOKING AGENCIES

Bear in mind that most booking agencies will only hook you up with their own members, so it pays to shop around.

Tourism Toronto (416 203 2500, www.torontotourism.com, 8.30am-6pm Mon-Fri) is the city's official booking service, while the **Greater Toronto Hotel Association** (416 351 1276, www.gtha.com) maintains comprehensive links on its website. **Travellers' Aid Society of Toronto** (416 366 7788, www.travellersaid.ca) can provide shelter and information in emergencies. This society also has booths at many rail and bus stations, as well as the airport. The **Downtown Toronto Association of Bed & Breakfast Guest Houses** (416 410 3938, www.bnbinfo.com) will be able to match your accommodation preferences – via a detailed online form or by phone – to B&Bs in central Toronto. **Toronto Bed & Breakfast Reservation Service** (1-877 922 6522 or 705 738 9449, www.torontobandb.com) helpfully brings together a handful of B&Bs, mainly in downtown areas.

> ❶ Green numbers given in this chapter correspond to the location of each hotel as marked on the street maps. *See pp270-275.*

Waterfront & Islands

Expensive

Radisson Plaza Hotel Admiral Toronto-Harbourfront

249 Queens Quay W, at Rees Street, Waterfront, ON M5J 2N5 (1-800 333 3333/416 203 3333/ fax 416 203 3100/www.radisson.com). Streetcar 509, 510. **Rates** $139-$289 single/double. **Credit** AmEx, MC, V. **Map** p271 E9 ❶

The nautically themed, eight-storey Radisson offers lakeside views over Toronto Harbour from the bar, promenade deck and outdoor pool. The lobby is all lacquered wood and brass, with a smattering of interesting marine art and artefacts. Nearby, there's a range of outdoor activities – tennis, cycling and sailing – and it's only a short walk to the CN Tower and other sights. When it comes to nightlife, the surrounding area is a bit of a wasteland – take a quick taxi or tram ride into downtown.

The best Hotels

For island breezes

Swan's End Guesthouse (*see p41*) has an idyllic location on the peaceful Toronto Islands.

For yoga fanatics

The **Cosmopolitan Toronto** (*see p47*) or **Pantages Suites Hotel** (*see p43*) come with incense menus, a meditation channel and yoga mats.

For culture vultures

At the hip **Gladstone** (*see p46*), every bedroom is a work of art.

For families

The **Delta Chelsea** (*see p44*) comes with a water slide, family pool and childcare centre.

For pomp and ceremony

The luxurious **Windsor Arms** (*see p43*) specialises in old-fashioned finery and top-notch service.

For a home away from home

With its communal rooms and garden, the cosy **Baldwin Village Inn** (*see p46*) makes every guest feel like part of the family.

For a sensational spa

At the **Park Hyatt** (*see p51*), the Stillwater Spa is a beautiful place to relax and rejuvenate.

Sutton Place. *See p44.*

Bar. Business centre. Concierge. Disabled-adapted rooms. Gym. Internet (wireless). No-smoking rooms & floors. Parking ($18). Pool (outdoor). Restaurant. Room service. Spa. TV (pay movies).

Westin Harbour Castle

1 Harbour Square, at Bay Street, Waterfront, ON M5J 1A6 (1-888 625 5144/416 869 1600/ fax 416 869 0573/www.starwood.com/westin/ index.html). Bus 6/streetcar 509, 510. **Rates** $150-$399 single/double. **Credit** AmEx, MC, V. **Map** p271 F9 ❷

Light, spacious rooms and glorious lake views are the big draws at this 38-storey hotel (request accommodation on the south side and upper floors). Sunlight glints off the glassed-in pool, and the day spa has a two-storey waterfall with lake views from the treatment rooms. The romantic Toula Restaurant offers fine Italian cuisine, all the better now that the rooftop dining room doesn't revolve any more. Because of its meeting spaces, the hotel draws a lot of convention business, but it also has good services for families with children. The waterfront area is not exactly bustling in the evening, but the Westin operates a shuttle service to downtown, which goes a long way to compensate. And should you want to get away from it all on the Toronto Islands, the ferry docks are next door.

Bar. Business centre. Concierge. Disabled-adapted rooms. Gym. Internet (high-speed, wireless). No-smoking rooms & floors. Parking ($17; valet $28). Pool (indoor). Restaurants (3). Room service. Spa. Tennis court. TV (DVD on request, pay movies).

Moderate

Swan's End Guest House

24 Omaha Avenue, Algonquin Island, ON M5J 1Z8 (416 364 5807/www.torontoisland.org). **Rates** $155-$175 including taxes; min 2-night stay. **No credit cards**

Perched on a lagoon, this island cottage is a ten-minute walk from the Ward's Island ferry dock. It has two bright and clean guest rooms with queen-sized beds, top-notch white linens and ensuite baths. A hearty breakfast is served in the sunny dining room. You can swim, bike, rollerblade or rent a canoe or kayak to explore the canals and lagoons. *TV (DVD).*

Budget

Studio Apartment

2A Nottawa Avenue, Algonquin Island, ON M5J 2C8 (416 203 9946/jeanniep@sympatico.ca). **Rates** $550-$600/wk. **No credit cards**.

Proud island resident Jeannie Parker rents out this self-contained one-room apartment by the week in the summer and by the month in the winter. With basic kitchen equipment, a private balcony (with a great view over the island) and a new garden, this home is a good base for a self-catering stay. *Internet (dataport). Non-smoking house. TV (VCR).*

Downtown West

Luxury

Fairmont Royal York Hotel

100 Front Street W, at University Avenue, Financial District, ON M5J 1E3 (1-800 441 1414/416 368 2511/fax 416 368 9040/www.royalyorkhotel.com). Subway Union. **Rates** $249-$429 single/double; $349-$569 suites. **Credit** AmEx, MC, V. **Map** p271 F8 ❸

When it opened in 1929, this was the largest and tallest building in the British Empire. Although it's now dwarfed by banking towers, the hotel's castle-like exterior still merits its royal name (as does the fact that three generations of England's royal family have napped here). Chandeliers and a decorated ceiling in the sumptuous lobby set a tone of regal awe (which is impossible to match in the rooms, where the once-spectacular lake views have been marred by a row of condo towers). The design of the EPIC restaurant shows grudging acknowledgement that the world has grown hipper (though, to please the traditionalists, it still serves a high tea every day). The gorgeous wood-panelled Library Bar serves a mean Margarita.

Bars (4). Business centre. Concierge. Disabled-adapted rooms. Gym. Internet (dataport, high-speed). No-smoking rooms & floors. Parking ($24; valet $31). Pool (indoor). Restaurants (5). Room service. Spa. TV (DVD on request, pay movies).

SoHo Metropolitan

318 Wellington Street, at Blue Jay Way, Entertainment District, ON M5V 3T4 (416 599 8800/fax 416 599 8801/www.metropolitan. com/soho). Streetcar 504/subway St Andrew. **Rates** $350-$750 single/double. **Credit** AmEx, MC, V. **Map** p271 E8 ❹

Sister to the original Metropolitan (*see p44*), the SoHo Met joins a clutch of swanky hotels in the Entertainment District. The ersatz name was a lame attempt to add cachet, but there was no need: the rooms are generously sized, and the decor is a winning combo of minimalism and cosiness (plenty of blond wood and hugely comfy beds); the sumptuous marble bathrooms come with Molton Brown toiletries. The hotel's location, in party central, means it's not far from bar to bed, but late-night revellers and traffic can sometimes be heard through the floor-to-ceiling windows. For eating and drinking, choose from Senses restaurant (in transition from fusion to Asian; *see p109*), the attached bar (beautifully lit at night) and Senses bakery (Euro-style breakfasts featuring excellent pastries and coffees). And if you've overindulged – or vegged out too much in front of your big flat-screen TV – burn off the calories in the gym or pool.

Bar. Business centre. Concierge. Disabled-adapted rooms. Gym. Internet (high-speed). No-smoking rooms & floors. Parking ($20; valet $25). Pool (indoor). Restaurants (2). Room service. Spa. TV (DVD, pay movies).

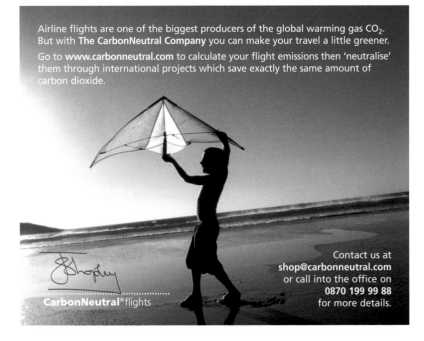

Windsor Arms

18 St Thomas Street, at Bloor Street W, University,
ON M5S 3E7 (1-877 999 2767/416 971 9666/fax
416 921 9121/www.windsorarmshotel.com). Bus 4/
subway Bay. **Rates** $295-$2,000 single/double/
suites. **Credit** AmEx, MC, V. **Map** p274 F4 **5**
In 1927, this tiny hotel opened its doors to the
world's celebrities and millionaires. It fell into
decline in the 1980s, but in 1995 developer-about-
town George Friedmann restored the Arms back to
its original neo-Gothic stateliness (though only the
stained-glass windows and the stone portico of the
entrance are original). The service is discreet, and
many rooms have 'private butlers' cupboards' (if you
want room service without having to interact with
another human being). Some have fireplaces for cosy
winter stays. In recent years, the hotel shrugged off
its haughtiness, repositioning itself to attract a
younger, hipper crowd. They can be found getting
pampered in the spa, swimming laps in the indoor
pool, or dancing to a band in the swanky bar. For
something more sedate, take tea in the lovely Tea
Room, or eat breakfast, lunch or dinner in the regal
Courtyard Café. **Photo** *p38.*
Bar. Concierge. Gym. Internet (high-speed).
No-smoking hotel. Parking ($25). Pool (indoor).
Restaurant. Room service. TV (DVD).

Expensive

Hilton Toronto

145 Richmond Street W, at University Avenue,
Financial District, ON M5H 2L2 (1-800 267
2281/416 869 3456/fax 416 869 3187/www.
hilton.com). Streetcar 501/subway Osgoode.
Rates $229-$419 single/double. **Credit** AmEx,
MC, V. **Map** p271 F7 **6**
The Hilton is a rarity in this town: a modern hotel
(1975) with character. The lobby, with its raised
wooden floor and hanging curtain, looks as though
it was created by stage designers (in fact, it was).
Exit stage left for the Canadian-themed Tundra
restaurant, and exit stage right for chunky glass
elevators. The latter carry you to hallways designed
to mimic the flow and activity of a river (note the
abstract fish, stones and ripples in the carpet
patterns). The rooms have asymmetrical furniture
and sleek fixtures that are both modern and comfy.
The Hilton shares its indoor/outdoor pool with a
nearby health club; in return, guests get access to
the club's squash courts and aerobics classes.
Bars (2). Business centre. Concierge. Disabled-
adapted rooms. Gym. Internet (high-speed). No-
smoking rooms & floors. Parking ($25; valet $30).
Pools (1 indoor/outdoor). Restaurants (3). Room
service. TV (DVD on request/pay movies).

Hôtel Le Germain Toronto

30 Mercer Street, at John Street, Entertainment
District, ON M5V 1H3 (1-866 345 9501/416 345
9500/fax 416 345 9501/www.hotelboutique.com).
Streetcar 504. **Rates** $225-$620 single/double.
Credit AmEx, MC, V. **Map** p271 E8 **7**

The Le Germain group specialises in creating
Euro-style boutique hotels; it owned award-winning
properties in Montreal and Quebec before opening
this Toronto counterpart in 2003. The service is
professional but personable, and the vibe is more
casual than institutional. The designers have got the
details right, from subdued lighting to luxury
showerheads that make you feel as if you're
soaping up in a tropical rainstorm. The small but
sumptuous rooms are designed to make guests
forget about the world outside (though clubbers
partying in the streets below can bring reality
crashing back in). The lobby boasts a massive glass
fireplace, sculptures and paintings, and, on the
raised floor above, a library of about 200 art books,
plus a self-service coffee machine. Free net access in
the rooms, proper hairdryers and friendly chamber
staff are further bonuses. The new restaurant Chez
Victor serves victuals as stylish as the decor;
breakfast is a tasty buffet.
Bar. Concierge. Disabled-adapted rooms. Gym.
Internet (high-speed, wireless in lobby). No-smoking
rooms. Parking (valet $28). Restaurant. Room
service. TV (DVD/VCR on request, pay movies).

InterContinental Toronto Centre

225 Front Street W, at Simcoe Street, Entertainment
District, ON M5V 2X3 (1-800 422 7969/416 597
1400/fax 416 597 8128/www.torontocentre.
intercontinental.com). Subway St Andrew or
Union. **Rates** $200-$420 single/double.
Credit AmEx, MC, V. **Map** p271 E8 **8**
Attached to the Toronto Convention Centre, this 586-
room hotel attracts a lot of business traffic. Don't let
the conference facilities fool you, though: it's great
for holidays, with a location in the heart of the
Entertainment District, the tropical Victoria Spa and
the colourful Azure bar. Services include high-speed
internet throughout the hotel.
Bar. Business centre. Concierge. Disabled-adapted
rooms. Gym. Internet (high-speed). Limited smoking
rooms available. Parking (valet $30). Pool (indoor)
Restaurant. Room service. Spa. TV (DVD on request,
pay movies, widescreen).
Other locations: 220 Bloor Street W, at Admiral
Avenue, The Annex (1-800 327 0200/415 960 5200).

Pantages Suites Hotel & Spa

200 Victoria Street, at Shuter Street, Dundas
Square, ON M5B 1V8 (1-866 852 1777/416
362 1777/fax 416 368 8217/www.pantages
hotel.com). Streetcar 501/subway Queen. **Rates**
$179-$349 double/suites. **Credit** AmEx, MC, V.
Map p272 G7 **9**
The timing was a bit off: the Pantages was named
after a neighbouring theatre that changed its name
just before the hotel opened. But this condo/hotel
tower is more chic than theatrical. The top floors are
condos, which makes for a mixed crowd in the lobby.
Rooms have a minimalist feel, with fluffy white
duvets and funky leather chairs in the larger rooms,
though the small bathrooms can be a letdown. The
mod cons are a forte: each room features a generous
kitchenette, with hob, refrigerator, dishwasher,

microwave, washer and dryer. While the home-from-home comforts might not be everyone's cup of tea (there's something odd about sleeping within arm's reach of the stove and fridge), these extras are useful. 'Serenity Rooms' come with yoga mats and air purifiers, and everyone is encouraged to tune into the meditation channel, while the salon (sorry, 'Anti-Aging & Longevity Spa') has a range of beautifying or relaxing treatments. The less health-conscious can sip Martinis in the new modish bar. If you're peckish, pop next door to Fran's diner, or, a better option, the Senator diner across the road.
Bar. Business centre. Concierge. Disabled-adapted rooms. Gym. Internet (high-speed, wireless). No-smoking rooms & floors. Parking (valet $30). Spa. TV (DVD on request, pay movies).

Renaissance Toronto Hotel Downtown

1 Blue Jays Way, at Front Street W, Entertainment District, ON M5V 1J4 (1-800 237 1512/416 341 7100/fax 416 341 5091/www.marriott.com). Streetcar 504/subway St Andrew or Union. **Rates** $229-$629 single/double. **Credit** AmEx, MC, V. **Map** p271 E8 ❿
The Renaissance is built into the fabric of the Rogers Centre, the stadium that's home to the Blue Jays baseball team, the Toronto Argonauts football team and various concerts. The hotel's claim to fame is that 70 of the rooms overlook the stadium (with opening windows), as do the bar and restaurant. It's a great way to see a game, or to stare out at an eerily empty stadium on non-game days. But be warned: the great views work both ways: once, the entire stadium watched an amorous couple getting down to business. The classy suites are split level, with comfortable lounges and marbled bathrooms.
Bar. Business centre. Concierge. Disabled-adapted rooms. Gym. Internet (high-speed). No-smoking hotel. Parking ($18; valet $25). Pool (indoor). Restaurant. Room service. Spa. TV (DVD on request, pay movies).

The Sutton Place Hotel

955 Bay Street, at Wellesley Street, University, ON M5S 2A2 (1-800 268 3790/416 924 9221/fax 416 924 1778/www.suttonplace.com). Bus 6, 94/subway Wellesley. **Rates** $179-$249 single/double; $279-$579 suite. **Credit** AmEx, MC, V. **Map** p274 F5 ⓫
The blocky, drab exterior of this celebrity hangout hides some of the most luxurious rooms in the city, and the central location is a distinct advantage. The hotel shoots for a European feel, with a ballroom lit by stunning Venetian-style chandeliers and suites studded with repro antiques. The intersection of Bay and Wellesley is no oil painting, but the hotel is located across the street from Bistro 990, the host restaurant for the Toronto International Film Festival. Sutton Place graciously receives stars year-round, especially in its penthouse suites, and the east-facing rooms have the added bonus of balconies. The hotel opened in 1967, and staff tell us they're still getting return visitors from the first year. **Photo** *p40.*

Bar. Business centre. Concierge. Disabled-adapted rooms. Gym. Internet (high-speed). No-smoking rooms & floors. Parking ($25). Pool (indoor). Restaurant. Room service. Spa. TV (DVD on request, pay movies, widescreen).

Moderate

Delta Chelsea

33 Gerrard Street W, at Bay Street, Chinatown, ON M5G 1Z4 (1-800 243 5732/416 595 1975/fax 416 585 4375/www.deltachelsea.com). Bus 6/subway College or Dundas. **Rates** $119-$369 single/double. **Credit** AmEx, MC, V. **Map** p272 G6 ⓬
With 1,590 rooms, the Chelsea is the largest hotel in the city. And it is something of a crowd-pleaser. It's handily located downtown near the Eaton Centre and the City Hall. The restaurants run the gamut from food court to fine dining, and the hotel has an affiliation with a nearby spa. The hotel is child-friendly in the extreme, with a well-equipped childcare centre, dedicated family suites with bunkbeds and kitchens, plus a huge water slide dropping into the all-ages pool. But it's also great for parents: there's an adults-only pool, which adjoins a fitness centre and a drinks lounge. The decor ranges from drab to comfortable, but there are bathrobes for all. **Photo** *p45.*
Bar. Business centre. Concierge. Disabled-adapted rooms. Gym. Internet (dataport, high-speed). No-smoking rooms & floors. Parking ($25). Pools (2 indoor). Restaurants (4). Room service. TV (pay movies, VCR on request).

Hotel Victoria

56 Yonge Street, at Wellington Street, Financial District, ON M5E 1G5 (1-800 363 8228/416 363 1666/fax 416 363 7327/www.hotelvictoria-toronto.com). Streetcar 504/subway King or Union. **Rates** $119-$179 single/double. **Credit** AmEx, MC, V. **Map** p272 G8 ⓭
Old and small are good qualities when it comes to hotels, and this one is both. Built in 1908, the Victoria is the second-oldest hotel in the city after The Gladstone (*see p46*). The 56 rooms are on the small side, and some views are better than others, but the place has character and a sense of intimacy. It has a breakfast room, and there are plenty of restaurants nearby for other meals. The location is great too: it is close to Union Station, the St. Lawrence Market, the Financial District and the Waterfront.
Internet (free wireless). No-smoking rooms. TV.

Metropolitan Hotel Toronto

108 Chestnut Street, at Dundas Street W, Chinatown, ON M5G 1R3 (1-800 668 6600/416 977 5000/fax 416 977 9513/www.metropolitan. com/toronto). Streetcar 505/subway St Patrick. **Rates** $139-$349 single/double; $229-$2,100 suite. **Credit** AmEx, MC, V. **Map** p272 F6 ⓮
This Asian-owned Metropolitan is less stylish than it likes to think it is, but it has tasteful and comfortable rooms with nary a floral in sight: think beige and beech, with intelligent touches such as double-decker

desks and good lighting. The rooms aren't huge, but they are comfortable. The restaurants are distinctly smart (gourmet Chinese Lai Wah Heen serves the best dim sum in town; *see p113*) and room-service meals of a high standard. The hotel is let down by its ordinary public areas, but business visitors probably don't mind. The central location is a bonus too: just steps from Nathan Phillips Square or shopping . For the SoHo Met, *see p41*.

Bar. Business centre. Concierge. Disabled-adapted rooms. Gym. Internet (dataport, high-speed). No-smoking rooms & floors. Parking ($19; valet $24). Pool (indoor). Restaurants (2). Room service. TV (DVD/pay movies, widescreen in some rooms).

Strathcona Hotel

60 York Street, at Wellington Street, Financial District, ON M5J 1S8 (1-800 268 8304/416 363 3321/fax 416 363 4679/www.thestrathcona hotel.com). Streetcar 504/subway King or Union. **Rates** from $125. **Credit** AmEx, MC, V. **Map** p272 F8 ⑮

Located in the heart of the Financial District, the Strathcona used to be a bargain alternative to the grander (and more famous) Royal York Hotel across the street. But times have changed: following recent renovations, it has gone upmarket. And it's usually packed when there's a big conference in town. Thanks to a deal with a nearby fitness club, guests

Get wet and wild, then sleep it off at the **Delta Chelsea**. *See p44*.

get cheap access to hot tubs, squash courts and a fully equipped gym. During the week, the basement pub is popular with the business crowd.
Bar. Concierge. Internet (high-speed). No-smoking rooms. Restaurant. Room service. TV (pay movies).

Travelodge Motor Hotel
621 King Street W, at Bathurst Street, Entertainment District, ON M5V 1M5 (1-800 578 7878/416 504 7441/fax 416 504 4722/ www.travelodgetorontodowntown.com).
Streetcar 504, 511. **Rates** $120-$180 single/double. **Credit** AmEx, MC, V. **Map** p271 D8 ⑯

A new name, some radical landscaping and a location in a suddenly trendy area of the city do nothing to quash the retro feel of this classic motor inn. It's a stone's throw from Susur (*see p109*), one of the city's top restaurants, but a world – and budget – apart. Rates include breakfast and parking comes at a nominal fee (a godsend this close to downtown). Though fancy wine bars are popping up all over the neighbourhood, this basic hotel still manages to keep its 1950s cool. And the shops of Queen Street West are a short walk away.
Internet (dataport, wireless). Parking ($7.50). TV.

Get on your glad rags

Teen queens, tree-huggers and wannabe rockers are bunking down on West Queen West, along with prudish Victorians, bikers and fans of faux fur. Following a major revamp, the themed rooms of the Gladstone Hotel (*see p52*) cover every fetish. And the city's oldest hotel, a landmark Toronto property, has been transformed from a flophouse to a fashionable destination.

Named after the English prime minister William Gladstone (1809-98), the hotel opened in 1889 across from a busy rail junction. Its design, in Richardsonian Romanesque style, is grand, characterised by red brick, rough cut stone and dramatic arches. But its past is less salubrious: in

the old days, it was the last place thirsty travellers could obtain hard liquor before reaching Hamilton, an hour to the west, and one of the few risqué hotels in town where patrons could drink while playing shuffleboard. During the late 20th century, the Gladstone declined into seediness.

In restoring the hotel in 2006, visual artist Christina Zeidler and her father, architect Eberhard (who created the Eaton Centre and Ontario Place) kept many of the original details intact, including plaster mouldings and faux marble pillars. The last remaining hand-operated elevator in the city rises up through a grand staircase like a gilded cage.

To reflect the artsy neighbourhood, Christina commissioned local artists to design the 37 guest rooms. You can preview each room on the hotel's website, so you don't end up in the Faux Naturelle Room – where 'lesbian separatist commune meets Storybook Gardens' – when you're in the mood for the Trading Post, a masculine room with a four-poster bed anchored by tree trunks. Hank, a Gladstone veteran from its flophouse days, is now the elevator operator; he may direct you to room 414, The Walls Are Speaking. Here, artists Day Milman and Bruno Billio pay homage to the Gladstone's past residents in toile wallpaper scenes.

All the eccentricity and eclecticism of West Queen West come together at the Gladstone, with cabaret and burlesque shows, magazine and CD launch parties, indie bands performing in the ballroom and, on the weekends, karaoke night in the Melody Bar. The second floor is devoted to art exhibits and festivals such as Come Up to My Room, the funky alternative interior-design fair held in February. The Art Bar continues to hold weekly figure-drawing classes begun in 1957.

Budget

Baldwin Village Inn

9 Baldwin Street, at McCaul Street, Kensington,
ON M5T 1L1 (416 591 5359/www.baldwininn.
com). Streetcar 506, 505/subway St Patrick.
Rates $85-$105 single/double. **Credit** AmEx,
MC, V. **Map** p271 E6 ⓱

In the heart of quaint Baldwin Street and steps from
Kensington's cafés and the university campus, this
pretty, six-room inn offers a good location – and
good value. In a converted house, it is occupied by
a retired couple who pay great attention to detail.
The rooms are clean and spacious (especially on the
second floor), with views over the street life or the
little garden in the back. A homely eat-in kitchen and
second-floor lounge encourage convivial gatherings.
Bathrooms are shared.
Bar. Internet (high-speed). Non-smoking property.

Bay Street Motel

650 Bay Street, at Elm Street, Chinatown, ON
M5G 1M8 (1-800 695 8284/416 971 8383/fax
416 971 8527/www.baystreetmotel.com). Bus 6/
streetcar 505/subway College or Dundas.
Rates $50 single; $65-$95 double. **Credit**
AmEx, MC, V. **Map** p271 F6 ⓲

Following some basic renovations, this low-end
hotel has been upgraded to 'pleasant'. Across the
street from the bus station, and close to the Eaton
Centre, it's one of the most affordable ways to sleep
in the heart of the action. Staff are friendly, and you
can get great bargains on longer stays – commit to
a week and cut your room rate by more than a third;
staying for a month brings it down by more than
two-thirds. Look at your room before you settle in
to check the amenities, as they tend to vary.
Bathrooms are shared.
Internet (free wireless). TV. Parking ($15)

Downtown East

Expensive

Cosmopolitan Toronto

8 Colborne Street, at Yonge Street, Financial
District, ON M5E 1E1 (416 350 2000/www.
cosmotoronto.com). Streetcar 504/subway King.
Rates $209-$539; penthouse suites from $2500.
Credit AmEx, MC, V. **Map** p272 G8 ⓳

Tucked away on a quiet downtown street, this new
boutique hotel cultivates its serenity seriously – and
stylishly. With an incense menu, yoga mats and a
guided relaxation CD gift, the Cosmo is all about
creating good karma. There are five suites per floor,
each with a washer/dryer and a kitchen. So you don't
have to leave, and you may not want to: the rooms
have hardwood floors, flat-screen TVs and Egyptian
cotton linens, plus floor-to-ceiling windows that
open and balconies with lake views. The Shizen Spa
and Doku 15 resto-lounge will get you in a Zen state,
as will the gemstone on your pillow. **Photo** *p50.*

Baldwin Village Inn

**OUR CLIMATE NEEDS
A HELPING HAND TODAY**

Be a smart traveller. Help to offset your carbon emissions
from your trip by pledging Carbon Trees with Trees for Cities.

All the Carbon Trees that you donate through Trees for Cities
are genuinely planted as additional trees in our projects.

Trees for Cities is an independent charity working with local
communities on tree planting projects.

www.treesforcities.org   Tel 020 7587 1320

Trees for Cities
Charity registration number 1032154

Bar. Business centre. Concierge. Disabled-adapted rooms. Gym. Internet (high-speed, wireless). No-smoking floors. Parking (valet $29). Restaurant. Room service. Spa. TV (DVD/CD).

Grand Hotel & Suites Toronto

225 Jarvis Street, at Dundas Street E, Downtown, ON M5B 2C1 (1-877 324 7263/416 863 9000/ fax 416 863 1100/www.grandhoteltoronto.com). Streetcar 505. **Rates** $179-$359 junior/deluxe suites; $399-$699 ambassador suites. **Credit** AmEx, MC, V. **Map** p272 G6 ⑳

Opened in 2000, this 177-room boutique hotel has become a firm favourite with business travellers who require longer stays. It boasts large, luxurious suites, complimentary breakfasts, a softly lit pool, and views of the lake from two rooftop hot tubs. The Citrus restaurant, meanwhile, sits elegantly between the limestone lobby and lush terrace. No wonder stars such as Gabriel Byrne and Shaquille O'Neal feel right at home here (trivia: this building was formerly the HQ of the Mounties).

Bar. Business centre. Concierge. Disabled-adapted rooms. Gym. Internet (high-speed, wireless). No-smoking rooms & floors. Parking ($18). Pool (indoor). Restaurant. Room service. Spa. TV (DVD/CD).

Le Royal Meridien King Edward

37 King Street E, at Victoria Street, St Lawrence, ON M5C 1E9 (1-800 543 4300/416 863 0888/ fax 416 863 4102/www.lemeridien-kingedward. com). Streetcar 504/subway King. **Rates** $225-$275 single/double; $350-$550 suites. **Credit** AmEx, MC, V. **Map** p272 G8 ㉑

Architect EJ Lennox, who also built Casa Loma and Old City Hall, sure knew how to show off. Guests look up in awe as they pass through the soaring marble columns of the four-storey lobby, overlooked by a portrait of King Edward VII himself. The King Eddie, as it's known to locals, is a designated historic building and retains all of its grandeur, from the original chandeliers to the high ceilings in the 292 sumptuous rooms. The business elite breakfast at the hotel's elegant Café Victoria. Although the hotel opened in 1903, it is up to date, offering wireless net access in the lobby and meeting rooms. *Bar. Business centre. Concierge. Disabled-adapted rooms. Gym. Internet (high-speed, web TV). No-smoking rooms. Parking ($30). Restaurant. Room service. Spa. TV (DVD on request, pay movies).*

Novotel Toronto Centre

45 The Esplanade, at Scott Street, St Lawrence, ON M5E 1W2 (1-800 668 6835/416 367 8900/ fax 416 360 8285/www.novotel.com). Subway Union. **Rates** $170-$340 single/double. **Credit** AmEx, MC, V. **Map** p272 G8 ㉒

The solid, unpretentious Novotel offers good value and location for the money. The traditional lobby comes with bar, gift shop and liveried concierge hustling theatre tickets; the bedrooms are simple and well kitted out. There is a dearth of style, but it is reliable and well run. The breakfast buffet cuts no

corners; if you're still peckish, the historic St Lawrence Market is nearby. The staff at this European chain are multilingual; try out your rusty Danish or Russian and they will be up to the job. *Bar. Concierge. Disabled-adapted rooms. Gym. Internet (high-speed). No-smoking rooms & floors. Parking ($20). Pool (indoor). Restaurant. Room service. TV (pay movies).*

Moderate

Bond Place Hotel

65 Dundas Street E, at Bond Street, Downtown, ON M5B 2G8 (1-800 268 9390/416 362 6061/ fax 416 362 6046/www.bondplacehoteltoronto. com). Streetcar 505/subway Dundas. **Rates** from $99 single/double. **Credit** AmEx, MC, V. **Map** p272 G6 ㉓

The Bond offers a central location and good value – and that's about it. Though it will never shrug off the drabness of the surrounding neighbourhood, the recent renovations give the place a little more style. In true Toronto fashion, staff serve travellers in many languages, including Cantonese and Tamil. While prices shoot up during special events, the hotel is usually a bargain, especially if your gang can fill a triple or quadruple occupancy, which costs only a bit more than a standard double. *Bar. Business centre. Concierge. Disabled-adapted rooms. No-smoking rooms. Parking ($15). Restaurant. Room service. TV (pay movies).*

Clarion Hotel & Suites Selby

592 Sherbourne Street, at Bloor Street E, Church & Wellesley, ON M4X 1L4 (1-800 387 4788/416 921 3142/fax 416 923 3177/www.hotelselby.com). Bus 75/subway Sherbourne. **Rates** $99-$199 single/double/suites. **Credit** AmEx, MC, V. **Map** p275 H4 ㉔

One of several hotels in town that claim Ernest Hemingway as their most distinguished guest (he used to write for the *Toronto Star* newspaper), this Victorian, red-brick hotel provides travellers with a characterful (and reasonably priced) alternative to the downtown high-rises. Originally built as a private home in 1880, this historic building now comprises 82 rooms (ranging from basic and small to suites with fireplaces or jacuzzis). It's close to Toronto's gay village, and also handy for the subway. Steer clear of the 'home office' rooms located in the basement: they are dark and gloomy. *Disabled-adapted rooms. Internet (free). No-smoking rooms. Parking ($13). TV.*

Ramada Plaza Hotel

300 Jarvis Street, at Carlton Street, Church & Wellesley, ON M5B 2C5 (1-800 567 2233/416 977 4823/fax 416 977 4830/www.ramada.ca). Streetcar 506/subway College. **Rates** $99-$149 single/double; $149-$259 1-bed suites. **Credit** AmEx, MC, V. **Map** p272 G6 ㉕

Cheap and cheerful is the best way to describe this chain hotel, situated across the street from Allan Gardens and its greenhouses. Built in 1929 as a block

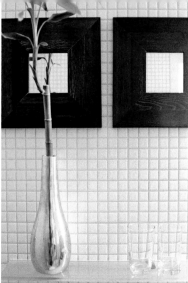

Zen and the art of hotel maintenance: **Cosmopolitan Toronto**. *See p47.*

of apartments and recently designated a historic building, it retains some quirks from the early days: the elevator shafts are smaller than average, while the old (refinished) cast-iron bathtubs are larger than average. The hotel shares its parking lot, pool and gym with an adjacent condominium complex. The neighbourhood is sketchy at night, but the downtown core is a short walk or ride by streetcar.

Bar. Business centre. Concierge. Disabled-adapted rooms. Gym. Internet (high-speed). No-smoking rooms & floors. Parking ($20). Pool (indoor). Restaurant. Room service. TV (pay movies).

Budget

Isabella Hotel & Suites

556 Sherbourne Street, at Isabella Street, Church & Wellesley, ON M4X 1L3 (1-888 947 2235/416 922 2203/fax 416 922 2204/www.isabellahotel.com). Subway Sherbourne. **Rates** $89-$209 single/double. **Credit** AmEx, MC, V. **Map** p275 H4 ㉖

A former flophouse that's riding Toronto's gentrification wave, the Isabella offers history and character for budget travellers. The original hotel was built in 1890, with a new tower added 25 years later. Its current incarnation preserves some of the 19th-century detail, including hand rails and external ornaments. The hallways are a bit drab, and the rooms on the small side. Some suites have fireplaces and a jacuzzi. The continental breakfast is basic but does the job.

Bar. Internet (high-speed). No-smoking rooms & floors. Parking ($15). Restaurant. Room service. TV.

Neill-Wycik College Hotel

96 Gerrard Street E, at Church Street, Church & Wellesley, ON M5B 1G7 (1-800 268 4358/416 977 2320/fax 416 977 2809/www.neill-wycik.com/

college_en). *Streetcar 506/subway College or Dundas.* **Rates** $45-$65 single/double; $85 triple; $100 quad/suite. **Credit** MC, V. **Map** p272 G6 ㉗

During the academic year this is a students' residence, but from May to August it becomes a tourist hotel. Rooms are arranged in groups of four or five, with each cluster sharing two common bathrooms, a kitchen and a living area. There's no bar, but a nearby pizzeria and an on-site café provide places to socialise. Discounts for students, seniors, hostel members and groups. Good value.

Internet (pay terminal). Parking ($10). TV (lounge).

Victoria's Mansion Guest House

68 Gloucester Street, at Church Street, Church & Wellesley, ON M4Y 1L5 (416 921 4625/fax 416 944 1092/www.victoriasmansion.com). Subway Wellesley. **Rates** $79-$145 single/double. **Credit** MC, V. **Map** p275 G5 ㉘

This sedate Victorian brick mansion, built as a residence in the 1880s, sits on a shady, picturesque street close to the gay village. It opened as a tourist hotel in 2000, and makes a nice change from the big international chains. The 23 characterful rooms all have a fridge and microwave; some are set up with kitchenettes to suit longer stays.

Internet (dataport, wireless). Parking (free). TV.

Midtown

Luxury

Four Seasons Hotel

21 Avenue Road, at Cumberland Street, Yorkville, ON M5R 2G1(1-800 819 5053/416 964 0411/fax 416 964 2301/www.fourseasons.com/toronto). Subway Museum. **Rates** $255-$570 single/double. **Credit** AmEx, MC, V. **Map** p274 F4 ㉙

For the flagship property of the Toronto-based luxury chain, this Four Seasons seems to be missing the X factor (little wonder they are building a brand-new one, scheduled to open this decade). The rooms are nice enough, the huge suites are good value if you can afford them, and there's a staff of 600 to serve a maximum of 764 guests, but it lacks a certain panache. That said, it's still the preferred resting spot for the upmarket Yorkville shopping crowd, not to mention countless A-list movie, opera and rock stars. The four restaurants include the swanky Truffles and the light and airy Avenue bar and lounge – an attempt to maintain a youthful image. The partial outdoor pool is kept at 35C (95F) in winter, so you can swim when it snows.
Bars (3). Business centre. Concierge. Disabled-adapted rooms. Gym. Internet (high-speed, web TV). No-smoking floors. Parking (valet $30). Pool (indoor/outdoor). Restaurants (4). Room service. TV (DVD, pay movies, video games).

Park Hyatt Toronto
4 Avenue Road, at Bloor Street, Yorkville, ON M5R 2E8 (1-800 778 7477/416 925 1234/fax 416 924 4933/http://parktoronto.hyatt.com). Subway Museum. **Rates** $250-$640 single/double. **Credit** AmEx, MC, V. **Map** p274 F4 ③⓪
The Park Hyatt is a classy affair, if a bit old-fashioned. From the marbled halls and capped bell-boys to the soft carpets and seamless service, the name of the game is tasteful comfort. Highlights include the renowned Roof Lounge bar (*see p139*), a coffee shop with the standards of an upmarket restaurant and the beautiful Stillwater Spa, where you can luxuriate in your own private changing room watching TV on a sofa. Bedrooms vary in size: the newer north wing offers a range of playful, bright and spacious rooms, including a blushing, overwhelmingly pink suite – while the more traditional south-wing rooms tend to be cosy and dark. Wooden repro antiques and fluffy duvets add a touch of home.
Bars (2). Business centre. Concierge. Disabled-adapted rooms. Gym. Internet (high-speed). No-smoking floors. Parking (valet $32). Restaurant. Room service (24hrs). Spa. TV (DVD/VCR on request, pay movies).

Moderate

Howard Johnson Downtown
89 Avenue Road, at Yorkville Avenue, Yorkville, ON M5R 2G3 (1-800 446 4656/416 964 1220/fax 416 964 8692/www.hojo-canada.com). Subway Museum. **Rates** $89-$179 single/double. **Credit** AmEx, MC, V. **Map** p274 F3 ③①
Your best bet for staying in Yorkville on a budget. Though located right next door to swanky Hazelton Lanes, this chain hotel has homely rooms – the checkered bedspreads say it all – with wooden furniture and exposed-brick walls (although some rooms have windows that look out on to more brick walls; views over Avenue Road are better). The lifts,

bathrooms and halls are on the small side. Although there's no restaurant, rates include breakfast, coffee and tea (available 24 hours a day in the lobby). *Gym. Internet (dataport, pay terminal). No-smoking rooms. Parking ($10). TV (pay movies).*

Budget

Ainsley House Bed & Breakfast
19 Elm Avenue, at Sherbourne Street, Rosedale, ON M4W 1M9 (1-888 423 3337/416 972 0533/fax 416 925 1853/www.ainsleyhouse.com). Bus 75/subway Sherbourne. **Rates** $49.50-$109 single/double. **Credit** MC, V. **Map** p275 H3 ③②
Staying at this century-old European-style guesthouse gives you rare access to a Rosedale mansion, though that access is limited. Guests are steered away from the living room, which is used by the Hannigan family, who run this B&B. The dainty rooms have high ceilings and iron beds, plus en-suite bathrooms. Hot breakfast is served every day. The gardens and tree-lined neighbourhood provide a welcome respite from the concrete jungle. *Internet (dataport). No-smoking hotel. Parking (free). TV.*

Global Guest House
9 Spadina Road, at Bloor Street W, The Annex, ON M5R 2S9 (416 923 4004/fax 416 923 4004/www.globalguesthousetoronto.com). Streetcar 510/subway Spadina. **Rates** $58-$68 single; $68-$78 double. **Credit** MC, V. **Map** p274 E4 ③③
In the heart of the Annex, this renovated 1889 house is a typical example of Toronto Victorian architecture, handily located next to Spadina subway station. With only ten rooms, the Global is intimate, but it's not a B&B. It doesn't serve breakfast, but there are free hot and cold drinks in the common room – presumably the reason owners Norman and Rhona Singer call the place a 'Bed and Tea'. Not all rooms have en-suite bathrooms; most are flamboyantly decorated. The backyard is available for use. There are two parking spots if reserved in advance.
No-smoking rooms. Parking. TV.

Madison Manor Boutique Hotel
20 Madison Avenue, at Bloor Street W, The Annex, ON M5R 2S1 (1-877 561 7048/416 922 5579/fax 416 963 4325/www.madisonavenuepub.com/madisonmanor). Subway St George or Spadina. **Rates** $99-$189 single/double/suites. **Credit** AmEx, MC, V. **Map** p274 E4 ③④
This historic Victorian mansion is tucked away on a quiet Annex road just off Bloor Street West. It has 23 rooms, each individually decorated by co-owner Isabel Manore (she and husband David also own the adjoining Madison Avenue Pub; *see p139*). Furnished with antiques found in Queen Street boutiques, the rooms possess character but vary in size, price and the number of amenities. Four have fireplaces and three have balconies (note that some are disturbingly close to the patios of the bar next

Drake Hotel

door, though staff say they have never had complaints). The hotel gives discounts to U of T students' parents, but people under 19 are not allowed. Rates include continental breakfast.
Bar. Internet (high-speed). No-smoking hotel. Parking ($10-$15). Restaurant.

West End

Expensive

Drake Hotel

1150 Queen Street W, at Beaconsfield Avenue, ON M6J 1J3 (416 531 5042/fax 416 531 9493/www.thedrakehotel.ca). Streetcar 501. **Rates** $179-$289 single/double. **Credit** AmEx, MC, V. **Map** p270 A7 ㉟

If you've spent more than three seconds in Toronto you'll have heard of the Drake. Once a flophouse, the 19-room property was transformed by ex-dotcommer Jeff Stober, who devoted $5 million and two years to building something Toronto lacked – a multi-purpose HQ of hipdom. Public rooms artfully blend the original trimmings of mahogany, terrazzo floors and steel railings with rotating art exhibits and the odd performance piece: don't be surprised to catch a striptease on the stairway or a spoken word act while you're eating your eggs Benedict. Though wired for the 21st century, with flat-screen TVs, CD and DVD players and high-speed net access, the 'crash-pads' are not for the claustrophobe. The basement provides a venue for eclectic performances. Queues form to get into the funky street-level bar and Sky Yard on the roof (heated in winter). The Corner Café, a restaurant and a raw bar round out the attractions. Naysayers say the Drake tries too hard to be cool, but it has certainly brightened up West Queen West. *See also p140 and p203.*

Bars (2). Concierge. Internet (high-speed, wireless). No-smoking hotel. Restaurants (4). Room service. TV (DVD/pay movies, widescreen).

Old Mill Inn

21 Old Mill Road, at Bloor Street W, ON M8X 1G5 (1-866 653 6455/416 236 2641/fax 416 236 2749/www.oldmilltoronto.com). Subway Old Mill. **Rates** $219-$379 single/double; $395-$695 suite. **Credit** AmEx, MC, V.

Nestled in a forested pocket of the West End, the Old Mill offers a tranquil break from urban grit. The original mill was built on this site next to the Humber river in 1793, the year that Toronto was founded. Today the wooded valley feels almost as secluded as it would have been then. This Tudor-style hotel, which only opened in 2001, incorporates the stone ruins of a later mill, and exudes history and luxury. The 47 individually designed rooms and 13 large suites encircle a wild, multi-level garden with trickling water. Tennis courts, a spa and easy access to trails and parks make you forget you're in the city. The grounds and large restaurant attracts wedding parties; in summertime the place is often a sea of taffeta and tuxedos. Afternoon tea is a long-standing tradition with tourists and residents alike.
Bar. Concierge. Gym. Internet (high-speed). No-smoking hotel. Parking (free). Restaurant. Room service. Spa. TV (DVD/VCR on request, pay movies).

Moderate

Gladstone Hotel

1214 Queen Street W, at Gladstone Avenue, ON M6J 1J6 (416 531 4635/www.gladstonehotel.com). Streetcar 501. **Rates** $175-$195 single/double; $375-$475 suite. **Credit** AmEx, MC, V. **Map** p270 A7 ㊱
For review, *see p46* **Get on your glad rags**.
Bars (2). Internet (high-speed, wireless). Restaurants (2). Room service. Spa. TV (pay movies, widescreen).

Palmerston Inn Bed & Breakfast

*322 Palmerston Boulevard, at College Street,
ON M6G 2N6 (1-877 920 7842/416 920 7842/
http://palmerstoninn.com). Streetcar 506.* **Rates**
$100-$225 single/double. **Credit** MC, V.
Map p270 C5 ③⑦
Sitting proudly on a grand old residential boulevard,
this pretty B& B is shaded by a canopy of mature
trees. The Georgian-style decor includes floral
prints, doilies and armoires. There are six rooms,
each one named after a Lady; some feature fireplaces
and private baths. After a hearty breakfast, relax in
a wicker chair on the front porch.
No-smoking house. Parking. TV (cable).

Hostels

College Hostel

*280 Augusta Avenue, at College Street, Chinatown,
ON M5T 2L9 (416 929 4777/fax 416 925 5495/
www.collegehostel.com). Streetcar 506, 510.* **Rates**
$55 single; $70 double; $25 (per person) dormitory.
Credit AmEx, MC, V. **Map** p271 D5 ③⑧
On the edge of Kensington Market, this popular
hostel is close to good bars, shops and restaurants.
The single and double rooms have cable TV and
phones, and the games room has a pool table and
pinball machine. There's also a decent sushi bar.
*Internet (wireless). No-smoking hostel. Parking (free).
Restaurant. TV.*

Global Village Backpackers

*460 King Street W, at Spadina Avenue,
Entertainment District, ON M5V 1L7 (1-888
844 7875/416 703 8540/www.globalbackpackers.
com). Streetcar 504, 510.* **Rates** $70 private room;
$28 (per person) quad; $25 (per person) dormitory.
Credit MC, V. **Map** p271 D8 ③⑨
Jack Nicholson, Mick Jagger and Canada's own
brooding poet Leonard Cohen slept here. It was a
hotel then; now it's a bright and friendly hostel with
dorms, quads and a few private rooms collectively
called 'the Village' (there are 190 beds in total). The
busy pub is a good place to meet fellow travellers,
and the staff organise events such as tours of the
Niagara Falls in rainbow-painted 'Magic Buses'. The
clubs of the Entertainment District are nearby.
Bar. Internet (pay terminal). No-smoking hostel. TV.

Hostelling International Toronto

*76 Church Street, at Adelaide Street E, St Lawrence,
ON M5C 2G1 (1-877 848 8737/416 971 4440/fax
416 971 4088/www.hihostels.ca). Streetcar 501,
504/subway King.* **Rates** $89 private; $24 (per
person) shared. **Credit** MC, V. **Map** p272 G7 ④⓪
This is a back-to-basics hostel whose 154 beds are
mostly in dorms; the few private rooms have
en-suite bathrooms. It's a social place, with an on-
site café, organised walking tours of the city and pub
crawls on a Wednesday. Barbecues are held on the
roof patio in high season.
*Disabled-adapted rooms. Internet (pay terminal).
No-smoking hostel. TV (lounge with VCR).*

Planet Traveler's Hostel

*175 Augusta Avenue, at Dundas Street W,
Chinatown, ON M5T 2L4 (416 599 6789/
www.theplanettraveler.com). Streetcar 505,
510.* **Rates** $60 private; $25 dormitory.
No credit cards. Map p271 D6 ④①
There's no sign outside this hostel, so look for the
garden planted in a vaguely planetary pattern and
the stained-glass planet earth above the door. It's a
small place – 18 dorm beds and two private rooms
– and subsequently very friendly. Complimentary
breakfast is provided; otherwise, Kensington
Market's cafés, bars and restaurants offer plenty of
places to nosh. Bathrooms are shared.
*Internet (shared terminal). No-smoking hostel.
TV (lounge).*

Global Village Backpackers.

LONDON　　SYDNEY　　LOS ANGELES

Sightseeing

Features

MOCCA. *See p98.*

Introduction

Easy streets.

Royal Bank Plaza. *See p65*.

Taking in Toronto is best done on foot. It is a pedestrian-friendly place full of characterful neighbourhoods that are best absorbed by meandering. Getting from one 'hood to another is easily achieved on public transport (get a day pass if you plan multiple journeys) and you can watch the districts change from a streetcar or bus (or just take the subway).

In terms of sights, Toronto is a work in progress. There is a clutch of must-sees, depending on your interests: the CN Tower, the Hockey Hall of Fame, Royal Ontario Museum, Rogers Centre (formerly SkyDome) and the Art Gallery of Ontario. The ROM and the AGO are getting major makeovers by Daniel Libeskind and Frank Gehry. Many of Toronto's attractions are natural, such as the Toronto Islands, the Beaches boardwalk, the Leslie Street Spit or High Park.

ORIENTATION

Toronto is easy to navigate. First, it borders a lake, so if you sense a slight slope downwards, then that's south. Second, it has the world's tallest freestanding building (at least until Burj Dubai is completed), acting as a handy marker near the lakefront, just west of centre. Third, it's built largely on a grid system, with just enough variation to keep it interesting, but not so much that getting lost is easy.

Point zero for east–west street designation and numbering is Yonge Street (pronounced 'Young'), famously if tenuously the longest street in the world. Yonge starts on the central lakefront and heads north – not quite to the North Pole; it veers westward and peters out at the border with Minnesota. So King Street, for example, which runs east–west, is called King Street West to the west of Yonge, and King Street East to the east, with numbers starting from zero at Yonge and running upwards along each arm. (North–south numbering starts at zero at the south end of roads and goes up as the road heads north.) On an east–west street, even numbers are on the north side, odd numbers on the south; on a north–south street, even numbers are to the west and odd to the east. The only mildly confusing factor is that numbers on either side of a street don't necessarily match up, or realign in any predictable way at intersections.

Some major thoroughfares have two names, notably Bloor Street, which turns into Danforth Avenue once you cross the Don River, and College Street, which becomes Carlton Street east of Yonge Street. Spadina ('Spad-*eye*-na') Avenue is arbitrarily downgraded to a mere Road in midtown, despite the presence of the august Spadina ('Spad-*ee*-na') House Museum.

Wandering at will is relatively safe: the dodgy bits of town are found in the suburbs. Keep your wits around you at transport terminals. For more on safety, *see p255*.

OVERVIEW

When Metropolitan Toronto amalgamated its five internal cities into one, it officially dropped the 'Metropolitan' moniker. That was in 1998. Now the whole shebang is simply known as the City of Toronto, or the 'mega-city', and stretches some 32 kilometres (20 miles) across and from the lakeshore to Steeles Avenue in the north. The population of the central city is 2.6 million and growing by the second. But there's another world on Toronto's doorstep with a population that now exceeds the city's own: the vast expanse of suburbs – Mississauga,

Sightseeing

Brampton, Richmond Hill, Markham and Pickering, to name a few – strung out on a concrete necklace of freeways and malls. Torontonians dismiss hinterland residents as '905-ers', referring to their telephone area code. Taken together, the city and its 'burbs are now called the GTA, or Greater Toronto Area, which is not a political entity and even less of a unified mindset. The population of the GTA is 5.9 million.

This book focuses principally on the area defined by the original city of Toronto, roughly bounded by Eglinton Avenue on the north side, Victoria Park Avenue to the east, the waterfront and Islington Avenue on the west (but we have extended the boundaries for certain attractions).

Toronto has few defined, named areas; often neighbourhoods are marked by a strip of businesses and named after their main artery – Queen West, the Danforth, Yonge & Eglinton, for example – or their character: Entertainment District, Little Italy and so on. Our Sightseeing chapters, and the rest of the book, follow an area schema that sticks closely to local use, but as there are no formal boundaries we have sometimes used arbitrary divisions.

Downtown Toronto, south of Bloor Street and between Bathurst and the Don Valley Parkway, is the business and civic heart of the city. Almost every main sight is here, along with the University of Toronto and the major arts venues. People still live here, so it is rarely dead. Next up is culturally diverse **Midtown**, where the money lives, plays and spends itself in tasteful fashion. Casa Loma and Spadina Historic House are here. The **West End** is the hipper side of town, with independent, individual shops, bars and restaurants and a boho lifestyle mainlining down Queen Street West and College Street (Little Italy). **East Toronto** is a little more unreconstructed, with traditional residential areas, the Greek-influenced Danforth, Little India and the Beach (the latter has a boardwalk, and a pleasant villagey feel. Finally, **North Toronto** has some good shopping, leafy neighbourhoods and lots of suburbia.

KEEP IT CHEAP

Toronto is relatively cheap. Americans and Brits usually get a favourable exchange rate and lots of city facilities are free, including swimming pools and ice rinks. If you're planning on doing much sightseeing, the **CityPass** ($49.50 adults, $33.30 children), available from Royal Ontario Museum, CN Tower, Art Gallery of Ontario, Casa Loma, Ontario Science Centre and Toronto Zoo or online at http://citypass.com/city/toronto, allows you in to these six main attractions.

Tours

Gray Line (416 594 3310, www.grayline. ca) and **Toronto Tours** (416 869 1372, www.torontotours.com) both do guided tours, and the latter also has a hop-on, hop-off bus.

In summer, uniformed touts around the Harbourfront jetties hawk boat tours. **Mariposa Tours** (416 203 0178, www.mariposacruises.com) offers one-hour cruises and dining tours; the **Great Lakes Schooner Company** (416 203 2322, www.tallshipcruisestoronto.com) will take you out on a three-mastered tall ship. **A Taste of the World** (416 923 6813, www.torontowalksbikes.com) runs offbeat, culturally oriented walks, such as foodie tours of Chinatown, and literary walks. For **Toronto Hippo Tours**, *see p174*.

Don't miss Toronto

Mainstream sights

CN Tower (*see p63*); **Kensington Market** (*see p74*); **Chinatown** (*see p70*); **Harbourfront** (*see p60*); **The Beach** (*see p101*); **Queen Street West** (*see p63*); **Royal Ontario Museum** (*see p78*); **Art Gallery of Ontario** (*see p73*); **Distillery District** (*see p85*); **Rogers Centre** (*see p62*); **Casa Loma** (*see p88*).

Lesser-known sights

Bata Shoe Museum (*see p79*); **RC Harris Filtration Plant** (*see p101*); **Elgin & Winter Garden Theatre Centre** (*see p69*); **Toronto Islands** (*see p76*); **Little India** (*see p101*); **Don Valley Brick Works** (*see p90*); **West Queen West** (*see p96*).

Quintessential Toronto experiences

A peameal bacon sandwich at St Lawrence Market (*see p150*); watching hockey in a bar; taking a streetcar; a dim-sum lunch in Chinatown; strolling the lakeside boardwalk; ice skating at Nathan Phillips Square or Harbourfront (*see p215*); taking a walk in High Park (*see p95*).

Viewpoints

CN Tower (*see p63*); **Canoe Restaurant & Bar** (*see p111*); looking back at the waterfront from a Toronto Islands ferry (*see p60*); the **Roof Lounge** (*see p139*); **Panorama Lounge** (*see p136*); **Scaramouche** (*see p122*).

Downtown

Bright lights, big city.

Waterfront

Maps p270, p271, p272 & p273

Streetcar 509, 510/subway Queens Quay or Union.
Keep your eye on Toronto's waterfront. There
is huge potential to show off the city's greatest
natural asset. And decades of mismanaged
growth and lost opportunities to bring the lake
to the people are finally about to be addressed.
There are now lofty plans to make the lake
more accessible with boardwalks, parks and
low-rise housing east of Yonge Street. The vast
Port Lands will also be transformed with even
more housing, parks, sand dunes and wetlands
(*see p70* **Green scene**).

These moves are long overdue. Cordoned off
by train tracks and highways, the water's edge
has never seemed accessible. The wall of
condos that rose over the past 30 years only
made the psychological barriers concrete.

Long before the city was founded, the
sheltered harbour served aboriginal peoples
as a base for trade and commerce. In the 18th
century, French and English settlers used the
inland port as a centre for the fur trade. By
the early 1900s the port was chugging with
steamboats that used Toronto as a starting

point for tours of the Great Lakes. The city
was the hub of Ontario's booming economy.

The opening of the St Lawrence Seaway in
1959 brought huge ocean-going freighters into
Toronto's harbour, and deep into the continent.
But trade by rail and road soon eclipsed the
city's hopes as an inland port, a trend
exemplified by the construction of the
Gardiner Expressway, an elevated highway
that runs beside the waterfront. An unending
debate over whether to tear it down and bury it
like Boston's leaky Big Dig is part of Toronto's
public discourse.

Meanwhile, visitors to the city tend to
wonder what all the fuss is about. While getting
to the waterfront (especially on bike or foot) can
be an alienating urban experience, once there
it's easy to spend time exploring the many
treasures along the shoreline. Where once were
warehouses, fuel stations and port machinery,
now there are shops, cafés, theatres, museums,
nature reserves, galleries, gardens and parks.

In addition to the lakefront attractions, one
of the best ways to experience (and photograph)
the waterfront is by taking the ferry to the
Toronto Islands (*see p76* **Bike on**), where a
variety of attractions await, including a car-free
residential community on Ward's Island.

A modernist masterpiece: the **Toronto-Dominion Centre** by Mies van der Rohe. *See p66.*

Though the harbour attractions are spread out across the waterfront, many of the best ones are clustered around a series of quays between Cooper Street and Lower Portland Street. A good central location to begin and to get a close-up look at the lake is at the terminus of Yonge Street, the longest street in the world. A small tribute here marks the names of towns along the 1,900-kilometre (1,100-mile) road. The town at the very end of the line is Rainy River, Ontario, on the Minnesota border. The esteemed address 1 Yonge Street belongs to the *Toronto Star*, Canada's largest newspaper.

Looking east, the cityscape devolves into an unattractive industrial stretch, with one sweet exception – the **Redpath Sugar Museum** (*see p61*). The **Waterfront Trail** for joggers, bikers and bladers is little more than a coat of faded paint on patchy asphalt (and therefore a bit hard to follow), but it improves further out towards the Beach (*see p101*). The trail also links up to other substantial recreational paths that meander for kilometres up the Don and Humber river valleys and out into the lake along the **Leslie Street Spit** (*see p70* **Green Scene**).

Where Bay Street joins Queens Quay, there is a path that leads behind the **Westin Harbour Castle** hotel (*see p41*) to the Island ferry docks and to **Harbour Square Park**. If you're looking for quiet green space in which to escape the crowds and the hustle of the city, this is not the place. Towers loom over the busy strip of grass, squeezing it against the water. If you follow the park around Harbour Square back to the main road, you'll find **Pier 6** (145 Queens Quay W, at the foot of York Street), the oldest surviving building on the waterfront dating from 1907. It now houses a coffee shop and a souvenir store. On warm days the former cargo depot opens its doors, allowing visitors to sip their latte while enjoying the sights and sounds of boats going to and fro.

In the 1970s the **Queens Quay Terminal** (207 Queens Quay W, 416 203 0510), just to the west, was a disused food warehouse, a casualty of hard times at the harbour. Today it's an affluent office/shopping mall complex with upscale boutiques and restaurants, some boasting harbourside terraces for alfresco noshing. The terminal also houses the **Premiere Dance Theatre** (*see p224*).

Next to Queens Quay is a large area known as **Harbourfront Centre**, a cultural destination that opened in 1974. The **Power Plant Gallery** (231 Queens Quay W, 416 973 4949) is easy to spot, thanks to its distinctive smokestack, a vestige from its days as a generating plant. Built in 1926, the Power Plant provided heating and cooling for the Toronto Terminal Warehouse (which later became Queens Quay Terminal). It was converted into an art gallery in 1987 and features contemporary works and installations by Canadian and international artists. A word to the credulous: the **Enwave Theatre** next

Sightseeing

to it (formerly known as Harbourfront Centre Theatre) is said to be haunted by up to three different ghosts.

You won't see any ghosts in the building to the west (yet another converted terminal building), but you will see plenty of live artists, performers and crafty types at the **York Quay Centre** (235 Queens Quay W, 416 973 4000), with its indoor and outdoor performance spaces and four art galleries. The Brigantine Room is where the Harbourfront Reading Series takes place (*see p170*). It's also home to a craft studio where you can watch sculptors, glass-blowers and artists practising their crafts in an open-studio setting. Their works are for sale at the nearby craft shop. On the south side of the building is an outdoor café with a small pond. Here hobbyists skipper remote-controlled model boats in the summer – in the winter it's a public skating rink. Also facing the lake, the **Harbourfront Centre Concert Stage** (*see p198*) is an outdoor venue that hosts performances during the summer-long annual **World Roots Festival** (*see p168*). While admission to Harbourfront is free, and there are frequent excellent free concerts, many events require tickets. Check the website and weekly listings.

Heading west, you will come to **HtO**, one of two parks to open on the waterfront in 2007. At the foot of Spadina Avenue, there is a small, whimsical beach, with a permanent forest of bright-yellow metal beach umbrellas and a staircase that descends into the water. A little further west is the **Toronto Music Garden** (475 Queens Quay W). Originally planned for Boston, the garden was inspired by Bach's 'Suites for Unaccompanied Cello' as envisioned by cellist Yo-Yo Ma, who collaborated with landscape designer Julie Moir Messervy to interpret the music in a natural garden. The Summer Music in the Garden series (www.harbourfrontcentre.com) presents classical and new music concerts. From June to September, when the garden is in full bloom, visitors can enjoy the garden using self-guide audio tours.

At the foot of Bathurst Street, behind the last standing grain elevator on the waterfront, is the other new public space, **Ireland Park**, a moving tribute to the thousands of Irish who arrived in Toronto in 1847 during the potato famine. Many perished during a typhus epidemic, but the city's Irish roots would grow stronger and take root in Cabbagetown (*see p81*). Next to this is the ferry that crosses to Toronto City Centre Airport on the island (*see p76*). A half-hour walk further west along the shore takes you to **Ontario Place** and **Exhibition Place** (for both, *see below*).

Exhibition Place

Lake Shore Boulevard W, between Strachan Avenue & Dufferin Street (416 263 3600/www.explace.on. ca). Bus 29/streetcar 509, 511. **Open** times vary; phone for details. **Admission** prices vary; phone for details. **Map** p270 B9.

The imposing Princes' Gates (named after Edward, Prince of Wales, and his brother George) rise up to meet you as you approach the grounds from the east and promise the pomp and circumstance befitting the grand old lady, born in 1879, known as the Canadian National Exhibition. The CNE is into its 13th decade, and the facilities have been upgraded to host not just the annual late summer festival and amusement park, but over 100 major events, from the Grand Prix of Toronto (*see p168*) to the Canadian National Exhibition (*see p169*).

Ontario Place

955 Lake Shore Boulevard W, between Aquatic Drive & Newfoundland Drive (416 314 9900/www. ontarioplace.com). Bus 29/streetcar 509, 511/subway Union. **Open** Dates & times vary; phone for details. Closed winter. **Admission** $22-$34; $12-$18 concessions; free under-3s. *IMAX tickets* $8-$10, $6 concessions. **Credit** AmEx, MC, V. **Map** p270 B10.

This public amusement park was built in the 1970s, when Canadian nationalism (and, some would say, government spending) was at its zenith. The private sector has since stolen all the thunder at Paramount Canada's Wonderland north of the city (*see p173*), but Ontario Place retains the pleasure of its lakeside location. The walkways, cafés and the world's first IMAX theatre are built out over the water, and many of the rides – from water slides to a nifty log-boat ride – involve getting at least a little wet. The pedal boats, normally the runt of the amusement park litter, are fun, as you can chug in and out of the futuristic structures that criss-cross the water. The park is also home to the Molson Amphitheatre (*see p200*), a 15,000-capacity alfresco venue, where fans spread out on the grass hill or take the reserved seats to watch top summertime touring acts.

Redpath Sugar Museum

95 Queens Quay E, between Yonge Street & Lower Jarvis Street (416 366 3561). Bus 6, 75/streetcar 509. **Open** 10am-noon, 1-3.30pm Mon-Fri. **Admission** free. **Map** p272 G9.

This unusual museum, housed in a converted sugar bag warehouse, was opened in 1979 and underwent a major revamp in 1996. In addition to generic exhibits on the history of the Redpath dynasty and of the sugar industry in general, there are also special programmes for groups. To the museum's credit, these have often delved into controversial issues of the sugar trade, including the role of child, immigrant and slave labour, and the introduction of women into the workforce. This is a working refinery, and sugar boats from the Caribbean are often in port unloading their cargo. They can interfere with access to the museum, so call ahead. And although its hours don't lend themselves to the

PATH. *See p65.*

weekend tourist trade, the sugar museum is free and worth a stop. The entrance is poorly marked, but when you sign in, the gate attendant will direct you.

Downtown West

Entertainment District

Maps p271 & p272
Streetcar 501, 504, 510/subway Osgoode,
St Andrew or Union.

Though the name is lame, the Entertainment District hosts a dense concentration of nightclubs centred on and around Richmond Street West between University Avenue and Spadina Avenue. For the purposes of this guidebook, we're expanding the district down to the Gardiner Expressway to include some of the top attractions in the city.

The **Air Canada Centre** arena (*see p63*), the thrusting needle of the **CN Tower** (*see p63*) and the **Rogers Centre** (aka **SkyDome**) stadium (*see p64*), with its famous retractable roof, form a mighty triumvirate of attractions. All are accessible via indoor walkways from **Union Station** (*see p65* – a good way to approach on foot. For the dome and the tower, the walkway has an exit on to Bremner Boulevard opposite the **Steam Whistle Brewing** company (*see p137*). Going in the other direction, the walkway can be entered at the corner of Front Street West and John Street.

The headquarters of the **Canadian Broadcasting Corporation**'s headquarters (250 Front Street W, live tapings 416 205 3700, museum 416 205 5574) are worth a look if you're interested in Canada's public broadcaster (considered the saviour of Canuck culture or a complete waste of time and money, depending whom you ask). The free self-guided museum in the lobby (open 9am-5pm Mon-Fri; 10am-4pm Sat) depicts the golden age of radio and TV. You can switch on, tune in or log on to CBC's many media outlets (*see p253*), or catch a free taping of a programme done before a live studio audience. In the same building, the **Glenn Gould Studio** (*see p197*) is an intimate venue for concert recordings.

Blue Jay Way was named after Toronto's baseball team, not the trippy Beatles track from *Magical Mystery Tour*. Running in a north–south direction, the street is called Peter Street north of King, and is home to clubs, bars and theme restaurants. King Street West caters to the theatre crowd, who take in shows at the **Royal Alex Theatre** (*see p221*), **Princess of Wales Theatre** (*see p221*) and **Roy Thomson Hall** (*see p200*). The strip is also geared to tourists, with restaurant touts luring pedestrian traffic their way.

In what must be one of the first – and hopefully last – examples of selling a cinema's name to a sponsor, the **Scotiabank Theatre**, formerly known as the **Paramount Cinema** (259 Richmond Street W; *see also p181*) garishly presents itself at the corner of Richmond Street West and John Street. If you can stand the sensory overload, you'll find an overlooked display at the top of the

pushing the funkier galleries, restaurants and bookshops further west in search of cheaper rent. Though its glory days are gone, Queen West is still a vibrant spot to walk, lunch, people-watch and shop for offbeat items – including vintage vinyl. Famous clubs like the Beverly have closed, but the **Rivoli** *(see p134, p203 and p215)*, the **Cameron House** *(see p202)* and the **Horseshoe Tavern** *(see p201)* keep the old Queen West spirit burning brightly.

The 'new' Queen West ('West Queen West') is further west, starting at Bathurst Street and running as far as Ossington.

Air Canada Centre

40 Bay Street, at Front Street W (416 815 5500/ www.theaircanadacentre.com). Subway Union. **Tours** *May-Aug* hourly 10am-4pm daily. *Sept-Apr* hourly 11am-3pm Wed-Sat (depending on events; phone to check). **Admission** $12; $8-$10 concessions. **Credit** AmEx, MC, V. **Map** p271/p272 F9.

The 21,000-seat arena offers regular behind-the-scenes tours that, schedule permitting, include a glimpse inside the dressing rooms of home teams the Raptors (basketball) and the Leafs (ice hockey), as well as a chance to try on a goalie outfit.

CN Tower

301 Front Street W, at John Street (416 868 6937/ www.cntower.ca). Subway Union. **Open** *Tower* Summer 8am-11pm daily. Winter 9am-10pm Mon-Thur, Sun; 9am-10.30pm Fri, Sat. *Other attractions* phone for details. **Admission** $21.49; $14.49-$19.49 concessions; free under-4s. **Credit** AmEx, MC, V. **Map** p271 E8.

Though soon to be eclipsed as the world's tallest structure (by the Burj Dubai), the CN Tower held the title for an impressive 30 years. Some quip that the best thing about the tower is that, when inside, you don't have to look at it. Completed in 1976 by the railway giant Canadian National, this pillar of hollow concrete stands 553m (1,815ft) high and is basically a big radio antenna – and tourist attraction. Visitors are in awe of its height, and locals are pleased to have such clear TV reception. The tower is twice as tall as its closest competitor in the city, and it's astounding to watch the surrounding 40- and 50-storey buildings fall away below you from the glass elevator. The basic ticket takes you up to the 346-metre (1,136-foot) Look Out Level, where there are indoor and outdoor observation decks, plus a nerve-jangling section of glass floor. The Horizons Café is cheaper than the tower's swanky, rotating restaurant, 360 (416 362 5411).

From here you can pay an extra $10 to reach the Sky Pod – another 30 storeys up – to a height of 447m (1,467ft). The experience is breathtaking, especially on windy days, when you can feel the building sway. Vertigo sufferers can head to the basement for a documentary on the construction of the tower, as well as a vast gift store.

long escalator that leads from the lobby to the cinemas. The Paramount Historic Railing includes sections of the bronze railing from the lobby of the original Paramount Theatre in Times Square, New York. A small collection of old photos and a video presentation recreate the grandeur of the 1920s movie experience.

Leave the Hollywood hype and cross Richmond Street for a taste of Canada's cinematic treasures at the **National Film Board Mediatheque** (150 John Street, *see also p181*). Established in 1939 with the help of British director John Grierson, it was meant to make war propaganda films but has become famous for its documentaries and animated movies, including classics by Norman McLaren. There are individual screening rooms where you can choose from 3,500 films.

One block north, the **MZTV Museum of Television** (277 Queen Street W, 416 591 7400 ext 2870, www.mztv.com) offers regular guided tours at noon, 2pm and 4pm. Founded by Moses Znaimer, who launched the feisty Citytv channel next door, the museum features the world's largest collection of television sets (about 200 in all) and TV memorabilia, including a 1928 General Electric 'Octagon', an experimental model never sold to the public, and the 1939 Phantom Teleceiver, which launched the television age in North America.

Home to an edgy, arty crowd in the 1970s and early '80s, **Queen Street West** (from University Avenue to Bathurst Street) is more about retail than revolution these days. Chain stores have cashed in on the area's vibe,

Dundas Square. *See p66.*

Rogers Centre (formerly SkyDome)

1 Blue Jays Way, at Front Street W (416 341 2770/www.rogerscentre.com). Streetcar 504/subway St Andrew or Union. **Tours** *Summer* hourly 10am-6pm daily. *Winter* 11am, 1pm, 3pm daily (dependent on events; phone to check). **Admission** $13.50; $8-$9.50 concessions; free under-5s. **Credit** AmEx, MC, V. **Map** p271 E8/E9.

Resembling a giant white beetle, the Rogers Centre (named after a local media and cable colossus) is a more significant building than the Air Canada Centre, and also has a more arresting tour. The walking tour, which starts with a 15-minute film about the construction, varies according to what's happening in the stadium, but, in addition to the boxes, media centre and memorabilia room, it can include a walk on the field, or a tour of the amazing roof. When the stadium opened in 1989, the fully retractable roof was the only one of its kind in the world. An efficient, quiet rail system allows it to open or close in only 20 minutes. The stadium holds up to 70,000 people, though few events actually draw that many fans, especially since the decline of resident ball team, the Blue Jays. One thing the tour does not cover is Toronto artist Michael Snow's sculpture, *The Audience*, on the outside of the stadium. You can find this frieze of 14 spectators high on the north-east corner of the building.

Steam Whistle Brewery

255 Bremner Boulevard, at Spadina Avenue (416 362 2337/www.steamwhistle.ca). Streetcar 509, 510. **Open** noon-6pm daily. **Tours** hourly 1-5pm Mon-Sat; 1-4pm Sun. **Admission** *Tours* $6. **Map** p271 E9.

Of the many microbreweries in Toronto, the Steam Whistle gets top marks for location, sandwiched between the ACC and the CN Tower in a railway roundhouse building. The brewery tour informs about combining hops and malt, as well as providing a glimpse of Toronto's railroading past. Steam Whistle offers tours, pours sizeable samples and hosts various events and exhibits. The products are available here, at most bars and taverns in town, and in the Beer Store (*see p156*).

Financial District

Maps p271 & p272

Streetcar 501, 504/subway King, Osgoode, Queen, St Andrew or Union.

Bay Street, the main drag of the Financial District, is synonymous with both Canadian monetary power and the dour Presbyterian work ethic that made Toronto such a dull city for so long. But it is worth braving the windswept concrete canyons and risking neck strain to take in the mighty towers – testaments to new and old money.

The **King** and **Bay** area is still money central. Four of the five major Canadian banks scrape the sky here, and the fifth, the Royal

Bank, maintains an iconic presence a block south, where its flashy golden towers bring an almost American glitz to the skyline.

Banks have clustered in the neighbourhood at least since the mid 1800s, but the first wave of 'skyscrapers' didn't arrive until the early 20th century, and the first biggies didn't appear until the 1920s and '30s, a period that produced the stunning **Commerce Court North** (the original Canadian Imperial Bank of Commerce building) at 25 King Street West. Completed in 1931 and comprising 34 storeys, it has a 20-metre (65-foot) high banking hall modelled on the Baths of Caracalla in Rome, and was once the tallest building in the British Commonwealth. The building dominated the neighbourhood until the mid 1960s, when the three original towers of the **Toronto-Dominion Centre** (*see p66*) arose on the south-west corner of King and Bay Streets. Designed by Mies van der Rohe, the giant of modernism, the austere black-steel and bronzed-glass towers are a Toronto landmark.

Other, taller structures soon followed, as rival banks sought to catch the public eye. But none of them can match the T-D Centre's austere pzazz. In fact, the neighbouring banks are mostly notable for their helpful colour coding: the shiny steel of the 57-storey tower of **Commerce Court West** (the CIBC's current home, designed by IM Pei); the white marble of the Bank of Montreal's **First Canadian Place** tower, with its 72 storeys; and the red granite of the **Bank of Nova Scotia**'s 66-storey tower. A more nondescript tower, at York and King Streets, houses the **Toronto Stock Exchange**, while the TSE's former home round the corner at 234 Bay Street is now the **Design Exchange** (*see p66*).

Further south at 200 Bay Street, the triangular towers of the **Royal Bank Plaza**, built in the mid-1970s, are shorter (41 and 26 storeys), but their mirrored golden windows (an apt metaphor for Bay Street's materialism) make the building stand out from the crowd. The towers' opulent reflections have enriched the pages of many a corporate calendar.

Across the street, the massive towers of **BCE Place** resemble a series of tin cans stacked haphazardly on top of one other. The complex incorporates the façades of several historic buildings on its Yonge Street side, and houses the remains of Toronto's oldest surviving stone structure, the former Commercial Bank of the Midland District (1845), within its bulk. The bank was designed by William Thomas, who is also responsible for two other important structures in old Toronto – **St Lawrence Hall** (built in 1850) and the old **Don Jail**. The centre's best feature is its

astonishing, light-filled galleria, designed by the Spanish architect Santiago Calatrava. The galleria's high white arches resemble the ribs of a giant whale or the vaulted roof of an old cathedral.

An underground mall leads to the **Hockey Hall of Fame** (*see p66*), part of which occupies a rococo bank building on the north-west corner of Front and Yonge Streets. Once the main Toronto office for the Bank of Montreal, it dates from 1886 and boasts a 14m (45ft) high banking hall and a striking stained-glass dome. Too bad that the architecture is now overshadowed by hockey memorabilia.

West on Front Street, the **Fairmont Royal York Hotel** (*see p41*) dominates the area. One of a string of railway hotels that spans the country, it has been one of Toronto's signature hotels since opening in 1929.

Across the street rises the massive colonnade of **Union Station**, a gateway to the city and a landmark in the struggle to preserve its past. Built between 1915 and 1927 in Classical Revival style, the railway hub was slated for redevelopment in the 1970s but was saved by determined preservationists. Today it's both the intersection point of subway, rail and commuter lines and an architectural landmark. It's almost (259 metres) 850 feet long and its celebrated Great Hall is considered one of the finest public rooms in Canada.

At the northern end of the Financial District, the handsome **Hudson's Bay Company** store anchors the south-west corner of Queen and Yonge Streets. Built in 1895-96, this old-school department store is the flagship of a national chain that struggles to live on in the face of big-box stores and can trace its origins as a trading company back to 1670. West on Queen Street, Toronto's first real opera house opened in 2006 at the corner of Queen Street and University Avenue opposite Osgoode Hall. Despite the city's reputation as an arts centre, Toronto had never had a designated opera house. Designed by Diamond + Schmitt, the **Four Seasons Centre for the Performing Arts** holds 2,000 people in a tiered horseshoe-shaped auditorium. *See also p198* **The curtain rises**.

PATH (*photos pp62-63*), a system of underground pathways, connects most of the major buildings in the downtown core, providing protection from the winter cold and summer heat. It stretches from the Metro Toronto Convention Centre in the south to the bus terminal at Bay and Dundas in the north. With 27 kilometres (16 miles) of shopping arcades and 1,200 shops, the maze-like system can feel disorienting. Despite poor signage, it's still a convenient way to get out of the rain.

Sightseeing

Design Exchange

234 Bay Street, at King Street W (416 216 2160/
www.dx.org). Streetcar 504/subway King. **Open**
9am-5pm Mon-Fri; noon-5pm Sat, Sun. **Admission**
$5; $4 concessions. **Credit** AmEx, MC, V. **Map**
p271/p272 F8.

The former home of the Toronto Stock Exchange,
this 1937 building is as notable for its deco design
as for its collection of post-war Canuck artefacts.
Noted Canadian artist Charles Comfort created the
eight murals on the former trading floor, as well the
the exterior stone frieze, which depicts different
kinds of workers. Check out the businessman in a
top hat (fourth in from the right) apparently picking
the pocket of the worker in front of him.

Hockey Hall of Fame

BCE Place, 30 Yonge Street, at Front Street W (416
360 7765/www.hhof.com). Streetcar 504/subway
King or Union. **Open** 10am-5pm Mon-Fri; 9.30am-
6pm Sat; 10.30am-5pm Sun. **Admission** $13; $9
concessions; free under-4s. **Credit** AmEx, MC, V.
Map p271/p272 F8.

A tribute to Canada's national game, this sports
shrine features more than 5,110 sq m (50,000 sq ft)
of games, displays and memorabilia, including
Olympic artefacts and information on the hall's 300-
odd inductees. Most people come to get their photo
taken with the Stanley Cup and other hockey
trophies, but you can also test your skills against a
couple of virtual greats.

Toronto-Dominion Centre

66 Wellington Street W, at Bay Street (416 869
1144/www.tdretail.ca). Streetcar 504/subway King or
Union. **Open** 10am-6pm Mon-Fri. **Admission** free.
Credit varies. **Map** p271/p272 F8.

Mies van der Rohe's late modernist masterpiece is a
close cousin to his famous Seagram Building in New
York, but the black-steel and bronze glass towers
are now very much a part of Toronto's self-image.
Together with new City Hall, the T-D Centre set the
pace for the rejuvenation of Toronto in the 1960s.
Later additions to the complex, one of them towering over the former Toronto Stock Exchange (now
the Design Exchange), have unbalanced the plaza in
which the towers are set, but the complex remains
one of the few architectural masterpieces in modern
Toronto. Most of the centre is off-limits to the public, but Canoe restaurant (*see p113*) is located on the
54th floor of the main tower. Two large outdoor
sculptures are noteworthy: Al McWilliams' eerie
circle-and-chairs (officially known as *Wall and
Chairs*) on the King Street side and Joe Fafard's
popular bronze cows in the central plaza. The latter
graze on a patch of grass west of the main tower.

South of the cows is the celebrated **TD Bank
Financial Group Gallery of Inuit Art** (Ground
Level, 79 Wellington Street W, 416 982 8473), housed
in the southernmost tower of the T-D complex. It's
part of the bank's vast worldwide collection of art
and was the first corporate art gallery in Canada
when it opened in 1986. **Photo** *p60*.

Maps p271 & p272

*Streetcar 501, 505/subway Dundas, Osgoode,
Queen, or St Patrick.*

Dundas Square (**photo** *p64*) the heart of
downtown, is a treeless granite park bathed
in the neon glare of billboards above Yonge
and Dundas. Built in 2004, the public square
bears an unfortunate resemblance to a bus
terminal and is in dire need of some greenery,
but it is an improvement on the tacky low-rise
shops that used to dominate this corner. There
are quirky fountains and chairs for people-
watching, but Times Square it ain't. Still,
this stretch of Yonge Street is filled with a
mix of people from all walks of life and a
varied array of businesses: strip joints, porn
cinemas, discount electronics shops, clothing
chains and music megastores. In 2008 the
Metropolis mall will open on the north-east
corner of Dundas and Yonge, anchored by a
new multiplex, a barrage of international
chains and a video-billboard exterior.

Across Yonge, just outside the **Toronto
Eaton Centre** shopping mall (*see p69*),
the pavement is inscribed with a map of Yonge
Street's meandering route. In this open area,
souvenir shills unload cheap baubles, while
Bible-thumpers foretell the Apocalypse. Escape
to tranquil **Trinity Square Park** behind the
mall, where the groovily progressive Anglican
Church of the Holy Trinity (10 Trinity
Square, 416 598 4521) offers a less intrusive
version of Christianity (the activist church
makes a point of welcoming marginalised
groups). The south entrance of the church
opens on to a small grassy copy of the 13th-
century stone labyrinth at Chartres Cathedral.
Walking the circuitous path is meant to be
meditative, not puzzling – the turf grass walls
are only a few inches high, so the only place
you'll get lost here is in your own thoughts.

North of the Eaton Centre, across Dundas,
is the **Atrium on Bay**, a mediocre mini mall
that houses the central office of the **Ontario
Travel Information Centre** (*see p257*).

South of here, Toronto's **Old City Hall**
(60 Queen Street W, 416 338 0338) offers a
spectacular example of Romanesque Revival,
the dominant style of architecture in the old
days. Designed by architect Edward James
Lennox, who also created Casa Loma, and the
King Edward Hotel, the castle-like hall opened
in 1899 and is now a National Historic Site.
The massive stone building features a 104-
metre (341-foot) clock tower and highly
ornamented Romanesque façades, with
gargoyles galore. It costs nothing to visit the
grand entrance hall, which boasts a mosaic

Mackenzie House. *See p69.*

Global village China

Population: 500,000
Home base: Spadina Avenue and Dundas Street W; Gerrard Street E and Broadview Avenue

The Gold Rush brought the first Chinese up from California to Canada (mainly Vancouver), but the construction of the Canadian Pacific Railway transported them to Toronto. After the last track was laid, many decided to stay. Not only did they struggle to find work and shelter, those early immigrants faced a degrading and racist 'head tax' of $500 levied solely on Chinese immigrants. When, at the turn of the last century, they became restaurant owners and shopkeepers, they found the cheap housing of Spadina Avenue to their liking. After an exclusion act was repealed following World War II, immigration began to surge, and what is now known as Chinatown became a boomtown.

By the 1960s and '70s, rents were so high many immigrants were lured to cheaper housing on the east side. The intersection of Broadview Avenue and Gerrard Street East is an alternative Chinatown favoured for its supermarkets, bakeries and restaurants. Meanwhile, the second and third generations, and those who came from southern China to invest in Toronto's future built up suburbs like Mississauga, Scarborough and Markham.
Trading places: Markham's Pacific Mall (*see p143*) is the place for bamboo, kitchen supplies, designer knock-offs and dim sum. Experience the wonders of brazen, Asian architecture at its extreme at the Dragon City Mall (280 Spadina Avenue W, 416 979 7777).

A taste of: Lee Garden (331 Spadina Avenue, 416 593 9524) attracts queues at peak times but it's worth the wait. Wah Sing Seafood (47 Baldwin Street, 416 599 8822), just off Spadina, lures with fresh seafood. Serious dim sum-ers get a high-end version at Lai Wah Heen in the Metropolitan Hotel (108 Chestnut Street, 416 977 9899).
Join in: The city's largest Chinese New Year celebration features the festive Dragon Dance. A huge dragon winds its way slowly down Dundas Street. A related pan-Asian fair is held on the last week of January or the first week in February: Toronto Celebrates Lunar Year (www.torontocelebrates.com) lasts for three days at the Automotive Building (105 Prince's Boulevard, Exhibition Place, *see p61*).
Local luminary: Member of Parliament Olivia Chow – a take-charge politician – emigrated to Canada from Hong Kong at the age of 13. Since 1985, when she was elected as a school trustee, then a city councillor, she has spoken out on key issues: the waterfront, health care, child care and the homeless. Olivia is one half of a celebrated power couple: she's married to the leader of Canada's left-wing NDP party, Jack Layton. She joined him in Ottawa after winning a federal seat in the 2006 election.

floor, wrought-iron grotesques, stained-glass windows and scagliola columns. Since 1965, when the new City Hall went up across Bay Street, this building has been used as a courthouse. Across Bay Street to the west is another period piece – the current **City Hall** (*see p73*), whose futuristic spaceship council chambers and curved office towers made the perfect (1960s) symbol for a burgeoning, confident city.

Back on Yonge Street you'll find two of Toronto's best-known theatres, the **Canon Theatre** (*see p220*) and the **Elgin & Winter Garden Theatre Centre** (*see below*). Just north-east, at the corner of Shuter and Victoria Streets, is **Massey Hall** (*see p198*), the legendary music venue; head north along Victoria (passing the lovely **Senator** diner; *see p113*) to Ryerson University, home of the **Ryerson Theatre** (44 Gerrard Street E, 416 979 5086). The university's grassy quad, accessible from Gerrard Street, between Yonge and Church, can provide respite from the bustle.

The area east of Yonge puts the 'church' in Church Street (although most of the entrances are in fact on Bond Street). **St George's Greek Orthodox Church** (115 Bond Street, 416 977 3342) is recognisable by its semi-circular mosaic of George slaying the dragon and by its hemispherical domes capped with distinctive Orthodox crosses. Across the road at No.116, the **First Evangelical Lutheran Church** (416 977 4786), erected in 1898 by German immigrants to the Toronto area, still offers services in both English and German.

The Gothic **St Michael's Cathedral** (65 Bond Street, 416 364 0234) is the principal church of Canada's largest English-speaking Catholic Archdiocese. Michael Power, Toronto's first Catholic bishop, laid the first cornerstone in 1845, and the building was completed three years later. The design was adapted from 14th-century English Gothic style by English architect William Thomas. Masses are sometimes graced by the boys of the St Michael's Choir School.

Metropolitan United Church (56 Queen Street E, 416 363 0331) places an emphasis on spreading the word through music. The first building on this site was constructed by Methodists and opened its doors in 1872. In 1925 the Methodists merged with the Congregational Union of Canada and most of the Presbyterian Church of Canada to form the United Church. Three years later this building was devastated by fire. Undaunted, the congregation rebuilt on the same foundation, resulting in the cathedral-style church that stands here today. The

building was dedicated in 1929, and the following year 'Met United' installed Canada's largest pipe organ, with some 8,000 pipes. In addition to their house (of God) performers, there are regular guest musicians, often with a new-agey, multicultural bent. The progressive United Church is also the most gay-friendly denomination in Canada.

Wedged among these sacred institutions, **Mackenzie House** (82 Bond Street, 416 392 6915; **photo** *p67*) is a densely packed museum devoted to the building's former tenant, William Lyon Mackenzie (1795-1861). Mackenzie was the first mayor of Toronto, a radical journalist and political reformer, but he is best known for leading the 1837 Upper Canada Rebellion (*see* History chapter). The rebellion failed and Mackenzie fled to the United States. Eventually, though, he was pardoned, and in 1850 he returned to Canadian politics and publishing. His home was converted into a museum in 1950.

Elgin & Winter Garden Theatre Centre

189 Yonge Street, between Dundas Street E & Queen Street (416 314 2871/www.mirvish.com). Streetcar 501, 505/subway Dundas or Queen. **Tours** 5pm Thur; 11am Sun. **Admission** $7; $6 concessions. **No credit cards. Map** p272 G7.
Billed as the last operating double-decker theatre in the world, this complex is also famous for its beauty. The two theatres have been painstakingly restored to their original luxury: the Elgin was readorned in ruby fabric and gilt, while the botanical fantasy of the Winter Garden's hand-painted walls was enhanced by thousands of leafy beech branches hung from the ceiling. A tour shows off both of the theatres, the lobbies and an exhibit of vaudeville-era scenery. *See also p221.*

Toronto Eaton Centre

1 Dundas Street W, at Yonge Street (416 598 8560/ www.torontoeatoncentre.com). Streetcar 501, 505/ subway Dundas or Queen. **Open** 10am-9pm Mon-Fri; 9.30am-7pm Sat; noon-6pm Sun. **Admission** free. **Map** p272 F6/G6.
While Dundas Square contains some of Toronto's most important places of worship, the biggest shrine here is devoted to consumerism. The Eaton Centre opened its doors in 1977, transforming Yonge Street from a tavern-lined, seedy street, into a tavern-lined, seedy street with a gigantic shopping mall. Actually, the mall paved the way for many other commercial enterprises in the area and also served as a model for a new breed of upmarket shopping centres across North America. Its offspring have outpaced it, and the Eaton is looking a bit dated these days.

The complex stretches a full block from Dundas to Queen Streets. At the south end, on the upper floors, look up at the sculpture *Flight Stop* by local artist Michael Snow. The flock of life-sized Canada geese (swooping down through the upper five storeys of the atrium) was created by affixing hand-tinted photographs on to fibreglass sculptures.

There are about 300 stores, restaurants and services in the mall. Eaton's, the flagship store, no longer exists (it declared bankruptcy in 1999). Sears Canada Inc bought the chain and changed the name. *See also p144.* **Photo** *p72.*

Chinatown

Maps p270 & p271

Streetcar 501, 505, 510/subway Osgoode, Queen's Park or St Patrick.

There are at least three major Chinatowns in Toronto, spawned by the suburban migration of second- and third-generation Asian-Canadians, who created enclaves in Markham's Pacific Mall (*see p143*) and the Chinatown of Broadview and Gerrard. But the original heart and soul of Toronto's large and dynamic Chinese community (*see p68* **Global village**) beats strongest along Spadina Avenue from Queen to College and along Dundas Street West from Bay Street almost as far west as Bathurst Street. Here you'll find a wonderfully manic, just-off-the-durian-truck intensity. As an added bonus, Chinatown links together some of downtown's major attractions in one neat, dumpling-like package.

There are more than a few non-Asian attractions in this enclave. **Osgoode Hall** (130 Queen Street W, 416 947 3300) was built in 1932 and held Canada's first law school (which has since moved up north to York University). The building's vintage wrought-iron gates were built in 1868 to prevent grazing cows from entering (and soiling) the hallowed grounds of the Law Society of Upper Canada (which is still housed here today). Tours of this classic example of Victorian Classical architecture are free (don't miss the rotunda).

Across University Avenue at 160 Queen Street West, **Campbell House** (*see p73*) sits in the shadow of the **Canada Life Building** (330 University Avenue, 416 597 1456), best-known for its famous beacon: the tower lights provide coded weather forecasts, which are updated four times a day. The **Canada Life Beacon** emitted its first signal on 9 August 1951 (back then the tower was more visible throughout the city, and by boaters far out on the lake). A cube-shaped light flashes red for rain, white for snow and shines a steady green for clear conditions and steady red for clouds. If the rows of white lights on the tower flash upwards, it means hotter weather is on the way. Similarly, descending or non-moving patterns indicate dropping or steady temperatures.

Green scene

Now that saving the planet is the mantra of politicians of all stripes, the greening of Toronto is taking shape. A 30-storey-high wind turbine at Exhibition Place provides power to about 250 households (though it also takes out a portion of the migrating bird population), and an initiative from Enwave Energy Corp taps the frigid waters in Lake Ontario to cool office buildings downtown. But it is the tactile, stop-and-smell-the-milkweed projects that are the most visible signs of local greening. These developments should make the residents, and the monarch butterfly population, happy for years to come.

The **Don Valley Brick Works** is an abandoned quarry in the heart of the city set amid wetlands, wild-flower meadows and forests. It's a good destination for cyclists heading up the bike trail in the Don Valley and for Rosedale dog-walkers who can access the site via wooded paths. The old brick foundry is being converted into a greenhouse that will revive native plants, and an organic vegetable garden will supply a restaurant on the premises. Ironically, the site is not accessible by public transport.

Toronto's waterfront is finally getting some respect after a feeding frenzy by developers, whose concrete curtain of condos blocked the city from the lake breezes and vistas. In June 2007, **HtO Park** opened at Spadina Quay. With whimsical features like stairs that descend into the lake and bright-yellow metal beach umbrellas, this park is a tiny wedge of inspiration.

Don River Park, scheduled to open in 2008, will mark the transformation of a toxic tributary into a green oasis. It's the first step in the transformation of Toronto's Port Lands, a sprawling area to the east of downtown dominated by old wharves and dump sites. The land was to be the site of the 2008 Olympic Games (Toronto lost to Beijing). But sports fans' loss is nature's gain. The park will feature wetlands, a sandbar, boating canals and a boardwalk promenade – a better legacy than a brief, debt-inducing spectacle.

The **Textile Museum of Canada** (55 Centre Avenue, 416 599 5321) is another curious sight woven into this eclectic neighbourhood, with over 10,000 textile artefacts from all over the world.

Heading west you'll find the **Ontario College of Art & Design** (100 McCaul Street, 416 977 6000), with Will Alsop's must-see, much talked-about, stilt-elevated **Sharp Centre for Design** building. Its neighbour to the north is the **Art Gallery of Ontario** (*see p73*), which is in the midst of receiving a Frank Gehry-designed makeover. Don't miss the Henry Moore sculpture at the corner of McCaul and Dundas Street West. At 2 Grange Avenue is the **Grange Modern** gallery (open by appointment only; call 416 596 8452), a showcase for well-known Canadian artist Charles Pachter.

Behind the gallery is the architectural period museum, the **Grange**, which is closed until 2008, and **Grange Park**. At the south end of the park, the ivy-covered **St George the Martyr Anglican Church** (197 John Street, entrance on Stephanie Street, 416 598 4366) is one of Toronto's oldest places of worship, dating from 1844. A fire in 1955 destroyed everything except the tower, which still looms over this urban park today. The congregation

meets in the original parish hall, which also holds some objects saved from the fire. This is also the home of the **Music Gallery** (416 204 1080), a publicly assisted centre for the creation and performance of new and unusual music, well known for a vibrant legacy of sonic innovation by the likes of John Oswald, Henry Kaiser and Michael Snow.

A couple of short blocks north of here is the Baldwin Street neighbourhood, between Beverley and McCaul, with its mix of earthy shops, bakeries, upscale bistros and boho cafés. It's a great spot to grab lunch before you head back down to Dundas into the chaotic, exotic flow of Chinatown proper. Year-round these busy blocks are crowded with shopkeepers and customers, who haggle and joust among barrels of beansprouts, unending varieties of dried fishes and crate upon crate of wonderful Chinese greens. At Chinese New Year the traditional parade features much noise-making and a giant dragon, which heads down this street and past the **Ten Ren Tea Company** (454 Dundas Street W, 416 598 7872), one of the world's largest tea producers. It's an excellent place to buy and taste a wide variety of teas, as well as teapots and cute little cups.

For many, the definitive Chinatown experience is the ritual of a leisurely dim-sum

To see an environmental triumph already in progress, head for the **Leslie Street Spit**. This five-kilometre (three-mile) urban wilderness is one of North America's most successful reclamation projects. Begun in the 1950s as a man-made breakwater to protect Toronto's outer harbour, the project was abandoned as the shipping business declined. But in the 1960s and '70s, as the city mushroomed, the spit was used as a dumping ground for building debris. The peninsula grew, and when the city transformed it into a wilderness preserve, nature took over. On weekends and holidays, the place draws walkers, birders, bladers and cyclists, who commune with an incredible variety of flora and fauna – some 400 varieties of plant and 300 bird species. Beavers, otters, red foxes and coyotes have also been sighted here. In 1974 a lighthouse was established to mark its terminus. Today the 'Spit' is known as Tommy Thompson Park, after a former parks commissioner.

Cars aren't allowed on to the Spit, but parking is available at the gate. A shuttle

van operates from early May to mid October, taking people to a footbridge located about halfway to the lighthouse. Otherwise, the walk from the park entrance to the lighthouse is five kilometres (two miles), but on a beautiful day it feels short. A map and brochure are available at the park entrance.

Don Valley Brick Works
550 Bayview Avenue, Midtown. Subway Castle Frank then a 30-minute walk (416 596 1495/www.evergreen.ca).

HtO Park
The foot of Spadina Avenue, Harbourfront. Streetcar 510 (416 392 1111/www. toronto.ca/harbourfront).

Leslie Street Spit
South of Lake Shore Boulevard, Harbourfront. Streetcar 501 east from Yonge (get off at Berkshire Street & go south on Leslie Street; 1.5km/1 mile walk to the gate). **Open** *early May-mid Oct 9am-6pm daily. Mid Oct-early May 9am-4.30pm daily.*

Sightseeing

A glass act: shoppers see the light at the **Toronto Eaton Centre**. *See p69*.

lunch. While serious aficionados scout for new terrain almost weekly (including in the other Chinatowns), **Yiu Wah** (421 Dundas Street W, 416 979 8833) provides a tempting array of dumplings and other freshly prepared delights. If budget is not an issue, head eastwards to the luxurious **Lai Wah Heen** (*see p114*) in the Metropolitan Hotel (*see p44*), which many believe serves the finest dim sum in town.

Continuing westbound on Dundas towards Spadina, the stores and trading companies spill out on to the sidewalks, hawking Cantonese CDs with cover versions of Madonna, animé-themed MP3 holders, vials of traditional medicine and Hello Kitty earmuffs.

Spadina

Streetcar 505, 509, 510.
In addition to the diverse regions of China, Toronto's Chinatown is home to a wide range of Asian cultures, from Thailand to Korea, Malaysia to Vietnam. The latter culture is well represented by the superb restaurants, soup kitchens and sandwich shops on Spadina Avenue. The **Dieu Ky Food Co** (336 Spadina Avenue, 416 979 7928) and **Pho Hung** (350 Spadina Avenue, 416 593 4274) are two reliable and well-priced options.

Once the centre of a booming garment industry, Spadina has a funky, industrial feel, with vintage warehouses and retail outlets lining the broad boulevard. At 50 metres (160 feet), it's also one of the widest streets in the city, but on weekends even these super-sized sidewalks are totally jammed. At the intersection of Dundas and Spadina the action really thickens: diminutive women crouch down low selling vegetables and fresh herbs, while seafood is somehow bought and sold from street-side stalls, and young Asian teens gab on mobile phones. As you go further up the street, the sidewalks are much less crowded, while the shopping gets even better. In addition to offering the cheapest souvenirs in the city, this section of Spadina is a great source for lots of handy items for the traveller: backpacks, suitcases and camera bags; international phone cards; herbal medicines; hats, inexpensive clothing and footwear. Just up the street at No.448 is another retail institution, **Gwartzman's Art Supplies** (416 922 5429). For fashion, walk south on Spadina from Dundas.

Art Gallery of Ontario

317 Dundas Street W, at Beverley Street (416 979 6648/www.ago.net). Streetcar 505/subway St Patrick. **Open** *Until June 2008* noon-9pm Wed-Fri; 10am-5.30pm Sat, Sun. **Admission** free during construction with ticketed special exhibit shows. Prices vary. **Credit** MC, V. **Map** p271 E6.

The AGO is staying open despite the fact that it's having its insides ripped out and transformed in a Frank Gehry-designed makeover. Specific galleries and wings will be closed on a rotating basis, so call ahead if you're keen on the Henry Moore sculpture gallery, the fine European collection, the Group of Seven or other stand-outs from the permanent collection. The AGO will unveil its new, expanded, titanium-clad self in June 2008.

Campbell House

160 Queen Street W, at Simcoe Street (416 597 0227/www.campbellhousemuseum.ca). Streetcar 501/subway Osgoode. **Open** *May-Oct* 9.30am-4.30pm Mon-Fri; noon-4.30pm Sat, Sun. **Admission** $4.50; $2-$3 concessions; $10 family. **No credit cards.** **Map** p271/p272 F7.

This is one of the city's older treasures of Georgian architecture, built in 1822 for Sir William Campbell, a judge who later became Chief Justice of Upper Canada. It passed through many hands over the ensuing century, until 1973, when the 300-ton house was moved from its original location on Adelaide Street to its current position. The operation was massive, but it saved the building from demolition. In 1974 it opened as a museum, although parts of the building are used as offices and therefore off-limits to the public. In addition to guided tours, the museum has a herb garden with explanations of how herbs were used for food and medicine.

City Hall & Nathan Phillips Square

100 Queen Street W, at York Street (416 338 0338/www.city.toronto.on.ca). Bus 6/streetcar 501/subway Osgoode or Queen. **Open** *City Hall* 8.30am-4.30pm Mon-Fri. **Admission** free. **Map** p271/272 F7.

Completed in 1966, Toronto's first City Hall was one of the city's first modernist buildings. The then-mayor Nathan Phillips had held an international competition, won by Finnish architect Viljo Revell. Revell designed the council chamber as a low, round building, embraced by two concave office towers of differing heights. The dramatic design has aged well, remaining bold and futuristic 40 years on. The ground floor is open to the public (check out the scale model of the city), and tours can be arranged by appointment (unfortunately, the observation deck at the top is not accessible).

City Hall faces south on to the concrete expanse of Nathan Phillips Square. Phillips' successor as mayor, Phil Givens, fought hard for the Henry Moore bronze on the hall's forecourt, believing prestigious art conferred a prestigious world image, but this vision proved his undoing. He won his battle against the philistines but lost the next election due to the outrage of the electorate at what was seen as a waste of public funds. History vindicates him: *The Archer*, as the sculpture is known, is the most popular public sculpture in the city. A makeover of the square is in the works, though designers know they're treading on hallowed ground; many features, including the unused elevated walkway, are off-limits to tinkering.

The square succeeds as a genuine gathering place. It's where Toronto rings in the new year. During the summer it's busy with concerts, dance performances, the annual Jamaican IRIE Music Festival (www.iriemusicfestival.com), the Toronto Outdoor Art Exhibition (*see p169*) and a summer farmers' market (*see p158* **The perfect picnic**). In winter the reflecting pool becomes a popular ice rink, and skaters whizz under the huge concrete arches that span it. Skates are available to hire (*see p215*).

Kensington Market

Streetcar 506, 506, 510.

The landing point for many new immigrants, Kensington Market has been the unofficial gateway to Toronto for over 200 years. Declared a National Historic District in 2006, the neighbourhood was once known as the 'Jewish Market', as it was the centre for thousands of Eastern Europe Jews. They worked in Spadina's busy garment industry and by the 1920s there were 30 synagogues in the area. The market evolved when merchants began selling their wares on their front lawns – and eventually in the converted storefronts that comprise the market today.

Kensington Market's main thoroughfares are Baldwin Street, Augusta Avenue, Nassau Street and Kensington Avenue. Stores are run by a mixture of Chinese, Italians, Greeks, Portuguese, East and West Indians, Koreans, Vietnamese, Filipinos, Africans from many countries, Mexicans, Spaniards and Latin Americans. A small Jewish presence also remains. The area is ever-changing, but that old market feeling lingers on: you still get the sense that many of the stores and restaurants were set up on a whim, with clothing racks and cardboard signs pitched up in front yards, along sidewalks and even down alleys. There are clubs here too, but Kensington's streets have a music of their own: dancehall reggae booms out from a Jamaican fruit store, mixing with mandolins emanating from a cheese shop and the discordant twang of Mandarin pop coming from a greengrocer. Kensington Market's cultural mix means that it has some of the city's best – and cheapest – shopping, including fresh and speciality food stores; an eclectic mix of vintage and discount clothing and snack foods from every continent.

Sanci's Wholesale Produce & Tropical Foods (66 Kensington Avenue, 416 593 9265) has been here since 1914, and is as popular now as it was then. Fans of vintage apparel should check out the crowded stretch of brightly painted brick storefronts along lower Kensington Street, where **Courage My Love** (*see p153*) is a virtual museum for obscure vintage clothing and accessories, while **Exile** (20 Kensington Avenue, 416 596 0827) and **Dancing Days** (17 Kensington Avenue, 416 599 9827) are offbeat, punky and funky alternatives. If you're in that special mood, check out the self-explanatory **Roach-O-Rama** (191A Baldwin Street, 416 203 6990) and its famous **Hot Box Café**.

You're better off visiting the market during the week or on a Saturday, as not all stores are open on Sundays. For more on the shops at Kensington Market, *see p148*.

Running parallel with Spadina Avenue, **Augusta Avenue**'s formerly dodgy blocks are being spruced up by authors, club promoters and movie types buying in and setting up shop with upscale new businesses, such as hip bar **Embassy** (No.223; *see also p136*); upscale bistro **La Palette** (No.256; *see also p114*), vibrant houseware shop **Bungalow** (No.273; *see also p151*) and diner/DJ club **SuperMarket** (No.268, 416 840 0501). If you need refuelling, grab a coffee at a local landmark, **Casa Acoreana & Luis Coffee** (235 Augusta Avenue, 416 593 9717), take a quick look at the wondrous self explanatory **House of Spice** (190 Augusta Avenue, 416 593 9724), then walk northwards for a taste of the funky new guard. While you're here, don't miss the **Pueblan** (Mexican regional) eatery or **El Trompo** (277 Augusta Avenue, 416 260 0097) for some tiny, perfect tacos.

The **Kiever Synagogue** (25 Bellevue Avenue, 416 593 9702) is one of Canada's oldest Jewish landmarks. Designed by an architect named Benjamin Swartz, the synagogue served a small congregation of immigrants from Kiev, Ukraine. The formal name of the congregation is the 'First Russian Congregation of Rodfei Sholem Anshei Kiev', but for entirely understandable reasons it is generally known simply as 'the Kiever'. The Kiever overlooks **Bellevue Square**, a small but pleasant community park at the corner of Wales and Augusta Avenues. Keep an eye out for a life-sized statue of a smiling Al Waxman. The Canadian actor and humanitarian, who died in 2001, is best remembered for playing Al King, the lead character in *King of Kensington*, a 1970s TV show set here in the market.

University

Map p274

Bus 94/streetcar 506, 510/subway Bay, Bloor-Yonge, Museum, Spadina or Wellesley.

The largest university in Canada comprises some choice downtown real estate, and for the tourist in search of either tranquil reflection or architectural interest, the campus is an oasis of old-fashioned beauty. Thanks to its many courtyards, quadrangles and large open spaces, the area feels like a park interrupted by chapels of learning. A stream once ran through the university, and while the Taddle Creek is long gone, the bucolic atmosphere remains.

Founded in 1827 as King's College, the university is one of the few local institutions that have done a decent job of conserving their heritage – turrets and all. In the past decade it has also been an incubator for new architecture, with talents from Canada and abroad designing dazzling new buildings.

Bordered on the north by Bloor Street and on the east by Bay Street, the downtown campus is divided into three sections by two imposing north-south avenues, Queen's Park and St George Street. Including its two suburban campuses – Erindale and Scarborough College – the University of Toronto is the third-largest public university in North America.

Central

The university's oldest and most iconic buildings lie directly north-west of Queen's Park and the provincial parliament building. **Hart House** was a gift from the wealthy Massey family and named after its chief patriarch, Hart Massey. With its Gothic arches, bay windows and great hall, it has an English Oxbridgey feel, yet is comfortingly old Toronto. Formerly an undergraduate men's centre, it's now open to women too. A small exhibition space, the **Justina M Barnicke Art Gallery**, is located in the west wing (*see below*). **University College** is one of the oldest buildings on campus and still very much a landmark. You can see its lone, asymmetrical spire and central tower from as far away as Yonge Street; the interior woodwork is worth a visit in itself. In the Laidlaw Wing is the **University of Toronto Art Centre** (*see below*), housing the eclectic and enjoyable art collection of New York psychoanalyst Dr Lillian Malcove Ormos. Cross the playing field in front of the college and you'll find **Convocation Hall**, a vast domed building from the 1920s that has seen its fair share of graduation exercises. Head further south to College Street and you'll hit the **Faculty of Architecture**, with its sleek modernist gallery, and the very different **Lillian H Smith Public Library** (*see below*), with its distinctly postmodern design.

Two even flashier buildings now herald the approach at College Street and University

Avenue: the **Centre for Cellular Biomolecular Research**, and the **Leslie Dan Pharmacy**, a flamboyant creation by the British architect Norman Foster (it's his first building in Canada).

Justina M Barnicke Art Gallery

Hart House, 7 Hart House Circle (416 978 8398/ www.utoronto.ca/gallery). Subway St George. **Open** *Sept-June* 11am-7pm Mon-Fri; 1-4pm Sat, Sun. *July, Aug* 11am-6pm Mon-Fri; 1-4pm Sat. **Admission** free. **Map** p274 E5.

Great Canadian art hangs in all corners of Hart House – in reading rooms, restaurants, even stairwells – but this is the official gallery, and though tiny, it often features interesting art shows.

Lillian H Smith Public Library

239 College Street, at Huron Street (416 393 7746/ www.torontopubliclibrary.ca). Streetcar 506, 510. **Open** *Sept-June* 10am-8.30pm Mon-Thur; 10am-6pm Fri; 9am-5pm Sat; 1.30-5pm Sun. *July, Aug* 10am-8.30pm Mon-Thur; 10am-6pm Fri; 9am-5pm Sat. **Admission** free. **Map** p274 E5.

A postmodern château with a dungeon-like basement and giant bronze griffins flanking the central doorway, this public library is a fanciful piece of architecture. It's also a must for fans of science fiction and/or children's literature, as it houses excellent collections of both.

University of Toronto Art Centre

Laidlaw Wing, University College, 15 King's College Circle (416 978 1838/www.utoronto.ca/artcentre). Bus 94/streetcar 506/subway Queen's Park. **Open** *Sept-June* 10am-6pm Tue-Thur, Sun; 10am-9pm Fri; noon-4pm Sat. *July, Aug* noon-5pm Tue-Fri. **Admission** free. **Map** p274 E5.

This little-known museum on the north side of the University College quad houses the private collection of New York City psychoanalyst Dr Lillian Malcove Ormos. Medieval ivories and a stunning 1538 panel painting of Adam and Eve by Lucas Cranach are on view, though regular exhibits are occasionally pushed aside by travelling shows.

Queen's Park & east

The provincial parliament building sits majestically in the middle of Queen's Park and is often referred to as **Queen's Park**. A fine example of Richardsonian Romanesque, the massive pinky-brown stone edifice was completed in 1892.

Another fine example of the genre, from 1892, lies north-east of Queen's Park in the middle of the Victoria College quadrangle, and is known as **Old Vic**. On the same quad is the **EJ Pratt Library**, named after the prominent Canadian poet. Check out the polka-dot walls of this 1961 building and the famous portrait of literary guru Northrop Frye. The eminent critic appears to be sitting on air.

Bike on Toronto Islands

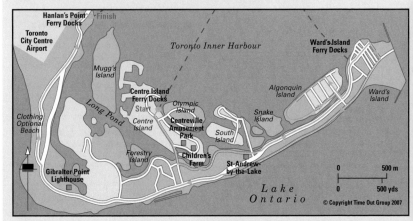

Start: Centre Island Ferry Terminal
Finish: Hanlan's Point Ferry Terminal
Length: About 16 kilometres (ten miles)
Time: 60-90 minutes, not including distractions
General information: 416 397 2628
Ferry timetable: 416 392 8193 ($6; $3.50 concessions; $2.50 under-15s)

The jewel of Toronto's parks, the Toronto Islands boast sandy beaches, sylvan glades and a funky residential village. They are accessed via ferry, which has three docking points: Ward's Island to the east; Centre Island in the middle and Hanlan's Point on the western tip. All three are connected, and you could walk from one end to the other in a couple of hours.

Though the ferry points suggest there are three islands, in fact there are 15 (the smaller ones are accessible only by boat). But 300 years ago there were no Toronto Islands (as we know them today). Back in 1791, when John Graves Simcoe chose the site of Toronto (then York) as Upper Canada's new capital, he noticed a long sandy isthmus adjoining the harbour's eastern mainland. His wife Elizabeth would while away the days galloping on horseback along the shore of that isthmus. But in 1858, a huge storm flooded the isthmus and blew out the connection to the mainland – and the islands were born.

Contemporary Torontonians should be thankful for that historic storm. These days,

the islands provide hours of outdoor fun: breezy parks, miles of golden sand, bike paths, paddle boats, tennis courts and the small amusement park on Centre Island. On the quirkier side, there is a bird sanctuary, a nudist beach and a bohemian residential community of 800 people (the latter live on Ward's and Algonquin Islands and are vividly described in Margaret Atwood's *The Robber Bride*).

While walking is pleasant in this car-free park, the six-mile (10-kilometre) length from end to end is best explored by bicycle, which can be rented in season at the pier on the far side of Centre Island or on the mainland near the ferry terminal. On summer weekends, however, passengers with bikes are restricted to the ferries bound for Ward's Island and Hanlan's Point, as the crowds swell for the most popular destination, Centre Island.

Take the Centre Island Ferry from the terminal behind Westin Harbour Castle Hotel at Bay Street and Queens Quay. The route begins from the ferry dock on Centre Island. Look carefully at the harbour and enjoy the breeze and the seagulls as the city slips away. 'Ah.' That's the first feeling as you take in the clean air of the Toronto Islands. *Stay on the paved path called Avenue of the Islands and cross over the white-and-pastel-green bridge (over a quiet canal).* The only real commercial diversion is **Centreville Amusement Park**, which you pass on your left just before the bridge. It's a great spot for the kids. Attractions include swan, pedal and bumper boats, plus a miniature train, a petting farm and a carousel. As you cross the bridge, note the Venetian inspiration of the balustrade and pretend you're crossing the Grand Canal. If you're renting a bike here, proceed to the end of this broad, flowerbed-lined boulevard – the rental shack stands near the lake.

Turn left on Cibola Avenue.
With the amusement park on your left across a channel, proceed under a canopy of trees to **St. Andrew-by-the-Lake Church** (416 203 0873). This small Anglican church, built in 1884, still offers regular Sunday services, as well as weddings and baptisms. The humble clapboard exterior forms a contrast with the Gothic arches of its stained-glass windows. If you've brought a frisbee, you can play a game of frisbee golf (tossing the disc into elevated mesh nets) further along Cibola Avenue.

Continue along Cibola Avenue then left over a wooden bridge onto Algonquin Island. The road is called Ojibway Avenue after it crosses Omaha Avenue. Keep following it north to the shore.
This bucolic residential community stands in stark contrast to the view, possibly the best anywhere, of Toronto's skyline. Swans, ducks, geese and kayakers are all commonly seen paddling through these still waters.

Turn left on Seneca Avenue. At Wyandot Avenue, a secluded trail leads off the path. This trail loops around and rejoins Omaha Avenue. Recross Algonquin Bridge and continue east on Cibola Avenue past Ward's island ferry dock along Bayview Avenue, the waterside concrete path. Turn right on to 1st Street.
These so-called 'streets' are just barely wide enough for two people to walk abreast. In the 1950s the city tried to chase the locals off the islands to make way for a park. Walking through this quiet paradise, hemmed by flower gardens, picket fences, spreading trees and small cottages, you can see why the residents fought so hard to keep the island community alive.

Follow 1st Street to Lakeshore Avenue, where you turn right.
Lakeshore Avenue, the major east–west thoroughfare, runs like a spine along the south side of the islands. It becomes a boardwalk from which you have a view across the water of a migratory bird sanctuary (on Muggs Island). A few hundred metres along on the right is the **Rectory Café** (416 203 2152). It's the best spot to eat on the islands, and offers home-made soups, sandwiches and other tasty treats.

Continue to rumble along the wooden boardwalk, which soon morphs into an asphalt path.
Gibraltar Point Lighthouse comes into view on the right. It is the oldest landmark in the city and the oldest lighthouse in the Great Lakes, dating from 1808. Naturally, it is haunted. In 1815, its lightkeeper JP Radan died a mysterious death here. He was presumed murdered, perhaps by soldiers from Fort York, though records are scant . The eerie lighthouse is closed to the public.

Proceed westward along Lakeshore Avenue.
The road bends to the right past a public school and a water-filtration plant. You'll notice boardwalks extending through the trees and over sand dunes to a 'clothing optional' beach. This popular nudist spot gets busy on summer weekends; boaters drop anchor and then drop their drawers, as do lots of gay men. Shower facilities, restrooms and a café are nearby.

Continue to the end of Lakeshore Avenue to the Hanlan's Point ferry dock.
Ned Hanlan was a world champion sculler in the late 19th century. His most famous victory, in 1880 against reigning Australian champ Edward Trickett on the Tyne river in England, made headlines around the world. When Hanlan visited London after his victory, brokers at the London Stock Exchange stopped trading and carried him aloft. A statue stands near the ferry dock. There's also a plaque marking the spot from which Babe Ruth hit his first home run as a pro baseball player in 1914 at the old Hanlan's Point Stadium.

Centre Island Bike Rental
Centre Island Pier, 416 203 0009.
Rates Bikes $6/hr; tandems $13/hr; quadracycles $28/hr.

Wheel Excitement
249 Queen's Quay West, Unit 110, behind Radisson Admiral Hotel, 416 260 9000/ www.wheelexcitement.ca. **Rates** Bikes or in-line skates $12/1st hr, then $3/hr (daily max $27).

Sightseeing

To the north lie Charles Street and two of the city's more interesting new buildings – the **McKinsey & Company** building and the **Isabel Bader Theatre**, a gift from Alfred Bader to the college in the name of his theatre-loving wife. The limestone-clad building echoes the scale and colour of Burwash Hall to the east and Emmanuel College to the west. Across Charles Street, on the north side, the West Coast-style **Wymilwood Student Centre** is the creation of Eric Arthur, the influential Toronto architect who helped save such early landmarks as St Lawrence Hall and Old City Hall, and who gave his name to the Faculty of Architecture's gallery at 230 College Street (416 978 5038). Arthur died in 1982, but his tome *Toronto: No Mean City* remains the bible of the city's historical architecture. **TheatreBooks** (*see p147*), a fine bookshop, sits in a brownstone just off Charles Street.

North of Charles Street, two of Toronto's most important museums face each other across the broad lanes of Queen's Park. The **Gardiner Museum of Ceramic Art** (*see below*) was founded by a local philanthropist and his wife in 1984; a big revamp opened in 2006 to glowing reviews. Its older cousin across the street, the **Royal Ontario Museum** (*see below*) explores both natural history and human cultures and is the largest museum in Canada, the fifth-largest in North America. While you're in the neighbourhood, take a glance at the **Royal Conservatory of Music** (273 Bloor Street W, 416 408 2825), also in the midst of a major revamp (it is adding a 1,000-seat recital hall). Originally the Toronto Baptist College, the hulking building does indeed look as if it could rain down hail and brimstone. Walk through the ornate iron gates to the east of the conservatory and down Philosophers Walk, and you can usually hear the sound of dozens of piano students practising, though hammers will likely dominate until 2008.

Gardiner Museum of Ceramic Art

111 Queen's Park, at Bloor Street W (416 586 8080/ www.gardinermuseum.on.ca). Subway Museum. **Open** 10am-6pm Mon-Thur, Sat; 10am-9pm Fri. **Admission** $12; $6-$8 concessions. Free every Friday 4-9pm. **Map** p274 F4.
The first specialist museum of ceramic art in North America. Following a $15-million revamp, the Gardiner now boasts three new galleries, a glass-covered atrium and Jamie Kennedy at the Gardiner (*see p117*), a restaurant overseen by the celebrity chef. Apart from the dining-room china, there is a fantastic collection of Italian maiolica, English delftware and other ceramics from Europe, Asia and the Americas. The museum has an expanded gift shop and offers classes at the clay studio.

Royal Ontario Museum

100 Queen's Park, at Bloor Street W (416 586 5549/www.rom.on.ca). Subway Museum. **Open** 10am-6pm Mon-Thur, Sat, Sun; 10am-9.30pm Fri. **Admission** $16; $10-$12 concessions; free under-5s; $5 4.30-9.30pm Fri. **Credit** AmEx, MC, V. **Map** p274 F4.
The ROM's new Michael Lee-Chin Crystal Wing was scheduled to open in June 2007, but before then it became the most controversial building in Toronto. Designed by Daniel Libeskind, the architect behind Berlin's Jewish Museum and Manchester's Imperial War Museum North, the glass-and-steel structure is, depending on your point of view, either a grand gesture or a God-awful folly. Still, it has kicked some life into the cultural scene and will draw more visitors to one of Canada's greatest museums.

Though it's known for its enormous Chinese collection, the museum surveys everything from natural history to human culture. Kids will love the bat cave, dinosaurs and mummies, not to mention the totem poles beside the main entrance. Adults may prefer the indigenous peoples' collections. For a literary view, read Margaret Atwood's *Life Before Man*, which features the ROM as the backdrop.

St George Street & west

A recently relandscaped St George Street is now the principal north–south axis of the university's western campus. Walk north from College Street and you'll pass everything from the Beaux Arts splendour of the **Koffler Student Services Centre** (originally a public reference library, now the home of the university's main bookstore) to the **Bahen Centre for Information Technology**; from the very '60s **Sidney Smith Hall** to the very '70s **Robarts Library**. The latter, sometimes referred to as 'Fort Book', is a bulky concrete structure that resembles an overloaded spacecraft attempting lift-off, but it is the largest of the U of T's 30 libraries. The beaked tower at the south end is home to the Thomas Fisher Rare Book Library.

Where St George joins Bloor Street is a collection of somewhat less academic interest, the **Bata Shoe Museum** (*see p79*), which makes for a surprisingly fun diversion. Directly opposite lies the new **Wordsworth College Residence**. A yellow-brick podium topped by a checkerboard tower of clear and opaque glass, it's a sassy addition to a traditional stretch of Bloor Street (the 19th-century home of the ultra-exclusive York Club is across the street).

North of Robarts library lies **Innis College**, named after the academic who inspired the communications theorist Marshall McLuhan, who baffled Toronto students for years while coining seminal phrases like the 'global village' and 'the medium is the message'. East of the library, at the corner of Hoskin and Devonshire Place, lies a celebrated re-imagining of the monastic ideal – **Massey College**. Conceived by former governor-general Vincent Massey, it was designed by Canadian architect Ron Thom.

Spadina Avenue marks the western edge of the university and here, near the junction of Harbord Street, lies the athletics centre and one of the most controversial buildings in the city, **Graduate House**. Built in an almost industrial style by a team of Toronto and Los Angeles architects, the residence offends and attracts people in almost equal degrees. The talking point is usually the sign-cum-cornice that overhangs Harbord Street and welcomes you to the university.

Bata Shoe Museum

327 Bloor Street W, at St George Street (416 979 7799/www.batashoemuseum.ca). Subway St George. **Open** 10am-5pm Tue, Wed, Fri; 10am-8pm Thu; noon-5pm Sun. **Admission** $8; $4-$6 concessions; free under-5s. **Credit** AmEx, MC, V. **Map** p274 E4. A playful take on a shoe box, Raymond Moriyama's oddly shaped building houses everything from native slippers to celebrity footwear (from Marilyn Monroe's red pumps to Elton John's platforms). A permanent exhibition traces the history of shoes.

Harbord

Map p274

Situated at the western edge of the university, Harbord Street is a bastion of upscale leftish liberalism. The street houses everything from the **Toronto Women's Bookstore** (73 Harbord Street, 416 922 8744) to a women-friendly sex shop **Good For Her** (*see p195*), not to mention some of the city's better restaurants and patios.

Downtown East

Church & Wellesley

Map p275

Bus 75, 94/streetcar 506/subway Bloor-Yonge, College or Wellesley.
Home to the local gay village, or 'the ghetto', as it's most commonly called, Church & Wellesley is a bustling district that is also a showcase for some of Toronto's best 19th-century architecture. Church Street was named after **St James's Church** (now a cathedral; 65 Church Street, 416 364 7865), one of the loveliest structures in the city, and some of the other buildings in this area (bounded by Yonge, Bloor, Gerrard and Sherbourne Streets) are equally dignified, imposing and graceful.

Their quiet grace stands in stark contrast to the massive apartment complexes erected in the 1950s and '60s after the opening of the Yonge Street subway in 1954. Buildings like the **City Park** co-op apartments at 484 Church Street, the city's first high-rise apartment complex, and the conical-shaped **Village Green** block of flats encouraged the arrival of many a confirmed 'bachelor' – so many that Village Green is often known as 'Vaseline Towers'.

But the area only took off in 1984, when the Second Cup opened near the corner of Church and Wellesley. Originally equipped with a broad set of steps suitable for lounging, chatting and cruising, the tiny coffee shop attracted a dedicated gay following, and 'the Steps' became a local landmark, mythologised by frequent references on the TV series *Kids in the Hall*. 'The Steps' fell victim to renovation a while back, but their effect lives on. In 1989, five years after Second Cup set up shop, **Woody's** (*see p191*) opened a block further south at Church and Maitland in a Queen Anne rowhouse originally built in 1893, and the gay gold rush was on. Rising rents and a proliferation of upscale condos may yet imperil the village's broad demographic, but for the moment it's almost impossible to run a gay business without a Church Street connection.

Tiny **George Hislop Park** commemorates the legendary gay businessman and activist. It runs parallel to Yonge Street between Charles and Isabella Streets.

The names of many more gay men are marked on the upright steel markers of the AIDS Memorial, erected in 1993, in **Cawthra Park**, located behind the **519 Church Street Community Centre** (*see p188*) at Church and Wellesley Streets. The original home of the ritzy Granite Club, 'the 519' is now home to innumerable support groups, community meetings and legal practices, as well as a beer garden during Pride Week (*see p168*) and a phoneline for reporting anti-gay violence.

At its southern end, the ghetto encircles what was one of Canada's premier jock palaces, **Maple Leaf Gardens**, at Church and Carlton Streets. Built in 1931, the blocky, yellow-brick building, mostly deco with Art Moderne details, was long home to the Toronto Maple Leafs hockey team, not to mention dozens of concerts by everyone from the Beatles and the Rolling Stones to touring circuses and occasional opera. But the Leafs moved to the **Air Canada Centre** (*see p63*) in the late 1990s, and the Gardens awaits redevelopment – most likely as a giant supermarket, which hockey fans decry as sacrilege.

A century ago this area, in particular Jarvis and Sherbourne Streets, was home to some of the city's eminent movers and shakers. Today it houses an oddball collection of historic homes, high-rise condos and hard-working hookers. The **Massey Mansions** at 515 and 519 Jarvis Street, north of Wellesley Street, are good examples of the old order. Originally designed for a dry goods merchant, the house at No.515, now a **Keg Mansion** restaurant (416 964 6609), was later home to the Masseys, the influential Canadian family who made their money in farm machinery and gave their name to several Toronto landmarks, including **Massey Hall** (*see p198*) and **Massey College** (at U of T; *see p78*). Hart Massey, the 19th-century Methodist patriarch who moved the family firm into the front ranks, lived at No.515. Two of his most famous grandsons resided next door at No.519, a

baronial home designed by EJ Lennox, the architect of Old City Hall. Vincent Massey grew up to become Canada's first native-born governor-general, while his younger brother Raymond became an actor famous for his portrayal of Abraham Lincoln.

The **National Ballet School** (105 Maitland Street, 416 964 3780) owns several historic buildings south of the Massey mansions, near the corner of Jarvis and Maitland Streets, including the classically inspired **Quaker Meeting House** at 111 Maitland Street and the Victorian home at 404 Jarvis Street. In a bid to triple its space and add new studios, classrooms and residences, the school has expanded south on to a heritage site formerly owned by the Canadian Broadcasting Corporation. Look for the twin 30-storey

Walk on Cabbagetown

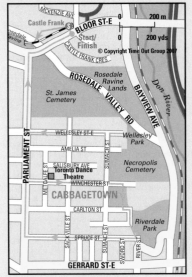

Start: Castle Frank Station
Finish: Castle Frank Station
Length: Six kilometres (four miles)
Time: two hours, not including distractions

Better homes and gardens of the 19th century and forested streets – that's what this walk is about. But it also includes strolls in parks and two of Toronto's most beautiful cemeteries.

Turn left out of Castle Frank Station (away from Bloor Street E). Find the steep unpaved trail leading down and to the west, passing under the subway bridge.
This short trail, leading from one busy street to another, is unexpectedly tranquil, but at the bottom traffic moves quickly. Cross Rosedale Valley Drive and turn left on the paved path. The path takes you deep into a wooded ravine, past St James' Cemetery. Unfortunately, the graveyard's lower gates are locked and there is no way out of the valley until you reach a flight of stairs where Rosedale Valley meets Bayview Avenue (note: homeless people sometimes congregate around the base of the stairs. They're generally friendly, but some can be too friendly, so you may want to do this walk with a friend) At the top of the staircase is the small, pleasing Wellesley Park.
Take Wellesley Street from the north-west corner of the park and turn south on Sumach Street.
Let the architecture fest begin: though Victorian architecture is found in pockets around the city, Cabbagetown boasts a high concentration of old buildings in a bucolic setting. Many fine 19th-century homes can be found on Sumach Street. The double house at 420-422 is a well-regarded Second Empire building, recognisable by its mansard roof, and dormers whose wooden ornaments are painted a soft, creamy white. Turn left on Winchester Street, to find the entrance to the historic **Toronto Necropolis** (*see p83*). Its name means city of the dead; public

80 Time Out Toronto

condo towers known as 'Radio City'. Designed by prominent local architect Peter Clewes, they're not part of the ballet school itself, but they do mark the revitalisation of this long-dormant part of the city. To the west of the towers, on Jarvis Street, the ballet school's new facilities wrap themselves around two historic buildings and offer passersby views of budding ballerinas at the barre.

Northfield House at 372 Jarvis Street was built in 1856 and was an early home of Oliver Mowat, later a Father of Confederation and a long-serving premier of Ontario. The wonderfully Jacobethan pile at **354 Jarvis**, built in 1898, looks like a set for *Jane Eyre* (with a proper perch for a madwoman in an attic), but it was actually once home to the Havergal Ladies College (now located in North Toronto) and later the Canadian Broadcasting Corporation; it was from here that Canada's first TV broadcast was transmitted in 1952.

Sherbourne Street houses many excellent 19th-century buildings, of which the most interesting is probably the **Clarion Hotel & Suites Selby** (*see p49*) at No.592. The mansion at the centre of the complex was built in 1883 for a member of the Gooderham liquor dynasty. At different times the hotel has housed everything and everyone from Ernest Hemingway to a gay backroom bar. The original macho man stayed here in September 1923, when the building was the Selby Hotel and Hemingway was a reporter for the *Toronto Star*. The place flourished during the building's long stint as a gay bar and hotel complex in the 1980s and '90s.

Sightseeing

washrooms, for the living, are located across the road from this Gothic site.

Cross Riverdale Park to Carlton Street. The park abuts **Riverdale Farm** (*see p83*), which you'll smell on your left.

The easternmost block of Carlton Street, approaching the lip of the lower Don Valley, is paved with red brick – matching the row of townhouses that line its southern side. One of the oldest houses on the street, at No.397, was built for a barrister named James Reeve in 1883, when the area was still rural. White-brick highlights and large decks on both storeys make this house as alluring now as it was in the old times.

Follow the path south between the houses and the Don Valley to Spruce Street. Walk west on Spruce.

The terraced houses at Nos.74-86 are successful public-housing projects, celebrated for their spacious design. Turning north on Parliament Street, you'll emerge in the heart of Cabbagetown. **Jet Fuel** (519 Parliament Street, 416 968 9982), a local coffee shop, is a good spot to get fired up for the rest of the walk. To pick up a terrific lunch (or dinner or snack), there's the gourmet take-away, **Daniel et Daniel** (248 Carlton Street, 416 968 9275), but Parliament Street offers options galore: fast food, international fare, juice bars, grocers, health-food shops and butchers.

Continue north and turn right on Winchester Street.

The former Presbyterian Church at 80 Winchester Street now houses the **Toronto Dance Theatre** (416 967 1365; *see p224*) and school. The red-brick Romanesque Revival structure (1891) looks like the mother of all the houses around it.

The home at 156 Winchester was originally owned by Daniel Lamb, founder of the Riverdale Zoo. The wonky porch recalls harder times, but now the trim is freshly painted blue and the garden is well kept, and there isn't a cabbage anywhere in sight.

Turn left back on to Sumach Street and left again on to Wellesley Street.

Wellesley Street has the quintessential mix of Cabbagetown's Edwardian and Victorian styles. This beautiful section of the street is also where you'll find the classic cottage-styled and bay-and-gable homes, some with perky picket fences. Briefly detour north on Sackville Street to Alpha Avenue. This quaint dead-end street is lined with tiny mansard-roofed houses from the 1880s. These dwellings are so tiny that you half expect a hobbit to emerge and invite you to tea.

Back on Wellesley Street, No.314 stands out from the crowd. Completed in 1890, the home's front façade is crammed with carved stone ornaments that must have been great publicity for the original owner, Thomas Harris, who owned a stone-cutting company.

Turn right on to Parliament Street.

On this side, you have access to **St James' Cemetery** (*see p83*).

Turn right on Bloor Street E, go over the bridge you passed under at the beginning, and back to Castle Frank Station.

At the junction of Sherbourne and Gerrard Streets, **Allen Gardens** contains a complex of conservatories dating back to 1909, beautifully planted with flora from various climatic zones.

Cabbagetown

Map p275

Bus 65, 75/streetcar 506/subway Sherbourne or Castle Frank.

In the 1840s many Irish families flocked to Toronto, fleeing the potato famine that was devastating their homeland. They settled in a working-class district of the city, and, mindful of their experience in Ireland, filled their front yards not with potatoes but with cabbages (hence the area's name). New waves of immigrants brought wealthier residents to the area, creating an unusually diverse economic mix that continues into modern times.

During a post-World War II push for urban renewal, Cabbagetown became both a proving ground for low-income public housing projects and a stomping ground for more affluent Torontonians, drawn by the beautiful fixer-upper homes at bargain prices. They set the bar for the gentrification of inner-city Toronto: homes that were purchased for $25,000 in the 1950s are now worth over half a million. Indeed, the tough, working-class neighbourhood, described by author Hugh Garner as 'North America's largest Anglo Saxon slum', is a thing of the past. The author grew up in the 'hood and his coming-of-age classic, *Cabbagetown*, sketches a bleak tableau of poverty, alcoholism and teen pregnancy.

While there are still a few gritty spots on its periphery, today's Cabbagetown is better characterised by its strong sense of community pride, as vintage hotels, cocktail lounges and industrial spaces are lovingly buffed up with a keen sense of maintaining the area's history and charm. Today the vast majority of houses have been modernised on the inside, but their historic façades remain.

Toronto's most neighbourly of neighbourhoods is full of hushed, leafy streets lined with red- and yellow-brick houses, thanks to the nearby **Don Valley Brick Works** (*see p71*). Parks and cemeteries line much of the northern and eastern borders, creating many cosy cul-de-sacs. It's difficult to single out one particular architectural masterpiece, as the entire neighbourhood boasts one of the best collections of 19th-century residences in North America (*see p80* **Walk on**).

The borders of Cabbagetown are somewhat fluid and much disputed, as they have gradually crept north over the decades. Originally extending down to

Queen Street East, Cabbagetown is now bounded by Gerrard Street on the south, Bloor/Danforth Street at its northern extreme, Sherbourne Street on the west and the Don Valley in the east.

Although some of the action is on Carlton Street, Cabbagetown's heart and main commercial artery is **Parliament Street**, named after Upper Canada's original parliament buildings, constructed at the base of the street in 1793. Recent efforts to develop the site of those buildings were stymied by archaeological preservationists – not surprising in this part of town, where even new condo developments are closely regulated to blend in with the local Victorian and Edwardian architectural texture.

Parliament Street retains a lively, urban neighbourhood feel, with many unusual cafés and shops. Restaurants are usually fairly priced and boast a smörgåsbord of international cuisine: Mexican, Sri Lankan, Japanese, Filipino, Indian and French fare, all within a few short blocks.

The area is thick with historic buildings, most of them private residences. One exception is the theatre at 509 Parliament Street, home to, among others, the **Canadian Children's Dance Theatre** (416 924 5657).

If you prefer to get your architecture quotient during prayer rather than performance, **Saint Luke's United Church** (353 Sherbourne Street, 416 924 9619) makes all the buildings around it seem plain in comparison. Originally known as Sherbourne Street Methodist, the church opened its huge wooden doors to worshippers in 1887. Its castle-like stonework exterior and stained-glass

BLDG. NO. 61

Distillery District. See p85.

panels are among the prettiest in the city. The church stands at the corner of Carlton Street, which boasts many fine examples of Second Empire and Gothic Revival buildings from the 1880s and '90s.

Carlton Street takes a turn north at Parliament and becomes a residential street culminating in **Riverdale Park**. Trails lead from the wooded park down to a footbridge (over the Don Valley Parkway) allowing access to the Don Valley park system and to more parks on the valley's east side.

Just to the north of Riverdale Park is **Riverdale Farm** (*see p83*). A hit with kids of all ages, the quaint city farm hosts cows, sheep and pigs, while the wetlands below are a haven for turtles and ducks. The farm holds all sorts of community events and family fun, such as pottery lessons, hayrides, cow milking and a weekly farmers' market in the summer (*see p158* **The perfect picnic**).

Within mooing distance of the farm is the **Toronto Necropolis** (200 Winchester Street, 416 923 7911). Opened in 1850, this majestic cemetery and crematorium replaced Potter's Field, Toront's first non-sectarian burial grounds. Located at Bloor and Yonge, Potter's Field was closed in 1855 as the city expanded. Nearly 1,000 of its esteemed denizens were uprooted and moved to the necropolis, where they now rest in peace once again. Among them are William Lyon Mackenzie (Toronto's first mayor), George Brown (founder of the *Globe*, now the *Globe and Mail*) and world champion sculler Ned Hanlan. Also resting here is celebrated Toronto architect Henry Langley, who designed the chapel at the entrance to the cemetery, as well as the attached lodge and

porte cochère – all built in 1872. Langley is noted for his Gothic Revival churches, of which he designed now fewer than 70 in Toronto alone (check out the **Metropolitan Methodist Church** at Queen and Church, or the **Jarvis Street Baptist Church** at 130 Gerrard Street E for nearby examples). Considered one of the best Gothic Revival structures in the country, the necropolis is haunting and ornate, with huge arching stained-glass windows.

On the north side of the necropolis is **Wellesley Park**, once an animal crematorium. A fire destroyed the main building in 1888, and now a row of tidy little homes sits two steps from the park. A paddling pool and small playground make it popular with local families.

To its north, **St James' Cemetery** (635 Parliament Street, 416 964 9194) completes Cabbagetown's collection of peaceful green spaces. Impressive crypts with historic Ontario names such as Brock and Jarvis cast shadows on broken tombstones, whose names have eroded away. Many of Toronto's original Irish immigrants are buried here, along with such luminaries as Sir William Pearce Howland, one of the Fathers of Confederation. At the entrance to the cemetery stands the Gothic yellow-brick Chapel of Saint James-the-Less, built in 1858.

Between Cabbagetown and St Lawrence is where the failed post-war public housing development **Regent Park** stood. It's being torn down to make way for the 21st-century version of low-income housing. Moss Park is below Dundas Street East and apart from a small strip of antiques shops along Queen Street East, this neighbourhood, notorious for junkies and hookers, is of marginal interest.

Riverdale Farm

*201 Winchester Street, east of Parliament Street
(416 392 6794/www.friendsofriverdalefarm.com).
Bus 65/streetcar 506.* **Open** 9am-5pm daily.
Admission free. Map p275 J5.

St Lawrence

Maps p271, p272 & p273

Bus 75/streetcar 501, 504/subway King or Queen.
This historic quarter dates back to the founding
in 1793 of what was then called the village of
York. Ever since, the area has been entwined
with Toronto's history, political life and
economic wellbeing. In the early days it was
designated the market block, and the shoreline
of Lake Ontario came right up to the backs of
warehouses along Front Street, where ships
could dock and unload their merchandise.

The area along Front Street between Church
and Sherbourne Streets has been gentrified over
the past two decades. Condos, apartments and
Crombie Park, a flourishing example of public
housing that has been studied by planners the
world over, have transformed the district into
one of the liveliest neighbourhoods in the city.

A browse around **St Lawrence Market** is
a quintessential Toronto experience. Enliven
your senses any day of the week except Sunday
and Monday by strolling through this vast two-
storey complex. This is where the crowds jostle
for supplies and load up for the coming week or
a dinner party, continuing a Toronto tradition
that began near this location in 1803. You can
get a sense of St. Lawrence's past at the
Market Gallery (*see p85*) on the second
level. Changing exhibits feature old photos,
documents and historical artefacts.

The gallery is also a good place to look
down on a bustling Saturday shopping spree.
Permanent vendors, including butchers,
fishmongers and seafood stands, plus stalls
selling fresh breads, spices and cheeses, attract
the mall-weary from all over town.

On the lower level, cooking supplies, pastries
and more greengrocers are found, as well as
many handmade crafts. At **Domino's Foods
Ltd** (95 Front Street E, 416 366 2178), you can
stock up on sweets and European foods.

St Lawrence Market is not just about filling
the larder. Many people drop in during the week
for an all-day breakfast speciality – peameal
bacon on a kaiser bun, a famous Canadian
delicacy. It is really a thick slice of ham, salt
and sugar cured and then rolled in cornmeal
and cooked on the grill. Bite into a warm

Hippy days

You're unlikely to find **Rochdale** (341 Bloor
Street West, the Annex) on any tourist
itinerary. Nor will you find any plaques or
markers on the building itself. But this drab
brutalist building – now known by the equally
drab name of the Senator David A Croll
Apartments – is a landmark in Toronto's
cultural history.

Built in 1968 as a bold experiment in
alternative education and communal
cohabitation, it was named after the town in
the north of England where the world's first
cooperative society was established in the
19th century. It quickly became a symbolic
beacon of love and general grooviness – the
bedrooms were called ashrams – feeding off
the scene in nearby Yorkville, then a thriving
stage for music, art, politics, protest and
poetry. Rochdale attracted like-minded spirits
from across the continent: rock stars, draft
dodgers, McLuhanites, writers, artists and,
especially, dopers. Cultural icons like Norman
Mailer, Allen Ginsberg, Alice Cooper and
Steve Miller partied here. When its residents
weren't strung out, they hosted poetry slams,
nude theatre, underground radio, workshops

in civil disobedience and experimental film
screenings. Within a few years Rochdale had
spawned a recording studio, at least one
major theatre group, a publisher and a
printing press.

But the good karma didn't last – a
combination of drugs, vagrants, vandals and
mismanagement ended the trip, and after
numerous overdoses and one 'jumper'
suicide, the building was closed in 1975 and
the remaining tenants forcibly evicted.
'Toronto the Good' had lost its innocence.

After lying dormant for years, the
hippie palace was transformed following a
frenzy of gutting, cleaning, destoning and
rezoning. Its current incarnation is, wait for
it, a seniors' apartment building (the new
residents seem unaware of the psychedelic
past). Other than the outer shell, all that
remains of Rochdale now is the sculpture
on the south-west corner of Huron and Bloor,
a giant slumping bronze called the *Unknown
Student* by Dale Heinzerling. Following the
building's renovation, authorities turned the
sculpture around – literally turning its back
on the building's sordid past.

peameal at **Carousel Bakery** (95 Front Street E, 416 363 4247) or **Paddington's Pump** (95 Front Street E, 416 368 6955). Crowds also gather at the little hole in the wall **Churrasco of St Lawrence** (95 Front Street E, 416 862 2867) for slow-roasted, specially seasoned, mouth-watering Portuguese chicken on a bun, accompanied by a bag of French fries, a soft drink and a couple of rich custard tarts.

On Saturdays, the North Market – an annex on the opposite side of Front Street – features a farmers' market selling fresh goods straight from the countryside. It opens at an ungodly hour – many farmers start setting up at 5am. Cured and fresh meats, Great Lakes fish, fruit and vegetables, herbs and even Ontario-grown peanuts are sold. The vendors like to call it a day by 1pm so don't arrive too late. On Sundays the building is transformed into an antiques market. For more details, *see p150*.

One of the city's most photographed vantage points lies between the north and south markets. Looking west, the skyscrapers are symmetrically lined up behind the **Gooderham Building** (49 Wellington Street E), or, as most people know it, the **Flatiron**. It was constructed in 1891, ten years before its more famous cousin in New York. On the opposite side of the building is a clever *trompe-l'oeil* painting by artist Derek Besant that fills the 'flat' side of the Flatiron. If you want to get inside, drop into the Flatiron & Firkin pub in the basement (416 362 3444).

Two important theatres are across Berczy Park, behind the Flatiron. The 3,000-capacity **Hummingbird Centre for the Performing Arts** (*see p221*) is a mid-century gem by architect Peter Dickinson. Now that the ballet and opera have decamped across town, the centre mainly presents touring shows. The **St Lawrence Centre for the Arts** (27 Front Street E, 416 366 7723) presents both music and Canadian Stage Theatre Company performances in two smaller, more intimate venues – the **Jane Mallet** and **Bluma Appel** theatres (*see p220*). While on Front Street East, look for the **Dixon Building** (Nos.45-49), featuring the city's only remaining cast-iron façade. The 1872 structure is a tribute to architectural illusion: what appears to be painted wood and stone is actually cast iron. Also note the 1877 warehouse at 67-69 Front Street East, distinguished by its ornate Renaissance Revival architecture style.

To get a feel for St Lawrence's history head to **Toronto's First Post Office** (1833; *see below*). It's a perfectly restored working post office, where you can sit by the fireplace and dip a quill in an inkwell to write a letter on old-fashioned paper.

Another gem is the classic Edwardian structure of the King Edward Hotel at 39 King Street East. The 'King Eddie' was the city's most fashionable hotel for some 60 years. The original property was developed in 1901 and received an additional 18 storeys in 1920. Now known as **Le Royal Meridien King Edward** (*see p49*), the grand old hotel suffered from decades of neglect before being returned to its former glory. Pop in for an elegant afternoon tea or a drink in the stately oak-panelled bar.

Though slightly off the beaten track, the **Distillery District** east of St Lawrence has the potential to become a major destination. The largest and best-preserved collection of Victorian industrial architecture in North America, the buildings now host a theatre, about 20 galleries, cafés, a brew pub, a day spa, unique shops and restaurants. It's all based around the Gooderham & Worts booze factory, which dates back to 1858. The distillery operated until the 1990s and served as a location for several Hollywood films – and no wonder. Strolling the bricked walkways around the 44 historic buildings, you feel as if you are in a Victorian village.

The pedestrian-only zone is worth a trip if only to sample the chocolates made at **SOMA** (*see p157*), the beer at the **Mill Street Brewery** (*see p137* **Brewhaha**), and the coffee at **Balzac's Coffee Roastery** (*see p115*). With the arrival of **Soulpepper Theatre** at the **Young Centre for the Performing Arts** (*see p222*), nightlife is also picking up in this atmospheric part of town. For more information on the district, stop in at the Distillery Visitor Centre.

Distillery District

55 Mill Street, at Parliament Street (416 364 1177/www.thedistillerydistrict.com). Streetcar 504. **Admission** free. **Map** p273 J8. **Photos** *pp82-83.*

Market Gallery

95 Front Street E, at Jarvis Street (416 392 7604). Streetcar 504. **Open** 10am-4pm Wed-Fri; 9am-4pm Sat; noon-4pm Sun. **Admission** free. **Map** p272 G8.

St Lawrence Market

92 Front Street E, at Jarvis Street (416 392 7120/ www.stlawrencemarket.com). Streetcar 504. **Open** *South Market* 8am-6pm Tue-Thur; 8am-7pm Fri; 5am-5pm Sat. *North Market* 5am-2pm Sat (farmers' market); 8am-5pm Sun (antiques market). **Admission** free. **Map** p272 G8.

Toronto's First Post Office

260 Adelaide Street E, at George Street (416 865 1833/www.townofyork.com). Streetcar 504. **Open** 9am-4pm Mon-Fri; 10am-4pm Sat, Sun. **Admission** free. **Map** p272 H8.

Midtown

Swanky shopping and park life.

Though characterised by leafy streets and neighbourhood charm, Midtown is starting to feel like Downtown in places. As more towers fill empty pockets of land, the high densities of downtown are creeping north. They are accompanied by a rise in NIMBY sentiment – 'not in my backyard', thanks. So far the developers are winning the fight, aided by a city council that sees high density as a remedy to urban sprawl.

Despite the plethora of cranes and construction sites, Midtown still has its fair share of picturesque villages. Once rich in hippy heritage, Yorkville is now rich in cash, with glamorous hotels, boutiques and restaurants lining its exclusive streets. The Annex boasts Victorian and Edwardian architecture, plus cafés, pubs and shops geared towards both students and yuppies. Further north, there's the exclusive Forest Hill, with its centre tidily concentrated around neat florists, prim boutiques, coffee shops and greengrocers along upper Spadina (note that it's Spadina Road up here, not Avenue). Rosedale's secretive, spiralling crescents still confound the map-wielding visitor, but this ravine-lined, tree-filled enclave for the privileged is worth seeking out: it's one of Toronto's most beautiful neighbourhoods.

Note that this guide takes Bloor Street as the dividing line between Downtown Toronto and Midtown: venues on the north of Bloor are covered here, but those on its south side (such as the Bata Shoe Museum and Royal Ontario Museum) will be found in the Downtown Toronto section (*see pp59-85*).

Yorkville

Map p274

Bus 6/subway Bay, Bloor-Yonge, Museum.
This chichi shopping district – bounded by Bloor Street, Yonge Street, Avenue Road and Davenport Road – has a history as rich as its customers. Incorporated as a village in 1853, Yorkville existed as its own entity for only 30 years before it became part of Toronto. And it later played a key role in the development of Toronto's counterculture. In the 1950s planners chose wisely to limit building density and prohibit high-rise development in the area, maintaining the

village's original character and encouraging street-level activities. It worked. In the '60s Yorkville mushroomed with artist-run studios, innovative shops and galleries. Buzzing coffee houses showcased the burgeoning talents of folkies such as Gordon Lightfoot, Neil Young, Bruce Cockburn, the Band and a young singer from the prairies named Joni Mitchell. These days the tie-dyed Trotskyites and beat poets have moved on, making way for some of the city's most exclusive boutiques and hotels.

The heart of Yorkville's shopping area lies on Cumberland Street and Yorkville Avenues between Bay Street and Avenue Road. The two streets are also joined by a few north–south lanes, which make for easy exploring.

On Cumberland, the **Village of Yorkville Park** is built on a former parking lot. Designed as a series of themed gardens, it's the perfect setting for an impromptu urban picnic, on a 650-ton chunk of pink granite lifted from the Canadian shield. As you reflect on the area's groovy days, you can browse the swingin' souvenirs from the era, like a 'genuine' Beatles

Village of Yorkville Park.

lunchbox at the memorabilia store **Retro Fun** (130 Cumberland Street, 416 968 7771).

Though many galleries have departed to trendy West Queen West (*see p97*), some of the finest and most innovative art in Toronto can still be enjoyed (free) in the galleries that cluster along Yorkville's streets, notably on Scollard Street and Hazelton Avenue. Stalwarts include **Mira Godard Gallery** (22 Hazelton Avenue, 416 964 8197; *see p185*) and **Beckett Fine Art** (120 Scollard Street; *see also p185*).

A small alleyway takes you from 14 Hazelton Avenue to the back entrance of the decadent **Hazelton Lanes** shopping mall (55 Avenue Road; *see also p143*). Inside there are upscale temptations in fashion, cars and the Canadian branch of the trendy, Texas-based supermarket chain **Whole Foods** (*see p159*).

Just up the street from Hazelton Lanes is one of the kookiest buildings in town – the **Toronto Heliconian Club** (35 Hazelton Avenue, 416 922 3618), a rare example of Carpenter's Gothic architecture, where wood rather than masonry reinterprets the grandiose vintage revival style. Originally a church (built in 1876), the building was bought by the THC in 1923 to provide a home for women in the arts, a function it fulfils to this day. A noticeboard outside announces events and exhibitions.

In Yorkville it's not uncommon to see autograph-seekers clustering around the exits of the area's five-star hotels, hoping for a brush with the many celebrities who stay in these parts, particularly during the Toronto International Film Festival, when the district serves as a sort of Hollywood North base camp. At the west end of Yorkville, **Alliance Atlantis Cumberland 4 Cinemas** (159 Cumberland Street; *see also p180*) screens quality (non-Hollywood) movies.

At the east end of Cumberland Street is a Toronto retail classic, the **Toy Shop** (62 Cumberland Street, 416 961 4870), going strong since 1908. The **Toronto Reference Library** (789 Yonge Street, 416 395 5577), another neighbourhood landmark, is the largest of its kind in Canada. **Yorkville Library** (22 Yorkville Avenue, 416 393 7660), around the corner, is a gentler and smaller, a nice spot to stop to read, and a good place to check out local events. Across the street at No.27 is another landmark, **Lovecraft** (*see p163*), which opened in 1971 and is the oldest 'adult boutique' in Canada.

The Annex

Map p274

Bus 26/streetcar 510, 511/subway Bathurst, Bay, Dupont, St George or Spadina.

This bustling, villagey district – roughly bounded by Avenue Road and Bathurst Street, Bloor Street West and Davenport Road – dates back to the 1880s. Back then, it was a suburb,

Sightseeing

and many of its Victorian houses still line its leafy backstreets, along with mock-Georgian and Tudor styles that were built in the period following 1910. But by 1930 the rise of the automobile meant that the smart money (or at least the big money) was moving further out to Rosedale and Forest Hill. Today the Annex is one of Toronto's most diverse communities, mixing the wealth of nearby Yorkville and the University of Toronto's student culture, with a bit of counterculture granola thrown in.

The neighbourhood's commercial hub is Bloor Street West, between St. George and Bathurst Streets, where most of the shopping, restaurants and nightlife can be found. The northern boundary, Davenport Road, follows a path that was originally a trail used by Toronto's first inhabitants, the native communities that commuted between the Don and Humber River valleys. Find out more with a visit to the nearby **Native Canadian Centre of Toronto** (16 Spadina Road, 416 964 9087), which organises public gatherings and events to promote First Nations' culture. Indeed, cultural institutions abound in the Annex: there's the **Alliance Française de Toronto** (24 Spadina Road, 416 922 2014), which showcases francophone culture throughout the year, and the **Italian Cultural Institute** (496 Huron Street, 416 921 3802), featuring rotating exhibits and seminars on contemporary Italian culture.

On the far side of the railway tracks you'll find the large warehouse and exhibition hall of the **City of Toronto Archives** (255 Spadina Road, 416 397 5000). The downstairs of this clean, modern building has rotating exhibits on Toronto's urban history and geography. To find out more about a topic, head upstairs to the research hall; registration is quick and free, and the staff are helpful.

Casa Loma

Map p274

Bus 7/streetcar 512/subway Bay, Rosedale, St Clair, St Clair W or Summerhill.
Toronto's grid system suddenly goes all twisty through this hilly neighbourhood, which stretches north from Davenport Road to St Clair Avenue between Yonge and Bathurst Streets. Early in the city's history, the outstanding view from this hilly summit led Toronto's wealthiest citizens to settle here.

Two remnants from those heady days, Casa Loma and **Spadina Historic House** (for both *see below*) are popular public attractions, conveniently located next door to one another. The former is the more famous

venue, and it's certainly more spectacular from the outside, but if you only have time to tour one of the two, choose Spadina House: it's actually more interesting. Between the two attractions, a small park leads to the **Baldwin Steps**. Named after the family who originally owned this land, these 110 stairs span a section of hillside that is too steep for a road. Stretch your legs on the way up for a fantastic view of Downtown.

Heading north along Spadina Road takes you to Sir Winston Churchill Park, at the corner of St Clair Avenue West. The park has floodlit tennis courts and a playground, and it's popular with joggers too. You can also gain access to **Nordheimer Ravine** (*see p90*) from the park, which has many good picnic spots, as well as a long tree-shaded trail.

Casa Loma

1 Austin Terrace, at Spadina Road (416 923 1171/ www.casaloma.org). Bus 7/streetcar 512/subway Dupont. **Open** 9.30am-5pm daily. Last entry 4pm. **Admission** $16; $8.75-$10 concessions; free under-4s. **Credit** AmEx, MC, V. **Map** p274 D2.
Some love it, others dismiss it as a kitsch folly. Either way, Casa Loma is a sight to behold, with its corbelled towers and battlements. Late 19th-century magnate Sir Henry Pellatt enlisted architect EJ Lennox to build this medieval-style castle with a stunning view of the city below. It was finished in 1914, but Pellatt hit hard times a decade later and had to move out; the house opened as a tourist attraction in 1937. Inside, the high ceilings and wide-open rooms feel oddly empty, despite the many displays from the heyday of the 'House on the Hill'. Check out the dome in the conservatory, which is made with Italian glass, cut and stained into images of grapes and trellises. Pendulous lights hang down from the dome, resembling bunches of grapes. The house also has a bona fide secret passage to the stables, which were carried out on an equally grand scale and are included in the price of admission. The gardens at the back of the building are lovely, dark, and steep, with fountains, waterfalls and woodsy pools. Ring the bells on the dragon sculpture in the so-called Secret Garden. If you're pure of heart, legend has it, the dragons will come to life. **Photo** *p89*.

Spadina Historic House & Gardens

285 Spadina Road, at Austin Terrace (416 392 6910). Bus 7/streetcar 512/subway Dupont. **Open** *Apr-early Sept* noon-5pm Tue-Sun. *Sept-Dec* noon-4pm Tue-Fri, noon-5pm Sat, Sun. *Jan-Apr* noon-5pm Sat, Sun. **Admission** $6; $4-$5 concessions. Free under-6s. **Credit** AmEx, MC, V. **Map** p274 E2.
This 50-room mansion was built for financier James Austin in 1866, but his son added even more space in the 20th century, so it now has elements of both Victorian and Edwardian architecture. The family sold the manse to the Ontario Heritage Foundation back in 1984, and Austin's descendants donated the

Casa Loma. See p88.

contents to the new museum; each room contains furniture, appliances, crockery and books that belonged to the original residents.

The museum gives a good sense of what high-society life was like a century ago. Enthusiastic staffers provide guided tours, and exhibits are changed frequently to suit a particular theme or season. The extensive historic gardens (free, if you don't enter the museum) are resplendent with the flowers, legumes and herbs of Austin's day. Don't miss the archaeological display on the lower level, which contains items from an even earlier house built on the same foundation by the Baldwin family (of Baldwin steps fame). On special occasions, appetising period dishes are prepared for visitors in the mansion's working kitchen.

Rosedale

Map p275
Bus 75, 82/subway Castle Frank, Rosedale, St Clair or Summerhill.

Rosedale is a fairy-tale world, characterised by winding, forested streets lined with old stone and brick mansions. In the 1820s Sheriff William Botsford Jarvis (after whom Jarvis Street is named) settled here with his wife Mary. William is credited with founding Rosedale, but it was Mary who named it, giving a nod to the wild roses that grew on the hills of their large estate. Mary spent many a day wandering these hills on foot and on horseback, and the trails she made are thought to form the template for modern Rosedale's roads. Visitors get lost here more than anywhere else in the city, and most of the locals like it that way.

Many of Toronto's wealthiest and most prominent citizens live in Rosedale. The area's Victorian, Georgian, Tudor and Edwardian mansions were built between 1860 and 1930, and many are listed in the Toronto Historical Board's Inventory of Heritage Properties. If you are interested in architecture, take a rambling walk through this pretty neighbourhood. Roughly speaking, its borders are Bloor Street East, Yonge Street, St Clair Avenue East and Castle Frank subway station in the east. For a tour, get off at Rosedale subway station and walk east along Crescent Road, taking detours along streets like Cluny Drive and South Drive. To get deep into the heart of Rosedale, cross over Mount Pleasant Road and explore streets such as Glen Road, Elm Avenue, Douglas Drive and Binscarth Road. Alternatively, approach Rosedale from the south: get off at Castle Frank station and walk north. Back on Yonge, Rosedale has a row of gourmet shops and restaurants north of Davenport

Sightseeing

and south of the railway tracks, where you can shop and eat alongside Toronto's rich.

Abutting Rosedale to the west is the pleasant neighbourhood of **Summerhill**, filled with high-end shops and services. Also here is the award-winning **Summerhill LCBO store** (10 Scrivener Square; *see p157*), the flagship shop for Ontario's publicly owned liquor board, housed in a restored vintage train station.

Back in Rosedale proper, well-manicured **Rosedale Park** has tennis courts, a playing field and a skating rink. This was also the location of Canada's first Grey Cup game in 1909, between the University of Toronto and the Parkdale Canoe Club.

A series of ravines forms a horseshoe shape through Rosedale. These woody crevasses bear names that further evoke a fairy-tale atmosphere: the Vale of Avoca, Moore Park and Rosedale Valley. The ravines also lead into the **Don Valley**, which forms the eastern boundary of the neighbourhood. One trail leads you right to the **Don Valley Brick Works Park** (*see below*).

Don Valley Brick Works Park

550 Bayview Avenue, at Pottery Road (416 392 1111/www.city.toronto.on.ca/parks). Subway Castle Frank then 20min walk.
Don Valley Brick Works Park is one of the most important geological sites in North America: the layers of sedimentary rock found in the quarry walls help scientists study the Ice Age, the environment

and climate change. The area was used centuries ago by indigenous communities as a source of clay, and between 1889 and 1984 the Don Valley Pressed Brick Works Company, one of Canada's biggest brickyards, operated here. It produced bricks that were used for some of the city's best-known buildings (Hart House, Casa Loma, Osgoode Hall and Old City Hall, among others).

It was only in 1995 that the park became a public space, and restoration of the site began. The old quarry has been transformed into a nature park featuring a wild-flower meadow and wetlands, paths and boardwalks – all ripe for exploring. Work is underway to convert the massive industrial buildings into a greenhouse and restaurant from the ubiquitous Jamie Kennedy (*see p118*).

Forest Hill

Bus 32B, 32C/subway Davisville, Eglinton, St Clair, St Clair W.
You won't see a forest, but you will see trees. Forest Hill was incorporated as a village in 1923, and its snooty status was assured in 1929, when **Upper Canada College** (200 Lonsdale Road, 416 488 1125), one of Canada's most respected private schools, opened its doors to young men; the rise of the automobile also allowed the wealthy to move up here from the city. In 1936, in an effort to retain the neighbourhood's classy feel, new building practices were introduced, requiring that a tree be planted at the front of each property. From

Ontario Science Centre. *See p91*.

little by-laws mighty oak trees grow, and Forest Hill, especially the lower part, still feels like an exclusive town in the middle of the country. That said, many of the area's grand old mansions have been torn down and rebuilt, which gives the area a more modern feel than Rosedale. Neo-Georgian, neo-Victorian and other 'neo-traditional' | forms are common along Forest Hill Road and Old Forest Hill Road. A cluster of pleasant shops and restaurants just north of St Clair on Spadina Road is known as Forest Hill Village. To get away from the mansions and back to nature, escape to the **Nordheimer Ravine** (*see p87*), which runs along the south-west section of Forest Hill.

Davisville

Bus 32B, 32C/subway Davisville, Eglinton or St Clair.
This largely residential area takes its name from John Davis, who arrived from England in 1840, and was Davisville's first postmaster.

The neighbourhood, east of Yonge and north of Davisville Avenue to Bayview Avenue, is architecturally less interesting than Forest Hill and Rosedale, and is home to yuppies rather than millionaires. The only real reason for visitors to come to Davisville is **Mount Pleasant Cemetery** (375 Mount Pleasant Road, 416 485 9129). The sprawling, leafy graveyard is a popular outing for everyone from Toronto's unicyclists to its goth community (in Toronto, even the goths have a slogan: 'Making Toronto a darker place'). The cemetery laid its first customer to rest in 1876 and by 1945 more than 117,000 interments had taken place, which is about twice the population of Toronto when the cemetery first opened. Many notable Canadians have found their final resting place here, including William Lyon Mackenzie King, Canada's tenth and longest-serving prime minister (1921-30; 1935-48). World-renowned pianist Glenn Gould lies here, as do Frederick Banting and Charles Best, whose experiments in the early 20th century led to the discovery of insulin. The cemetery also offers access to the **Belt Line Trail**. This 4.5-kilometre (2.8-mile) path follows the line of a belt-line railroad from the 19th century, and is now a popular cycling path.

The intersection of **Yonge and Eglinton** is the heart of North Toronto. It is brimming with shops, bars, restaurants – probably the most densely packed consumer section north of Downtown. There are a couple of major cinemas here, and the stretch of Yonge between Eglinton and Lawrence offers some characterful independent shops. Once home

to a thriving singles scene, the area is still known as Young & Eligible by some locals, probably owing to the large number of high-rise apartment buildings in the area, but the dominant demographic is now yuppie families.

Leaside

Bus 51, 56, 100/subway Davisville, Eglinton or St Clair.
This neighbourhood is named after a farming family headed by John and Mary Lea, who emigrated here from England in 1819. As often happens, it was the second generation that rose to prominence: their son William Lea opened a tomato cannery, became town councillor, and built an octagonal house that he called Leaside. Part residential and part industrial, the streets of Leaside proper don't have much to offer. Just north of Eglinton, however, a bike path leads from Broadway Avenue down into **Serena Gundy Park**. If you cross back south under Eglinton Avenue, you'll end up in **Ernest Thompson Seton Park**. Seton was an eccentric naturalist, and author of *Wild Animals I Have Known*, reputedly one of the inspirations for Rudyard Kipling's *Jungle Book*. When Seton moved to Toronto in 1870, this part of the Don Valley was still wilderness, and it became a natural research laboratory for his zoological studies. Today it's tamer, with picnic tables dotting grassy areas along the West Don River, but scientific endeavour still has its place. In the park, by Taylor Creek where the Don Valley Parkway meets Don Mills Road, there is a series of sculptures that resemble giant exposed molars. Filled with soil and plants, they actually make up an experimental water purification system. Further north is the **Ontario Science Centre** (*see below*).

Ontario Science Centre

770 Don Mills Road, at Eglinton Avenue (416 696 1000/www.ontariosciencecentre.ca). Subway Eglinton then bus 34. **Open** *Sept-June* 10am-5pm daily. *July, Aug* 10am-6pm daily. **Admission** $17; $10-$12.50 concessions; free under-4s. *Omnimax* $12 adults; $8-$9 concessions. **Credit** AmEx, MC, V.
The multi-level centre houses 800 or so science exhibits, plus Toronto's only planetarium and an Omnimax movie theatre. The OSC opened in 1969, and some exhibits now have a retro feel. But the interactive Science Arcade and the temporary shows are consistently engaging and topical. The new $40-million Weston Family Innovation Centre, described as a 'scientific Times Square', highlights new developments via multimedia displays. The excellent gift shop will please science junkies, but the food is not great. If weather permits, pack a picnic and eat in the park that lies behind the museum. **Photo** *p90*.

West End

For a life on the edge, go west.

The cutting edge: **Museum of Contemporary Canadian Art.** *See p98.*

Map p270

Streetcar 501, 504, 505, 506.

Any cross-town rivalry in Toronto is mostly kept to friendly bar-rail banter. The East arguably has better beaches, plus the bluffs and the Danforth. The West End has plenty of parks, shopping and sights, but best of all its neighbourhoods are ideal for charting out the city's kaleidoscopic cultural diversity. Of the 80 or so different communities in the city, many settled in the expanse west of Bathurst Street stretching to the Humber River.

The trend factor tilts in the West End's favour too, though this would be contested by some east-side dwellers. Pockets of bohemia arise spontaneously amid the vintage storefronts and industrial warehouse spaces: just look at the formerly bleaker-than-bleak strip of **Dundas Street West** (*see p97* **Walk on**). Sandwiched between West Queen West and Little Italy, a small but seminal scene is awakening – offering a fresh alternative to both areas. Further out, the **Junction**, in the Dundas and Keele area, is where displaced artists from West Queen West (*see p97* **Walk**

On) have been settling, with several storefront galleries marking it out as the next cool 'hood.

The West End may be wild, but it's also wide. Plan your exploration by area, according to your interests and time frame. The breezy **Waterfront Trail** (*see p60*) allows cyclists and walkers to zip through a corridor of parks, sports facilities and historic sites in one almost seamless, car-free strip. High Park and the Humber River are accessible from the trail.

The West End's four major vectors – Bloor, College, Dundas and Queen Streets – lead to a variety of urban diversions, from vital nightspots to the best pierogi in town.

Bloor Street connects a series of diverse neighbourhoods – with the added bonus of the subway line below. At Bloor and Bathurst Street, both locals and visitors love to shop at the crazy, must-see **Honest Ed's** (*see p145*). Round the corner is Markham Street's **Mirvish Village**, and its funky mix of arty bookstores, restaurants and shops.

Walking west (in the direction of Christie), **Koreatown** – some call it Little Korea – is in your face with its peppy retail strip (at its most intense at Euclid and Manning Streets). Check out the bakery window at Uni Kim (680 Bloor Street), where tiny walnut cakes pop out of a mechanised mini-assembly line. Koreatown halts abruptly at Christie Street, where **Christie Pitts Park** and the Christie subway provide further options: heading westwards on Bloor there are waves of smaller international enclaves to explore – you'll find a mix of Latin, African, Indian and Sri Lankan communities, which are currently adding new life to the strip.

College Street is home to the oldest of several Italian pockets (see p94 **Global village**). This patch of Little Italy buzzes on an espresso-induced high, with plenty of places to sip and nosh. Some of the tree-lined residential streets off College hide tiny shops, ice-cream parlours and galleries.

The transformation of **Dundas West** near Ossington Avenue is slowly taking hold. Once the preserve of hardware and plumbing supply stores, sports bars and fish vendors, the area

has suddenly sprouted edgy, bohemian spots like the **Dakota Tavern** (see p140), **Sweaty Betty's** (see p141) and the **Communist's Daughter** (see p140), which bring a street-level rec-room aesthetic all their own.

Today **West Queen West** is the talking point of the town because its shabby-chic vibe is now threatened by condo developments so grossly out of scale with their surroundings that they will surely change the character of the area. The prospect of displacing old industrial space, where a good number of local artists live and work, with pseudo-trendy cut-out condos has infuriated locals; even the mayor has vowed to stop the projects. For now, though, Toronto's down-and-outers rub shoulders with its up-and-comers and once-divey hostels have become the city's most desirable hotels. The **Drake Hotel** (1150 Queen W; see p52) offers myriad salon-styled diversions and has brought business and a touch of glamour to WQW. The

Global village Poland

Population: 150,000
Home base: Roncesvalles Avenue, between Lake Shore Boulevard W and Bloor Street W

The first Polish émigrés settled in the city in the 18th century, but it wasn't until 1850 that peasants began to arrive in large numbers, attracted by advertisements for railway and land development (a number headed westwards towards Saskatchewan to take up beet farming). Determined to express themselves religiously and culturally, they established a community of churches, bakeries and butchers near the railway yards.

A lull in immigration between the world wars was followed by an influx of political refugees; defecting athletes and performers – along with accredited doctors, engineers and professors – chose this fast-growing city as their harbour from communist rule. Today Toronto's Polish community supports two newspapers and several TV and radio time slots, and has grown beyond the confines of Roncesvalles Avenue to the West End (Bloor West Village, Etobicoke) and Mississauga.
Trading places: Though the Roncesvalles neighbourhood, between the churches of St Casimir (156 Roncesvalles Avenue) and St Vincent de Paul (263 Roncesvalles Avenue), continues to trade heavily in Polish delicacies, books and videos, the focus is now shifting to suburban strip malls.

A taste of: Toronto's largest Polish population now resides outside the city proper, in adjacent Mississauga, home to Plaza Wisla (named after the longest river in Poland), at Dundas Street West and Dixie Road, and the cheapest baked goods this side of Warsaw. The downtown pedestrian can find his mecca at Dundas Street W and Roncesvalles Avenue, where 80 per cent of businesses are run by Polish Canadians and residential streets are flooded with the sounds of Polish pop. Though threatened by mass gentrification (a trendy antiques strip flourishes at Queen Street West), the stretch still remains sausage central. Copernicus Delicatessen (79 Roncesvalles Avenue, 416 536 4054) is the best link to superlative spicy kielbasa, while Czechowski Polish Sausage (935 The Queensway, 416 252 4567) in Etobicoke serves fancy varieties stuffed with cheeses.
Join in: The Feniks Polish Film Festival is an on-again, off-again occurrence. To find out where to see the latest Polish offerings to the big screen is to go to www.feniks.net.
Local luminary: Late radio and TV broadcaster Peter Gzowski is the great-great-great-grandson of one of Canada's first Polish immigrants, Sir Casimir Gzowski, a military and civil engineer who oversaw the building of bridges, canals and railways across Ontario.

Global village Italy

Population: 500,000
Home base: College Street and Bathurst Street, St Clair Avenue W and Dufferin Street

Italy's World Cup victory in 2006 served as a reminder of the strength of Italian culture in Toronto. The parties rivalled the last cup victory in 1982, to this date the largest street party ever held in the city. The first Little Italy grew up in the early 1900s along College Street, where Italians from the poverty-stricken south of Italy made new lives building Toronto's railways, streetcar lines and sewers.

After World War II Canada opened up its borders, and Torontonian Italians sponsored the arrival of family members. At the same time, a building boom attracted huge numbers to the construction trade. Another zone consisting of mostly northern Italians formed at St Clair Avenue W and Dufferin Street, and is now even bigger and more Italian in flavour than its downtown counterpart. Migration continued north-west into the suburbs of Woodbridge, where many of the city's construction royalty have built their estates. Today the community supports the CHIN television and radio station, and a newspaper (*Corriere Canadese*). The Italian Cultural Institute (*see p88*) runs screenings, exhibitions and other events.

Trading places: Motoretta (554 College Street, 416 925 1818) sells enough gelato-coloured Vespas to give you a Federico Fellini flashback. Riviera Bakery (576 College Street, 416 537 9352) has ice-cream, and supplies most of the neighbourhood with baked goods.

Grab some Calabrese rolls and head to Centro Formaggio (578 College Street, 416 531 4453), or any of the other food shops on the street, and dine alfresco at the Piazza Johnny Lombardi (at the intersection of Grace Street and College). The parkette is a loving tribute to the late great CHIN founder – a man who championed both multiculturalism and bikini contests. Venture to Faema (672 Dupont Street, 416 535 7147) for great Italian coffee.

A taste of: Grab a seat on the patio at Café Diplomatico (594 College Street, *see p125*) in the heart of Little Italy and savour the streetscape. While you're people-watching, check for signs of Old World Italian life. You'll find the soul of Little Italy at places like Sammy Joes, Café Bar Azzurri and local sports bars; as well as Italian people, there's often a good card game or soccer match to watch. For a real veal meal deal head down Clinton Street, taking the alleyway at the bottom for a block, to the original California Sandwich Bar (244 Claremont Street, 416 603 3317). This is one of Toronto's great culinary institutions; these messy buns of meatball, aubergine, steak and veal are revered by all – as testimonials on the walls (from hockey players, police and firemen, celebrities and film crews), gleefully attest.

For serious shopping, strike uptown to the St Clair and Dufferin 'Corso Italia' retail strip. Here you'll find all things Italian – including designer clothing, jewellery and furniture. It's also a sweet

---

Gladstone Hotel (1214 Queen Street West; *see p52* is a funky 19th-century railroad hotel lovingly restored by the Zeidler family in 2006 and now the nexus of the local art scene.

King Street West is a thriving hub for Toronto's graphic arts, design, animation and communication firms. Developers have their sights set firmly on this area too. They're busily converting it from a trendy studio warehouse district into a trendy studio condominium district.

Further west is **Parkdale**. Once a majestic lakeside village, it spiralled into decline after World War II, as the nearby lake was filled in and developed with tracks and roadways. The current renovation generation is busy rebuilding this classic Toronto neighbourhood,

which is still scenic and full of lovely old homes. Further west, it's a shopper's haven for all kinds of vintage goods, from serious antiques to much thriftier second-hand wares. At the bottom of the hill, Queen Street ends abruptly (the streetcars, however, keep on going) and on your left you'll see Lake Ontario. To the right is **Roncesvalles Avenue**, which has a strong sense of community and a diverse shopping scene in Polish 'Roncesvalles Village' (*see p93* **Global village**).

Further west is **High Park**. At two square kilometres (0.8sq mile), it's Toronto's biggest park – a remarkable gift to the city by John Howard. He purchased it in the 1830s, building his residence, **Colborne Lodge** (*see p96*), on a fine hilltop overlooking the lake. The

haven, with many pasticcerie (try Tre Mari Bakery, 1311 St Clair Avenue W, 416 654 8960); or go further west for cannoli at Messina Bakery (19 Scarlett Road, 416 762 2496). For a cultural experience and the city's finest *gelato*, don't miss La Paloma Gelateria & Café (1357 St Clair W, 416 656 2340). Try one or more of the 50 varieties of ethereal handmade gelati that vary with the seasons, including old-world faves like spumante, fig and glazed chestnut.

Join in: College Street is shut to traffic for two days in June, when the Taste of Little Italy festival (www.tasteoflittleitaly.com) swells with thousands of people enjoying music and street performances. Local businesses offer a feast (from Italian to Brazilian to Thai). Rides for children and beer gardens are further attractions.

Local luminary: Italian-Canadian Nino Ricci, author of *Lives of the Saints*, has lived in the city for years.

house/museum is one of the many great features that complement the unusually diverse park, which is home to an astonishing array of plants, animals and birds. Trails spool through rolling hills, paths are well maintained (but steep and muddy here and there), with informative markers along the way. Nature-loving adults will enjoy Grenadier Pond; the kids may prefer the duck pond over at the park's popular little zoo.

To the west of High Park is **Bloor West Village**. Once a run-down retail strip, it's now a fashionable shopping district bordered by tree-lined residential streets. Trendy cafés, upscale markets and classy clothiers join Ukrainian bakeries and Euro-styled delis – the perfect place for a post-park wind-down.

A popular breakfast spot is the **Bloor-Jane Diner** (2434 Bloor Street W, 416 766 5383).

To the south of Bloor Street, **Riverside Drive** runs through the neighbourhood of Swansea and is a trove of Tudor-style houses. Keep an eye out for 210 Riverside, identifiable by the spreading oak tree on the front lawn. The home's first owner was Lucy Maud Montgomery, the Canadian author most famous for her *Anne of Green Gables* books. Montgomery nicknamed her house 'Journey's End'. Swansea itself was one of the last independent villages to be assimilated by the city of Toronto, and the hilly, affluent neighbourhood retains its character. Its individuality is aided by its being bounded on three sides by water: Grenadier Pond,

Sipping point: scenesters swill at the **Drake Hotel**. *See p52 and p140.*

Lake Ontario and the Humber River. You can walk – or better still, cycle – along the Humber through an almost unbroken chain of parks all the way to the northern limits of the city.

To explore the western lakefront, walk or bike along the **Waterfront Trail** (*see p60*). One option for an excursion is to visit **Historic Fort York** (*see p96*) and head down to the lakeside path. You'll see the grand buildings and gates of **Exhibition Place** (*see p61*) as the trail rounds Humber Bay, as well as the vintage arches of the **Sunnyside Pavilion**, with its large public swimming pool (*see p217*) and beachside restaurant. It's a quiet spot to watch beach volleyball or gaze at the lake.

The **Palais Royale** (1601 Lake Shore Boulevard W, 416 533 3553) is where the giants of swing once swung Toronto crowds. This deco dancehall got a facelift in 2006, keeping its sprung dancefloor and adding a massive deck overlooking Lake Ontario. The Rolling Stones threw a surprise gig here on a hot August night in 2002.

Heading west along the water's edge past picnic tables, green space and ice-cream vendors, you can cut under the Gardiner Expressway on **Colborne Lodge Drive** for an excursion into High Park.

Look out for two monuments. In **Sir Casimir Gzowski Park**, a few miles along from Bathurst, you'll find a bust of Sir Casimir himself, along with biographical information (*see p93* **Global village**). Half a mile further along the trail, the **Queen Elizabeth Monument** commemorates a visit by King George VI and his wife Elizabeth (later the Queen Mother) to Canada in 1939, when they officially opened the stately highway known as the Queen Elizabeth Way.

Way out west – on the outer limits of the city, you'll find the **Montgomery's Inn Museum**

(*see p98*). Even further away is the **Black Creek Pioneer Village** (*see below*), a step back in time, and a day trip in itself.

Black Creek Pioneer Village

1000 Murray Ross Parkway, Jane Street at Steeles Avenue (416 736 1733/www.trca.on.ca). Bus 35, 60. **Open** May-Dec. **Admission** $12; $7-$10 concessions; free under-5s. **Credit** AmEx, MC, V.
This quaint re-creation of 19th-century village life could easily have become 'Ye Olde Disneyesque Embarrassment', but it's actually an interesting place to spend an afternoon. The property was a farm during the 1800s; today, there's a working mill, a blacksmith, a printing house and a weaver's shop. The barns, workshops and other restored buildings are staffed by costumed craftspeople.

Colborne Lodge

Colborne Lodge Drive & the Queensway (416 392 6916/www.toronto.ca/culture/colborne.htm). Streetcar 501/subway High Park. **Open** *Jan-Feb, Apr* noon-4pm Fri-Sun. *Mar* noon-4pm Thur, Sat, Sun. *May-Aug* noon-5pm Tue-Sun. *Sept* noon-5pm Sat, Sun. *Oct-Dec* noon-5pm Tue-Sun. **Admission** $4; $2.75 concessions. **Credit** MC, V.
Architect John G Howard knew a thing or two about making a house a home. Shortly after becoming Toronto's first surveyor, he designed a villa for himself and his wife Jemima on the highest point of land overlooking the Humber Bay (prompting Jemima to dub the area 'High Park'). Howard made several additions to the house, including installation of the city's first indoor toilet. Their home is now a museum, chock-full of the Howards' furniture, kitchen gadgets and other possessions, arranged as they would have been in the 1860s.

Historic Fort York

100 Garrison Road, between Bathurst Street & Strachan Avenue (416 392 6907). Streetcar 511. **Open** 10am-4pm Mon-Fri; 10am-5pm Sat, Sun. Closed last 2wks Dec. **Admission** $6; $3-$3.25 concessions; free under-6s. **Credit** AmEx, MC, V. **Map** p270 C8.

Walk on West Queen West

Start: Queen Street West, at Dufferin Street
Finish: Queen Street and Ossington Avenue
Length: About five kilometres (three miles)
Time: Three hours, including gallery time
and a meal break.

This downtown stroll takes in the arty
West Queen West scene and up-and-coming
Ossington Avenue and Dundas Street West.
The walk incorporates art, history, street
culture and architecture.

*Take the 501 streetcar to Gladstone
Avenue or the subway to Dufferin station,
then bus 29 southbound. Get off at Queen
Street West. Cross Dufferin to the east at
the lights and enter the Gladstone Hotel
(see p52).* Stroll through the public rooms
of the oldest hotel in the city, beautifully
restored in 2006 and now home to a chock-
a-block calendar of art exhibitions, burlesque
shows and bands.

*Turn to your left when you exit, heading
east.* West Queen West is by and large a
one-sided story – all the action takes place
on the north side of the street. The south
side is a mishmash of car washes, vacant
lots and some government service buildings.
Strongly contested condo developments will
rise directly across from the Gladstone and
a little further east. The candy-coloured
building with teardrop windows is a condo
sales office designed by Will Alsop and may
become a gallery in its after-life. Contrasting
forces give the area its gritty energy –
appliance stores, flophouses, print shops
and greasy spoons of yesteryear underscore
the bars and boutiques of the moment.

*Walking east a couple of blocks, to
Beaconsfield Street, you'll find the Drake
Hotel (see p52).* The chic boutique hotel
has been a major contributor to the area's

resurgence; pop in for breakfast or a drink
on its SkyDeck. Just past Dovercourt Road,
the south side is taken up by the large Centre
for Addiction and Mental Health (CAMH). This
has been a 'lunatic asylum', as the hoardings
around its reconstruction call it, since the
1850s. The centre is building a new urban
village that will open on to the street. Wicked,
at the corner of Brookfield Street, is a
storefront swingers' club. Dozens of galleries
have collectively arisen in a creative cabal:
Stephen Bulger (No.1026; *see p187*), SPIN
Gallery (No.1100; *see p187*) and MOCCA
(No.952; *see p98*) among them.

*Turn north on Ossington Avenue towards
Dundas Street West.* Bars and galleries
are spreading north amid wholesalers,
Vietnamese diners and a cigar factory.
Sweaty Betty's (No.13; *see p141*), Crooked
Star (No.202; *see p140*) and the Dakota
Tavern (No.249; *see p140*) are staking out
turf on a street in transition.

*Turn east on Dundas Street W and enter
Trinity-Bellwoods Park.* This is the largest
downtown park between Yonge Street and
High Park, and it is home to the former
Trinity College, as well as another lost
treasure – the Garrison Creek, now buried
deep below. Meander along its tree-lined
paths and dip into the dog playground.

*Exit through the restored gates at Queen
Street W and head west.* Restaurants and
cafés are concentrated at this end of WQW.
Try one of the restaurants nearby – Brazilian
at Caju (No.922; *see p129*); Italian at Bar
One (No 924; *see p128*), Malaysian at Kei
(No.936; *see p130*), or Canadian classics
like Oyster Boy (No.872; *see p129*), or
Sugar (No.942; *see p127*) for weekend
brunch with the locals.

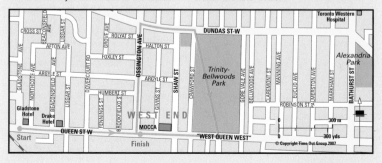

This historic site is where present-day Toronto began. Lt-Governor John Graves Simcoe founded the fort in 1793 to protect the town of York, as Toronto was then known (the town was incorporated the same year). The fort only saw real military action once, at the Battle of York in 1813. It was sacked by the Americans, but rebuilt shortly thereafter (and the English went on to win the larger war, thus ensuring the future of the Canadian nation). In the 20th century, many of the forts' vintage buildings were destroyed to make way for the Gardiner Expressway, but a few gems survived. The museum offers guided tours and historical re-enactments, and performances of period music and dance.

Montgomery's Inn Museum

4709 Dundas Street West (416 394 8113). Subway Islington then 10min walk. **Open** 1-4.30pm Tue-Fri; 1-5pm Sat, Sun. **Admission** $4; $1-$2 concessions. **No credit cards**.

It's a shame that this inn, the main part of which dates from 1830, is so far from anywhere else. But if you're in the area, it's well worth a visit. Thomas Montgomery operated the inn and tavern for 25 years. When Thomas's wife Margaret died in 1855, he shut down the shop and closed up shop. The late Georgian stone house fell into disrepair, until it was opened as a museum in 1975.

The old sign emblazoned with a picture of a plough, is one of the few artefacts that have survived from Montgomery's day. It now hangs in the museum. Tea is served from 2pm until 4.30pm from Tuesday to Sunday.

Museum of Contemporary Canadian Art (MOCCA)

952 Queen Street W, at Shaw Street (416 395 0067/www.mocca.toronto.on.ca). Streetcar 501. **Open** 11am-6pm Tue-Sun. **Admission** by donation. **Credit** V. **Map** p270 B7.

After years in the hinterland, the arrival of MOCCA on West Queen West serves to reinforce the street cred of the arts movement on Queen. Exhibits in the two large rooms are eclectic and draw on resources from across the country. Oddly, the local press ignores its presence, while gallery-goers consider it a must-see. There's a small lounge where catalogues and art books are for sale. **Photo** *p92.*

Global village Portugal

Population: 350,000
Home base: College Street and Dundas Street W, between Ossington Avenue and Dufferin Street

Mass Portuguese immigration didn't hit Toronto until the mid 1960s and '70s, yet today the group is the third-largest in the city by mother tongue. Originally settling in Kensington Market, where they opened rice, bean and fruit stands, the community soon shifted south to the area around St Mary's Church (589 Adelaide Street W, 416 703 2326), the city's largest Portuguese parish, and westwards to the inexpensive village surrounding Trinity-Bellwoods Park along Dundas Street West. Difficult though it was to find employment in a city teeming with immigrants, the Portuguese eventually rose above their station as construction workers and cleaners, finding jobs in the hospitals, schools and restaurants in their community.

At Dundas Street West and Dovercourt you'll see plenty of mom-and-pop grocery shops banks, tiny travel outfits and used-car dealerships.

The local churches reflect the local population. The Santa Cruz Parish Church (142 Argyle Street, 416 533 8425) rivals the Church of St Patrick (at Dundas and Grace Streets) as the district's spiritual nucleus; both hold Mass in Portuguese.

Trading places: The rise of Little Brazil on Dundas Street west of Ossington Avenue is lending the district a tropical flavour.
A taste of: Start on Dundas, west of Ossington, ordering a beer at one of the local sports bars; it will usually arrive with a plate of marinated beans, shrimp or peanuts. Then walk west into carnivore country, Portugal-style: *churrasqueiras* proffer grilled and roasted chicken with sides, and rows of butcher shops, with bright signs, boast meat specials. Find snacks aplenty at Caldense Bakery & Pastries (1209 Dundas Street W, 416 534 3847) or back up to Golden Wheat Bakery & Pastry (652 College Street, 416 534 1107) for breads, coffee and ethereal custard tarts. There's plenty to explore along College Street, west of Ossington.
Join in: In the second weekend of June, Trinity-Bellwoods Park gets jammed with Portuguese Day revellers – expect giant barbecues of chicken and fish, folk dancing, live music, sports and activities for the kids.

If you fancy watching footie with a cool beer, try College Street. Outlets such as Bairrada Churrasqueira Grill, at No.1000 (416 539 8239) offer spicy grilled meat churrasco-style.
Local luminary: Now that Nelly Furtado is gunning for Madonna's pop crown, she may spend less time in her old neighbourhood.

North Toronto

Mansions and museums on the northern fringe.

Most visitors to Toronto focus on the city's core, but those who go north can get away from it all without leaving town. All that space, though, means distances are spread out, and while transit services do exist, you might want to consider renting a bike or a car for destinations off the subway line.

Lawrence subway station, the first stop north of midtown, is the gateway to the leafy and affluent neighbourhood of **Lawrence Park**. The main attraction here is **Alexander Muir Gardens**, a ten-minute walk south of the subway station on the east side of Yonge Street. The entrance is through a pretty rose garden, which descends into a bucolic wooded ravine whose walking trails stretch for miles, overlooked by stately houses. Back on Yonge Street, the smart stretch between Lytton Boulevard and Eglinton Avenue is a yuppie shopping and eating district.

Continuing north, the built-up area around Yonge Street and Sheppard Avenue is where the beauty gives way to blandness. Up here, it's a busy commuting zone, where subway lines meet and Highway 401 cuts across the city. North York, its own separate city before it was amalgamated into Toronto, grew into a so-called satellite downtown under the stewardship of its then mayor, Mel Lastman. 'His Melness' gave the people a central gathering point and modestly named it **Mel Lastman Square** (5100 Yonge Street). A fountain features a bell-ringing, kinetic sculpture nicknamed 'Mel's Bells'. The square is in front of the **North York Civic Centre** (416 338 0338), which, before amalgamation, was North York's city hall. It's home to a hotel, shopping mall and public library, but the whole place feels grey and desolate.

Culturally, there are few offerings up here to entice tourists or Torontonians, with a couple of exceptions. The **Toronto Centre for the Arts** (5040 Yonge Street, 416 733 9388) houses three theatres, including the acoustically superlative **George Weston Recital Hall** (*see p197*). North of the square, **Gibson House** (5172 Yonge Street, 416 395 7432; closed Mon, Sun) commemorates David Gibson, one of the major figures from the failed Rebellion of 1837 (*see p15*). A Scottish immigrant, Gibson built his first family home here in 1826. Following his exile and subsequent pardon, he returned

to the site with his wife and children in 1851, building the farmhouse that stands here today. Supplementing the exhibits, costumed tour guides demonstrate such 19th-century skills as spinning yarn and making ice-cream by hand. Just to the west of all of these sites, **York Cemetery** (101 Senlac Road, 416 221 3404) is a peaceful place to walk.

Grazing cattle was a common sight for the first residents of the **Lawrence Manor** neighbourhood back in the 1950s. Today the section of Bathurst Street north of Briar Hill Avenue up to the 401 highway is the (very) bustling home to Toronto's Jewish community. David Bezmozgis, a Toronto author, profiles Jewish immigrant culture in his award-winning *Natasha: And Other Stories* (2004). Orthodox synagogues and schools abound, and stores offer kosher foods (including bagels and deli fare), books, gifts and Judaica. The **Holocaust Centre of Toronto** (4600 Bathurst Street, 416 635 2883) has exhibits and a library. Admission is free, but by appointment only.

Just down the road, at 4588 Bathurst Street, the **Bathurst Jewish Community Centre** (416 636 1880) is a well-equipped complex that houses the respected **Koffler Gallery**, the **Leah Posluns Theatre** and **My Jewish Discovery Place Children's Museum**. South of Sheppard Avenue, in **Earl Bales Park** (*see p217*), stands a **Holocaust Memorial** monument created by Toronto sculptor and Holocaust survivor Ernest Raab. Another monument, also by Raab, commemorates Raoul Wallenberg, the Swedish diplomat who saved the lives of thousands of Jews in Budapest.

The **Toronto Aerospace Museum** (65 Carlhall Road, at Keele Street & Sheppard Avenue W, 416 638 6078, closed Mon) is west of here, located in the original 1929 home of the de Havilland aircraft company. Among the flying boy toys in its hangar you'll find a full-size replica of the Avro Aero, Canada's contribution to supersonic flight, and a Lancaster MKX, plus vintage flight paraphernalia and equipment. It's the oldest surviving aircraft factory in Canada.

Though its name conjures up images of equestrian elegance, the **Bridle Path** is a monument to excess. Toronto's answer to Beverly Hills, it's worth a good gawk. The homes on this street (south of York Mills Road, east of Bayview Avenue) are monsters, costing up to $20 million. Many owners buy a lot, tear down the existing house and custom-build a new dream home. The resulting pastiche of building styles is Disneyesque. Maybe that's why the Artist Now Known Again As Prince picked up a palatial pad here after marrying Torontonian Manuela Testolini (check out the grey stone mansion at No.61, said to have cost around $7 million). The couple split in 2006 and there haven't been many Prince sightings since. Newspaper baron Conrad Black owns palatial digs on adjacent Park Lane Circle.

Just south-east of here is **Edwards Gardens**, at Leslie Street and Lawrence Avenue East. Dotted with annuals, roses, wild flowers and rockery, it's a lush oasis and a standby for wedding pictures. Its winding ravine paths are popular with cyclists and walkers. Within the grounds, the **Toronto Botanical Garden** (777 Lawrence Avenue East, 416 397 1340), due to open in 2007, will feature more gardens, courses and a shop.

Built in 1952, **Don Mills** – named after the Don River, and just east of the Bridle Path – was a modernist's dream. The first post-war planned community in Canada is ageing well with its mid-century retro look, but the heart was removed when the shopping plaza came down in 2006 to make way for more condos. The area is home to the striking **Japanese Canadian Cultural Centre** (6 Garamond Court, at Wynford Drive, 416 441 2345), which houses a performance theatre and gallery.

The **David Dunlap Observatory** (123 Hillsview Drive, at Major Mackenzie Drive, 905 884 9562) is north of the city in **Richmond Hill**. Here students and researchers ponder the astronomical mysteries of the universe – and so can you. Evening tours include a chance to look at the night sky through the largest optical telescope in Canada. The multi-domed observatory is located in a large park, dotted with white-tailed deer. Children under seven are not permitted on the evening tours.

Southbrook Farm (1061 Major Mackenzie Drive, at Bathurst Street, 905 832 2548) provides a chance to visit a country farm and winery on the edge of town. In summer and autumn you can pick your own fresh fruit, and hot baked pies and fruit wines are sold.

Global village Jamaica

Population: 300,000
Home base: Throughout the Toronto area

As part of a historic peace treaty with the British, the first immigrants from Jamaica came to Canada in 1796 to help build a fort in Halifax. But it wasn't until the 1960s that they started arriving in significant numbers, when new laws were passed, favouring educated and skilled immigrants.

In the 1970s Toronto became home to an A-list of Jamaican musical talent: Stranger Cole, Jackie Mittoo, Leroy Sibbles, Ernie Smith and Carlene Davis are just a few who left a mark on the local soundscape.

Today there are many communities living in the far-flung fringes of Toronto: Don Mills, Scarborough, Brampton, Rexdale, Ajax and Mississauga. 'Little Jamaica' proper runs along Eglinton Avenue West (for a few blocks) past Oakwood.

Trading places: Kensington Market (see p148) is a vibrant hub. It is home to Patty King Bakery (187 Baldwin Street, 416 977 3191), which sells hot patties, pastries and breads. And the market's stalls offer everything from coconuts to vinyl to hand drums. Another small pocket of Jamaican-run stores, hairdressers and grocers is found on Bathurst Street, north of Bloor Street...

A taste of:... which is where you'll also find Wong's Restaurant (930 Bathurst Street, 416 532 8135). It has been dishing up excellent Jamaican cuisine for 30 years.

Join in: Toronto's Jamaicans keep in touch with the island via weekly publications like Pride, The Gleaner, Share and the monthly Word magazine (www.wordmag.com), which hosts the annual IRIE Music Festival (www.iriemusicfestival.com); also check out the annual Caribana festival (see p169). The Jamaican Canadian Association (995 Arrow Road, 416 746 5772) is a hub for the community and hosts frequent events.

Local luminary: Toronto is still home to some high-profile Jamaicans, among them Louise Bennett ('Miss Lou'), the first dub poet. Michael Lee-Chin, meanwhile, is the poster boy for overachieving Jamaicans. One of nine children growing up in Port Antonio, Jamaica, he now runs one of the largest mutual-funds companies in Canada. Lee-Chin donated enough dosh to the Royal Ontario Museum that the Daniel Libeskind-designed addition bears his name.

East Toronto

Go Greek and catch a wave.

The Don Valley cuts through the heart of Toronto, and its wide green gap is more than a geographical division: it separates a mentality. Head east across the graceful five-arch span of the Bloor Viaduct (Prince Edward Viaduct on the map, but nobody calls it that), and you leave downtown behind and enter a world of old-fashioned, small-town neighbourhoods – quiet streets canopied by lines of trees, sprawling parks, mom-and-pop cornerstores – and some of the best skyline views in the city. East Toronto is also home to a large **Greektown** (*see p104* **Global village**) and **Little India** (*see p103* **Global village**), as well as the most accessible stretch of city shoreline along Lake Ontario in **the Beach** neighbourhood.

While East Toronto lacks any major attractions, the city is on course to regenerate a large industrial wasteland into a showcase of urban planning and design. The mouth of the Don River, a virtual no-man's-land for decades, is being transformed into a park setting. Even more ambitious is Lake Ontario Park, a sprawling 'dunescape' sandbar that will be bordered by Cherry Beach in the west and Tommy Thompson Park (*see p70*) at the

foot of Leslie Street in the east. Over time, housing will fill in the Portlands area now home to a strange mix of Great Lakes freighter ships, hulking incinerators and scrap heaps.

For now, though, it's a short hop from heavy industry to a scene of bucolic sailboats bobbing on the lake at Ashbridge's Bay. The park of the same name is a gateway to the Beach. Boasting acres of sand, the latter is one of the largest sites of beach volleyball action in North America (*see p213*). On warm summer nights, buff bodies in skimpy attire take face plants in the sand under a sea of volleyballs on 85 courts.

The Beach

Bus 64, 92/streetcar 501.
This community was created during the 19th century, when the gentry decided they needed homes 'outside' the city and built small mansions by the lake. In summer they would close up their downtown Rosedale homes and relocate here. Since then the city has sprawled out to swallow them, and it's a direct 30-minute trolley ride from Yonge Street straight along Queen Street East. But the Beach remains a separate community, with the feeling of a resort

town. In summer, the crowds escape the heat by packing on to the boardwalk and beaches and filling every outdoor patio along Queen.

The area occupies the stretch of Queen Street between Woodbine Avenue and Victoria Park Avenue, after which you will find yourself in Scarborough (a mainly residential district that turns into a land of fast-food outlets and strip malls). After years of local debate over what to call this neighbourhood, the Beach or the Beaches, the singular-minded folk prevailed in 2006. This despite the fact that there are many differently named beaches along the four kilometres (two miles) of wooden boardwalk: Balmy Beach, Kew Beach and Woodbine Beach, all pleasant places to get away from the city on a sweltering day. The stretch of Queen Street East near the boardwalk is filled with smart shops, cafés and bars, casual restaurants serving wings and beer and more well-heeled dining. Downtowners envy the secluded cottage-style homes nestled at water's edge (never mind the fact that the boardwalk is a constant parade of strollers, joggers, dog walkers, bikers and bladers). Manicured parks with bandstands and gazebos make for idyllic picnics under the shade of weeping willows.

For kicking back, smearing on the suncream and pretending you're on South Beach, Queen Street has several joints with patios, including the **Lion on the Beach** (1958 Queen Street E, 416 690 1984; *see also p141*). The **Sunset Grill** diner (2006 Queen Street E, 416 690 9985; *see also p125*) serves an all-day breakfast. The **Garden Gate** (2379 Queen Street E, 416 694 3605) serves up portions of Chinese-Canadian cuisine (think chow mein with grilled cheese sandwiches). It's also across the street from a fine rep house, the **Fox Theatre** (*see p178*).

As unlikely as it may seem, fans of art deco should pay a visit to the **RC Harris Filtration Plant** (2701 Queen Street E, at Victoria Park Avenue), the monolithic building at the east end of the beaches. Designed by English architect Thomas Pomphrey in the 1930s, this operational water-treatment plant is all towers and arched doorways, sitting incongruously in a park setting. The plant has been used in many movies. Tours are offered haphazardly; call 416 338 0338.

Equally unexpected are the **Scarborough Bluffs**, dramatic cliffs that plunge into the lake a couple of miles east of the water plant (you can see the cliffs in the distance). You can make your way along the beach to get there, or it's a 10-minute walk down Brimley Road from the Kingston Road 12 bus stop. **Bluffers Park** has a community of houseboat dwellers, and you can scamper about the base of the cliffs.

The Danforth

Streetcar 504/subway Chester or Pape.
Bloor Street changes names to Danforth Avenue (locals call it the Danforth) on the east side of the Don Valley and, typically, the neighbourhood changes as well. This is where a large Greek immigrant population settled. Peppered with Greek shops, restaurants and cafés, Greektown is not a cutesy, ethnic tourist trap… yet, but as the forces of gentrification have their inevitable effect and the original inhabitants move out, it is at risk of becoming a second Little Italy. It already has a similarly fashionable bar and restaurant scene.

The Danforth is a pleasant place to amble, but you do have to be hungry to get the most out of the area. Greeks like to feed you, and the irresistible aroma of souvlaki, feta and moussaka wafts from storefronts. Most of the restaurants stay open late, so you can always get a plate piled high with kebabs, roast potatoes, savoury rice and Village Salad (the 'real' Greek salad of onions, tomatoes, cucumber and feta cheese – no lettuce) after the bars close at 2am. The classic experience is **Mr Greek** (568 Danforth Avenue, 416 461 5470), serving heaped platters at decent prices.

The Danforth is also known for a little shopping complex known as **Carrot Common** (348 Danforth Avenue, 416 466 3803), anchored by the **Big Carrot** (*see p159*) health food shop.

Gerrard Street East

Streetcar 506.
When you start to notice signs with the titles Mo Pa, Hoi Tan and Wing Kee, you know you have wandered into the city's second Chinatown, though many other cultures, including Vietnamese and Cambodian, have since joined the neighbourhood. The bargains are good in the restaurants, groceries and little speciality shops, especially those dispensing Chinese herbs and medicines, such as **Dai Kuang Wah Herb Market** (595 Gerrard Street E, 416 466 9207). At the **Grand Sea Food House** (615 Gerrard Street E, 416 778 8888) you can order a fresh lobster dinner for a mere $18. Be warned: most of these restaurants feature Chinese characters – which at least means the food is authentic.

Little India

Bus 22, 31/streetcar 506.
A few blocks further east along Gerrard Street, between Greenwood and Coxwell Avenues, is Little India. With its garish advertising signs,

Global village India

Population: 200,000
Home base: Gerrard Street E, west from
Coxwell Avenue

In Toronto, immigrants tend to flock
downtown, settle, prosper, then shift their
focus to spacious suburbs as the next
displaced culture moves in. Toronto's Indian
community, however, is an exception to the
rule. They colonised a remote patch of the
east end, and were off the radar of most
Torontonians until the numbers exploded.

Indian immigration began in earnest in the
1960s and '70s, mostly in the form of young
men who drove taxis, took over convenience
stores, opened restaurants and laboured in
construction while upgrading professional
studies that didn't translate from the old
country. Families followed – parents,
grandparents, cousins, children – and
soon the population that occupies the two-
kilometre (1.25 mile) stretch of Gerrard
Street East near Coxwell Avenue had
fragmented, with many families moving
further east into Scarborough, west by the
airport and into the suburb of Bramalea.

Of course, the community itself is divided
into Sikhs, Tamils and the Hindu majority,
the traditional Southern Indians (who adorn
their temples with black granite icons) and
the more liberal northerners (who prefer
lighter marble). In all, there are 45 Hindu
temples in the city, the neighbourhood of

Richmond Hill claiming the largest – the
Hindu Temple Society of Canada (10865
Bayview Avenue, 905 883 9109) – where
not a week goes by without some fête.
Trading places: Though more of Toronto's
Indians make their home outside the
Gerrard/Coxwell community than within it,
business there is overwhelmingly Indian,
with silks and saris luring seamstresses
and fashion mavens taken with Bollywood
style. There are dozens of sari shops along
Gerrard Street East (most in the 1400s).
A taste of: On Gerrard Street you're
best keeping it simple: stalls sell authentic
street treats, and there are good takeaways
and caffs, but some of the restaurants are
mediocre. For pastries and sweets, comb
Gerrard Street East or the area around
Albion and Islington in Etobicoke, the only
other concentrated Indian community.
Join in: Meditate at the Vedanta Society
of Toronto (120 Emmett Avenue, 416 240
7262) in Etobicoke, daily from 6pm to 7pm.
In mid May, for 15 days, Hindus celebrate
Rathotsawam (the Chariot Festival), during
which processions of lotus-shaped wood
chariots circle around the neighbourhood.
Local luminary: Film director Deepa Metha
lives in Toronto, where she explores the
Indian immigrant experience in her movies.
She has probed the subcontinent in her
well-received trilogy, *Fire, Earth, and Water*.

Sightseeing

Global village Greece

Population: 150,000

Home base: Danforth Avenue towards East York; Scarborough, Markham and Mississauga

It could hardly be mistaken for the motherland, but the Danforth, aka Greektown, possesses a discernible Mediterranean feel, especially in the summer, when patios with no concept of last orders spill on to the street and Hellenic music (not just 'Zorba the Greek') can be heard from open kitchens, private homes and passing cars. The neighbourhood of modest homes and shops was settled by Greek immigrants who had escaped Turkish occupation in the early 20th century to toil away – not unlike other ethnic groups – on the Canadian National Railway, and as miners or farmers. Successive waves in the mid century brought over women sponsored by their husbands and fathers, who worked as domestics for the city's establishment. Whereas in 1907 only two dozen Greek names appeared in the city's phone books, today the Greek population on the Danforth and beyond is the second-largest outside Greece (Queens, New York, is the first). As a result, the local flavour is authentic, with Greek-language signage, blue-and-white flying flags and Mediterranean banks and manufacturers. Restaurants – the favoured business of first-generation émigrés in the latter half of the century – are plentiful and the quality of the cooking is high.

In the 1990s this social scene, along with low house prices, made the area attractive to Toronto's upwardly mobile, who gutted and reno'ed to yuppie standards. More Greeks have shifted eastwards than remain, with thousands of families moving to Scarborough, Markham and Mississauga.

Trading places: Those who have forsaken the quarter have nonetheless remained faithful to Mister Greek Meat Market (801 Danforth Avenue, 416 469 0733), purveyor of lamb and pig for backyard spits and wedding feasts.

A taste of: Though the Danforth is still buzzing, the strip is in danger of becoming a wax museum of Greek life, its souvlaki joints and pastry shops mere kitsch amid new-era coffee dens and health-food houses. A few high points remain: Sun Valley Fine Foods (583 Danforth Avenue, 416 469 5227) is a modest fruit shop-cum-produce bazaar in the Danforth's hectic heart, and Pan (see p131) offers a decent meal.

Join in: Early each August stone ovens and grills are towed on to the pavement for the week-long Taste of the Danforth festival (see p169). St George's Greek Orthodox Church (see p69), in Downtown West, is the main venue for Greek Easter celebrations and St George's Day, both in April.

Local luminary: Greek prime minister Andreas Papandreou resided in the Danforth while in exile in the early 1970s, and also taught economics at Toronto's York University.

---

the neighbourhood is famous for its **Indian Bazaar**, where you can buy saris, silks and brightly coloured scarves, and spices and foods. Both professional and weekend chefs peruse these markets regularly. Festivals during the year bring a Bollywood-style excess to the area.

Riverdale/Leslieville

Streetcar 501, 506.

Riverdale faces Cabbagetown across the Don Valley, and like its neighbour, it is favoured by the city's liberal chattering classes. It stretches from Broadview Avenue to Pape Avenue, and Mortimer Avenue to the lake. As affordable real estate in Riverdale proper becomes scarce, more families are buying less expensive homes further east in largely immigrant neighbourhoods as far as

Coxwell Avenue. If you like to house-browse, take a stroll down any of the streets that surround the impressive Withrow Park, located between Logan and Carlaw Avenues.

Another nice walk is through **Leslieville** (Queen Street E, between Logan and Connaught Avenues). It has become world famous among interior decorators for its high concentration of mid-century modern furniture. A string of antiques shops sells groovy teak furniture and other 1950s and '60s kitsch. Foodies come here for brunch (**Bonjour Brioche**, 812 Queen Street E; *see also p131*; **Edward Levesque's Kitchen** 1290 Queen Street E, 416 465 3600; *see also p132*) and more upscale dinner options (**Tomi-Kro**, 1214 Queen Street E, 416 463 6677; *see also p130*). These businesses are helping this stretch to shed its reputation as the poor cousin of Queen Street West.

Eat, Drink, Shop

Jamie Kennedy Wine Bar. *See p118.*

Restaurants & Cafés

Eat to a global beat.

Toronto's restaurant scene is at a turning point. While it has always satisfied the needs of those who eat to live, it is becoming a destination for those who live to eat. With a steady supply of new talent, the scene is constantly expanding, and as the city's population and wealth increase, so too does the quality of restaurants. The city's multicultural make-up is reflected in the myriad cuisines, which are being blurred to great effect: most kitchens of traditional ethnic restaurants are now in the hands of the younger generations, who are updating old-country cooking with interesting takes on fusion.

No longer the Big Apple imitator – always a pointless pursuit – Toronto has more than a handful of its own celebrity chefs, most of them with starring roles on home-grown TV fodder. Locals know their Donna Dooher (of Mildred Pierce, see p129) from their Mark McEwen (of Bymark, see p111). And Susur Lee, of Susur (see p110), has embraced the spotlight, even appearing on American TV cooking show *Iron Chef*. Other stars shy from the cameras: they're busy raising haute cuisine to new heights.

True, this city has yet to produce something so original it takes the world by storm, but lately the emphasis is on taste, rather than trends. And there's a real movement towards developing a distinct Canadian cuisine: cooks and producers are concocting a range of dishes that highlight raw materials as much as technique. For starters, try Yukon bison, Quebec foie gras, Canadian caviar, crates of locally grown heirloom carrots and wedges of artisan cheeses. For a taste of the land, see p112 **Local flavour**.

To get oriented to the foodie scene, you need a compass. Generally speaking, the neighbourhood defines the food. The ethnic patchwork means you can count on finding Chinese in Chinatown, Greek on the Danforth, funky cafés on West Queen West and snazzy eateries in the Entertainment District. But there are exceptions – you can sometimes find French in Little Italy, say, or Italian on the Danforth.

Dressing for dinner in Toronto is easy: keep it casual or dress it up as you like. Smoking is forbidden in Toronto restaurants. A new law allows you to bring your own bottle of wine, but the programme, with some high corkage fees, has received mixed reviews. Best to check in advance. Anyone under 19 is restricted from entering restaurants that declare bar status.

The best Restaurants

For breakfast or brunch
Czehoski (*see p129*); **Edward Levesque's Kitchen** (*see p132*); **Lai Wah Heen** (*see p114*); **Senator** (*see p113*); **Sugar** (*see p127*); **Xacutti** (*see p128*).

For lunch
Bistro & Bakery Thuet (*see p109*); **Bymark** (*see p111*); **Gamelle** (*see p127*); **Nami** (*see p118*); **Osgoode Hall** (*see p111*); **Phil's Original BBQ** (*see p129*); **Sidhartha** (*see p142*).

For afternoon tea
Kalendar (*see p125*); **Pangaea** (*see p121*); **Pain Perdu** (*see p127*); **Patachou** (*see p123*); **Red Tea Box** (*see p127*).

For a patio setting
Allen's (*see p132*); **Bar One** (*see p128*); **Café Diplomatico** (*see p125*); **Drake Hotel** (*see p106*); **Jules** (*see p129*); **Trattoria Giancarlo** (*see p128*); **The Fifth Grill** (*see p109*).

For late-night eats
Bar Mercurio (*see p117*); **Kei** (*see p130*); **Kultura** (*see p119*); **Lee Garden** (*see p114*); **Mona's Shwarma & Falafel** (*see p127*); **Ouzeri** (*see p130*); **7 West** (*see p121*).

Entertainment District

Cafés & coffee houses

Jules
147 Spadina Avenue, at Queen Street W (416 348 8886). Streetcar 501, 510. **Open** 11.30am-9pm Mon-Fri; noon-5pm Sat. **Main courses** $12-$19. **Credit** AmEx, DC, MC, V. **Map** p271 D7 ❶

❶ Purple numbers given in this chapter correspond to the location of restaurants on the street maps. *See pp266-275.*

The sheer gaul: **Le Select Bistro** sticks to classic French cooking. *See p109.*

A simple French café and bistro on the Queen West strip. The quaint dining room has a distinctively buttery scent (it must be the quiches and crêpes). Popular at lunchtime, it attracts office types and local artists who are taking a break from the rat race, dining on flavourful sandwiches and hearty salads. Most mains are served with frites, and the tarte tatin will leave you humming the *Marseillaise*. With all the trendy restaurants and fusion overkill in town, it's refreshing to find good, hearty French fare. **Other locations**: 617 Mount Pleasant Road, at Davisville Avenue, North Toronto (416 481 1666).

Le Gourmand
152 Spadina Avenue, at Queen Street W (416 504 4494/legourmand.com). Streetcar 501, 510. **Open** *7am-8pm Mon-Fri; 9am-6pm Sat; 9am-5pm Sun.* **Main courses** *$6-$17.* **Credit** *DC, MC, V.* **Map** *p279 D7* **2**
This small, sunny café and gourmet food shop bustles midday with a trim menu of grilled sandwiches, a selection of baked butter-rich goods and a wide array of coffees. Service is friendly, and the mood relaxed: you can linger over a latte or a seasonal bowl of ice-cream. In summer, tables and

chairs out front offer prime people-watching. Sit back and watch the colourful pedestrian parade of suits and leather that meets along Queen West.

Continental

Amadeus

111 Richmond Street W, at York Street (416 366 3500). Streetcar 504, 510. **Open** 11am-11pm Mon-Sun. **Main courses** $9-$39. **Credit** AmEx, DC, MC, V. **Map** p271 F7 ❸

With a dearth of good restaurants in the surrounding area, Toronto's new opera house might as well be in the middle of the lake. That's where Amadeus, an authentic taste of Vienna, has the edge – all the better when Mozart is on the bill. The beer hall, or *stubbe*, pours some fine brews, including Austria's Spiegl, to wash down perfect pretzels, Wiener schnitzel, parsley potatoes and blood sausage dumplings. Too bad the women servers have to wear traditional Alpine *drindl* outfits – think *Sound of Music* meets Hooters – but it's all part of the macho vibe (except for those dainty little pastries). By contrast, the dining room next door – with its stiff white linens – is an exercise in sobriety.

Bistro and Bakery Thuet

609 King Street W, at Portland Street (416 603 2777/www.thuet.ca), Streetcar 504, 511. **Open** 11.30am-2.30pm Tue-Sat; 5-11pm Mon-Thur; 5pm-midnight Fri, Sat; 11am-3pm Sun. **Main courses** $27-$39. **Credit** AmEx, MC, V. **Map** p271 D8 ❹

True bistro fare, just like top chef Marc Thuet likes it – but with an Alsatian twist. Thuet, who rose to fame on the haute-cuisine scene with Centro and The Fifth Grill (*see p109*), has always had a passion for artisan breads, foie-gras feasts, succulent game and pretty puds – and it shines through here. Riesling-based sauces are heady, portions are generous, and the romantic Gallic ambience could have made even Edith Piaf happy, had that been possible. For indulgent take-out – from boeuf bourguignon to the chef's own demi-glace gourmet doggie biscuits – go to Atelier Thuet, his prepared-food shop. **Other locations**: 171 East Liberty Street, West End (416 603 2777).

Crush

455 King Street W, at Spadina Avenue (416 977 1234/www.crushwinebar.com). Streetcar 504, 510. **Open** 11.30am-11pm Mon-Fri; 5pm-midnight Sat. **Main courses** $23-$43. **Credit** AmEx, DC, MC, V. **Map** p271 D8 ❺

This airy, chic bar-bistro excels at wines by the glass, with more than 30 selections, and a robust menu. At midday, sizzling steak sandwiches are served with buttery mushrooms, melted brie and roasted garlic. Eat your greens and add a side of rapini (similar to Chinese broccoli). At night, meaty mains dominate, with hearty oxtail stew, succulent lamb saddle and roast whole chicken. Food is sourced from top producers, including a fine Niagara prosciutto and Oyster Boy's bivalves.

Fifth Grill

5th Floor, 225 Richmond Street W, at Duncan Street (416 979 3005/www.easyandthefifth.com). Streetcar 501/subway Osgoode. **Open** 6-11pm Thur-Sat. **Set menu** $85; terrace $50. **Credit** AmEx, DC, MC, V. **Map** p271 E7 ❻

Haute cuisine has gone casual in Toronto, so little wonder this posh gourmet palace has been reworked as a steak house. Diners enter via the Easy and the Fifth nightclub. A freight elevator elevator swoops them away from the dancefloor and up to the elegant dining room. The meat ranges from pure Canadiana – bison rib-eyes – to a chateaubriand for two. Former chef JP Challet has returned to the stove, adding a soupçon of adventure to the menus. And the Fifth Grill still has one of the best terraces in the city. Reservations recommended.

Le Select Bistro

432 Wellington Street W, at Bathurst Street (416 596 6405/www.leselect.com). Streetcar 511. **Open** 11.30am-10.30pm Mon-Wed, Sun; 11.30am-midnight Thur-Sat. **Main courses** $22-$33. **Set menu** $29. **Credit** AmEx, DC, MC, V. **Map** p270 C8 ❼

This quintessentially Paris-style bistro, long a haunt of the Queen West set, packed up in the summer of 2006 and headed to a new, discreet location. The romantic ambience has survived, along with the extensive and impressive wine cellar. And decent French fare still rules: garlicky escargots, sunny pissaladière and smoked whitefish mousse for starters, followed by confit of duck leg, braised oxtail and, *bien sûr*, steak frites. **Photo** *p107*.

Fusion

Lee

603 King Street W, at Portland Street (416 504 7867/www.susur.com). Streetcar 504, 511. **Open** 5.30-11.30pm Mon-Sat. **Dinner** $35. **Credit** AmEx, MC, V. **Map** p271 D8 ❽.

Susur Lee, the local fusion superstar, has given his fans a gift: an affordable alternative to his more famous restaurant, Susur (*see p110*). The master works closely with well-groomed chef Jason Carter to create beautifully composed tapas-sized dishes, each one showing off his trademark intricate combinations. Chillis, citrus, tropical fruits and myriad tastes engage all senses. The open, casual room gets noisy but the clatter, combined with lively waitstaff, creates an air of excitement. The plates are small, so order many and share.

Rain

19 Mercer Street, at John Street (416 599 7246/www.rainrestaurant.ca). Streetcar 504/subway St Andrew. **Open** 5.30-10.30pm Mon-Sat. **Main courses** $36. **Credit** AmEx, DC, MC, V. **Map** p271 E8 ❾

Entrepreneurs Michael and Guy Rubino are known for their playful, dramatic style. But their *Barbarella*-meets-*Tarzan* decor (think Lucite and jungle bamboo) belies their serious, carefully crafted Asian menus. Peking-style partridge, aromatic hotpots and a seafood-heavy menu keep diners coming. The vibe is luxe: plan to make it a leisurely stay.

Senses

SoHo Metropolitan Hotel, 318 Wellington Street W, at Blue Jays Way (416 935 0400/www.metropolitan. com/soho/restaurants.asp). Streetcar 504/subway St Andrew. **Open** 6-10pm Tue-Sat. **Main courses** $28 and up. **Credit** AmEx, DC, MC, V. **Map** p271 E8 ⑩

Under the guidance of former chef Claudio Aprile, the SoHo Metropolitan's restaurant and bar gained notoriety for being stiff and formal. Hong Kong star Patrick Lin, a native Torontonian, has returned and stepped behind the stove, shifting the culinary gaze to the East. Lin's delicate Chinese gastronomy pairs classical techniques with modern influences. At press time, the chef had yet to announce his menus.

Susur

601 King Street W, at Portland Street (416 603 2205/www.susur.com). Streetcar 504, 511. **Open** 6-10pm Mon-Sat. **Dinner** $110. **Credit** AmEx, MC, V. **Map** p271 D8 ⑪

Susur Lee is a celebrity on a scale like no other Canadian chef: witness his role as a contestant on the American TV game show *Iron Chef*. And the

glamour can be felt at this minimalist haven, which offers a feast for the senses. Main courses might appear to be standard haute-cuisine fare – lamb and pork tenderloin, lobster tail and roast quail – but are treated to Lee's unique take on Asian fusion. His famous six-course tasting menu – $120 and three delicious hours – starts with mains and is followed by appetisers, soup and dessert (you can also dine the traditional way). Not for the timid of palate – or small of appetite – and best consumed by those with wallets as expandable as their belts.

Indian

Babur

273 Queen Street W, at Duncan Street (416 599 7720). Streetcar 501/subway Osgoode. **Open** 11.30am-2.30pm, 5-10.30pm daily. **Main courses** $8-$11. **Credit** AmEx, DC, MC, V. **Map** p271 E7 ⑫

Good lunch buffets don't come any cheaper: Babur's is $11 and offers all the standards, along with bottomless rice and tender naan. The location is also a crowd-pleaser – arty types working along Queen and King enjoy easy access, as do the suits across University Avenue. The butter chicken is a good bet for timid palates, Goan fish curry is a seafood classic, and shashlik paneer will please vegetarians.

Italian

La Fenice

319 King Street W, at John Street (416 585 2377/www.lafenice.ca). Streetcar 504/subway St Andrew. **Open** 11.30am-2.30pm, 5.30-10.30pm Mon-Fri; 5.30-10.30pm Sat. **Main courses** $18-$21. **Credit** AmEx, DC, MC, V. **Map** p271 E8 ⑬

One of Toronto's pioneering northern Italian establishments, La Fenice offers old-world service in a sleek 1980s setting (which has held up better than big shoulder pads). Diners slide into comfy leather chairs and tuck into fresh pastas such as melt-in-the-mouth gnocchi in a sweet tomato sauce. Jumbo shrimp are properly grilled and veal chops are juicy. Though no longer a trend-setter, this pre-theatre fave is nonetheless refined and reliable.

Tutti Matti

364 Adelaide Street W, at Spadina Avenue (416 597 8839/www.tuttimatti.com). Streetcar 504, 510. **Open** noon-3pm, 6-10.30pm Mon-Fri; 6-10.30pm Sat. **Main courses** $9-$24. **Credit** AmEx, DC, MC, V. **Map** p271 D7 ⑭

Chef Alida Solomon spent years training in Tuscan trattorias, and then returned home to spread the good news: there's more to Italian cooking than tomato sauce and cheese (or even sun-dried tomatoes and buffalo mozzarella). Solomon's small open kitchen excels at rustic bean soups and fresh pastas (which most of Toronto's chefs cannot master) matched with deep, earthy sauces such as wild-boar ragoût. Cheese plates laden with top-notch Italian imports and local delights outshine the desserts. The wine list also yields some bold and unusual choices.

Don't miss Cuisine

Canoe Restaurant & Bar
A celebration of Canadian ingredients – Albertan beef, Nova Scotia lobster, Quebec cheeses – in a lofty, luxurious setting. *See p113.*

Hiro Sushi
A seafood feast prepared by a master. *See p118.*

Jamie Kennedy Wine Bar
Exquisite fare in a convivial bistro setting. *See p118.*

Lai Wah Heen
Dim sum so fine it has Hong Kong talking. *See p114.*

Lee
If you can't afford Susur (*see p110*), sample Susur Lee's complex fusion concoctions at a bargain price. *See p109.*

Scaramouche
A room with a view – with a luxurious menu to match. *See p122.*

Starfish Oyster Bed & Grill
The oyster is your world at this stellar spot. *See p119.*

North American

Bluepoint Oyster Bar & Supper Club

291 King Street W, at John Street (416 599 9995/www.bluepointoysterbar.ca). Streetcar 504/ subway St. Andrew. **Open** noon-11pm Mon-Thur; noon-1am Fri; 5pm-2am Sat; 5-11pm Sun. **Main courses** $16-$50. **Credit** AmEx, DC, MC, V. **Map** p271 E8 ⑮

This trendy seafood spot is a crowd pleaser: there's a first-floor raw bar, an upstairs lounge and a private party room. The dramatic lighting and look-at-me design are complemented by a beautiful crowd of shell-diggers. The molluscs are of high quality, sourced from Canada's rich coasts as well as from far-flung locales like New Zealand.

Rodney's Oyster House

469 King Street W, at Spadina Avenue (416 363 8105/www.rodneysoysterhouse.com). Streetcar 504, 510. **Open** 11.30am-1am Mon-Sat. **Main courses** $16-$50. **Credit** AmEx, DC, MC, V. **Map** p271 D8 ⑯

A transplant from the East Coast, Rodney Clark imported his dad's oysters before opening his own joint. Rodney's is one of the city's first, and most traditional, oyster bars; after you've drizzled a dazzling array of sauces on the molluscs, tuck into Dungeness crab, lobster and other seafood chowders, along with a range of pastas and mains. There is a cheery maritime ambience, and the fish is the freshest in town.

Ultra Supper Club

314 Queen Street W, at Peter Street (416 263 0330/ www.ultrasupperclub.com). Streetcar 501, 510. **Open** 6-11pm Mon-Sat. **Main courses** $26-$36. **Credit** AmEx, DC, MC, V. **Map** p271 E7 ⑰

As in 'ultra trendy'. If you like your dining room to be a dance club, then this is the spot for you. Glossy to the extreme, Ultra is set in an open room with high ceilings, stone columns and 'privacy curtains' that wrap around tables (it's supposed to make you feel like a Roman emperor). The menu items – veal loin with veal sweetbreads and truffle risotto, for one – are suitably rich. This was one of the city's first resto-lounges, and it has aged well.

Financial District

Cafés & coffee houses

Great Cooks on Eight

8th Floor, 401 Bay Street, at Queen Street (416 861 4333/www.greatcooks.ca). Streetcar 501/subway Queen. **Open** 11am-3pm Mon-Sat. **Main courses** $7-$18. **Credit** AmEx, DC, MC, V. **Map** p271 F7 ⑱

The 'Eight' refers to location: the eighth floor of the downtown department store The Bay, overlooking downtown. The bustling lunchtime spot is a modern update of the department store restaurant. Part cafeteria, part tea room, it has menus that are as casual as the decor: no-fuss quiches, egg-and-tuna sarnies and cheesy lasagne that puts frozen counterparts in their place. After hours, it becomes a cooking school where celebrity chefs conduct classes for amateurs and corporate clients.
Other locations: Lower level, The Bay, 176 Yonge Street, at Queen Street, Dundas Square (416 861 4727).

Continental

Bymark

Toronto Dominion Bank Tower, 66 Wellington Street W, at Bay Street (416 777 1144/www. bymarkdowntown.com). Subway King. **Open** 11.30am-2.30pm, 5-11pm Mon-Fri; 5-11pm Sat. **Main courses** $35-$45. **Credit** AmEx, DC, MC, V. **Map** p271 F8 ⑲

In the heart of the Financial District, the Toronto Dominion Tower offers some of the best modernist eye candy in town. Now celebrity chef Mark McEwen has created a split-level dining room at the base of the towers. Sleek and glamorous, it's a favourite with the high rollers of Bay Street, who dine on contemporary, finely crafted dishes. Even the burger is sumptuous: an eight ounce beauty topped with melted brie and porcini mushrooms. There is a staggering, 5,000-bottle wine cellar and the menus offer suggested pairings. Foie gras and champagne are staples.

Osgoode Hall

2nd Floor, 130 Queen Street W, at University Avenue (416 947 3361). Streetcar 501/subway Osgoode. **Open** noon-2pm Mon-Fri. Closed July, Aug. **Main courses** $11-$19. **Credit** AmEx, DC, MC, V. **Map** p271 F7 ⑳

Set behind a great lawn and cast-iron fence, the stately Osgoode Hall houses the Law Society of Upper Canada. Past a security check – no passport needed – and up a creaky staircase lies a hidden restaurant where the walls are lined with books, and the most popular dress code, after suits, calls for wigs and robes. Bistro fare highlights fresh, often organic ingredients in delectable dishes. The fairly priced menu ranges from fine soups and sandwiches to satisfying mains such as cassoulet and daily fish entrées. This is also your best chance to taste the famous Canadian butter tart (with flaky pastry, caramel filling and warm vanilla sauce).

North American

beerbistro

18 King Street E, at Yonge Street (416 861 9872/ www.beerbistro.com). Subway King. **Open** 11.30am-1am Mon-Wed; 11.30am-2am Thur, Fri; 4pm-2am Sat. **Main courses** $10-$22. **Credit** AmEx, DC, MC, V. **Map** p272 G8 ㉑

For those who like to eat beer as well as drink it, beerbistro serves it braised, basted and barbecued. The Belgian Ale burger is caramelised by sugars in the ale; the Coq au Bier substitutes wine with a German-style wheat beer. The waitstaff suggests pairings from the 20 brews on tap and over 100

Local flavour

Eat, Drink, Shop

The fad for Canadian foods is no fleeting trend. Many Toronto chefs have always taken great pride in making the most of seasonal goods that are native to these parts. Raw materials range from tiny greens to heirloom tomatoes, lake perch to farm-raised wild boar and more. Artisan producers abound: cheese-makers from across the country turn out creamy wheels worthy of any European dairy with wines to match from British Columbia and Ontario. Cooks and farmers alike are showing a new talent for charcuterie, from in-house smoked sausages at **Cava** (*see p123*) to succulent prosciutto aged by Niagara producer Mario Pingue.

Anthony Walsh at **Canoe Restaurant & Bar** (*see p112*) has a field day sourcing Canadiana flavours: Nunavut caribou, rare-breed piggies from Manitoba, foie gras from Quebec and lobsters from Nova Scotia. A read through the menu is like taking a cross-country tour with stops at the best farms and vineyards: ask your waiter to tell you the stories that come with these ingredients. If you dare, prepare to challenge preconceptions about Canadian wines: foods are made to match with the best the country has to pour.

Walsh keeps good company. His mentor, chef Jamie Kennedy (**Jamie Kennedy Wine Bar; Jamie Kennedy at the Gardiner**, *see p118*) proudly displays a dazzling wall of home-grown preserves. These savoury and sweet flavours garnish Ontario lamb, local sheep cheeses and tender greens from local outfit Manic Organic. Frites are made with the Canadian variety of Yukon Gold potato.

Marc Thuet (**Bistro and Bakery Thuet;** *see p109*) gets his foie gras from Quebec, his black cod from British Columbia and his beef locally. And Thuet's brand-name breads

appear on menus around town, such as **Czehoski** (*see p129*), where you can get Alex Farms cheddar (*see p150* **St Lawrence Market**) and Cumbrae pork.

Canadian content also dominates at **Niagara Street Café** (*see p127*) where the menu boasts local, naturally raised meats and organic dairy.

Chris McDonald marries native goods with Spanish tradition at **Cava** (*see p123*), while **Edward Levesque's Kitchen** (*see p132*) fries up organic eggs, bacon and other treats. Take in Andrew Milne-Allan's passion for local produce whipped into fresh pastas, homely soups and bracing salads at **Zucca** (*see p124*). Small French bistro **Gamelle** (*see p127*) pays patriotic tribute with succulent roast venison, while **Scaramouche** (*see p122*) features a wide selection of home-grown ingredients. **Trattoria Giancarlo** (*see p128*) is similarly strong on top-notch produce sourced from nearby organic farms. And each new season yields a fresh crop of Canadian-themed restaurants.

bottled varieties – just don't ask to smell the cap (though if you fancy extending your knowledge of brilliant brews, beer meister Stephen Beaumont holds beer school and tastings).

Canoe Restaurant & Bar

54th Floor, Toronto Dominion Tower, 66 Wellington Street W, at Bay Street (416 364 0054/ www.canoerestaurant.com). Bus 6/subway King or St Andrew. **Open** 11.30am-2.30pm, 5-10.30pm Mon-Fri. **Main courses** $29-$44. **Credit** AmEx, DC, MC, V. **Map** p271 F8 ㉒

Canoe is a Toronto showpiece, both for the lofty setting and superlative cuisine. It's also a favourite with the CEOs who toil in the concrete canyons of Bay Street: they habitually hit the bright, wood-panelled dining room between marathon meetings. But even if you're on a budget, you too can enjoy the panoramic view, a glass of Niagara chardonnay and light posh nosh at the bar. Should you seek further fulfilment – and you should, this is one of the country's best restaurants – we recommend the tasting menus, which show off the talents of executive chef Anthony Walsh. Canoe is also famous for using top Canadian ingredients – Albertan beef, Nova Scotia's lobster, Quebec cheeses and seasonal produce from local growers, plus superior local vintages. *See p112* **Local flavour**.

Dundas Square

North American

Barberian's Steak House

7 Elm Street, at Yonge Street (416 597 0335/www. barberians.com). Streetcar 505/subway Dundas. **Open** noon-2.30pm, 5pm-midnight Mon-Fri; 5pm-midnight Sat, Sun. **Steaks** $22-$46. **Credit** AmEx, DC, MC, V. **Map** p272 F6 ㉓

Fine steakhouses are a thing of the past. But for a bit of nostalgia, and a succulent slab of grilled cow along with the essential side of starch, forgo the chain establishments for this storied destination. In its day, it attracted the top nobs and it still draws visiting beef-eating celebrities . The impressive wine cellar, collected by Aaron Barberian the Younger, reflects a desire to keep the big spenders coming. Good for holidays, when most places are closed: Barberian's is open every night of the year.

The Senator

253 Victoria Street, at Dundas Street E (416 364 7517/www.thesenator.com). Streetcar 505/subway Dundas. **Open** 7.30am-2.30pm Mon-Fri; 8.30am-2.30pm Sat,-Sun. Evening hours vary. **Main courses** $9-$24. **Credit** AmEx, DC, MC, V. **Map** p272 G6 ㉔

In the shadow of the Toronto Eaton Centre sits this nostalgic slice of history. The diner looks much as it has since its start in the '50s – chrome-and-Bakelite counters, leatherette banquettes and a bar with swivel stools – and the menu is made to match. A hearty breakfast – eggs, home fries, beans, toast

and bacon – sets you up for marathon shopping excursions. Lunch and pre-theatre choices abound, whether it's a giant BLT or the kitchen's famous crab cakes puffed with more sweet meat than filler. The evening hours change according to what shows are in town, so call ahead.

Superior

253 Yonge Street, at Dundas Square (416 214 0416/www.superiorrestaurant.com). Subway Dundas. **Open** 11.30am-9pm Mon; 11.30am-10pm Tue-Sat. **Main courses** $17-$32. **Credit** AmEx, MC, V. **Map** p272 G7 ㉕

Just steps from the Elgin and Winter Garden theatres and Massey Hall, this airy, laid-back restaurant offers a welcome alternative to the strip's overpriced, underwhelming tourist traps. The home-cooking menus stick to standard pastas, salads and meat-focused mains. Prepared under the watchful eye of owner Tom Lexovsky, dishes range from the reliable to the inspired, and the ingredients are fine. The extensive wine cellar, which offers options for connoisseurs and budget-minded patrons alike, has won awards from the *Wine Spectator*.

Thai

Salad King

335 Yonge Street, at Gould Street (416 971 7041/ www.saladking.com). Streetcar 505/subway Dundas. **Open** 11am-9pm Mon-Fri; noon-9pm Sat. **Main courses** $8-$15. **Credit** DC, MC, V. **Map** p271 G8 ㉖

Immune to the trends of what's hot and not, this long-standing Thai diner has always delivered the goods: fresh spring rolls, lively noodles and tropical-flavoured salads for the masses. The prices are bargain basement, so midweek the bright, noisy room is packed with students from nearby Ryerson University and office workers, with everyone elbowing each other for a seat. The chicken coconut curry is a sensory trip in a bowl.

Chinatown/Kensington Market

Asian

Matahari Grill

39 Baldwin Street, at Beverley Street (416 596 2832). Streetcar 505, 506. **Open** noon-3pm Tue-Fri; 5-10pm Tue-Fri; 5-10pm Sat, Sun. **Main courses** $12-$20. **Credit** AmEx, DC, MC, V. **Map** p271 E6 ㉗

Bordering Kensington Market and Chinatown, this small Malaysian hotspot offers the best of both worlds: fiery Asian fare in a hip setting. Also, in keeping with the area, it's easy on the pocket. The Matahari Platter – a selection of satays, spring rolls, wontons and pickles – is a good place to start, though curries and seafood are equally tasty. Service is helpful, especially when navigating some of the more exotic menu items. Best to reserve.

Chinese

Lai Wah Heen

Metropolitan Hotel Toronto, 108 Chestnut Street, at Dundas Street W (416 977 9899/www.metropolitan. com/lwh). Streetcar 505/subway St Patrick. **Open** 11.30am-3pm, 5.30-10.30pm Mon-Fri, Sun; 11am-3pm, 5.30-11pm Sat. **Main courses** $20. **Credit** AmEx, DC, MC, V. **Map** p272 F6 ❷❾

Dim-sum trolleys are wheeled out all over Chinatown at the weekend in Toronto, but none of the food is as fine as the fare at Lai Wah Heen (though you'll pay for the quality). Although the dining room is somewhat institutional – it is, after all located in the business friendly Metropolitan Hotel (*see p44*) – the Cantonese cooking is so good that the setting matters little. Sunday brunch's tasting menu comprises six dim-sum selections and one noodle dish. Portions and presentation are the epitome of delicate: alligator-loin dumplings, banana-and-shrimp mousse and mini abalones to start. The belle of the dinner menu is crispy Peking duck. Midtown visitors can try new sister incarnation Lai Toh Heen (629 Mount Pleasant Road, 416 489 8922).

Lee Garden

331 Spadina Avenue, at Baldwin Street (416 593 9524). Streetcar 505, 510. **Open** 4pm-midnight Mon-Thur, Sun; 4pm-1am Fri, Sat. **Main courses** $12-$16. **Credit** AmEx, DC, MC, V. **Map** p271 D6 ❷❾

Locals decided long ago that Sunday would be the night for Chinese food. And so, while the rest of the city grinds to a halt, the restaurants in Chinatown gear up for their biggest evening of the week. Lee Garden is markedly more popular than its competitors, and its dishes are characterised by their freshness rather than by their fiery temperature – this is Cantonese, after all. Prepare to wait, and then to be whisked to a table by staff who deliver your order swiftly and with gusto.

Mother's Dumplings

79 Huron Street, at Dundas Street (416 217 2008). Streetcar 505, 506, 510. **Open** 11am-11.30pm Mon-Sat; noon-11:30pm Sun. **Main courses** $4. **Map** p271 E6 ❸⓪

Though it's a hole in the wall, the spartan Mother's Dumplings attracts crowds of locals, who come for silken dumplings stuffed with chicken and mushrooms, pork with pickled cabbage or chives and other gustatory goodies. Fresh delights made onsite – in a tiny, semi-open kitchen – are comfort food from northern China. Wonton soup speckled with ginger and coriander will brighten the greyest day. Ditto for the pork and beef buns, which often sell out. The plastic tables and chairs tend to make this bargain meal a quick affair. **Photo** *p115*.

Wah Sing Seafood

47 Baldwin Street, at Henry Street (416 599 8822). Streetcar 505, 506, 510. **Open** 11.30am-10.30pm daily. **Main courses** $8-$15. **Credit** MC, V. **Map** p271 E6 ❸❶

Seafood junkies with a soft spot for Cantonese cuisine are drawn to Wah Sing. Many of the Far East restaurants in the area claim to serve the best seafood in town (notice the profusion of fish tanks in windows), but Wah Sing is the real deal. It will draw you in with its two-for-one lobster deal, and keep you there with all manner of low-priced bottom-feeder specialities. You may not want to hang around after the last claw or tail (the ambience is spartan), but there's plenty more to enjoy (bars, cafés and shops) in Baldwin Village, a secret, tree-lined enclave just north of Dundas Street.

Continental

La Palette

256 Augusta Avenue, at Oxford Street (416 929 4900). Streetcar 506, 510. **Open** 6-10pm Mon-Fri; 11am-4pm, 6-11pm Sat; 11am-4pm, 6-9pm Sun. **Set menu** $30. **Credit** AmEx, DC, MC, V. **Map** p271 D6 ❸❷

This pre-boho bistro is an old Kensington Market standby, a throwback to the days of hearty French cooking. The classic menu includes a prix fixe featuring warm salads, steak frites and various dishes with wine sauces, all meant to be washed down with a good selection of vino. Save room for the home-made fruit tarts. With just 26 seats, it's best to reserve for weekend dinners.

Torito Tapas Bar

276 Augusta Avenue, at College Street (647 436 5874). Streetcar 506. **Open** 6-11pm Mon-Sat. **Dinner** $35. **Credit** DC, MC, V. **Map** p271 D5 ❸❸

Toronto has finally warmed to tapas. Although many interpretations stray far from the genuine Spanish article, this Kensington hangout balances Latin tradition with invention – with finger-licking results. In true tapas style, each plate is small in size and big on flavour, whether it's citrus-fresh ceviche, Spanish tortillas, shrimps swimming in garlic or the signature tripe soup. Even the small selection of desserts verges on bold. Arrive early, stay awhile and knock back some vino.

Japanese

Ematei

30 St Patrick Street, at Queen Street (416 340 0472). Streetcar 505/subway St Patrick. **Open** noon-2.30pm, 5pm-midnight Mon-Fri; 5pm-midnight Sat, Sun. **Main courses** $22-$46. **Credit** AmEx, DC, MC, V. **Map** p271 E7 ❸❹

The craze for sushi might have spawned a wealth of cheap imitations, but Ematei offers an authentic taste of Tokyo. In spite of an obscure location on a blah street and a decor that is more tacky than traditional, Japanese tourists and local diehards have worn a path here in search of generous hotpots, top-grade hand rolls and airy tempura. Good deals are found with the three-course menus. Near the Art Gallery of Ontario (*see p73*).

Eat, Drink, Shop

Stuff yourself with **Mother's Dumplings**. *See p114.*

Vegetarian

Café 668

668 Dundas Street W, at Bathurst Street (416 703 0668/www.cafe668.com). Streetcar 505, 511. **Open** 12.30-4pm, 6-9pm Tue-Fri; 1.30-9pm Sat, Sun. **Main courses** $10-$13. **No credit cards.** **Map** p271 D6 ③⑤.
Restaurants for vegetarians often advertise 'fresh' and 'raw' as selling points, but flavour is low on the priority list. Thankfully, the vegetarian Asian fare served at this café has a bent for biting spice. There are plenty of mock meats, as well as fine noodles. Yet another reason to check out Kensington Market.

Vietnamese

Pho Hung Restaurant

350 Spadina Avenue, at St Andrew Street (416 593 4274). Streetcar 505, 510. **Open** 10am-10pm daily. **Main courses** $5-$10. **No credit cards.** **Map** p271 D6 ③⑥
If you're looking for Asian but want to avoid thick, heavy sauces, try a warm tureen of *pho* washed down with cheap beer. Noodles are a speciality, but they aren't the only dishes on the menu – other delicacies come wrapped in shrimp rice paper or golden buns, and you can also get a mean curry. **Other locations**: 200 Bloor Street W, at Queen's Park, University (416 963 5080).

University/Harbord

Cafés & coffee houses

Aunties & Uncles

74 Lippincott Street, at College Street (416 324 1375). Streetcar 506, 511. **Open** 9am-4pm Tue-Sun. **Main courses** $7-$8.50. **No credit cards.** **Map** p271 D5 ③⑦
Bearing an uncanny resemblance to your granny's kitchen, with mismatched Arborite tables and vinyl seats, Aunties is classic 'what you see is what you get' territory. Grilled cheese sandwiches and French toast are made from fresh, chubby challah bread. Club sarnies are impossible to eat neatly for all their chunky cuts of chicken breast and tomato. Potato salad goes with everything; prices are blissfully low.

Continental

Bistro 990

990 Bay Street, at Wellesley Street (416 921 9990/www.bistro990.ca). Subway Bay or Wellesley. **Open** noon-3pm Mon-Fri; 5.30-11pm Mon-Sun. **Main courses** $18-$42. **Credit** AmEx, DC, MC, V. **Map** p274 F5 ③⑧
The strip between Yorkville and Queen Street is a dust bowl for diners, but this old-style bistro offers a good place to park your appetite. During the film festival, the small dining room and narrow patio

Izakaya. *See p118.*

attract the A-list stars for aromatic bowls of mussels and plates of frites and other charmers. Over a fish-bowl glass of Beaujolais, eavesdrop on the barflies for local gossip.

Gallery Grill
7 Hart House Circle, at King's College Circle (416 978 2445/www.harthouse.utoronto.ca/English/ gallery-grill.html). Bus 94/subway Museum. **Open** *Sept-June* 11.30am-2.30pm Mon-Fri; 11am-2pm Sun. Closed holiday weekends. **Main courses** $14-$16. **Credit** AmEx, DC, MC, V. **Map** p274 E5 ③⑨
From the vertiginous balcony, you can look down into Hart House's elegant oak-panelled Great Hall and ponder the academic life. U of T faculty and students who can afford it lunch here on refined continental fare, prepared with a light touch by chef Suzanne Baby. At Sunday brunch, the smartest picks are the poached eggs with a wild mushroom sautée or arctic char frittata. Other midday options include smoked trout salad and Stilton flan. Leave time to tour the university campus, which features some of Toronto's best Gothic architecture.

Italian

Bar Mercurio
270 Bloor Street W, at St George Street (416 960 3877). Subway St George. **Open** 7am-11pm Mon-Sat. **Main courses** $22-$32. **Credit** AmEx, MC, V. **Map** p274 E4 ④⓪
Among a sea of fast-food chains and pubs spilling over with students, this European bar stands out from the crowd. Lean on the marble counter as the day begins, sip a latte and nibble on a brioche. Food is available all day – through lunch and late into the evening for dinner. Best bets are the home-made pastas, especially gnocchi in a gorgonzola sauce and the Pasta Mercurio, broad noodles in a duck ragoût scented with black truffle. Wines are plentiful and the place hums with a low-key buzz. Kitty-corner is the bar's stylish cousin, L'Espresso; in good weather, lounge on the street-side patio.
Other locations: 321 Bloor Street West, at Spadina Avenue, The Annex (416 585 2233).

Middle Eastern

Kensington Kitchens
124 Harbord Street, at Robert Street (416 961 3404). Bus 94/streetcar 510. **Open** 11.30am-10pm Mon-Thur, Sun; 11.30am-10.30pm Fri, Sat. **Main courses** $10-$18. **Credit** AmEx, DC, MC, V. **Map** p274 D4 ④①
Popular with university students and profs, this long-standing Lebanese eaterie is a notch above most fast-food falafel joints. The pretty dining room, decorated with antique toy planes, offers falafel platters, vegetarian fare, fresh fish and tasty desserts. While away the hours on a summer afternoon on the upstairs patio, shaded by a lovely old tree. The neighbourhood is full of secondhand bookshops.

93 Harbord
93 Harbord Street, at Spadina Avenue (416 922 5914). Bus 94/streetcar 510. **Open** 5.30-10pm Tue-Thur, Sun; 5.30-11pm Fri, Sat. **Main courses** $20-$30. **Credit** AmEx, MC, V. **Map** p274 D4 ④②
The best of the neighbourhood's Middle Eastern restaurants. Palestinian chef Isam Kaisi presents a bold fusion menu – the Middle East meets Africa – in a demurely stylish room. The menu is a kaleidoscope of flavours: cumin and tamarind, liquorice and mint, citrus and chillies. Start with a plate of duck ragoût or any number of savoury salads, and don't miss the lamb tagines of slow-cooked shank tossed in an aromatic couscous, or the vegetable tagine. Some dishes pour on the heat, so ask in advance.

St Lawrence/Distillery District

Cafés & coffee houses

Balzac's Coffee Roastery
Building 60, 55 Mill Street, at Parliament Street (416 207 1709/www.balzacscoffee.com). Bus 65. **Open** 7am-10pm daily. **Credit** V. **Map** p273 J8 ④③
If entering this retro coffee house feels like walking on to a movie set for a Paris café, then Balzac's designers will pat themselves on the back. This was once ground zero for Hollywood North, before the Distillery District emerged as a tourist destination. The java is made from beans that are roasted on the premises. For caffeine addicts with a conscience, there are fair-trade and organic blends. A small selection of sweet breads, tarts and cookies is provided by decent pastry shop Dufflet Pastries.

Brick Bakery
Building 45A, 55 Mill Street, at Parliament Street (416 214 4949). Bus 65. **Open** *Summer* 9am-7pm daily. *Winter* 10am-6pm Tue-Sun. **Main courses** $6-$7. **No credit cards. Map** p273 J8 ④④
Another conspicuously conceptualised spot in the smart Distillery District, this British-style pasty-and-pie take-out has good grub at fair prices. Especially tasty are the savoury pies – steak and stout, ma'am – and Eccles cakes. Turkey chilli is an odd, and bad, idea – a low-fat option on an otherwise fine menu that also includes braised lamb sarnies with apricot chutney. Staff are harried but friendly. Narrow benches favour design over comfort; outside there are two picnic tables.

SOMA
55 Mill Street, at Cherry Street (416 815 7662/ www.somachocolate.com). Bus 65. **Open** 11am-6pm Tue-Fri; 11.30am-6pm Sat, Sun. **Desserts** $4-$12. **No credit cards. Map** p273 J8 ④⑤
A café, chocolate shop and epicurean temple rolled into one, this unique spot is the brainchild of a pastry chef and his designer wife. David Castellan and Cynthia Leung decided the meaning of life was found in chocolate, so in their new expanded shop

Eat, Drink, Shop

they have laid bare the dark arts. Through Plexiglas windows you can watch staff grinding cocoa beans, crafting choccies and making ice-cream (find your inner Charlie here). The open room has a few stools and a piazza-inspired set of stairs – perfect for lounging while you sip top-grade coffee or spicy hot chocolate, and nibble on delicious cakes. Afterwards, stroll through the quaint Distillery District and poke around the galleries and shops.

Continental

Perigee

Cannery Building, 55 Mill Street, at Parliament Street (416 364 1397/www.perigee restaurant.com). Bus 65. **Open** from 5.30pm Tue-Sat; closing times vary. **Set menus** $85-$105. **Credit** AmEx, DC, MC, V. **Map** p273 J8 ⑥
The best restaurant in the Distillery District. Although the foodie ambience can be precious, the open-kitchen dining room offers a memorable meal. Chef Patrick Riley toils away for all to see and, as he serves the food, encourages round-table discussions of the finely prepared classical French dishes. Perigee accommodates only 30 people, so the concept often works. Tasting menus only. For Soulpepper theatre-goers (*see p222* **Spicing up the scene**), there's a pre-show menu too.

Italian

Romagna Mia

106 Front Street E, at Jarvis Street (416 363 8370/ www.romagna-mia.com). Streetcar 504/Subway Union. **Open** noon-2.30pm, 5-10.30pm Mon-Fri; 5-10.30pm Sat. **Main courses** $15-$30. **Credit** AmEx, DC, MC, V. **Map** p272 G8 ⑰
Though named after Emilia Romagna, a foodie region in central Italy, this trattoria sets off warning bells with its red-checkered tablecloths and bright lighting. But have no fear: superior cooking is offered here. The antipasto plates are loaded with the owner's fine charcuterie. The risotto is excellent and, in keeping with the region, there are plenty of pasta dishes rich with prosciutto and parmesan – a taste of *la dolce vita* in the heart of Hogtown.

Japanese

Hiro Sushi

171 King Street Street E, at Jarvis Street (416 304 0550). Subway King. **Open** noon-2.30pm, 6.30-10.30pm Mon-Sat. **Main courses** $20-$30. **Credit** AmEx, DC, MC, V. **Map** p272 G8 ⑱
Hiro Sushi is destination number one for raw fish. But the fans, who come from near and far, snub the handsome dining room; they've come to sit at Hiro Yoshida's bar and eat straight from the master chef's selection. If you'd like the same food, ask for the *omakase* menu. Translucent soups, tempura and sashimi, and bento boxes round out the choices.

Izakaya

69 Front Street E, at Church Street (416 703 8658). Subway King or Union Station. **Open** 11.30am-10.30pm Mon-Thur; 11.30am-11.30pm Fri, Sat; noon-10pm Sun. **Main courses** $10-$20. **Credit** AmEx, DC, MC, V. **Map** p272 G8 ⑲
Bill Murray would be at home in this futuristic and chic Tokyo temple. The name refers to the Japanese equivalent of a pub: it's where you go for that happy hour saké. And to mop up the drink, the foods are varied and portions more generous than typical snacks. The crowd is a mix of fashionistas and plebs: everyone comes for the playful ambience and quality tempura, dumplings, noodles and *katsu* curry. The drink list is equally impressive. Prices are surprisingly low. **Photo** *p116.*

Nami

55 Adelaide Street E, at Church Street (416 362 7373). Subway King or Queen. **Open** noon-2.30pm, 5.30-10.30pm Mon-Fri; 5.30-10.30pm Sat. **Main courses** $25-$30. **Credit** AmEx, DC, MC, V. **Map** p272 G7 ⑳
A classic Japanese meeting place, where diners sit at sushi bars or tucked into discreet alcoves shielded by rice paper or curtains. For a long time Nami offered some of the freshest sushi in town – and it's still up there in the rankings. A 'sushi pizza' is an interesting – if disturbing – choice. For the purists, there's sashimi, *makimono* and sushi all present and correct. Tender teriyaki off the menu is perfectly matched by beautifully seasoned, grilled accompaniments from the *robata* bar.

North American

Jamie Kennedy Wine Bar

9 Church Street, at Front Street E (416 362 5586/www.jkkitchens.com). Subway Union then 10 mins walk. **Open** 11.30am-11pm daily. **Main courses** $6-$14. **Credit** AmEx, DC, MC, V. **Map** p272 G8 ㉑
Chef Jamie Kennedy is a local legend. His superlative cooking is inspired by a passion for local, artisan-produced foods. Now there are three spots for fans of 'JK'. The convivial wine bar is vibrant, casual and affordable. Pick a seat at either of the two bars – one faces an open kitchen where you can watch the chefs at work – and choose from the tapas-style menu. Courses are expertly paired with wines – sommeliers tour the world in search of gems, but also offer Niagara and other Canadian vintages. Plates range from whimsical, delicious takes on Quebec *poutine* (the most popular is topped with succulent lamb) to house-cured charcuterie. A wall of preserves in mason jars flags the chef's commitment to seasonal offerings. Next door is the intimate, more upscale restaurant, where luxurious French dishes are updated. Kennedy's dazzling modern restaurant in the Gardiner Ceramic Museum (*see p78*) offers great views and exquisite food. **Other locations**: 111 Queen's Park, at Bloor Street West, University (416 362 1957).

Where's the beef?

If you like 'em meaty, big and bouncy, Toronto is the place to take care of that burger fix. Never mind that the city was once nicknamed Hogtown – the love of ground beef, cooked sizzling on an open flame, reigns supreme. From a vegan impostor to a mile-high beauty oozing French cheese, it's all here.

In the heart of the financial district, **Bymark** (*see p111*) takes the cake, with the most expensive and excessive meat-on-a-bun: eight ounces of ground round topped with melted brie and sautéed porcini mushrooms – and it might just call for a glass of the finest red available to mankind (you'll find it here). **Czehoski** (*see p129*) offers the second-priciest burger – served with heapings of truffles and foie gras to top a meat mix of bison and beef. On a more modest scale, **Allen's** (*see p132*) has been serving excellent burgers for years – perfect for the purist. The burgers at **Edward Levesque's Kitchen** (*see p132*) are a nod to diner's specials, though they come with a healthy organic twist. The popular **Utopia Grill** (586 College Street, West End, 416 534 7751) has something for everyone, from basic to bison to veggie. If you want a treat without the meat, try the chaste miso burger at **Fresh by Juice for Life** (*see p121*). Alternatively, go the other way and head for **Langdon Hall** (*see p242* **Spa trek**), where the burgers are served with garlic-mayo fries. The diet can wait till next week.

Kultura

169 King Street E., at Jarvis Street (416 363 9000/ www.kulturarestaurant.com). Subway Union. **Open** 5pm-closing times vary Mon-Sat; 10am-3pm Sun. **Courses** $5-$14. **Credit** AmEx, DC, MC, V. **Map** p272 G8 ⑤.

Attitude and attire are emphasised at this slightly pretentious restaurant/lounge. The stylish rooms are designed to beautify the hipsters, but what about the food? Thankfully, the substance matches the style: the global menu turns out highly praised dishes. There are no 'mains' but a random collection of tapas-sized plates.

Starfish Oyster Bed and Grill

100 Adelaide Street E, at Church Street (416 366 7827/www.starfishoysterbed.com). Subway King. **Open** noon-3pm, 5-11pm Mon-Fri; 5-11pm Sat. **Main courses** $23-$29. **Credit** AmEx, DC, MC, V. **Map** p272 G7 ⑤.

You know you're in good hands when the owner holds the title of world champion shucker. Patrick McMurray relishes all things briny. The maritime decor and unpretentious atmosphere are a magnet for bivalve slurpers, who take a seat at the long raw bar for a taste of the world's best. Other ingredients, from salads to frites to snapper, are top-grade.

Eat, Drink, Shop

chez **VICTOR**

CHEZ VICTOR INSPIRES A NEW APPRECIATION OF "L'ART DE VIVRE"

Join us for a delicious array of unique flavours with a focus on local produce. Simplicity yet we court the adventurous.

CHEZ VICTOR : L'ART DE LA TABLE RÉINVENTÉ

Pour vos repas entre amis, en tête-à-tête ou en solo, Chez Victor marie avec succès style, chaleur et convivialité dans un cadre intimiste.

Hôtel Le Germain 30 Mercer Street, Toronto | www.germaintoronto.com | **Reservations** 416 982 2421 | chezvictor@germaintoronto.com

Yorkville

Cafés & coffee houses

Café Nervosa

75 Yorkville Avenue, at Bellair Street (416 961 4642). Bus 6/subway Bay or Bloor-Yonge. **Open** 11.30am-11pm Mon-Sat; 11.30am-10pm Sun. **Main courses** $20-$25. **Credit** AmEx, DC, MC, V. **Map** p274 F4 ❸.

Celebs in town lounge at the Four Seasons or Windsor Arms hotels. Wannabe celebs loll here, at the gateway to posh Yorkville. If you're coiffed, bleached, manicured and/or animal-printed, you'll blend right in – particularly with the leopard-tinged upstairs refuge. In good weather, smokers get a prime perch on the terrace. The food takes a back seat, although it is fair: thin-crusted pizzas and light dishes such as spinach salad and angel-hair pasta.

Coffee Mill

99 Yorkville Avenue, at Bellair Street (416 920 2108). Subway Bay or Bloor-Yonge. **Open** 10am-11pm Mon-Thur; 10am-1am Fri, Sat; noon-11pm Sun. **Main courses** $10-$14. **Credit** AmEx, DC, MC, V. **Map** p274 F4 ❺.

This Hungarian café is about as old-world as the city gets. It's an institution in a neighbourhood once crowded with hippies; now it's the designer divas who squeeze into leatherette banquettes or sip espresso on the outdoor terrace. If you've never had *palascinta*, an Eastern European sweet crêpe filled with soft cheese, now's your chance. Leave room for one of the many hot drinks made with chocolate.

MBCo

110 Bloor Street W, at Bellair Street (416 961 6226). Subway Bay or Bloor-Yonge. **Open** 8am-7pm Mon-Sat; 8am-6pm Sun. **Main courses** $5-$14. **Credit** AmEx, DC, MC, V. **Map** p274 F4 ❺.

This hip Montreal bakery chain (the name stands for Montreal Bakery Company) is taking off in Toronto. The narrow, sleek spot faces Yorkville's oddly pleasing concrete park. Grilled sandwiches, wraps such as a wholewheat pittas stuffed with organic chicken, thin-crust pizzas, fresh salads and comforting egg dishes attract the neighbourhood's upper crust. Petal teas and a small selection of Niagara wines add a note of sophistication. If the place is crammed, you can get lunch boxed to go. A second location is in the TD Towers (416 361 5055) and a third at Summerhill is in the oven.

7 West

7 Charles Street W, at Yonge Street (416 928 9041). Subway Bloor-Yonge or Wellesley. **Open** 24hrs daily. **Main courses** $10-$15. **Credit** MC, V. **Map** p275 G4 ❺.

A 24-hour standby that makes the best of a great location near the crossroads of Bloor and Yonge. Happily for its neighbours in the umpteen condo complexes, the homey café (it occupies all three storeys of a charming Victorian house) stays open late. It's also open early. In fact, you can count on it being open whenever you pop round for middling sarnies, various pastas, the usual salads and generous-portion platters. Good grub that offers an alternative to all-night chain restaurants.

Chinese

The Dynasty

Second Floor, 131 Bloor Street W, at Avenue Road (416 923 3323). Subway Bay, Museum. **Open** 11am-4pm Mon-Fri; 10am-4pm Sat, Sun. **Main courses** $24-$39. **Credit** AmEx, DC, MC, V. **Map** p274 F4 ❺.

Far removed from the busy streets of Chinatown, this much-loved dining room shares the block with Tiffany's along the city's Mink Mile. Get a table by the window on a sunny Sunday and join the multi-cultural crowd, who come for excellent dim sum. Steamed spare-ribs in black-bean sauce; sticky rice crêpes, pudgy dumplings and a selection of over 70 dishes will leave you sated. Linger and watch the Gucci-clad passers-by below (the restaurant is on the second floor of the Colonnade Mall). Rumour has it Wolfgang Puck will be opening across the hall.

Continental

Pangaea

1221 Bay Street, at Bloor Street W (416 920 2323). Bus 6/subway Bay. **Open** 11.30am-11.30pm daily. **Main courses** $24-$39. **Credit** AmEx, DC, MC, V. **Map** p274 F4 ❺.

Although this is one of the busiest parts of town, there are precious few places to eat around Bay and Bloor, so upmarket Pangaea stands out. Join the suits – some of them Chanel – for a wild taste of the North American continent. Caribou, venison and cat-tail hearts (the edible parts of bull rushes) are handled with care. Pastry chef Joanne Yolles, one of the best, creates exquisite sweets.

The Annex/Casa Loma

Cafés & coffee houses

Fresh by Juice for Life

326 Bloor Street W, at Spadina Ave (416 531 2635/www.juiceforlife.com). Streetcar 511/subway Spadina. **Open** 11.30am-10.30pm Mon-Fri; 10.30am-10.30pm Sat, Sun. **Main courses** $10-$15. **Credit** AmEx, DC, MC, V. **Map** p274 E4 ❻.

Blenders are always whirring at this juice bar-cum-vegan paradise. If you can ignore the noise – and get past the queues by the entrance – you'll find Fresh a welcome departure from the usual bistros and trattorias. The establishment that introduced wheatgrass to Bloor Street (and then to Queen West) has grown into much more than a juice bar (though there are 50 varieties). Wraps, rice bowls and miso burgers are mainstays; spicy Cajun fries are a calorie-laden relief from the wholesome theme.

Future Bakery

483 Bloor Street W, at Brunswick Avenue (416 922 5875). Streetcar 510, 511/subway Bathurst or Spadina. **Open** 8am-1am daily. **Main courses** $7-$10. **Credit** AmEx, MC, V. **Map** p274 D4 **61**.

There's nothing futuristic about this place: the food harks back to granny's childhood in Poland, the desserts are enormous and the beer is basic. Wobbly tables are scattered about the vast layout and patio, floors are grungy, and the walls are stained with decades of cigarette smoke (though smoking is no longer allowed). The one thing Future has going for it is its location – on the main strip of the Annex; in the summer, the patio is a neighbourhood hotspot. And, if you happen to like mashed potatoes and pierogi (Polish dumplings), welcome home.

Continental

Scaramouche & Scaramouche Pasta Bar

1 Benvenuto Place, off Edmond Avenue, at Avenue Road (416 961 8011). Streetcar 512/ subway Summerhill. **Open** *Restaurant* 5.30-10pm Mon-Sat. *Pasta Bar* 5.30-10.30pm Mon-Sat. **Main courses** *Restaurant* $36-$42. *Pasta Bar* $19-$26. **Credit** AmEx, DC, MC, V. **Map** p274 F1 **62**.

The old guard of the Toronto restaurant scene overlooks the city from a midtown hill. Scaramouche still has the look of a grandiose '80s hotspot: furnishings – and clientele – are brassy. Book ahead for a window seat, and a striking view of downtown

(especially in leafless winter). The food is stellar, as refined as can be found in Toronto; for a (slightly) more modestly priced meal, visit the the Pasta Bar next door. Chef Keith Froggett has overseen this gem for more than two decades, and it shows; some things are best left unchanged.

Indian

Indian Rice Factory

414 Dupont Street, at Howland Avenue (416 961 3472). Bus 7, 26/subway Bathurst or Dupont. **Open** noon-2.30pm, 5-10.30pm Mon-Fri; 5-10.30pm Sat, Sun. **Main courses** $10-$15. **Credit** DC, MC, V. **Map** p274 D2 **63**.

Though hidden on a quiet residential stretch in the Annex, the Indian Rice Factory has become a hub for those who favour clean, classy Indian cuisine over the more rugged, gritty kind you get in Little India. Some complain that such sophistication comes at too high a price, but a bite of the butter chicken usually shuts them up. The lamb is cooked just right, tender and carefully spiced; the light, flaky samosas won't sabotage the main course. Book ahead if you don't want to wait.

Nataraj

394 Bloor Street W, at Brunswick Avenue (416 928 2925). Subway Bathurst or Spadina. **Open** noon-2.30pm, 5-10pm Mon-Fri; 5.30-10.30pm Sat. **Main courses** $8-$10. **Credit** AmEx, DC, MC, V. **Map** p274 D4 **64**.

Grano. *See p124.*

With Little India so far off the subway line, there's much debate over where to find the best Indian cuisine in the city centre. Many vote for Nataraj. Grab a Cobra beer, then order the fragrant saffron rice with piquant tandoori and palak paneer, and you'll soon see why it's always busy.

Italian

Mistura

265 Davenport Road, at Avenue Road (416 515 0009/www.mistura.ca). Bus 5/subway Museum. **Open** 5.30-10pm Mon-Wed; 5.30-11pm Thur-Sat. **Main courses** $25-$30. **Credit** AmEx, DC, MC, V. **Map** p274 F3 ⑥⑤
Chef Massimo Capra and partner Paolo Paolini have created a restaurant that is elegant enough for a special occasion, but friendly enough for a casual meal. Everyone comes for home-made pastas, traditional fare such as veal *scaloppine* and fish soup. Standouts include a red-beet risotto and melt-in-your-mouth gnocchi. There is a fine selection of vino. Upstairs is Sopra Upper Lounge, a jazz lounge where lasagne is served with live music. The jury is still out on whether this particular combination works.

Korean

Korea House

666 Bloor Street W, at Manning Avenue (416 536 8666). Subway Bathurst. **Open** 11am-midnight daily. **Main courses** $10-$15. **Credit** MC, V

Restaurants in the Annex tend to be mainstream. But if the occasion calls for something more exotic than comfort food or continental, stray a few blocks west to Little Korea. Order a soju (Korea's answer to saké) and watch the dishes of *kimchi* and its cousins appear. *Be bim bop* gives you all your food groups – and all your calories – in one bowl, while *bulgogi* beef surpasses your typical Chinese shredded kind. Queues aren't unusual.

Midtown/Davisville

Cafés & coffee houses

Patachou

1120 Yonge Street, at Roxborough Street (416 927 1105). Subway Rosedale or Summerhill. **Open** 8.30am-7pm Mon-Fri; 8.30am-6pm Sat. **Main courses** $7-$12. **Credit** MC, V. **Map** p275 G2 ⑥⑥
Few of the New World patrons had ever seen a croissant when Patachou opened its doors a quarter of a century ago. To this day, Patachou's pastries are fit for aristocracy – fruit tarts as pretty as jewels, ganache-layered cakes and éclairs filled with mocha cream. Seated at bistro tables, outside and in, diners tuck in to fine soups, sarnies such as croque monsieur and a salad niçoise worthy of its name. This new location has a lovely design, although the dazzling tiles make for a noisy room. Another location on St Clair West is a quieter lunch spot. **Other locations:** 835 St Clair Avenue W, at Hendrick Avenue, West End (416 927 1105).

Continental

Cava

1560 Yonge Street, at St Clair Avenue (416 979 9918/www.cavarestaurant.ca). Subway St Clair. **Open** noon-2pm, 5-10pm Mon-Fri; 5-10pm Sat. **Dishes** $5-$18. **Credit** AmEx, MC, V. **Map** p275 G1 **⑥**

Sometimes Toronto latches on to trends in an embarrassing way – too late, too much, not too good. The city's new-found love of tapas is a case in point, but Cava proves to be an exception to the rule. Tucked away in a nondescript mall in a nondescript neighbourhood, its tapas and wine bar is not trendy, but it will outlast the pretenders. Take the charcuterie: the house-made, cured and dried salamis and chorizos are outstanding. The salt cod cakes, beef cheeks and chocolate desserts possess inventive flair, courtesy of chef Chris McDonald. House brand bubblies – Spanish Cavas, of course – top a hefty wine list of Latin labels. A smart midtown crowd laps it all up.

Didier

1496 Yonge Street, at St. Clair Avenue (416 925 8588/www.restaurantdidier.com). Subway St Clair. **Open** 11.30-2pm, 6-10pm Tue-Fri; 6-10pm Sat. **Main courses** $26-$36. **Credit** AmEx, DC, MC, V. **Map** p275 G1 **⑥**

This elegant, wood-panelled destination attracts local admirers who love their French food classic, unfussy and perfect. After years of working at other people's restaurants, Didier LeRoy, a winner of France's prestigious Chevalier medal, is finally doing it his way. Menus are a cut above the norm– a gateau of pickerel in beurre blanc and the trio of duck stray far from bistro norms. At the charming Didier boutique, you can buy duck confit and tender cornish hens (but it is only open during the summer). If you crave classy French cuisine, Didier is worth a trip to Midtown.

Fat Cat Bar & Bistro

376 Eglinton Avenue W, at Avenue Road (416 484 4228/www.fatcat.ca). Subway Eglinton West. **Open** 5.30-10pm Mon-Wed; 5.30-10.30pm Thur-Sat. **Main courses** $23-$35. **Credit** AmEx, DC, MC, V

Fat cats proliferate in Forest Hill, where mega-mansions are routinely bulldozed to make way for even bigger palaces. So it's no surprise that Fat Cat, a classy neighbourhood joint, keeps the focus on rich goods – foie gras or sweetbreads for starters; bison, veal tenderloin and black grouper for seconds. Flavours are culled from around the world: curries, salsas and succotash all play their part. The aim is to live large and eat well. This is first and foremost a local hangout – and a fashionable one at that – so expect to hear locals discussing their BMWs, holidays in Aruba and the best private schools. For swanky dos, it also does catering. **Other locations**: Fat Cat Wine Bar, 331 Roncesvalles Road, at Dundas Street West, West End (416 535 4064).

Italian

Grano

2035 Yonge Street, at Lola Road (416 440 1986/ www.grano.ca). Subway Davisville or Eglinton. **Open** 10am-10pm Mon-Sat. **Main courses** $10-$25. **Credit** AmEx, DC, MC, V.

This neighbourhood trattoria, going strong for 20 years, is a family affair – in many ways, the fifth child of owners Robert and Lucia Martella. Regulars fill the varied rooms day and night, taking in the warm hospitality and Italian culture (antique posters, Claudio Villa's serenades and Fellini flicks on a screen behind the bar). The food follows suit: soups like mama makes, lively pastas and rich risottos. The long display case of antipasti – a cornucopia of salads and starters – is a highlight. Breads are baked on the premises – all the better for soaking up reasonably priced wines. The festivities continue well past suitable family hours. **Photos** *pp122-123.*

Zucca Trattoria

2150 Yonge Street, at Eglinton Avenue (416 488 5774). Subway Davisville or Eglinton. **Open** 5.30-10pm daily. **Main courses** $22-$32. **Credit** AmEx, DC, MC, V.

Amid a concentration of middling so-called Italian eateries, this warm spot is the real deal. It's frequented by a well-heeled neighbourhood crowd, but the hubbub is generated by the creations from the kitchen. Zucca is the baby of chef Andrew Milne-Allan (who pioneered good Italian on College Street) and has been going for a decade. Tuck into a just-right portion of hand-rolled noodles in a sauce of duck ragoût or seasonal vegetables. Follow through with finely braised meats or grilled whole fish – each dish a tribute to a region of the boot country – and save room for chocolate-and-ricotta cheesecake.

Japanese

EDO

484 Eglinton Avenue W, at Avenue Road (416 322 3033). Bus 32/subway Eglinton. **Open** 5-11pm daily. **Main courses** $18-$25. **Credit** AmEx, DC, MC, V.

Though operated by a non-Japanese restaurateur, this Forest Hill stalwart nevertheless knows what its diners want: generous portions; relaxed, attentive service; and none of the harsh lighting and dubious offerings of many fast-food sushi joints. On the contrary, you'll want to spend the night savouring the plump sashimi, hand rolls and tempura that won't wilt in your grasp. And you may learn a thing or two from the staff about saké.

Middle Eastern

Jerusalem

955 Eglinton Avenue W, at Rostrevor Road (416 783 6494). Bus 32/subway Eglinton West. **Open** 11.30am-10.30pm Mon-Fri, Sun; 11am-midnight Sat. **Main courses** $11-$20. **Credit** AmEx, MC, V.

Niagara Street Café. *See p127.*

Before falafel became the standard pub-crawler's snack, there was Jerusalem, frequented mainly by local Jewish families. It's not quite as dowdy as its environs would suggest. And its menu flows from meze to mains to fresh seafood. You won't find dips this tantalising on most of the finer Middle Eastern menus. There are more tasting platters than dishes, which appeals to the adventurous diner.

West End

Cafés & coffee houses

Café Diplomatico

594 College Street, at Clinton Street, Little Italy (416 534 4637/www.diplomatico.ca). Streetcar 506, 511. **Open** 8am-2am Mon-Fri; 8am-3am Sat, Sun. **Main courses** $5-$15. **Credit** AmEx, DC, MC, V. **Map** p270 C5 ❻❾

It's a trade-off: the Dip wins hands down for the best people-watching platform in Little Italy, inside or on the vast patio. But you'll have to contend with poor service and below-average food. One menu surprise is the french fries – a cut above the rest. Otherwise, don't expect culinary miracles and you won't be disappointed – the Dip is all about sitting back with a Stella and watching the world strut by.

Caffé Brasiliano

849 Dundas Street, at Euclid Street, Little Portugal (416 603 6607). Streetcar 505. **Open** 6am-11pm Mon-Sat. **Main courses** $5-$10. **No credit cards.** **Map** p270 C6 ❼❶

Cabbies always know where to find good food on the go and they can often be found here, on this up-and-coming stretch of Dundas West, along with young families and other fans. This new, expanded location is just across the street from the 1960s original, but the joe is the same. The house blend is dark and delicious – and about one third the cost of a Starbucks creation. Tables are laden with homey fodder: meaty stews, cheesy lasagnes and filling soups. Don't miss the rich custard tarts from the Portuguese bakery Caldense: the common man's crème brûlée in a soft pastry shell.

Kalendar

546 College Street, at Euclid Avenue, Little Italy (416 923 4138/www.kalendar.com). Streetcar 506, 511. **Open** 8am-midnight Mon-Wed; 8am-1am Thur, Fri; 10.30am-2am Sat; 10.30am-midnight Sun. **Main courses** $10-$19. **Credit** AmEx, DC, MC, V. **Map** p270 C5 ❼❶.

Easily the winner of the beauty contest on the College strip, this café is more than just a pretty face. Amsterdam and that city's Indonesian influences inspire the menu's main feature: hand-rolled scrolls or crêpe-style rotis filled with roast veggies, herbed mayo, curries and chicken. Naan bread and pizzas satisfy bar-hoppers and other weekend strollers. In the summer, the patio out front is a great place to watch the scene over a draught or a mocha coffee. Consistently voted best date restaurant.

Eat, Drink, Shop

Terroni. *See p128.*

Mona's Shwarma & Falafel

661 College Street, at Grace Street, Little Italy (416 535 8466). Streetcar 506, 511. **Open** noon-10pm Mon-Thur; noon-3am Fri, Sat; 1-7pm Sun. **Main courses** $4-$10. **No credit cards. Map** p270 C5 **72**.
Little Italy's best Middle Eastern take-out is one of the friendliest spots along the College Street strip. If the place is hopping, you might be offered a hot slice of crispy potato while you wait for that heaped falafel platter. The tiny place is located just west of the trendiest bars, and it wisely takes advantage of its location by staying open late. As a result, it attracts the late-night, post-bar crowds. Rumour has it that celebrity chef Susur Lee drops by.

Pain Perdu

736 St Clair Avenue W, at Christie Street (416 656 7246). Streetcar 512. **Open** 7am-7pm Tue-Fri; 7am-5pm Sat; 8am-4pm Sun. **Main courses** $5-$7. **Credit** DC, MC, V.
Toronto's reputation for unusual foodie destinations receives another endorsement with this Basque boulangerie. Be sure to take a healthy appetite to the small and casual neighbourhood café: everything, from buttery croissants to egg-rich quiches and pastries, is irresistible. The namesake dish is a type of French toast: yesterday's baguette soaked in cream, oven-baked and served with fruit. Don't forget to sample some of the city's finest gateau Basque, a custard-filled tart.

Red Tea Box

696 Queen Street W, at Tecumseth Street (416 203 8882). Streetcar 501. **Open** 10am-6pm Mon, Wed, Thur; 10am-7pm Fri, Sat; noon-5pm Sun. **Main courses** $5.50-$17. **Credit** MC, V. **Map** p270 C7 **73**.
This old coach house has been transformed into a scented, pretty boîte with exquisite teas. Artfully prepared sweets are whimsical and delicious – chocolate cake decorated with lavender, for instance. A limited fusion menu proposes aromatic soups, sandwiches and a good-value bento box. The summertime patio, situated between small front and back dining rooms, is a quiet retreat from the bustling West Queen West neighbourhood, a trendy shopping destination. Upstairs is a small shop selling fine Asian tableware and linens.

Sugar

942 Queen Street W, at Ossington Avenue (416 532 5088). Streetcar 501. **Open** 6-10pm Wed-Fri; 10am-3pm, 6-10pm Sat; 10am-3pm Sun. **Main courses** $9-$23. **Credit** MC, V. **Map** p270 B7 **74**.
With its simple menu, cheery room and friendly vibe, Sugar is a popular spot for brunch on trendy West Queen West. All generations feel at home here, from young journalists to yuppie families. The atmosphere is conducive to lingering, and diners sit at communal tables. Typical brunch fare includes lemony eggs Benedict, french toast and generous bowls of granola. Fresh orange juice and strong coffee take the edge off a hangover (though the view of the local mental does not inspire). There is also a dinner menu.

Continental

Chiado

864 College Street, at Ossington Avenue, Little Italy (416 538 1910/www.chiadorestaurant.ca). Streetcar 506, 511. **Open** 11am-4pm, 5-10pm Mon-Fri; 5-10pm Sat. **Main courses** $25-$35. **Credit** AmEx, DC, MC, V.
Some people forget that College Street is as Iberian as it is Italian. And this elegant, formal restaurant is devoted exclusively to Portuguese cuisine. The modern rooms carry some traditions from the old country: family parties, girls in frilly dresses and awkward boys in their suits. But the traditionalists eat alongside trendy young couples and business-men. They all come for one thing: the fish, which is flown in fresh most days of the week (including marinated sardines, octopus salad, giant shrimp). Side orders of vegetables are done to perfection. If you are not a seafood eater, choose from farm-raised capon and organic chicken. The wine list, purported to be the biggest collection of Portuguese grapes on the continent, has something for everyone (madeira and port are a forte). The bar next door has a more relaxed vibe.

Gamelle

468 College Street, at Markham Street, Little Italy (416 923 6254/www.gamelle.com). Streetcar 506, 511. **Open** 6-11pm Mon, Sat; noon-2.30pm, 6-11pm Tue-Fri. **Main courses** $22-$30. **Credit** AmEx, DC, MC, V. **Map** p270 C5 **75**.
Just up the street from Little Italy's collection of middling eateries and fleeting darlings is this charming Mediterranean bistro. Owner Jean-Pierre Centeno has seen the mercurial nature of Toronto's restaurant scene over his long career. So he opened Gamelle (over a decade ago) with an eye to keeping it small and consistent. The plan has worked: the warm room encourages leisurely dining, and you can see and smell your carefully crafted dishes as they are prepared in the tiny open kitchen. In the back, the leafy patio is a summertime haven.

Niagara Street Café

169 Niagara Street, at King Street, Little Italy (416 703 4222/www.niagarastreetcafe.com). Streetcar 504, 511. **Open** 6-10pm Wed-Thur; 6-10.30pm Fri , Sat; 10.30am-3pm, 6-10pm Sun. **Main courses** $18-$20. **Credit** AmEx, DC, MC, V. **Map** p270 C8 **76**.
In the past, calling a restaurant organic was about as tantalising as advertising trans fats. And so it was that this romantic little boîte ran into tough times under previous management. But Anton Potvin knows better: while he sticks to a clean course of ethical foods, he and chef Michael Caballo focus on taste. So you can have your hangar steak and eat it too – guilt-free. Wild-caught fish and rare-breed piggies round out the simple but inventive menus. Owing to reasonable prices, lack of pretension and a deliciously eclectic wine list, the word is out (reservations are suggested; brunch fills up fast). Watch for the opening of an upstairs bar.

Fish & chips

Chippy's

893 Queen Street W, at Strachan Avenue (416 866 7474). Streetcar 501. **Open** 11.30am-8pm Mon-Wed, Sun; 11.30am-9pm Thur-Sat. **Main courses** $8-$10. **No credit cards. Map** p270 B7 ❼.

The blaring Led Zeppelin soundtrack keeps the cooks happy – and the customer reaps the rewards, because Chippy's takeaway fish and chips is one of the city's finest. Working with top-grade vegetable oil, halibut, cod and haddock and a stout-spiked batter, the two-person team fries to order. Potatoes are hand-cut and double-fried, which means crispy and light on the grease. The garlic mayo is delicious, but the tartare is dull. Don't stray too far from the mainstream: deep-fried salmon is oily. Opposite Trinity Bellwoods Park, this is a great place for picnic fixings.

Other locations: 490 Bloor Street W, at Bathurst Street, the Annex (416 516 7776).

Fusion

Mildred Pierce

99 Sudbury Street, at Lisgar Street (416 588 5695/www.mildredpierce.com). Streetcar 501, 504. **Open** noon-2pm, 5.30-10pm Mon-Thur; noon-2pm, 5.30-11pm Fri; 11am-3pm, 5.30-11pm Sat; 10am-3pm, 5.30-10pm Sun. **Main courses** $17-$26. **Credit** AmEx, DC, MC, V. **Map** p270 A7 ❼.

This Indian-Mediterranean fusion restaurant has survived countless trends and changed little – nor should it. The namesake is the Joan Crawford classic film noir, and drama is embraced here: rich textiles drape down from high ceilings like something out of a romantic movie. Favourites include sweet-and-spicy roast chicken and roast rack of lamb, as well as some tasty vegetarian dishes. Some items and cocktails are named after movie characters – be prepared to have fun. Mildred Pierce is a stone's throw from the Queen West strip west of Bathurst, but hidden away, so check your map before setting off.

Xacutti

503 College Street, at Palmerston Boulevard (416 323 3957/www.xacutti.com). Streetcar 506, 511. **Open** 6.30pm-1am Mon-Thur; 6.30pm-2am Fri, Sat; 10.30am-4pm Sun. **Main courses** $19-$37. **Credit** AmEx, DC, MC, V. **Map** p270 C5 ❼.

Pretty Xacutti ('sha-koo-tee') is named after a spicy curry from India's west coast, but this chic spot is by no means a traditional Indian. Both the dining room and Bird (*see p140*), the romantic bar upstairs, are bustling with Toronto's young and beautiful crowd. It's easy to be distracted by the glamour (orders are taken on Palm Pilots by sleek waiters) but the contemporary Indian-Western fusion is surprisingly inventive and seductive (as in cinnamon-scented pork ribs with guava and lobster in a star-anise champagne butter). Sunday brunch is no less cheeky: try the macadamia-nut pancakes topped with whipped banana butter.

Italian

Bar One

924 Queen Street W, at Shaw Street (416 535 1655). Streetcar 501. **Open** 11.30am-4pm, 5-11pm Tue-Fri; 9am-4pm, 5-11pm Sat; 9am-4pm Sun. **Main courses** $5-$28. **Credit** AmEx, DC, MC, V. **Map** p270 B7 ❽.

Now that they've made their mark on Little Italy with Bar Italia (582 College St, 416-535 3621), the Barone family are working on Queen West. This place is more intimate than its College cousin, with communal seating at the marble-topped counter and curved-wood booths. Dinners range from squash-stuffed ravioli to fillet of salmon. The back patio is a delight; come for brunch, as evenings are busier.

Terroni

720 Queen Street W, at Claremont Street (416 504 0320/www.terroni.ca). Streetcar 501. **Open** 9am-10pm Mon-Wed, Sun; 9am-11pm Thur-Sat. **Main courses** $8-$13. **Credit** V. **Map** p270 C7 ❽.

Despite its pejorative name, Terroni (Italian for 'bloody southerners') manages to attract countrymen in their droves. In fact, waiting for a table (and wait you will at peak times) is a lesson in dialect. The most popular offerings are the pizzas, 23 old-school configurations that average $10 but could feed two and leave scant room for the fine antipasti, good pastas and famed *cannoli*. Conspicuously absent from Little Italy, Terroni nevertheless occupies similarly fashionable ground in its other locations. **Photo** *p126*.

Other locations: 1 Balmoral Avenue (416 925 4020); 106 Victoria Street, Dundas Square (416 955 0258).

Trattoria Giancarlo

41 Clinton Street, at College Street, Little Italy (416 533 9619). Streetcar 506, 511. **Open** 6-11pm Mon-Sat. **Main courses** $20-$25. **Credit** AmEx, DC, MC, V. **Map** p270 C5 ❾.

Under leafy branches, the summertime patio more than doubles the size of this Italian neighbourhood restaurant. Regulars return time after time for lemon-cream pasta, shrimp in delicate broth and a tender veal chop big enough for two. Giancarlo sometimes gets too comfortable with its success, but the kitchen always pulls its socks up. Local ingredients are sourced from some of the area's finest, small farms. The show-off wine list carries some stand-outs; house wines are cheaper.

Japanese

Sushi Kaji

860 The Queensway, at Plastics Avenue (416 252 2166). Bus 123. **Open** 6-9pm Wed-Sun. **Set menus** $85-$120. **Credit** AmEx, MC, V.

It's a schlep to the Queensway, an extension of King Street that heads westwards into the suburbs. But enough locals are raving about Sushi Kaji that it's worth alerting intrepid foodies. Still something of a secret, Kaji may yet have space at the intimate eight-seat sushi bar for your party. There you'll watch masters at work slicing seafood in wonderful ways. There are also plenty of vegetarian options and a couple of choices for meat-and-potato types.

Korean

San Korean Restaurant

676 Queen Street W, at Euclid Avenue (416 214 9429/www.sankoreanrestaurant.com). Streetcar 501, 511. **Open** 11.30am-4pm, 5-10pm Tue, Wed; 11.30am-4pm, 5-10.30pm Thur, Fri; noon-4pm, 5-10.30pm Sat; 5-10pm Sun. **Main courses** $12-$17. **Credit** AmEx, DC, MC, V. **Map** p270 C7 ❸

You don't normally find this kind of thing outside Little Korea, but San serves fine Korean fare on Queen West, packing in customers nightly and spitting them out satisfied every time. You'll spot the similarities with Japanese food in the bento boxes, stuffed with dumplings, tempura, tuna rolls and teriyaki. But San also does shredded beef and barbecued ribs with distinctly Korean flavours. Linger over beer, wine and complimentary tea.

Latin American

Caju

922 Queen Street W, at Shaw Street (416 532 2550/www.caju.ca). Streetcar 501, 511. **Open** 11.30am-2.30pm, 5.30-11pm Tue-Fri; 5.30-11pm Sat. **Main courses** $14-$28. **Credit** AmEx, MC, V. **Map** p270 B7 ❹.

Every Saturday evening, to the beat of the bossa nova, this Brazilian fusion restaurant goes native and serves feijoada, the nation's signature dish, a stew of pork, black beans and collard greens. To whet your appetite, sip a Caipirinha and sample *pao de queijo*, puffy popovers made with cassava flour. Other dishes unite Caribbean and Portuguese influences, while desserts draw on exotic fruits.

Julie's Cuban Restaurant

202 Dovercourt Road, at Foxley Street (416 532 7397). Streetcar 505. **Open** 5.30-11pm Tue-Sat. **Main courses** $13-$20. **Credit** DC, MC, V. **Map** p270 A6 ❺.

A well-kept secret, owing to its remote location, Julie's has a devoted following. If you can't squeeze on to the patio, sit at one of the old kitchen tables indoors. Cuba is not usually known for its culinary flair, but Julie's fried green plantains and corn fritters always please. Otherwise, expect traditional Cuban rice dishes, fried with pork, chicken or beef.

North American

Czehoski

678 Queen Street W, at Strachan Avenue (416 366 6787). Streetcar 501. **Open** noon-2am Mon-Fri; 11am-2am Sat, Sun. **Main courses** $9-$17. **Credit** AmEx, DC, MC, V. **Map** p270 C6 ❻.

This hip and friendly restaurant and bar has a knack for transforming staid ideas into clever creations. Take the setting: formerly a historic butcher shop (thus the tongue-twisting name, pronounced *cha-haw-ski*), it has been reworked with a groovy design (though they've kept the old sign out front). On the menu, consider the Mediterranean Diet, an all-veggie antipasti platter. Or the Canadian diet: mac and cheese. The Bourgeois Burger, also listed as the city's 'most ridiculous burger,' is an exercise in excess – and with a price tag to match ($36.75). This playful theme runs throughout the three-storey venue. Upstairs, an open room pulses with live DJs and cocktail-tipplers. The formula is a hit: across the street is the offshoot Coca, where the Spanish flavour of the tapas menus is reflected in saffron-leather banquettes and olive-coloured chairs. **Other locations**: 783 Queen Street W, at Manning Avenue, Queen West (416 703 0783).

Drake Hotel

1150 Queen Street W, at Beaconsfield Avenue (416 531 5042/www.thedrakehotel.ca). Streetcar 501. **Open** 11am-2.30pm, 6-11pm Mon-Sat; 10.30am-2.30pm, 6-11pm Sun. **Main courses** $16-$36. **Credit** AmEx, DC, MC, V. **Map** p270 A7 ❼.

The menu items are as varied as the places to eat at this multi-purpose hotspot. There's the sidewalk café, lunch and evening lounges, a sushi bar, a dining room, a couple more bars, a terrace and, if all else fails, room service. The Drake's globe-trotting menus range from yummy tuna sandwiches to funky veggie cassoulet to a way-out combo of braised lamb with mint and chocolate. The Drake is surprisingly low on the attitude barometer and high on value. Sometimes the relaxed approach can mean impossibly slow or inept service – chalk it up to the Drake's boho groove. *See also p52, p270.*

Oyster Boy

872 Queen Street W, at Strachan Avenue (416 534 3432). Streetcar 501. **Open** 5-10pm Mon-Wed; 5-11pm Thur-Sun. **Main courses** $11-$17. **Credit** AmEx, DC, MC, V. **Map** p270 B7 ❽.

This narrow hideaway in the heart of West Queen West supplies superior seafood in a friendly retro bar. The menu has few surprises, and not many options for those averse to crustaceans, but Oyster Boy is a great place to slurp your Malpeques, and the warm atmosphere will tempt you to linger longer. Fine brews take the lead over wines.

Phil's Original BBQ

838 College Street, at Ossington Avenue, Little Italy (416 532 8161). Bus 63/streetcar 506. **Open** 5-9pm Mon-Thur; 5-10pm Fri, Sat. **Main courses** $11-$19. **Credit** MC, V. .

The division between Little Italy and Little Portugal is nebulous. But Phil's (formerly Dipamo's Barbeque) clearly occupies the latter. Though the plattered chicken and ribs reference the American South, the experience aligns itself with the *churrasquerías* of neighbouring Ossington, Dovercourt and Dundas. The dining room is no-frills, but the cool jazz soundtrack is a nice touch. Dishes burst with flavour, particularly the beef brisket, stewed in its own juices and served with barbecued beans.

Southern Accent

595 Markham Street, at Bloor Street W (416 536 3211/www.southernaccent.com). Streetcar 511/subway Bathurst. **Open** 5.30pm-1am Tue-Sun. **Main courses** $14-$29. **Set menus** $25. **Credit** AmEx, DC, MC, V **Map** p274 D4 ⓭.

Tucked in behind Honest Ed's, not far from the Annex, Southern Accent is a quirky gem. It would be right at home down in the Bayou, with its eccentric decoration, colourful staff and resident fortune-teller. Offerings are not for the faint-hearted: blackened livers and spicy sausage will set your tongue on fire. Side orders include fried green tomatoes and crunchy calamares. The bar does a superb bourbon sour.

South-east Asian

Kei

936 Queen Street W, at Shaw Street (416 534 7449). Streetcar 501. **Open** 6-10pm Mon-Thur; 6-11pm Fri, Sat. **Main courses** $15-$23. **Credit** AmEx, DC, MC, V. **Map** p270 B7 ⓮.

Subtle Malaysian flavours dominate this restaurant's compact menu of silken miso soups, good *gado-gado*, light-as-air curry puffs and satisfying main dishes. The singular dessert, in keeping with the minimalist vibe, is a fragrant fried-banana tapioca. A casual, intimate spot, Kei attracts savvy locals for a casual supper or an affordable romantic evening. Unselfconsciously cool, it often turns into more of a hangout as the night wears on, and Kei, the owner, cranks the world beat tunes.

Lalot

200 Bathurst Street, at Queen Street (416 703 8222). Streetcar 501. **Open** 6-10pm Mon-Thur; 6-11pm Fri, Sat. **Main courses** $15-$23. **Credit** AmEx, DC, MC, V. **Map** p270 C7 ⓭.

A contrast to its location – the gritty corner of Bathurst and Queen – Lalot is a stylish Vietnamese eaterie, as small and sleek as a Kate Spade bag. After a long day at the drawing board – and before a long night on the dancefloor – upscale neighbourhood thespians and other characters arrive en masse to sup on simple Asian feasts. The catfish caramelised in a clay pot is a knockout. Wines are up to par.

East Toronto

Cafés & coffee houses

Bonjour Brioche

812 Queen Street E, at DeGrassi Street (416 406 1250). Streetcar 501, 504. **Open** 8am-5pm Tue-Fri; 8am-4pm Sat; 8am-3pm Sun. **Main courses** $6-$9. **No credit cards. Map** p273 L7 ⓬.

A beacon in Leslieville, Bonjour Brioche is easily spotted – just look for the queues outside the door.

Even on slushy winter mornings, supporters of this French-style bakery-café huddle on the street outside, dreaming of brioche, buttery croissants and warm baguettes. For brunch, try baked french toast or a croque madame with a bowl of café au lait.

Myth

417 Danforth Avenue, at Arundel Avenue, The Danforth (416 461 8383/www.myth.to). Subway Chester. **Open** 4pm-midnight Mon-Thur; 4pm-2am Fri; noon-2am Sat; noon-midnight Sun. **Main courses** $14-$26. **Credit** AmEx, DC, MC, V.

Brawny east-enders with a penchant for the pool cue hang around for hours drinking beer, while others sip trendy cocktails or dine alfresco. The food is a tasty mix of the Greek Isles (typical of a Danforth joint) and California (read: fish, fish and more fish).

Continental

Provence Délices

12 Amelia Street E, at Parliament Street (416 924 9901/www.provencerestaurant.com). Streetcar 506. **Open** 6-10pm Mon-Fri; 10am-3pm, 6-10pm Sat; 10am-3pm Sun. **Main courses** $19-$26. **Credit** AmEx, DC, MC, V. **Map** p275 J5 ⓭.

Cabbagetown has a dearth of good places to eat, so little wonder this charming slice of Southern France has the neighbourhood *artistes* enthusing about the steak frites and cassoulet. Even the liver and onions is delicious. Set in a restored cottage, the pretty room encourages the armchair traveller to imagine the same spot, transported to the sunny Med. The warm tarte tatin, pro service and dulcet tones of Gallic chansons help with the voyage.

Fusion

Tomi-Kro

1214 Queen Street E, at Leslie Street (416 463 6677). Streetcar 501. **Open** 6-11pm Tue-Thur; 6pm-midnight Fri, Sat. **Main courses** $18-$26. **Credit** AmEx, DC, MC, V.

This stretch of Queen East used to be considered dull, but the survival of this Mediterranean-Asian fusion bistro suggests that things are looking up. John Coronius, a former partner in Danforth favourite Lolita's Lust, named this (in Greek) 'the little place'. A bold sense of fun greets you at the door: lamps covered in hearts, blaring music and nonsensical declarations on the menu. Thankfully, the food is more serious, but it is not for those with timid palates. Pairings include octopus with saké, duck with kaffir lime leaves, and venison with cocoa.

Greek

Ouzeri

500A Danforth Avenue, at Logan Avenue, The Danforth (416 778 500/www.ouzeri.com). Subway Chester. **Open** 11am-midnight daily. **Main courses** $12-$20. **Credit** AmEx, DC, MC, V.

Something fishy

Go figure. Toronto is hundreds of miles from salt water and situated on the shores of a deeply polluted lake. But its residents wolf down seafood like a ravenous mermaid at a subterranean banquet.

First and foremost, Toronto loves the oyster. Case in point: a year-round supply of wild and cultivated molluscs from both Canadian coasts is served in chowders, stews and on their own at **Bluepoint** (*see p110*), **Oyster Boy** (*see p129*), **Rodney's** (*see p111*) and **Starfish** (*see p119*). But you can also get good oysters across the city in pubs and general restaurants; Oyster Boy supplies dozens of eateries, including neighbourhood diner **Swan** (892 Queen Street W, West End, 416 532 0452).

Beyond the bivalve, there are plenty of other piscivorous options. The eccentric **Joso's** (202 Davenport Road, The Annex, 416 925 1903) serves platters of fish in a decadent dining room; customers peruse the raw selections, pick a jewel and send it back to the kitchen for prep. At Vietnamese **Lalot** (*see p130*), catfish comes caramelised in a clay pot. Caviar – of the Canadian sturgeon variety – appears on the menu at **Jamie Kennedy Gardiner** (*see p118*). Atlantic sardines are expertly grilled at **Cava** (*see p124*) or **Niagara Street Café** (*see p127*) and served raw at **Chiado** (*see p127*). Black cod is a perennial favourite: try it paired with braised oxtail at **Canoe** (*see p113*). The fish and chips at **Penrose** (600 Mount Pleasant Road, Davisville, 416 483 6800) are a favourite of Barbra Streisand, but our vote goes to **Chippy's** (*see p128*). As for sushi, the choices are endless. For a cut above, try **Hiro Sushi** (*see p118*) or **Sushi Kaji** (*see p128*. Note: the **Endangered Fish Alliance** (416-323-952/www.endangeredfishalliance. org) publishes a guide to ethical fish eating.

Budget eaters tend to opt for pseudo-Greek platters of souvlaki, fries and salad at generic eateries throughout Greektown. But if you spend a bit more, you can enjoy the real deal, in a smarter setting: the clean scheme of white with coloured tiles makes a change from the area's usual checked tablecloths. Magnificent dips and oven-warmed pitta are the prelude to a seafood list of Aegean proportions, so pace yourself. Ouzeri is also a popular watering hole, where younger crowds wash down snacks with bottles of Greek wine. Friendly and buzzy.

Pan
516 Danforth Avenue, at Ferrier Avenue, The Danforth (416 466 8158/www.panonthedanforth. com). Subway Pape. **Open** 11.30am-11pm Mon-Thur, Sun; 11.30am-midnight Fri, Sat. **Main courses** $13-$23. **Credit** AmEx, MC, V.
At Pan, fine dining is crossed with southern European warmth. Staff are genuinely glad to see you, and attend to your every whim. The place is hopping weekend nights, and in winter a roaring fireplace adds a note of warmth. Lovers of lamb will

Eat, Drink, Shop

be happy, and mains are superior to most on this resto-heavy strip. Meat and fish platters are generous. Appetisers are conventional.

Indian

Sidhartha

1450 Gerrard Street E, at Coxwell Avenue, Little India (416 465 4095). Bus 22/streetcar 506. **Open** 11am-10.30pm daily. **Main courses** $8-$10. **Credit** MC, V.

Little India offers its fair share of mediocre food. Sidhartha, however, is an appealing and affordable choice. The warm tones and friendly service set the stage. Skip the buffet, though chep, and go à la carte. The bhajie is an airy pastry filled with sautéed onions and the vegetarian biryani with mint and tamarind sauces is recommended, as is the lamb biryani (or any lamb dish). Desserts underwhelm.

Italian

Seven Numbers

307 Danforth Avenue, at Broadview Avenue (416 322 5183/www.sevennumbers.com). Subway Broadview. **Open** 5-11pm Tue-Sat; 5-10pm Sun. **Main courses** $7-$17. **Credit** AmEx, DC, MC, V.

Transplanted from its popular Eglinton West location, this popular family trattoria has won over the east-enders with generous dishes of grilled veggies, pastas and seafood. Rosa Marinuzzi cooks up Old World specialities with a zeal and timing that only an Italian mama could muster. The atmosphere is as lively as the flavours.

Japanese

Akane-ya

2214 Queen Street E, at Fernwood Park Avenue, The Beaches (416 699 0377). Streetcar 501. **Open** 5-10.30pm Mon-Sat; 5-9pm Sun. **Main courses** $15-$20. **Credit** AmEx, DC, MC, V.

Rosy-cheeked and windswept from a day on the boardwalk, you might crave something fresh and fast – and local legend Akane-ya serves both purposes. Sidle up to the sushi bar for the usual fare – which is so fresh you may forget you're not by the sea. A five-course dinner for two can be had for $35.

Lily

786 Broadview Avenue, at Danforth Avenue, The Danforth (416 465 9991). Streetcar 504, 505/subway Broadview. **Open** 5-10pm Mon-Thur; 5-11pm Fri, Sat. **Main courses** $16-$60. **Credit** AmEx, MC, V.

The decor is as close to art deco as Japanese gets – possibly because the venue was formerly a Belgian bistro. There's also artistry in the preparation, from the sushi to the black cod. Every traditional Japanese dish is done with a twist: lime is a favourite, adding a flourish to soups and mains. Ingredients are layered and layered again; the result is delicious.

North American

Allen's

143 Danforth Avenue, at Broadview Avenue, The Danforth (416 463 3086/www.allens.to). Streetcar 504, 505/subway Broadview. **Open** 11.30am-1am Mon-Fri; 11am-1am Sat, Sun. **Main courses** $10-$26. **Credit** AmEx, DC, MC, V.

Toronto has no shortage of Irish pubs; this one's classy, polished-oak Manhattan feel is a nod to New York's famous bar of the same name. Regulars crowd the brass-rail bar, banquettes and, further back, the dining room. The open and cool back patio seats dozens more. The menu is sophisticated, including Kerry lamb and bistro specialities such as Atlantic salmon; the burgers are among the best in town. Draught beers flow; choose from more than a dozen excellent labels, plus dozens more in bottles.

Edward Levesque's Kitchen

1290 Queen Street E, at Alton Avenue (416 465 3600/www.edwardlevesque.ca). Streetcar 501. **Open** 6-10pm Tue; 10am-3pm, 6-10pm Wed-Fri; 9am-3pm, 6-10pm Sat; 9am-3pm Sun. **Main courses** $15-$22. **Credit** AmEx, DC, MC, V.

This casual diner/dining room excels at breakfasts (using mostly organic products) and basic fare like burgers. Depending on your perspective, the menu is puzzling or varied: tandoori chicken, grilled sandwiches, diner standards and hearty salads. Italian dishes are the weakest link; the burgers and breakfasts, the strongest. Good homestyle pies.

Tulip Steak House

1606 Queen Street E, at Coxwell Avenue (416 469 5797/www.tulipsteakhouse.com). Bus 22/streetcar 501. **Open** 8am-11pm Mon-Wed; 8am-midnight Thur; 7am-midnight Fri, Sat; 7am-11pm Sun. **Main courses** $15-$18. **Credit** AmEx, DC, MC, V.

This dowdy diner is just off the beaten track, west of the Beaches – which is probably one reason it hasn't changed in over 50 years. You can dine on scrambled eggs or schnitzel, but the sell-out is the beef: Tulip is a proper steakhouse, without the heavy drapery and white-shirted waiters. Don't leave without sharing one of the giant T-bones, or a brisket. And save room for the rich chocolate cake.

Vietnamese

Mi Mi Restaurant

688 Gerrard Street E, at Broadview Avenue (416 778 5948). Streetcar 504, 506. **Open** 10am-10pm Mon, Tue, Thur, Fri; noon-10pm Wed; 10am-10.30pm Sat, Sun. **Main courses** $5-$15. **No credit cards. Map** p273 K6.

There are only a few good Vietnamese joints in Toronto, and Mi Mi is one of the best. With sweet service and cheerful pink walls, this family-run place offers a welcome alternative to the Chinatown standards. Better yet, they excel here in barbecued meats and shrimp as well as rice and noodle dishes and pho soups. Don't miss the rice rolls.

Bars

From grungy dives to luxe lounges, Toronto swills and thrills.

When planning a night on the tiles, you won't need to splash out on taxis. Most districts have enough variety to keep the drinker occupied until the wee hours, so you can choose one area and stick to it. The section of College Street that runs through Little Italy is crammed with more cocktail and wine bars than you can shake a swizzle stick at. The whole area positively glows with the warm light of candles, and patios abound. Indeed, many rate Little Italy as Toronto's best drinking region, but other strips, such as West Queen West, the student-powered Annex and St Lawrence, are coming on strong. New boozing destinations include the area around Dundas West and Ossington, characterised by low-key bars such as **Dakota Tavern** and **Crooked Star**, and, further west (and south), Parkdale, whose gentrification continues apace, with trendy but cosy hipster bars sprouting every which way. Old reliable areas include the swanky Yorkville and the Entertainment District, which is crowded with mainstream bars and clubs. Thankfully, most

bars eschew cover charges, obnoxious doormen and dress codes (any exceptions are noted below). Toronto comes up short in the brew-pub department largely due to restrictive provincial liquor laws but the handful that are here make suds worth seeking out (*see p137* **Brewhaha**), and nowadays even run-of-the-mill pubs often have a good selection of imported beers on tap.

Toronto is also near the Niagara wine region (*see p235*), and many bars carry a good selection of Ontario vintages. Niagara has an ideal climate for icewine – an extremely sweet dessert wine made from grapes that have been left on the vine to freeze in winter. A glass of icewine from the Strewn or Peller wineries is a pricey but delicious local treat. And don't overlook the rieslings, pinots and baco noirs.

For information on buying alcohol from stores, *see p156*. For bars that also double as music venues, *see p202*.

The best Bars

For a drink with a view
Canoe Bar & Restaurant (*see p111*); Panorama Restaurant & Lounge (*see p136*); Roof Lounge (*see p139*).

For patio drinking
Allen's (*see p131*); Black Bull Tavern (*see p133*); Café Diplomatico (*see p125*); Drake Hotel (*see p140*); Hemingway's (*see p139*); Rivoli (*see p134*).

For decadent lounging
Foundation Room (*see p139*).

For decent pub grub
Irish Embassy Pub & Grill (*see p139*); Rebel House (*see p139*).

To preen and be seen
Bird (*see p140*).

For film noir ambience
Laurentian Room (*see p137*); Paddock (*see p134*).

Entertainment District

Banu
777 Queen Street W, at Euclid Avenue (416 777 2268). Streetcar 501. **Open** noon-10pm Tue, Wed; noon-11pm Thur; noon-1am Fri- Sun. **Credit** AmEx, MC, V. **Map** p270 C7 ❶
When Iranians partied under the shah, this is what a cool Tehranian bar looked like (the bar is subtitled Iranian Kabob Vodka Bar). Transplanted to the 21st century, it still looks hip, with mod sectionals and beige vinyl booths set against tables tiled in turquoise ceramics. Mid-East downtempo beats keep the groove going while hipsters and Iranians scoff lamb testicles between vodka shots.

Black Bull Tavern
298 Queen Street W, at Soho Street (416 593 2766). Streetcar 501, 510. **Open** noon-2am daily. **Credit** MC, V. **Map** p271 E7 ❷
This British-style pub has one of the largest and best patios in the city: thanks to a parking lot across the street, it gets plenty of afternoon sunshine. The Bull used to be a serious biker bar (in summer you'll still see rows of hogs parked outside), but these days it's more popular with the regular Queen Street crowd. Grab a pint on the patio and watch the world go by.

> ❶ Pink numbers given in this chapter correspond to the location of each bar on the street maps. *See pp265-275.*

Cameron House

408 Queen Street W, at Cameron Street (416 703 0811/www.thecameron.com). Streetcar 501, 510. **Open** *4pm-2.30am daily.* **Credit** V. **Map** p271 D7 ❸

Old-cool and new-school Queen Street mix in this dark, friendly bar. Artists and musicians haunt the former flophouse, gaining inspiration from the faded ceiling murals, cheap drinks and free conversation. Indie bands perform weekly, and the back room gets booked for art and spoken word happenings.

The Charlotte Room

19 Charlotte Street, at King Street West, Entertainment District (416 598 2882). Streetcar 504. **Open** *3pm-1am Mon-Thur; 3pm-2am Fri; 6pm-2am Sat.* **Credit** AmEx, MC, V. **Map** p271 E8 ❹

The Charlotte Room is a pool hall you could take your mother to. It's smart, clean and well lit – there's even a carpet (and it's not sticky). Sandblasted brick walls and sconce lighting give this downtown bar an uptown feel. No wonder it's popular with an after-work crowd, who come to relax on comfy chairs, sip draught beer (ten on tap) and nosh on nachos ($11), Caesar salads ($8) and pizza ($11). The immaculate tables cost $12 an hour. **Photo** *p136*.

Paddock

178 Bathurst Street, at Queen Street W (416 504 9997/www.thepaddock.ca). Streetcar 501, 511. **Open** *11.30am-2am Mon-Sat; 5pm-1am Sun.* **Credit** AmEx, MC, V. **Map** p270 C7 ❺

Once seedy, the Paddock has gone upscale: it has a beautiful curved bar, dim lights and cool jazz, plus an artsy-media crowd, who come to drink posh cocktails and imported and local beer.

Rivoli

332-334 Queen Street W, at Spadina Avenue (416 596 1908/http://rivoli.ca/2003). Streetcar 501, 510. **Open** *11.30am-1am daily.* **Credit** AmEx, MC, V. **Map** p271 E7 ❻

A classic Queen Street bar, the Rivoli has one of the best patios in the city, a popular restaurant and a long martini bar, which is often crowded with fashionable types. The pool hall upstairs has less attitude, and the back room is one of the city's great music venues. *See also p175, p203.*

Smokeless Joe's

125 John Street, at Richmond Street W (416 591 2221). Streetcar 501, 504/subway St Andrew. **Open** *4pm-2am daily.* **Credit** AmEx, MC, V. **Map** p271 E7 ❼

Dakota. *See p140.*

It's easy to miss this tiny bar, which is overshadowed by the surrounding strip of massive meat-market joints. What makes this hole in the-wall (it holds 28 people) so great is the availability of more than 250 types of beer, many of which are not found anywhere else in Ontario.

Squirly's
807 Queen Street W, at Manning Avenue (416 703 0574). Streetcar 501. **Open** 11am-1am Mon, Sun; 11am-2am Tue-Sat. **Credit** MC, V. **Map** p270 C7 ❽
A favourite student and budget watering hole, with time-worn velveteen armchairs and, in summer, a pleasant, spacious back patio stuffed with mid-century furniture that's seen better days.

Wheat Sheaf Tavern
667 King Street W, at Bathurst Street (416 504 9912). Streetcar 504, 511. **Open** 11am-2am daily. **Credit** AmEx, DC, MC, V. **Map** p270 C8/p271 D8 ❾
Situated at the junction of King Street West and Bathurst Street for over 150 years, the Wheat Sheaf (opened in 1849) proudly and loudly trumpets its status as Toronto's oldest bar. A beer-drinking tradition is palpable, especially in the historic neon signs advertising Molson Canadian, not to mention ye olde giant-screen TV.

Financial District

For **Canoe Restaurant & Bar**, *see p113.*

Library Bar
Fairmont Royal York Hotel, 100 Front Street W, at University Avenue (416 368 2511/www.royal yorkhotel.com). Subway St Andrew or Union. **Open** noon-1am daily. **Credit** AmEx, DC, MC, V. **Map** p271 F8 ❿
The Library Bar – all wood panelling, leather chairs and bookshelves – is a classy, atmospheric retreat, just off the busy lobby of the Fairmont Royal York. It's a particularly cosy place on a cold winter's day; martinis are the tipple of choice all year round.

Pravda Vodka Bar
36 Wellington Street E, at Yonge Street (416 306 2433/www.pravdavodkabar.ca). Streetcar 504/ subway King. **Open** 5.30pm-2am Mon-Sat. **Credit** AmEx, MC, V. **Map** p272 G8 ⓫
Behind a glacial white façade, Russian dolls nestle under the hammer-and-sickle flag and portraits of Lenin. There's a sofa lounge at the back, and premium vodkas are served in shot glasses made of ice, with taster trays for the more adventurous. Caviar and exotic roe feature on the short menu.

Stick people aim for the **Charlotte Room**. *See p134.*

Dundas Square

Imperial Pub & Library Tavern

54 Dundas Street E, at Victoria Street (416 977 4667). Streetcar 505/subway Dundas. **Open** 11am-3am daily. **Credit** AmEx, MC, V. **Map** p272 G6 ⓬

This slice of faded grandeur is not trendy but it's got character. Behind its dull brick exterior, the tavern glows with soft colours, photos of James Dean and paintings of Parisian whores. A large aquarium hangs above the bar – a reminder to drink like a fish.

Chinatown/Kensington Market

Embassy

223 Augusta Avenue, at Baldwin Street (416 591 1132). Streetcar 505, 506, 510. **Open** 3pm-2am daily. **No credit cards. Map** p271 D6 ⓭

This small, hip bar offers a retreat from the Kensington Market crowds, but it too gets jammed at peak times. The decor – brick walls, old sofas – is spartan but cool, as is the indie soundtrack. Boho boozers choose from eight draught beers.

Last Temptation

12 Kensington Avenue, at Dundas Street W (416 599 2551). Streetcar 505, 510. **Open** 11am-2am daily. **Credit** AmEx, MC, V. **Map** p271 D6 ⓮

A shady oasis by day, a beacon of light by night, the Temp is a favourite with Toronto's alternative media people, as well as old-timers who quietly sip their beer and stare into space. The pool table still sees some action from time to time, though the rickety bohemian patio is more popular.

Red Room

444 Spadina Avenue, at College Street (416 929 9964). Streetcar 506, 510. **Open** 11am-2am daily. **No credit cards. Map** p271 D5 ⓯

From the people who brought you the Green Room (*see below*) comes another student-friendly pub. Old-fashioned street lamps light the patio, and inside the

casually hip crowd populates the booths and tables, or slouches on the couches at the back. If you don't feel like boozing, try an avocado milkshake instead.

University/Harbord

Green Room

296 Brunswick Avenue, at Bloor Street W (416 929 3253). Subway Bathurst or Spadina. **Open** 11am-2am daily. **No credit cards. Map** p274 D4 ⓰

The Green Room's back-alley entrance leads into a large space cluttered with mismatched chairs and couches, and wobbly tables. The latter are covered in wax from candles jammed into beer bottles. There's more boho fun upstairs, and in the courtyard. Located in the heart of the Annex, it's popular with the alternative student crowd.

Insomnia

563 Bloor Street W, at Bathurst Street (416 588 3907/www.insomniacafe.com). Streetcar 511/subway Bathurst. **Open** 4pm-2am Mon-Fri; 10am-2am Sat, Sun. **Credit** AmEx, DC, MC, V. **Map** p274 D4 ⓱

Insomnia started out as an internet café, but the only vestiges are one computer and the late opening hours. The lounge is busiest in the winter, when all the neighbourhood patios are closed and the Annex trendies descend. Local DJs play each night between 10pm and 2am. Thursday is cheap martini night, and beer costs less on Mondays.

Panorama Restaurant & Lounge

51st Floor, Manulife Centre, 55 Bloor Street W, at Bay Street (416 967 0000/www.panoramalounge. com). Subway Bay or Bloor. **Open** 5pm-1am daily. **Credit** AmEx, MC, V. **Map** p274 F4 ⓲

At the top of a skyscraper, Panorama lives up to its name, offering expansive views of the city. The crowd is conservative: thirtysomething power-suited power-brokers and their arm candy, catching drinks after a movie, thankful for this quiet, civilised midtown watering hole. The bar is at its best in the summer, when the large rooftop patio is open. A Midtown alternative to Canoe (*see p113*).

Ye Olde Brunswick House

*481 Bloor Street W, at Brunswick Avenue
(416 964 2242). Subway Bathurst or Spadina.*
Open 4pm-2am Thur-Sat. **Credit** AmEx, MC, V.
Map p274 D4 ⑲
The slogan 'party where your parents did' sums up
this century-old collegiate drunk tank, distinguished
by cheap pitchers, queues, betting and live music at
weekends. Behind its historic brownstone façade,
rowdy frat boys in baseball caps embark on
drinking binges, shoot pool or dance with hot chicks
on the sticky dancefloor. Warning: this is not the
place for a quiet drink and conversation, or a first
date. But if you're feeling rowdy, welcome home.

Cabbagetown

Laurentian Room

*51A Winchester Street, at Parliament Street
(416 925 8680/www.thelaurentianroom.com).
Bus 65/streetcar 506.* **Open** 6pm-2am Wed-Sat.
Credit AmEx, MC, V. **Map** p273 J5 ⑳
With its original mahogany floor and lacquered oak
bar, this atmospheric art deco room is a time cap-
sule from the Prohibition era. Al Capone was said to
frequent the joint when in town. He'd love it today:
on most nights, a performer swings over the room
on a hoop that is dangling from the ceiling. There's
a lively burlesque show every Saturday after 11pm.

St Lawrence

C'est What

*67 Front Street E, at Church Street (416 867
9499/www.cestwhat.com). Streetcar 504/subway
King or Union.* **Open** 11.30am-2am daily. **Credit**
AmEx, MC, V. **Map** p272 G8 ㉑
This cosy subterranean bar is a beer drinker's
delight, offering 40 brews on tap, including the
house's own hemp ale and coffee porter. Linger over
backgammon, Scrabble, darts and pool. On
Saturday afternoon, there is live jazz music.

Esplanade Bier Markt

*58 The Esplanade, at Church Street (416 862
7575). Streetcar 504/subway King or Union.*
Open 11am-2am daily. **Credit** AmEx, DC, MC, V.
Map p272 G8 ㉒
This faux-Belgian brasserie has more than 100
brands of beer and lots of space in which to drink
them. On a strip of bars and restaurants that
includes Fionn MacCool's (*see below*), it's a popular
spot for after-work drinking and flirting.

Fionn MacCool's

*70 The Esplanade, at Church Street (416 362
2495/www.fionnmaccoolstoronto.com). Streetcar
504/subway King or Union.* **Open** 11am-1am Mon,
Tue, Sun; 11am-2am Wed-Sat. **Credit** AmEx, MC, V.
Map p272 G8 ㉓

Eat, Drink, Shop

Brewhaha

Not that we're biased, but Canadian beer is
generally stronger and more interesting than
the watery and tasteless stuff found in the
United States. Even so, beer connoisseurs
usually steer clear of the popular, mass-
market brands (anything by Labatt and
Molson). But they don't have to resort to
ordering imports, either. During the past
decade, several local microbreweries have
sprung up, boasting superior varieties that
are big on flavour and depth.

Amsterdam Brewing Co (21 Bathurst
Street, at Lakeshore Boulevard W, 416
504 6882) produces a couple of stalwarts
(Natural Blonde and Nut Brown) that are
found on tap in pubs across the city, as well
as at branches of the Beer Store (*see p157*).
On site, try the Framboise (raspberry), the
stronger Avalanche, or any of the seasonal
specialities. Brewery tours are conducted
daily at 5pm (on Sundays at 1.30pm) and
include eight beer samples for $6.

Uptown, the **Granite Brewery** (*see p140*)
makes a select batch of bitters, ales and
stouts, available only on the premises.
Beer lovers make the trek for the Best Bitter

Special, Traditional IPA, stout, and Peculiar, a
dark ale. If brewmaster Ron Keefe is around,
he's happy to talk shop.

On the atmospheric cobblestone streets
of the Distillery District, look out for the
Mill Street Brewery (Building 63, 55 Mill
Street, 416 681 0338). The organic brew
(pesticide- and insecticide-free) is crafted in
large copper vats, then poured into delicate
little bottles. The Tankhouse Ale is a fragrant
fine ale with zesty malt; Coffee Porter is
deep, with mocha undertones; and Belgian
Wit is a wheat beer made with coriander
and orange peel. There's a new on-site pub
as well as a shop that pours free samples.

Housed in the historic John Street
Roundhouse, a former repair shop for
steam trains, the **Steam Whistle** (*see p64*)
has a vintage Canadian setting. Staff even
make deliveries in period trucks decorated
with retro graphics. The brewery makes just
one elixir: a humble and now ubiquitous
pilsner. Tours are available, and there are
exhibitions by local artists. Knock back a few
brews and give yourself some Dutch courage
for the CN Tower (*see p63*) next door.

LOUNGE
CORE
FREE @ 7PM
TAG TEAM
TUESDAY
FREE @ 10PM

EMERGENCY EXIT UNLOCKED B

Drake Hotel. *See p141.*

It's as if the owners ordered the complete product line from 'The Authentic Irish Pub Catalogue' – Guinness posters, a snug, plenty of dark wood, and corned beef and cabbage on the menu. Live Irish music ranges from U2 covers to a traditional reels.

Foundation Room

119 Church Street, at Front Street E (416 364 8368/www.foundationroom.ca). Subway King, Union. **Open** 5pm-2am Mon-Fri; 6pm-2am Sat, Sun. **Credit** AmEx MC V. **Map** p272 G8 ㉔

Taking its cue from the Moroccan casbah, this subterranean dine-and-dance cave is awash in warm hues, pillow-lined banquettes and Buddha Bar muzak. Thirtysomethings unwind and sip pomegranate martinis; a North African-inspired tapas menu may induce impromptu bellydancing.

Irish Embassy Pub & Grill

49 Yonge Street, at Wellington Street (416 866 8282/www.irishembassypub.com). Streetcar 504/subway King or Union. **Open** 11.30am-2am Mon-Fri; 11am-2am Sat, Sun. **Credit** AmEx, MC, V. **Map** p272 G8 ㉕

This historic British colonial building, dating from 1873, was the first merchant bank in Toronto. Now an upscale Irish pub, it has retained its original vaulted ceiling and marble columns. At lunchtime, stockbrokers and corporate lawyers come here to consume Guinness and Irish stew.

Laide

138 Adelaide Street E, at Jarvis Street (416 850 2726/www.laide.ca). Streetcar 501 or 504. **Open** 5pm-2am Tue-Fri; 7pm-2am Sat. **Credit** MC V. **Map** p272 G7 ㉖

Feeling frisky? The nude sculptures and grainy old soft-core playing above the bar should get you in the mood. The dark, candlelit lounge is not first-date material, but it's a good rendezvous for secret lovers.

Yorkville

Hemingway's

142 Cumberland Street, at Bay Street (416 968 2828/www.hemingways.to). Bus 6/subway Bay. **Open** 11am-2am daily. **Credit** AmEx, MC, V. **Map** p274 F4 ㉗

New Zealander Martin McSkimming opened this friendly restaurant and bar in 1980, and you'll still find him hanging around chatting with the regulars. The rooftop patio is open year-round (it's enclosed in the winter), and there's live music at weekends.

Lobby Bar

Four Seasons Hotel, 21 Avenue Road, at Cumberland Street (416 928 7332/www.four seasons.com/toronto). Subway Bay or Museum. **Open** 3-8pm daily. **Credit** AmEx, DC, MC, V. **Map** p274 F4 ㉘

To see and be seen: that's the raison d'être of this Four Seasons bar, which offers a front-row seat for watching A-list comings and goings. Though known for its high tea, they also pour a good stiff

one. You can also quaff a gorgeous martini, the speciality of the Avenue Bar across the lobby. Move to the latter after this bar closes (at 8pm), and watch the street from a leather club chair. **Photo** *p141*.

Roof Lounge

18th Floor, Park Hyatt Hotel, 4 Avenue Road, at Bloor Street W (416 324 1568/www.parktoronto. hyatt.com). Subway Bay or Museum. **Open** noon-1am daily. **Credit** AmEx, MC, V. **Map** p274 F4 ㉙

A mere 18 storeys off the ground, this is by no means the loftiest bar in the city. But it is possibly the nicest of Toronto's high-altitude drinking establishments, with a large fireplace, leather-lined bar and deep-green marble tables. In summer, the terrace is crowded with patrons enjoying the view of the University of Toronto and the skyscrapers beyond.

The Annex

Bedford Academy

36 Prince Arthur Avenue, at Bedford Road (416 921 4600). Subway St George. **Open** 11am-2am daily. **Credit** AmEx, MC, V. **Map** p274 E4 ㉚

This old townhouse is one of the more civilised drinking establishments in the Annex. The bar gets plenty of the university trade in the shape of graduate students sipping local Steam Whistle brew. In addition to a good range of beers on tap and generous martini portions, the Academy also offers a better-than-average pub menu.

Duke of York

39 Prince Arthur Avenue, at Bedford Road (416 964 2441/www.thedukepubs.ca). Subway St George. **Open** 11am-2am daily. **Credit** AmEx, MC, V. **Map** p274 E4 ㉛

Tartan carpet covers one big room after another at this British-style pub. The Duke's quiet vibe attracts teachers and students alike; Thursday's beer-tasting sessions are popular with everyone.

Madison Avenue Pub

14 Madison Avenue, at Bloor Street W (416 927 1722/www.madisonavenuepub.com). Streetcar 510/subway Spadina. **Open** 11am-2am daily. **Credit** AmEx, MC, V. **Map** p274 F4 ㉜

The Frankenstein's monster of the frat scene, the Maddy is made up of three Victorian mansions grafted together into five patios, six rooms (each of which holds about 200 people), 137 beer taps, a kitchen, a Scotch bar and, inevitably, a merchandise stand. Like Mary Shelley's creation, this beast isn't quite as scary as it at first seems, and you can enjoy a drink and a meal in relative peace.

Rosedale

Rebel House

1068 Yonge Street, at Roxborough Street (416 927 0704/www.rebelhouse.ca). Subway Rosedale. **Open** 11.30am-2am Mon-Fri; 10.30am-2am Sat, Sun. **Credit** AmEx, MC, V. **Map** p275 G2 ㉝

Eat, Drink, Shop

This smart pub has a beer garden patio in the back, with 17 local brews on tap. Hearty pub grub (try the buffalo burger) and easy access from the Rosedale subway station make it a popular destination.

Davisville

Bow and Arrow
1954 Yonge Street, at Davisville Avenue (416 487 2036/www.arrowpub.com) Subway Davisville. **Open** 11am-1am Mon-Wed, Sun; 11am-2am Thur-Sat. **Credit** AmEx MC V

The half-timbered front suggests Ye Olde England, and inside, homesick Brits and Anglophiles gather for the real ale (including 27 locally made microbrews). Try the Arkell Best Bitter from Wellington County Brewery or the Durham Triple X IPA. Pub fare and satellite footie keep the expats happy.

Granite Brewery
245 Eglinton Avenue E, at Mount Pleasant Road (416 322 0723/www.granitebrewery.ca). Bus 54/ subway Eglinton. **Open** 11.30am-1am Mon-Sat; 11am-1am Sun. **Credit** AmEx, MC, V

Beer aficionados travel great distances for a taste of Peculiar, the strongest of the Granite's bold, own-brewed ales. They also come to nosh on beer-infused dishes. You can also buy their beer to take home.

West End

Beaconsfield
1154 Queen Street W, at Beaconsfield Avenue (416 516 2550). Streetcar 501. **Open** 5pm-2am daily. **Credit** MC, V. **Map** p270 A7 ❸❹

The chandeliers glow and reflect in the stainless-steel bar of the Beaconsfield, which is within staggering distance of the Drake (*see below*). Housed in a former bank building, it's a lovely restoration, with a menu of comfort food and a few beers on tap.

Bird
2nd Floor, 503 College Street, at Palmerston Blvd, Little Italy (416 323 3957). Streetcar 506/subway Queens Park then 15 min walk. **Open** 8pm-2am Wed-Sat. **Credit** AmEx, MC, V. **Map** p270 C5 ❸❺

Above the trendy Xacutti restaurant (*see p127*), this romantic bar attracts a chic crowd, who can be found lounging around and sipping pricey cocktails.

Cadillac Lounge
1296 Queen Street W, at Brock Avenue (416 536 7717/www.cadillaclounge.com). Streetcar 501. **Open** 11am-2am daily. **Credit** MC, V.

Denim-clad drinkers down bourbon and listen to country music in this appealingly shabby bar. There's a band playing most Saturday nights, and a honky-tonk Sunday matinée. *See also p202.*

Chelsea Room
923 Dundas Street W, at Grace Street (416 364 0553/www.canteena.ca). Streetcar 505. **Open** 7pm-2am daily. **Credit** AmEx, MC, V. **Map** p270 C6 ❸❻

Dundas West has a few quietly hip bars, and Chelsea Room is a gem. You could easily miss this gently lit space, but it's worth seeking out for its (tiny) patio, brightly tiled martini bar and comfy banquettes. It's friendly and offers locally brewed beers.

Cocktail Molotov
928 Dundas Street W, at Grace Street (416 603 6691). Streetcar 505. **Open** 5.30pm-2am daily. **No credit cards. Map** p270 C6 ❸❼

With oak panelling, repro Eames stools and no attitude, this simple bar is the essence of the city's laid-back cool, with heavy-rock tunes (no bossa nova here), plenty of different beers and elaborate cocktails for the glamour pusses in the group.

College Street Bar
574 College Street, at Manning Avenue, Little Italy (416 533 2417). Streetcar 506, 511. **Open** 5pm-2am daily. **Credit** AmEx, MC, V. **Map** p270 C5 ❸❽

Exposed brick and dark wood set the tone for this old favourite. Less formal than some of its swanky neighbours, it's still a place where the young and fashionable come to see and be seen. The seafood-intensive menu has a good reputation.

Communist's Daughter
1149 Dundas Street W, at Ossington Avenue (647 435 0103). Bus 63/streetcar 505. **Open** 5pm-2am daily. **No credit cards. Map** p270 B6 ❸❾

Tucked away among the area's macho Portuguese soccer bars and Catholic churches, this tiny bustling bar is as unpretentious as its surrounding neighbourhood, but somehow very cool. The retro interior is short on fancy decor but big on character, right down to the well-curated jukebox.

Crooked Star
202 Ossington Street, at Dundas Street W (416 536 7271). Streetcar 505. **Open** 3pm-2am Mon-Fri; 2pm-2am Sat, Sun. **Credit** AmEx, MC, V. **Map** p270 B6 ❹⓿

On a burgeoning strip, this comfy lounge attracts a mix of locals and hipsters who are venturing west. Roomy wooden booths invite lounging; the soundtrack is a mix of alternative DJs and the odd acoustic act. During Sunday brunch, episodes of *Coronation Street* are shown to loyal fans.

Dakota Tavern
249 Ossington Avenue, at Dundas Street W (416 850 4579/www.thedakotatavern.com). Streetcar 501. **Open** 5pm-2am Mon-Sat; noon-2am Sun. **No credit cards. Map** p270 B6 ❹❶

Countrified trendiness is the idea at this western-themed watering hole, which features Sunday night barn dances and a bluegrass brunch. Settle into a barrel-shaped bar stool for live music (most nights) and tasty inexpensive grub. **Photos** pp134-135.

Drake Hotel
1150 Queen Street W, at Beaconsfield Avenue (416 531 5042/www.thedrakehotel.ca). Streetcar 501. **Open** 8pm-2am daily. **Credit** AmEx, DC, MC, V. **Map** p270 A7 ❹❷

Chic and sleek: **Lobby Bar**. *See p139.*

This trendy boutique hotel got the buzz going in West Queen West a few years ago, and it's still going strong. There's a Euro-style lounge, sushi bar, café, rooftop patio bar and entertainment space (the Underground), which offers bands, performance art and retro nights. *See also p52 and p202.*

Gladstone Hotel

1214 Queen Street W, at Gladstone Avenue (416 531 4635/www.gladstonehotel.com). Streetcar 501. **Open** 11am-2am daily. **Credit** MC, V. **Map** p270 A7 ㊸
This restored Victorian hotel is ground zero for the indie arts scene. The Melody Bar is a large, wood-panelled room with faux-marble columns and leatherette banquettes. It plays to all tastes, from a gay night (Wednesday) to the city's best karaoke (Thursday to Saturday). On other nights, there are bands and DJs. See also *p52.*

Lot 16

1136 Queen Street W, at Lisgar Street (416 531 6556). Streetcar 501. **Open** 5pm-2am daily. **Credit** MC, V. **Map** p270 A7 ㊹
This low-key bar is literally and figuratively in the shadow of the Drake (*see p140*). The retro light fixtures, simple cocktails and plain decor make a welcome change from its more contrived neighbour.

Press Club

850 Dundas Street W, at Euclid Avenue (416 364 7183). Streetcar 505. **Open** 6pm-2am daily. **No credit cards.** **Map** p270 C6 ㊺
The vintage typewriter in the window may reflect the neighbourhood's gaggle of scribes, but you don't have to be a starving novelist to sidle up to the bar here. Occasional live music and a backyard patio give this neighbourhood hangout a homely feel.

Souz Dal

636 College Street, at Grace Street, Little Italy (416 537 1883). Streetcar 506. **Open** 8pm-2am daily. **Credit** MC, V. **Map** p270 C5 ㊻

This small cocktail bar holds only 50 people (but another 25 can squeeze on to the back patio). It's dark and seductive, with red plush chairs and candlelight reflecting off the copper trim. Down a martini from the long list and you can't help but get a romantic glow, even if you're here on your own.

Sutra

612 College Street, at Clinton Street, Little Italy (416 537 8755). Streetcar 506, 511. **Open** 8pm-2am daily. **Credit** AmEx, MC, V. **Map** p270 C5 ㊼
This long sliver of a room is a great date bar. Order champagne and oysters and take a pew on a cushion cube seats. A heated patio has a Polynesian theme, with bamboo walls and sand underfoot.

Sweaty Betty's

13 Ossington Avenue, at Queen Street West (416 535 6861). Streetcar 501. **Open** 5pm-2am daily. **Credit** AmEx, MC, V. **Map** p270 B7 ㊽
This tiny, two-room dive is indeed sweaty. Its popularity may come from its location: at the cross-roads of Queen West and funky Ossington. DJs spin, and so will the room after some absinthe or tequila.

Wild Indigo

607 College Street, at Clinton Street, Little Italy (416 536 8797). Streetcar 506, 511. **Open** 8pm-2am Tue-Sun. **Credit** MC, V. **Map** p270 C5 ㊾
In the tranquil backyard patio, a blue-lit Buddha sets the tone for this mellow martini bar. Wild Indigo also has a good range of wines and imported beers.

East Toronto

For **Allen's** pub, *see p131.*

Dora Keogh Traditional Irish Pub

141 Danforth Avenue, at Broadview Avenue, The Danforth (416 778 1804/www.allens.to/dora). Streetcar 504, 505/subway Broadview. **Open** 4.30pm-2am daily. **Credit** AmEx, MC, V.
Favoured by locals for a pint of Guinness or a glass of Jameson's, this low-key Irish bar has a handsome wood and copper decor, a fireplace and a snug.

Lion on the Beach

1958 Queen Street E, at Kenilworth Avenue, The Beaches (416 690 1984). Bus 92/streetcar 501. **Open** 11.30am-2am daily. **Credit** AmEx, MC, V.
This casual pub is a Beaches staple, and a popular gathering spot for large groups. There are two quiet patios and top 40 cover bands at the weekend.

Only Café

972 Danforth Avenue, at Donlands Road (416 463 7843/www.theonlycafe.com). **Open** 10am-2am Mon-Fri; 9am-2am Sat, Sun. **Credit** MC, V.
A popular spot for breakfast and brunch, the Only Café lures beer lovers later in the day, boasting more than 120 different bottled varieties. There are occasional acoustic sets and open mic sessions for singer/songwriters. Neighbourhood regular Ron Sexsmith has tried out new tunes on the tiny stage.

Eat, Drink, Shop

Shops & Services

Hey big spenders.

Honest Ed's. *See p145.*

From mega-malls to mini boutiques, Toronto is a shopping town. It's easy to part with your cash here. Discover new tunes in indie record shops or smart titles in niche book stores, try on up-and-coming designers in quirky Canadian boutiques or A-list labels in swanky design houses. While Toronto doesn't claim to be on a par with London, New York or Tokyo as a consumer destination, there is enough to entice – and surprise – seasoned shopaholics .

WHERE TO GO

If it's fashion you're after, the Mink Mile along Bloor Street West in Yorkville (*see also p86*) deals in high-end labels from Gucci to Chanel – with the bargain designer fashion of Winners thrown in for good measure (*see p145*), while the streets to the north (Cumberland Street and Yorkville Avenue) are home to a clutch of lesser-known but equally pricey names. The area of Queen Street West around Spadina Avenue, once an edgy fashion destination, has now achieved high-street status, forcing the adventurous, low-rent boutiques further west on Queen (from Bathurst Street to Ossington). A pocket of Canadian fashion has also emerged on the burgeoning Dundas Street West strip

(*see p155* **Canadian couture**). The vintage hub remains **Kensington Market** (*see p148*), also a centre for food shopping, as is the indoor **St Lawrence Market** (*see p150*).

PRICES AND SALES

Costs depend on where you come from and exchange rates. Canadians find Toronto expensive, but Americans and Brits find their currencies go a long way here.

Expect a 15 per cent goods and service tax on most non-essentials (not included in the prices marked), but there is a visitor refund scheme (*see p253*) that is flexible and easy to use.

Sales are held in summer (July to August) and winter (from 26 December to late January).

One-stop

Department stores

Holt Renfrew

50 Bloor Street W, at Bay Street, Yorkville (416 922 2333/www.holtrenfrew.com). Subway Bay or Bloor-Yonge. **Open** 10am-6pm Mon-Wed, Sat; 10am-8pm Thur, Fri; noon-6pm Sun. **Credit** AmEx, DC, MC, V. **Map** p274 F4.

The epitome of la-di-da, Holt Renfrew is a glittering temple for high-end attire and pampering products. The Canadian retail dynasty, which owns Brown Thomas in Dublin and London's Selfridges, attracts visiting celebs and local gentry, who have been known to send their chauffeurs inside to collect goods while they wait in their limos. There's no need to though: hotel-style suites coddle the stars and keep them from the hoi polloi. Not that they need much protection: hotel-style suites coddle the stars and charge their purchases of Armani, Jimmy Choo or the latest European denim to their platinum cards. Following a facelift, more designers were added to the brimming portfolio, including Juicy Couture, Marc Jacobs, Mercy and others. World Design Lab (for emerging and experimental international fashion) and vintage couture are also here, and, on the ground floor, there's a glossy new fragrance and handbags pavilion for Jo Malone, Susanne Lang, Kate Spade, Lulu Guinness and other top brands. There's more to come: another plush expansion with the promise of more poshness. Holt's also has a concierge on the ground floor to assist in anything from booking flights to getting theatre tickets. **Other locations**: Yorkdale Shopping Centre, 3401 Dufferin Street, at Highway 401, North Toronto (416 789 3261).

Malls

Hazelton Lanes

55 Avenue Road, at Bloor Street, Yorkville (416 968 8680/www.hazeltonlanes.com). Bus 6/subway Bay or Museum. **Open** 10am-6pm Mon-Wed, Fri, Sat; 10am-7pm Thur; noon-5pm Sun. **Credit** varies. **Map** p274 F3/4.

A 1970s eyesore on the outside, a quaint web of courtyards within, Hazelton Lanes was once fashion central for the rich and glamorous, but in recent years it has declined: expect to find more than a few vacant shops. But things are looking up: there's an upscale gym-cum-yoga space and a high-end Whole Foods Market in the basement (celeb spotting in the aisles is now a regular pastime for locals). At Andrew's you'll find well-curated designer sportswear and evening wardrobes for the carriage trade. The trendy TNT offers exclusive LA labels (Teenflo, Theory) for both male and female fashionistas and visiting celebrities; the tranquil Teatro Verde is an upmarket home accessories shop and florist. To provide fuel for flagging shoppers, Lettieri café serves a wicked espresso.

Pacific Mall

4300 Steeles Avenue E, at Kennedy Road, Markham (1-905 470 8785/www.pacificmalltoronto.com). Bus 43, 53. By car: Don Valley Parkway northwards to route 404, take Woodbine Avenue/Steeles Avenue exit, turn right on Steeles. **Open** 11am-8pm Mon-Thur, Sun; 11am-9pm Fri, Sat. **Credit** varies.

A sea-blue monstrosity in an industrial area on Toronto's northern fringes, the Pacific Mall is North America's largest shopping centre selling Asian goods. Indeed, it could take a day to explore this village of toys, togs and treats. On the ground floor, wares are housed in a streetscape of 150 fishbowl-style kiosks. Expect shelf upon shelf of candy-coloured mobile phones, sneakers, T-shirts, school supplies and Hello Kitty products. As a reward for making the trek, goods are offered at discount prices. A second level is devoted to Far Eastern edibles – pastries, dim sum, noodles – and counters of sticky candy, which shoppers consume with gusto.

The best Shops

The Beguiling
An alternative comics and indie culture emporium that goes way beyond superheroes. *See p147.*

Courage My Love
Vintage treasures and second-hand style in a family-run institution. *See p153.*

Dinah's Cupboard
Delicious seasonal foods. Great for picnic fixings. *See p159.*

Georgie Bolesworth
This stylist-turned-retailer has her finger on the pulse of emerging Canadian fashion talent. *See p155* **Canadian couture**.

Honest Ed's
An eccentric discount emporium with a flair for shameless self-promotion. *See p145.*

Lileo
Destination for well-heeled lifestyle gurus. A *de rigueur* stop-off in the Distillery District. *See p151.*

La Paloma Gelateria
A gelato-lover's dream, with a constantly evolving roster of new flavours. *See p160.*

San Remo
Out of the way, yes, but this jewel-box of offbeat and feminine fashion – all Canadian designed – is worth the trip. *See p150.*

Shelly Purdy Studio
When it comes to buying bling, this Canadian diamond specialist caters to every budget. *See p154.*

Soundscapes
The best indie record shop in Toronto. Hard-to-find gems from local and international artists are the name of the game. *See p163.*

Eat, Drink, Shop

Toronto Eaton Centre

220 Yonge Street, at Dundas Street, Dundas Square (416 598 8560/www.torontoeatoncentre.com). Streetcar 501, 505/subway Dundas or Queen. **Open** 10am-9pm Mon-Fri; 9.30am-7pm Sat; noon-6pm Sun. **Credit** varies. **Map** p272 G6.

One of Toronto's top tourist destinations is, ahem, a shopping mall. Long frequented by bargain-hungry Americans spending their super-charged bucks, the mall still draws the crowds despite the surging Canadian dollar. The Eaton name comes from a family dynasty done in by the dinosaur status of their nationwide department store chain in 1999. Though bargain chain Sears picked up the pieces of this flagship store, the Eaton name lives on. The south, or Queen Street, end is anchored by the venerable 400-year-old Hudson's Bay Company. Between these retail titans are hundreds of shops, from mid-range international chains (including H&M and Zara) to more pedestrian, home-grown styles like B2 by Browns designer footwear, kitchenware and lifestyle shops such as Williams-Sonoma and Pottery Barn or trendy cosmetics boutique Sephora. The basics are covered, including books at Indigo, and middling fashions at The Gap and Banana Republic. There is also a low-key food court packed with chain outlets.

Winners: dress for success without losing your shirt. *See p145.*

Yorkdale Shopping Centre

3401 Dufferin Street, at Highway 401, North Toronto (416 789 3261/www.yorkdale.com). Subway or GO Yorkdale. **Open** 10am-9pm Mon-Fri; 9.30am-9pm Sat; 11am-6pm Sun. **Credit** varies.

The first mall in North America, this sprawling neon structure has been expanding since it opened in 1964, leaving no retailer (local or foreign) uninvited. Once a hangout for teens from local working-class neighbourhoods, Yorkdale has scrubbed up, and now houses a Holt Renfrew, Coach, Harry Rosen, Pottery Barn, Aveda, MAC, Foot Locker, HMV and 200 other shops, plus a large cinema, restaurants and professional services, such as valet car parking.

Discount malls

Honest Ed's

581 Bloor Street W, at Bathurst Street, The Annex (416 537 2111). Streetcar 511/subway Bathurst. **Open** 10am-9pm Mon-Fri; 10am-6pm Sat; 11am-6pm Sun. **Credit** AmEx, MC, V. **Map** p274 D4.

For a memorable bout of bargain shopping, don't miss Honest Ed's. It is owned by Ed Mirvish, the 90-something proprietor and theatre impresario who brought London's Old Vic Theatre back to life in the 1980s. And his showmanship shines through: the emporium is decked out in Vegas vaudeville-meets-old school merchandising style, with flashing lights and garish signs. Autographed publicity shots of old West End stars stare out across the heaps of under-garments and rubber boots. The impresario's artier side can be seen around the corner on Markham Street, where Mirvish Village houses artists' studios, galleries and speciality bookstores. **Photo** *p142*.

Winners

110 Bloor Street W (416 920 0193/www.winners.ca). Subway Bay or Bloor-Yonge. **Open** 9am-9pm Mon-Fri; 9.30am-6pm Sat; 11am-6pm Sun. **Credit** AmEx, MC, V. **Map** p274/p275 G5.

Toronto loves this chain of bargain fashions. After ruling in the suburbs – and drawing downtown dwellers out to the sticks for knock-down prices – Winners has arrived in the heart of the city. Drop by for a cheap and cheerful pair of denims to pair with that new rock from Tiffany's jewellers just across the street. Designer dresses, casual sportswear and men's and children's clothing can all be found at hefty discounts. Among 20 locations, another huge shop is at the corner of Yonge and College Streets. **Other locations**: throughout the city. **Photo** *p144*.

Antiques

Butterfield 8

235 Danforth Avenue, at Playter Boulevard, East Toronto (416 406 5664). Subway Broadview or Chester. **Open** 10am-6pm Mon-Wed, Sat; 10am-7pm Thur, Fri; noon-4pm Sun. **Credit** AmEx, MC, V.

The name – and inspiration for the stock – comes from the Liz Taylor melodrama of the '60s. Sure, you can comb the Toronto Antiques Centre (*see below*) or stake out the junk shops on Queen, but you're unlikely to come across the high-quality kitsch you get here. True collectibles can be found in cigarette paraphernalia (enamel cases and lighters) and celebrity-themed jewellery (Bruce Lee cufflinks anyone?), and neo-kitsch appears in the form of cute, brightly coloured carry-alls and home accessories.

Passion for the Past

1646 Queen Street W, at Wilson Park Road, West End (416 535 3883). Streetcar 501, 504. **Open** noon-6pm Tue-Sun. **Credit** V.

A market vibe rules at Passion, where haggling is not frowned upon. The quality Victorian furnishings that once dominated the shop are now scarce – the range of offerings now dates up to the 1960s – but they do exist, and are worth seeking out.

Sticks & Stones Antiques

1854 Queen Street W, at Roncesvalles Avenue, West End (416 699 9611/www.sticksandstonesantiques. com). Streetcar 501, 504. **Open** 10am-6pm Tue-Fri; 10am-5pm Sat, Sun. **Credit** AmEx, DC, MC, V.

As the name suggests, this family-owned business specialises in gems and furnishings. It's a favourite with fashion stylists: it would take a whole day to peruse the vast rows of vintage jewellery. Thankfully, computerisation means that staff know exactly what they have in stock, even if they can't immediately locate it.

Toronto Antiques On King

276 King Street W, at Duncan Street, Entertainment District (416 345 9941/www.torontoantiquecentre. com). Streetcar 510. **Open** 10am-6pm Tue-Sat. **Credit** AmEx, MC, V. **Map** p271 E8.

Toronto does not have too many markets, but this antiques arcade is enough to sate any enthusiast. The usual collections of china, silver and jewellery are worth sifting through if you're a collector. Twentieth-century curios include silk-tasselled lamps from vaudeville days, magazines, old tin advertisements, wedding gowns and gloves. Antique maps and natural-fibre rugs are also sold.

Books, newspapers & magazines

Book City

663 Yonge Street, at Charles Street, Church & Wellesley (416 964 1167). Subway St Clair. **Open** 9.30am-10pm Mon-Sat; 11am-10pm Sun. **Credit** MC (over $25), V. **Map** p275 G1.

Even with five locations citywide, Book City is still the ideal small bookshop. Sophisticated, hard-to-find literary magazines and low-budget Canadian upstarts all feature, and there are few better places to pick up a Sunday *New York Times* (though copies sell quickly). It sells new hardcover books at 10% off the cover price and offers more discounts with a loyalty card. Staff are bright and helpful.

Other locations: 348 Danforth Avenue, at Broadview, East Toronto (416 469 9997); 2350 Bloor Street W, at Jane Street, West End (416 766 9412); 501 Bloor Street W, at Spadina, The Annex (416 961 4496); 1950 Queen Street E, at Woodbine, The Beaches (416 698 1444).

Indigo Books & Music

55 Bloor Street W, at Bay Street, University (416 925 3536/www.chapters.indigo.ca). Bus 6/subway Bay. **Open** 9am-10pm Mon-Wed, Sun; 9am-11pm Thur-Sat. **Credit** AmEx, MC, V. **Map** p274 F4.

The upmarket twin of Chapters, Indigo is the better looking of the two huge book outlets, with a clean colour scheme and snazzy design. Still, rummaging through Indigo is like shopping at IKEA: you're there because you have to be (it has virtually monopolised the market). Still, most locations have a café and this branch is actually a pleasant meeting place. New release fiction is on the main level and the lower level has a CD store and a great selection of travel books. Apart from its huge selection of books and magazines, Indigo's best asset is its book-signing events – celebrity authors often make pitstops for signings or promotions.

Other locations: 2300 Yonge Street, at Eglinton Avenue, North Toronto (416 544 0049); Yorkdale Shopping Centre, 3401 Dufferin Street, at Highway 401, North Toronto (416 781 6660); Toronto Eaton Centre, 220 Yonge Street, at Dundas St, Dundas Square (416 591 3622).

Nicholas Hoare

45 Front Street E, at Church Street, St Lawrence (416 777 2665). Streetcar 504/subway Union. **Open** 10am-6pm Mon-Wed; 10am-8pm Thur, Fri; 9am-6pm Sat; noon-6pm Sun. **Credit** AmEx, MC, V. **Map** p272 G8.

A handsome pastiche of a traditional English bookshop, Nicholas Hoare offers the most intelligent selection in town. The books are stacked right up to the ceilings and accessed by dark oak ladders on brass rails. Classical music streams out from speakers, while an erudite bunch peruse poetry, coffee-table books and new home-grown literature. Skylights illuminate a space that otherwise resembles a well-worn manor study; plush seating is strategically located in front of a stone fireplace that crackles and scents the shop on cold winter days.

Pages

256 Queen Street W, at John Street, Entertainment District (416 598 1447/www.pagesbooks.ca). Streetcar 501/subway Osgoode. **Open** 9.30am-10pm Mon-Fri; 10am-10pm Sat; 11am-8pm Sun. **Credit** AmEx, MC, V. **Map** p271 E7.

A Queen West bookstore with a Queen West sensibility. Its strengths are art tomes, obscure magazines and quirky postcards. Staff are savvy, and likely to be poets or novelists in progress. The cultural agenda is evident at the store's funky (and free) This Is Not a Reading Series, held at the Rivoli (*see p134*).

Nicholas Hoare.

Type

883 Queen Street W, at Gore Vale Road, West End (416 366 8973/www.typebooks.ca). **Open** TBA. **Credit** AmEx, MC, V. **Map** p270 C7.

In an era of big box retailing, it's refreshing to see a quirky independent store claim its own turf. Stocking titles that reflect its West Queen West neighbourhood (design, fashion, urban issues, kids and cutting-edge indie fiction), this new bookstore hosts enough literary events and readings to keep the bookworms coming. Pick up a title and head for a bench in Trinity-Bellwoods Park across the road.

Comics

The Beguiling

601 Markham Street, at Bloor Street, West End (416 533 9168/www.beguiling.com). Streetcar 511/subway Bathurst. **Open** 11am-7pm Mon-Thur, Sat; 11am-9pm Fri; noon-6pm Sun. **Credit** MC, V.

Behind elaborate window displays, the interior is dark and clandestine, the vibe avant-garde and underground. On the main floor, there are graphic novels, mini comics and children's books, plus European comics such as the Tin Tin series. Mainstream comics occupy the upstairs, as well as a growing collection of manga and anime. On the walls, there's a selection of original comic book art by artists like underground legend Kim Deitch, Paul Pope and renowned locals such as Seth and Chester Brown, who call this shop home. Staff are knowledgeable. A local legend in Mirvish village.

The Silver Snail

367 Queen Street W, at Spadina Avenue, Entertainment District (416 593 0889). Streetcar 501, 510. **Open** 10am-6pm Mon, Tue; 10am-8pm Wed-Fri; 10am-7pm Sat; noon-6pm Sun. **Credit** AmEx, MC, V. **Map** p271 D7.

Situated on the cool Queen West shopping strip, the Silver Snail is an atypically smart comic book store, with modern decor and high ceilings on two floors. Staff are suitably opinionated; stockwise, it's small-press reads, mainstream comics and graphic novels, manga and Japanese toys (including figurines and action figures for adults as much as kids), and the requisite back issues for collectors.

Speciality books

The quaint thoroughfare of Harbord Street has is a used-book haven, owing to its proximity to the University of Toronto. The highest concentration of booksellers runs west from Spadina Avenue. Specialists in texts and academic (**Atticus Books**, 84 Harbord Street, 416 922 6045, www.atticus-books.com; **Caversham Booksellers**, 98 Harbord Street, 416 944 0962, www.cavershambooksellers.com) and women's studies (**Toronto Women's Bookstore**, 73 Harbord Street, 416 922 8744, www.womensbookstore.com) can be found

among the stores selling new books. Billed as Canada's largest used book store, **BMV** (471 Bloor Street West, 416 967 5757), a few blocks north, keeps customers browsing under the fluorescent lights late into the night. A little further west on Markham Street in Mirvish Village, you'll find tiny **Ballenford Books on Architecture** (600 Markham Street, 416 588 0800) and its airy, skylit neighbour **David Mirvish Books on Art** (596 Markham Street, 416 531 9975), selling significant new releases and out-of-print art books under a giant pop-art mural by Frank Stella. East along Bloor to Yorkville, there's **TheatreBooks** (11 St Thomas Street, 416 922 7175), housed in an elegant Victorian brownstone, and, a few blocks along, a foodie favourite: the self-explanatory **Cookbook Store** (850 Yonge Street, 416 920 2665). For a travel bookshop extraordinaire, pop into **Open Air Books and Maps** (25 Toronto Street, 416 363-0719). Hidden in a basement down a sidestreet just east of Yonge and King, it is one of the city's best-kept secrets, packed to the rafters with travel guides of all kinds.

Electronics

Bay Bloor Radio

55 Bloor Street W, at Bay Street, University (416 967 1122/www.baybloorradio.com). Bus 6/subway Bay. **Open** 10am-7pm Mon-Wed; 10am-9pm Thur, Fri; 10am-6pm Sat. **Credit** AmEx, MC, V. **Map** p274 F4.

The city's best-known purveyor of audio and visual equipment. Though it's in the upmarket ManuLife Centre, you'll rarely hit a weekend without a sale.

Future Shop

355 Yonge Street, at Elm Street, Dundas Square (416 971 5377/www.futureshop.ca). Streetcar 505, 506/subway College or Dundas. **Open** 10am-9pm Mon-Fri; 10am-6pm Sat, Sun. **Credit** AmEx, MC, V. **Map** p272 G6.

First-time renters are Future's desired customer, and B-rated models its stock in trade. If you need a basic DVD player or a boom box for the beach, Future is the place. Ask about extra costs before you buy. **Other locations**: 2400 Yonge Street, at Eglinton Avenue, North Toronto (416 489 4726); 10 Old Stock Yards Road, West End (416 766 1577).

PCUsed & CPUsed

488 Dupont Street, at Bathurst Street, The Annex (416 537 2001/533 2001/www.pcused.com or www.cpused.com). Subway Bathurst or Dupont. **Open** 9am-6pm Mon-Wed; 9am-8pm Thur, Fri; 10am-6pm Sat; noon-5pm Sun. **Credit** AmEx, MC, V. **Map** p274 D2.

This store carries a good selection of PCs and Macs, but the best deals are often second-hand goods: notebooks go for a song. Technicians speak in layman's terms (thankfully), and can also do repairs.

Eat, Drink, Shop

Fashion

See also p148 **Kensington Market**.

Boutiques

Anne Hung Boutique

829 Queen Street W, at Claremont Street, West End (416 364 7251/www.annehung.com). Streetcar 501, 511. **Open** 12.30-7pm Tue-Fri; 12.30-6.30pm Sat; noon-5pm Sun. **Credit** MC, V. **Map** p270 C7.
Designer Anne Hung's boutique is a tall, narrow space with blonde wood floors and brick walls. She has been singled out by French *Vogue* as the most promising Canadian designer, and her clothes – slinky, sexy jersey pieces and dresses – are characterised by a bold colour palette and fair prices.

Clandestino

249 Crawford Street, at Dundas Street W, West End (647 436 4761). Streetcar 505. **Open** noon-6pm Tue-Sun. **Credit** MC, V. **Map** 270 B6.

Outside, in summer, a red Mayan hammock beckons from under a colourful garland flapping gently in the breeze. Inside, it's a riot of cheerful kitsch worthy of a Mexican fiesta, from the terracotta-tile floors to painted tin decorations. Figurines of *luchadores* (Mexican wrestlers) and large masks share space with handmade wooden toys and *lotería* (lottery) boards; a display case houses handmade silver and turquoise jewellery. In addition to clothing from Nepal and beyond, the shop carries a selection of silk-screened Ts and separates by local designers.

Kitsch Boutique

325 Lonsdale Road, at Spadina Road, Forest Hill (416 481 6712). Subway St Clair West. **Open** 10am-8pm Mon-Fri; 10am-6pm Sat; noon-5pm Sun. **Credit** AmEx, MC, V.
This flamboyant neighbourhood shop specialises in 11th-hour cocktail attire – wrap, shoes and faux jewels – by a range of US labels. Glamorous evening gowns are another forte. A 'bargain' basement sells designer duds at a large discount.

Kensington Market

Kensington Market isn't everyone's cup of tea. If your budget is suited more to a Chanel store than a charity shop, go shopping in Yorkville (*see p86*). But if you have a penchant for bohemia and browsing for bargains, you'll be in your element here. A cluster of narrow, shop-lined streets, the market oozes character, and it is home to a mixed bag, from the dowdy (racks of rags and kiosks of cheap luggage) to the delightful (hippy chic fashion and foodie favourites).

Begin with a quick and tasty bite at **Mother's Dumplings** (the Chinese version of comfort food; *see p114*) or a leisurely brunch at the lovely **La Palette** (*see p114*), then find your way to the top of Augusta Avenue to start your walk. Knitwear specialist **Fresh Baked Goods** (274 Augusta Avenue, 416 966 0123)

Lilith

541 Queen Street W, at Augusta Avenue, Entertainment District (416 504 5353). Streetcar 501, 511. **Open** 11am-7pm Mon-Wed; 11am-8pm Thur-Sat; noon-6pm Sun. **Credit** AmEx, MC, V. **Map** p271 D7.

Few local designs make it out of the country, but the funkiest find their way to Lilith, an authority on urban frocks and accessories. If basic black is your thing, you might want to skip this lively den of mauve, turquoise, orange and all tones between – never mind the playful prints of frolicking animals and toy trucks. The Yummy Mummy line of maternity wear defies the norm.

Peach Berserk

507 Queen Street W, at Spadina Avenue, Entertainment District (416 504 1711/www. peachberserk.com). Streetcar 501, 510. **Open** 10am-7pm Mon-Sat; noon-5pm Sun. **Credit** AmEx, MC, V. **Map** p271 D7.

Boutique owner and designer Kingi Carpenter is the monarch of Queen Street, working the mosaic floors

of her fabulous shop for the past 15 years. The fare is girly, kitschy and catchy, with themed silkscreen prints such as I Love A Man in Uniform, punk ephemera and excerpts from Helen Gurley Brown's novel *Sex and the Single Girl* found on everything from velvet coats to playful bias-cut skirts. Emblazoned on frocks are the faces of Kim Jong-il, George W Bush and other targets.

Propaganda

686 Yonge Street, at Isabella Street, Church & Wellesley (416 961 0555/www.propaganda.bz). Subway Wellesley. **Open** 11am-7pm Mon-Sat; 1-5pm Sun. **Credit** AmEx, MC, V. **Map** p275 G4.

Regulars walk through the orange door to see what hip designer/owner Regina Sheung has uncovered next. Favouring niche brands, she might stock kitschy, sparkly belts, buckles and brooches by locals Barbie's Basement Jewellery or an appliqué leather bag emblazoned with 'I Heart Bacon' or a unique silk-screened T. Unusual accessories rule here, and the selection is always ahead of the curve.

is a punchy start, with its flamboyant angora outfits. Styles are funky by nature, sleeves fashionably long and hems flared. Next door is **Bungalow** (*see p153*), a must for fans of mid-century modern furnishings (teak tables, shag rugs, vintage barware) and groovy retro outfits. The quirkiest corner shop in town is **Casa Acoreana** (235 Augusta Avenue, 416 593 9717), a general store stocked with

glass jars of candy, nuts, grains and baking goods on one side and the charmingly shambolic **Louie's Coffee Stop** on the other.

Turn left on Baldwin Street. A holdover from the market's days as a Jewish textile centre, **Tom's Place** (*see p151*) is a famed no-frills discount fashion outlet. Women's clothing (German sportswear classics Kasper and Gina B) and Italian designer samples from brands like Versace hold court on the ground floor, but the upstairs men's department is the real draw, offering suits by Zegna, Boss and Armani at low prices.

Market odors can be pungent, but you'll find an interesting mix of aromas at **My Market Bakery** (172 Baldwin Street, 416 593 6772), **European Quality Meats & Sausages** (174 Baldwin Street, 416 596 8691) and **Cheese Magic** (182 Baldwin Street, 416 593 9531).

Kensington Avenue, on your right, is where the sartorial grit begins. The string of vintage boutiques is impressive, but virtually indistinguishable from each other, with racks of denim and leather pouring onto the sidewalk. **Asylum** (62 Kensington Avenue, 416 595 7199) is a typical stopoff, but **Exile** (20 Kensington Avenue, 416 596 0827) is a hotspot for outlandish retro and new fetish wear. And it has its own press for iron-on T-shirts. The legendary **Courage My Love** (*see p153*) is at the end of the row. Note: not every outlet is open on a Sunday.

Risqué

404 Bloor Street W, at Brunswick Avenue,
The Annex (416 960 3325). Subway Bathurst or
Spadina. **Open** 11am-7pm Mon-Fri; 11am-6pm Sat;
noon-6pm Sun. **Credit** AmEx, MC, V. **Map** p274 D4.
The Annex is better known for patchouli and batik
than the cleavage-enhancing blouses and hip-hug-
ging trousers, but the latter are the stock in trade of
this boutique. The designer denim is by Dish, a
Vancouver label with a loyal following. More in tone
with the neighbourhood are cosy sweaters and
earthy frocks. Prices are high, but the clothes are so
pretty, they're hard to resist.

San Remo

23 St Thomas Street, at Sultan Street, University
(416 920 3195). Bus 6/subway Bay or Museum.
Open 10am-6pm Mon-Wed, Sat; 10am-8pm Thur,
Fri; 1-5pm Sun. **Credit** AmEx, MC, V. **Map** p274 F4.
A ready-to-wear antidote to mass-produced
designer collections, San Remo's house label is
created by the boutique's down-to-earth owner, with
input from Italian artisans. The feel is a return to
ladylike glam, from the elegant dresses to the
swanky stilettos, and the staff help to coordinate the
daring pieces. Prices are as high as the concepts.

Scarlet

363 Eglinton Avenue W, at Avenue Road, Forest
Hill (416 480 0330). Bus 32/subway Eglinton.
Open 10am-4pm Tue-Fri; 10am-6pm Sat.
Credit AmEx, MC, V.

These funky, upscale clothes are geared towards
career women. The selection is witty, with Peter Som
mixed in with Canadian Lida Baday, and Brit
designers Alice Temperley and Ann-Louise
Roswald's unique textiles. There's a comfy sofa and
kid-friendly area near the changing rooms

Children

Chocky's

352 Queen Street W, at Spadina Avenue,
Entertainment District (416 977 1831). Streetcar
501, 510. **Open** 10am-7pm Mon-Sat; noon-6pm Sun.
Credit AmEx, MC, V. **Map** p271 D7.
Chocky's former shop in Chinatown was a local
institution for parents, who went there to stock up
on kids' underwear, T-shirts, pyjamas and rain gear.
At this smaller downtown space, the cut-rate pric-
ing system remains, along with trendier clothing.
Other locations: 2584 Yonge Street, at Eglinton
Avenue, North Toronto (416 483 8227).

Misdemeanours

3222 Queen Street W, at Spadina Avenue,
Entertainment District (416 351 8758). Streetcar
501, 510. **Open** 10am-7pm Mon-Wed; 10am-8pm
Thur, Sat; 10am-9pm Fri; noon-6pm Sun. **Credit**
AmEx, MC, V. **Map** p271 D7.
Like their mums, who wear the theatrical Fashion
Crimes label from mother store across the street,
little girls just wanna have fun. Expect to see a feath-

St Lawrence Market

Named one of the world's 25 best markets
by *Food & Wine* magazine, St Lawrence is
a foodie favourite. Going strong for 200
years, it is as popular now as it ever was,
with a huge range of fresh local produce
and great take-out stands, plus international
and deli items.

Take a tour before you buy. On the ground
floor, sample the wheels and wedges of
international cheeses from **Alex Farms** or
Chris Cheesemonger, a specialist in creamy
Québecois provisions and pâtés including
Canadian foie gras. The **Mustard Emporium**
offers more than 80 gourmet varieties (our
tip: Rib-B-Que). Seafood is everywhere; if
you're here for a quick bite, buy a slice or two
of Arctic char at **Mike's**, then queue up for a
bagel at **St Urbain**, one of the few bakers in
the city offering the Montreal style: dense,
chewy and salty. **Churrasco of St Clair** makes
a killer chicken sandwich on a kaiser roll.

The hottest fast-food offering here is a
peameal sandwich – thick slices of cornmeal-
crusted bacon on a doughy kaiser, best

smothered in mustard. You can't miss the
queues at **Carousel** bakery along the west
wall, though these sarnies are served at other
stands too. Fruit and veg are downstairs, with
some exotic picks, along with barrels of bulk
food – nuts, chocolate, confectionery – at
Domino's. Across the street, a farmers'
market takes place on Saturdays (5am-5pm),
hosted by rural cheesemakers and sausage
kings who make a special trip. On Sundays
the space is taken over by an antiques fair.

Special events and exhibitions are held
frequently on site, and there are two-hour
guided tours ($20) of the market and
surrounding area. Upstairs there is a small
gallery and archive of city history.

St Lawrence Market

92 Front Street E, at Jarvis Street, St Lawrence
(416 392 7219/Tours 416 392 0028/www.
stlawrencemarket.com). Streetcar 504. **Open**
8am-6pm Tue-Thur; 8am-7pm Fri; 5am-5pm Sat.
Antiques market 8am-5pm Sun. *Tours* 10am
Wed-Sat. **Map** p272 G8.

er boa and tiara paired with these outfits, which are trimmed with marabou, faux fur or other amusing synthetics; here, colourful tutus and crinolines are considered everyday wear.

Designer

The strip of Bloor Street West from Yonge Street to Avenue Road, once known as the 'mink mile', is heaven for lovers of luxury labels, with branches of everything from Chanel to Tiffany, via Gucci, Prada, Hermès and more. Discount chain Winners (see p145) provides designer duds for the masses.

General

Club Monaco

157 Bloor Street W, at Avenue Road, Yorkville (416 591 8837/www.clubmonaco.com). Subway Bay or Museum. **Open** 10am-8pm Mon-Wed; 10am-9pm Thur, Fri; 10am-7pm Sat; 11am-7pm Sun. **Credit** AmEx, MC, V. **Map** p274 F4.
CM was one of the first fashion chains to recognise the elegance of Japanese lines and simple, pattern-less colour. And its outstanding pricing made it an international star. Designs are wearable and affordable: buy a pair of jeans and a ribbed turtleneck and you'll have them for more than a season – and neither will you suffer embarrassing out-of-fashion stigma. Sale items are ubiquitous. This Bloor Street flagship, in a Greek Revival heritage building, has the best pedigree and selection.
Other locations: throughout the city.

Lileo

Building 35, 55 Mill Street, at Parliament Street, Distillery District (416 413 1410/www.lileo.ca). Bus 65. **Open** 11am-7pm Mon-Wed; 11am-8pm Thur-Sat; 11am-6pm Sun. **Credit** AmEx, DC, MC, V. **Map** p272 H8.
This lifestyle and fitness emporium occupies a sprawling space in the historic Distillery District. From glitter-encrusted cashmere hoodies to faux-retro Ts; from classic brands like Lacoste to recherché garments hand-dyed and woven in Africa; from handmade soaps and skincare to designer Birkenstocks – it's all here. The yoga gear is worn by urbanites as much for work as for work-outs, while some of the price tags prove that chic healthy living comes at a premium. There's also a juice bar.

Over the Rainbow

101 Yorkville Avenue, at Hazelton Avenue, Yorkville (416 967 7448). Subway Bay or Museum. **Open** 10am-6pm Mon-Wed, Sat; 10am-8pm Thur, Fri; noon-5pm Sun. **Credit** AmEx, MC, V. **Map** p274 F4.
Push past bratty teens with mums in tow to discover the latest in denim (the fact that the kids actually want to shop here proves that the jeans are up to date). Styles are stacked with precision from floor to ceiling. Also available are fun and sporty T-shirts, sweats and accessories from Juicy, Paul Frank, Triple Five Soul, Chip & Pepper, Miss Sixty and

Diesel. After 30 years – and myriad styles of jeans from peg-leg to elephant and back again – this is still a Yorkville standard.

Roots

Toronto Eaton Centre, 220 Yonge Street, at Dundas Street, Dundas Square (416 593 9640/www.roots. ca). Streetcar 505/subway Dundas. **Open** 10am-9pm Mon-Fri; 10am-7pm Sat; 11am-6pm Sun. **Credit** AmEx, DC, MC, V. **Map** p272 G6.
Every Torontonian remembers a favourite Roots possession, whether it's a sweatshirt, a fleece or a pair of clunky boots. The Canadian icon started cobbling reverse-heel shoes in the '70s, then branched out into leisurewear – to the joy of outdoor folk everywhere. Today styles are spicier, including the kids line, but you can still find the basics.
Other locations: throughout the city.

Menswear

Boomer

309 Queen Street W, at John Street, Entertainment District (416 598 0013). Streetcar 501/subway Osgoode. **Open** 10.30am-7pm Mon-Wed, Fri; 10.30am-8pm Thur; 10.30am-6pm Sat; 1-5pm Sun. **Credit** AmEx, DC, MC, V. **Map** p271 E7.
Boomer offers the best names (Boss, Ted Baker et al) from finer department stores, and stock is chosen with the Queen Street crowd in mind. Own-brand output is restricted to French-cut dress shirts.

Grreat Stuff

870 Queen Street W, at Massey Street, West End (416 533 7680). Streetcar 501. **Open** 11am-7pm Tue, Wed, Fri; 11am-8pm Thur; 10am-6pm Sat; noon-5pm Sun. **Credit** DC, MC, V. **Map** p270 B7.
The clothing at Grreat Stuff looks vintage, but the retro feel comes from the choice of designer samples and line ends (by the likes of Kenneth Cole, Mexx, Tony Bahama). Fitted shirts, silk sweaters and Swedish suits are part of the changing inventory, with prices well below the norm. **Photo** p152.

Harry Rosen

82 Bloor Street W, at Bellair Street, Yorkville (416 972 0556/www.harryrosen.com). Subway Bloor-Yonge. **Open** 10am-7pm Mon-Wed; 10am-9pm Thur, Fri; 10am-6pm Sat; noon-6pm Sun. **Credit** AmEx, DC, MC, V. **Map** p274 F4.
Some might snub Harry Rosen for being on the conservative side of the spectrum (let's face it, he's been around for 50 years), yet there was a time when he was the only game in town for respectable men's fashion – one brogue-shod step from Savile Row. Service is also top-notch.
Other locations: throughout the city.

Tom's Place

190 Baldwin Street, at Augusta Street, Kensington Market (416 596 0297). Streetcar 505, 510. **Open** 10am-6pm Mon-Wed; 10am-7pm Thur, Fri; 9am-6pm Sat; noon-5pm Sun. **Credit** AmEx, DC, MC, V. **Map** p271 D6.

RICHARD JAMES
SAVILE ROW

KENNETH COLE
new york

Grreat Stuff. *See p151*.

Although the exterior of Tom's Place is tatty, Kensington strollers shouldn't be put off – especially those with a knack for bartering. Step inside up to the second floor (past racks of designer samples for women) for a good selection of top-notch men's suits sold at discount prices. Choose from designer-label woollen classics or the house brands, made from Italian fabrics. Don't forget shirts, in all the colours of the rainbow.

Street/clubwear

Châteauworks

340 Queen Street W, at Spadina Avenue, Entertainment District (416 971 9314/www.le-chateau.com). Streetcar 501, 510. **Open** 10am-9pm Mon-Fri; 9.30am-7pm Sat; noon-6pm Sun. **Credit** AmEx, MC, V. **Map** p271 D7.

The Montreal-based trend machine Le Château claimed this as its Toronto flagship years ago. Anything the clothier offers can be had here: men's polyester club shirts with trendy embellishments, loads of shiny, sexy stuff for women, the latest in kids' hipsters… If you don't mind the patchy quality, you can get away with buying a season's wardrobe for under $300.

Vintage/second-hand

Bungalow

273 Augusta Avenue, at Nassau Street, Kensington Market (416 598 0204/www.bungalow.to). Streetcar 506, 510. **Open** 11am-6.30pm Mon-Fri; 11am-6pm Sat, Sun. **Credit** MC, V. **Map** p271 D6.

This airy, spacious Kensington Market shop is an ode to mid-century modern, with affordable teak furnishings, shag rugs, sofas and barware scattered among its racks of second-hand clothing. Regular browsing pays off: in among the rockabilly cowboy shirts, Levi's cords and leather jackets, you might unearth a Lilly Pulitzer shirtwaist and a Russell Wright jug or retro blender to go with. There's no musty smell, just a clean, well-edited selection.

Courage My Love

14 Kensington Avenue, at Dundas Street W, Chinatown (416 979 1992). Streetcar 505, 510. **Open** 11.30am-6pm Mon-Fri; 11am-6pm Sat; 2-5pm Sun. **Credit** AmEx, MC, V. **Map** p271 D6.

Courage came along decades ago and made Kensington Market a centre for vintage chic. It's a family affair, and still the cheapest ticket in town for frumpy but fabulous eveningwear, tuxedos, cuff links, leather, crafts, exotic costume jewellery and whimsical buttons. The store also creates on-trend, limited runs of retailored threads, made from charity shop odds and ends.

Paper Bag Princess

287 Davenport Road, at Bedford Road, The Annex (416 925 2603/www.thepaperbagprincess.com). Bus 26/subway Dupont. **Open** 11am-7pm Mon-Fri; 11am-6pm Sat. **Credit** AmEx, MC, V. **Map** p274 E3.

Collector and owner Elizabeth Mason was dealing in vintage couture long before it became a red-carpet staple (Julia Roberts, Madonna, Beyoncé Knowles and Kelly Lynch are just a few of her famous fans). Happily, Mason keeps her Toronto outpost as well stocked as her LA shop. Alaia, Pucci and Missoni are recent favourites.

Preloved

613 Queen Street W, at Bathurst Street, Entertainment District (416 504 8704/ www.preloved.ca). Streetcar 501, 511. **Open** 10am-7pm Mon, Tue, Sat; 10am-8pm Wed-Fri; noon-6pm Sun. **Credit** AmEx, MC, V. **Map** p271 D7.

Preloved's star is rising across Canada. The sell-out signature collection for men and women is creatively cut and pasted from clothing discards – a fashionable way to recycle. The edgy and unpretentious gear is fashioned from old sweaters, jeans and coats. The T-shirts are the most fun, bearing logos and embellishments from defunct bands and summer camps. **Photo** *p154.*

Fashion accessories

Handbags

Jeanne Lottie Fashion

106 Yorkville Avenue, at Bay Street, Yorkville (416 975 5115/www.jeannelottie.com). Bus 6/subway Bay. **Open** 10.30am-6pm Mon-Sat; noon-5pm Sun. **Credit** AmEx, MC, V. **Map** p274 F4.

Designer Jane Ip is Canada's answer to Kate Spade – and her perky must-have bags are sold at her Yorkville store, and shops around the country. Thankfully (because it's hard to leave with less than two), Ip's on-trend accessories – made from tweed, fun fur or faux shearling – can cost less than $100.

M0851

23 St Thomas Street, at Bloor Street, Yorkville (416 920 4001/www.mo851.com). Subway Bay or Museum. **Open** 10am-6pm Mon-Wed; 10am-7pm Thurs-Sat; noon-5pm Sun. **Credit** AmEx, MC, V. **Map** p274 F4.

This Montreal chain has stores from Taipei to New York. Its fashion is characterised by muted tones, clean lines and sleek bags. Made with buttery leather from Italian calf-skin, and treated in lanolin, the bags are highly coveted. Prices are reasonable.

Hats

Lilliput Hats

462 College Street, at Bathurst Street, Harbord (416 536 5933). Streetcar 506, 511. **Open** 10am-6pm Mon-Fri; 11am-6pm Sat; by appointment Sun. **Credit** MC, V. **Map** p271 D5.

Milliners are an endangered breed in Toronto, but the lust for vintage has brought hats back. Lilliput makes the classic cloche, a summer straw hat and the felt fedora redux, plus other hip headgear.

Jewellery

Birks

55 Bloor Street W, at Bay Street, Yorkville (416 922 2266/www.birks.com). Bus 6/subway Bay. **Open** 10am-6pm Mon-Thur, Sat; 10am-7pm Fri; noon-5pm Sun. **Credit** AmEx, DC, MC, V. **Map** p274 F4.

Celebrating nearly 130 years in the business, this venerable Canadian jewellery house is still going strong. Occupying a stately corner of the upmarket ManuLife Centre, this branch is the most pleasant. In an attempt to shed its conservative reputation, the company recently hired noted fashion journalist Holly Brubach (former style editor of the *New York Times Magazine*) for a revamp. The 'new Birks' now offers more bling, from diamond-studded strands to glittering glam charm bracelets to sleek everyday silver. An ever-changing selection of fine vintage jewellery and homeware is also a draw.
Other locations: Toronto Eaton Centre, 220 Yonge Street, at Dundas St, Dundas Square (416 979 9311); First Canadian Place, 100 King Street W, at Bay Street, Financial District (416 363 5663); Yorkdale Shopping Centre, 3401 Dufferin Street, at Highway 401, North Toronto (416 782 6311).

Experimetal Jewellery

588 Markham Street, at Bloor Street, West End (416 538 3313/www.annesportun.com). Streetcar 511/subway Bathurst. **Open** 11am-6pm Tue, Wed; 11am-7pm Thur, Fri; 10am-6pm Sat; noon-5pm Sun. **Credit** AmEx, MC, V.

Even if organic shapes and unusual settings aren't your thing, this petite boutique is still worth a peek for its undulating metals studded with stones. Designer Anne Sportun's hands and rings have even been featured on a Canadian postage stamp.
Other locations: 742 Queen Street W, at Bathurst Street, West End (416 363 4114).

Made You Look Jewellery Studio & Gallery

1338 Queen Street W, at Dufferin Street, West End (416 463 2136/www.madeyoulook.ca). Streetcar 501, 504. **Open** 10am-6pm daily. **Credit** MC, V. **Map** p270 A7.

Just a block from the new hipster central of Parkdale lies Sarah Dougall's showcase for more than 50 home-grown jewellery designers. Prices cover the range, and each artist is a find, working in such varied materials as resin, copper, glass, pearls and crystal. Designs veer between classic and delicate and bold and funky. The in-house studio offers a sneak preview of the work in progress.

Shelly Purdy Studio

Suite 501, 296 Richmond Street W, at John Street, Entertainment District (416 340 7581/www. shellypurdy.com). Streetcar 501/subway Osgoode. **Open** 10am-6pm Tue-Fri; 11am-5pm Sat. **Credit** MC, V. **Map** p271 E7.

Shelly Purdy has specialised in beautiful diamonds since 1987. She sells AURIAS diamonds (extracted from the Ekati mine in the chilly Canadian tundra), which are coveted by her upmarket international

Preloved. *See p153.*

Canadian couture

There's more to Canadian fashion than lumberjack shirts, mukluks and parkas. With home-grown designers like Dean & Dan Caten of DSquared, Arthur Mendonça, Paul Hardy and Lida Baday cutting a dash internationally, Canadian fashion is growing up. It's doing a roaring trade on Milan's runways – and is available at a cut-rate price in Toronto. A new wave of Canadian designers has opened shops around the city (especially in trendy West Queen West).

The renaissance in Canadian chic boutiques began with **Georgie Bolesworth** (891 Dundas Street W, at Bellwoods Avenue, West End, 416 703 7625) on an up-and-coming strip surrounded by Portuguese soccer bars and karaoke rooms. Designers are sourced – and often discovered – by bohemian fashion stylist Georgia Groome (the shop is named after her grandfather), way before they make it on to the radar of the mainstream fashion press. From Cincyn's sexy jersey to Lydia K's folk costume skirts and boleros and Mercy's vintage-look creations, there's plenty to please, complemented by exotic jewellery and Véronique Miljkovitch's wearable textile art.

A few doors down at the darling boutique **Skirt** (903 Dundas Street W, at Bellwoods Avenue, West End, 647 436 3357), owner Jamie Dowdles will regale you with the story behind each and every label, in a whitewashed space topped by a pink chandelier. The stock is more affordable and everyday than Georgie, with gauchos by Quip, Dagg & Stacey's cute culottes and Tryna's exotic jewellery.

In the artsy West Queen West district, **Willow Grant** (960 Queen Street W, at Shaw Street, West End, 416 533 7553) is worth a look. The Canadian fashion gallery is named after the shop's two iguanas, which roam the front window when it's sunny. The focus here is on designers from Toronto, Montreal and Vancouver. One-of-a-kind handbags from My Old Pants and SDG 033 are a highlight, but young fashion designers are always renting racks so offerings change regularly.

For those who pair fashion with fitness, **Lululemon**'s line of yoga-ready sweats, pretty Ts and snug jackets are something of a local uniform (342 Queen Street W, at Spadina Avenue, Queen West, 416 703 1399).

clientele. Thankfully, she can cater to most price brackets: the Achievement stackable nesting diamond rings, created to celebrate each of life's milestones, start at a reasonable $350. Collections include Celtic Rune (inspired by symbols of fertility and love) and Canadian Jungle (ornate foliage surrounding cultured pearls and coloured stones).

Leather

Augustina

5 Old York Lane, 138 Cumberland Street, at Avenue Road, Yorkville (416 922 4248). Bus 6/subway Bay. **Open** 10am-6pm Mon-Wed, Sat; 10am-7pm Thur, Fri; noon-5pm Sun. **Credit** AmEx, MC, V. **Map** p274 F4.

Most designer handbags have a knock-off twin somewhere in the world. But few pirates could mimic Augustina's imports – gasp-worthy bags that are rarely spotted elsewhere, from some of the world's most underrated designers. Lauren Merkin is a perennial favourite, along with perfumes from Miller Harris. Sweaters are another forte: they come in whisper-soft cashmere, merino wool and cotton, and range from $200-$400. A good selection of top-end accessories also includes costume jewellery, belts and underwear. The shop only stocks a few of each item, and the location, hidden down a Yorkville laneway, adds to the sense of exclusivity.

Lingerie

Nearly Naked

749 Queen Street W, just west of Palmerston Avenue, West End (416 703 7561). Streetcar 501, 511. **Open** 11am-6pm Mon-Wed, Sat; 11am-7pm Thur, Fri; noon-5pm Sun. **Credit** AmEx, DC, MC, V. **Map** p270 C7.

Nearly Naked is a hip but no-fuss neighbourhood lingerie shop. Everything is here, from boy-cut briefs to boulder holders from reputable speciality brands (including Scandinavian label Change, known for its microfibre bras). The emphasis is comfort, though there's a dash of ruffled satin and racy black lace. It also sells hosiery, comfy sleep and loungewear.

Secrets From Your Sister...

476 Bloor Street W, at Bathurst Street, The Annex (416 538 1234). Streetcar 511/subway Bathurst. **Open** 11am-7pm Mon-Wed, Fri; 9.30am-8pm Thur; 10am-6pm Sat; noon-6pm Sun. **Credit** AmEx, MC, V. **Map** p274 D4.

Another neighbourhood favourite, especially with busty gals and those with a thirst for lingerie that is exotic, pretty and funky. The styles, fabrics and outlandish colours are unlike anything your mother ever recommended, though sensible nursing bras and cosy flannel and cotton pyjamas bring things back down to earth.

Eat, Drink, Shop

Shoes

B2

399 Queen Street W, at Spadina Avenue,
Entertainment District (416 595 9281). Streetcar
501, 510. **Open** 10am-7pm Mon-Wed, Sat, Sun;
10am-9pm Thur, Fri. **Credit** AmEx, MC, V.
Map p271 D7.

This boutique's parent company, Browns, can be
found in swish department stores and upscale malls.
But B2 is more fun – if only for gawking at eccentric four-inchers you know you can't afford. It carries the international – Costume National, Miu Miu,
Hush Puppy, Camper and Frye – along with its own
Euro-style brands at more reasonable prices. Unlike
Browns, it also carries a strong selection of fashionable trainers by the likes of Puma, Lacoste and
Diesel. Glam handbags are also sold.

Bootmaster

609 Yonge Street, at Gloucester Street, Church &
Wellesley (416 927 1054/www.bootmaster.com).
Subway Wellesley. **Open** 10am-7pm Mon-Sat; noon-5pm Sun. **Credit** AmEx, MC, V. **Map** p275 G5.

The giant red cowboy boot has been parked on the
sidewalk here since 1986; staff ship to loyal customers worldwide, and the walls are lined with photos autographed by celeb clients. Bootmaster is
known for fair prices and a huge selection of cowboy leather gear, from jackets and accessories, such
as hand-tooled silver belt buckles inlaid with lapis
and turquoise, to the main event: boots from Tony
Lama, Justin and Boulet, all types of Frye (plus
Small Frye for the kids), Chippewa for the motorcycle set, and colourful handmade boots from the Old
Gringo. Macho retro western shirts, Stetson hats and
jackets trimmed with alligator and stingray will also
help you achieve the John Wayne look.

Davids

66 Bloor Street W, at Yonge Street, Yorkville (416
920 1000). Subway Bloor-Yonge. **Open** 9am-6pm
Mon-Wed, Sat; 9am-8pm Thur, Fri; noon-5pm Sun.
Credit AmEx, MC, V. **Map** p275 G4.

The most glamorous shoe shop in town. If the currency exchange is working in your favour, you'll
find Davids rewarding. The spotlight is on high-end
European designs – including impressively high
stilettos – in buttery leathers, brought in from Milan
and Paris. Men's shoes are sold upstairs.

John Fluevog Shoes

242 Queen Street W, at John Street, Entertainment
District (416 581 1420/www.fluevog.com). Streetcar
501/subway Osgoode. **Open** 11am-7pm Mon-Wed,
Sat; 11am-8pm Thur, Fri; noon-6pm Sun. **Credit**
AmEx, MC, V. **Map** p271 E7.

The Vancouver-based cobbler with goth beginnings
is now something of a legend, as much for his inventive, colourful curlicues and oddball shapes as his
irreverent marketing and kitschy style names. The
fact that the shoes (men's, women's and unisex) are
also comfortable enhances their cult fashion status.

Fashion services

Dry-cleaners

Dove Cleaners

1560 Yonge Street, at Heath Street, Forest Hill (416
413 7900/www.dovecleaners.com). Subway St Clair.
Open 7.30am-8pm Mon-Fri; 9am-6pm Sat. **Credit**
AmEx, MC, V.

With home and office pick-up and delivery (an easy
net-based system is in place), Dove's high-end
service is ideal for the moneyed customer.
Other locations: 40 King Street W, Financial
District (416 869 3000).

Splish Splash

590 College Street, at Clinton Street, Little Italy (416
532 6499). Streetcar 506. **Open** 8am-10pm Mon-Fri;
9am-8pm Sat, Sun. **No credit cards. Map** p270 C5.

This launderette/convenience store is a friendly
meeting place for young urban types.

Shoe repair

Nick's Shoes & Custom Footwear

169 Dupont Street, at St George Street, The Annex
(416 924 5930/www.nickscustomboots.com). Subway
Dupont. **Open** 8am-6.30pm Mon-Fri; 9am-5pm Sat.
No credit cards. Map p274 E2.

Nick is known for his reliability and skill: you're
unlikely to lose a heel twice if he's in your little black
book. His auxiliary talent is for imitation – he can
craft fancy footwear for a snip of the usual price.

Novelty Shoe Rebuilders

119 Yonge Street, at Adelaide Street, St Lawrence
(416 364 8878). Streetcar 501, 504/subway King or
Queen. **Open** 8.30am-5.30pm Mon-Fri; 8.30am-5pm
Sat. **Credit** MC, V. **Map** p272 G7.

Shoe styles come and go, but this institution has
been taking care of wayward soles for 70 years at
the same location in the Financial District. Repairs
are done while you wait or slip into one of the funky
wooden booths for a quick polish.

Flowers

The strip of sidewalk along Avenue Road just
south of Davenport Road is known for its
buckets of fresh and flamboyant cut flowers.
Also doubling as mini grocers, the Chinese
shops that line the west side of the street teem
with inexpensive stems and bunches.

Food & drink

Alcohol

Every now and then the provincial government
considers letting Ontarians buy their booze
from the private sector. But then the $1 billion
generated by the Liquor Control Board of

Ontario (LCBO) every year brings the bureaucrats back to their senses. Efforts to spruce up the stores are impressive, but there never seems to be one open when you need it. The newly refurbished LCBO store in a landmark train station (10 Scrivener Square, Rosedale, 416 922 0403) boasts vintage rooms and cooking classes. LCBOs stock a full range of wines and spirits, plus some domestic and imported beers, and can be found at 87 Front Street East, St Lawrence (416 368 0521), 337 Spadina Avenue, Chinatown (416 597 0145), in the Atrium on Bay (595 Bay Street, Dundas Square, 416 979 9978), 545 Yonge Street, Church & Wellesley (416 923 8498) and in the Manulife Centre, Yorkville (416 925 5266). For general information, call 1-800 668 5226. Most shops open at 10am weekdays and noon on weekends.

The only competition comes from **Wine Rack** (560 Queen Street W, Entertainment District, 416 504 3647), a small chain licensed to sell Ontario wines.

Beer Stores are a separate monopoly, owned and operated by the big breweries. Downtown branches include 572 Church Street (Church & Wellesley 416 921 6036); 452 Bathurst Street (Little Italy, 416 923 4535); 614 Queen Street West at Bathurst (Queen West, 416 504 4665) and 534 Parliament Street (Cabbagetown, 416 925 1915).

Bakeries

Clafouti

915 Queen Street W, at Gore Vale Avenue, West End (416 603 1935). Streetcar 501. **Open** 8am-6pm Tue-Sat; 9am-5pm Sun. **No credit cards. Map** p270 C7.

Tarts come in individual or family size, glazed and irresistibly fresh. There's a selection of imported French jams, jellies and candies, and the fabled buttery croissants (plain, or with rose or cinnamon flavourings) are gone by 11am on weekends.

Harbord Bakery

115 Harbord Street, at Major Street, Harbord (416 922 5767). Bus 94/streetcar 510. **Open** 8am-7pm Mon-Thur; 8am-6pm Fri, Sat; 8am-4pm Sun. **Credit** MC, V. **Map** p274 D4.

This Jewish bakery has been here since the mid 1900s, when Eastern Europeans began arriving in the neighbourhood. You can still find some of the city's freshest chollah, rye bread and bagels (with huge, twisted variations), and a selection of pastries, strudels and tarts.

Confectioners

Nostalgia is a sweet thing, and various sugary testaments to childhood memories have cropped up around town over the past ten years. The first **Sugar Mountain** opened in clubland (320 Richmond Street W, Entertainment District, 416 204 9544) but soon expanded into the Yonge Street, St Clair and Queen West areas. The copycat **Suckers** (450 Danforth Avenue, East Toronto, 416 405 8946) tends to be patronised by Greektown yuppies. Chocolate and fudge nuts in the Beaches head for the **Nutty Chocolatier** (2179 Queen Street E, 416 698 5548), while in the Distillery District, **Soma** (Building 47, 416 815 7662) serves up the brown nectar in the form of Mayan hot chocolate, spiced with chilli and cinnamon, as well as mainstream flavours. **Laura Secord** (Yorkdale Shopping Centre, 3401 Dufferin Street, North Toronto, 416 789 5697, plus other mall locations) is a local institution as a purveyor of bite-size candy bars. **JS Bonbons** (811 Queen Street W, West End, 416 703 7731) is a local favourite for hand-sculpted works of chocolate art with a contemporary twist on flavourings; it also has a branch in Midtown.

Soma.

chocolate laboratory

Eat, Drink, Shop

The perfect picnic

Torontonians are masters at making the most of the good weather. From the first day of spring right through to crisp autumn days, you'll spot picnickers of all varieties: families spread out on the lawns of Centre Island, say, or couples sharing gourmet sandwiches and fruit smoothies on a bench.

If you want to shop for your own fixings, any of the farmers' markets will do. At Saturday's **St Lawrence Market** (*see p150*), vendors sell fresh fruit and veg, meat pies, cheeses and more. Alternatively, grab a back bacon sarnie at the Carousel Bakery, while perusing the goodies at the more than 50 food stands.

Across town, **Kensington**'s outdoor bazaar (*see p148*) stretches for blocks. It's perfect for organic coffees, samosas, cheeses, falafels and wholesome breads, with a little reggae thrown in for atmosphere. Fresh produce ranges from the local to the exotic and prices are good.

If you're strolling along Queen West, try the barbecue chickens and meaty sandwiches from the all-organic **Healthy Butcher** (565 Queen Street W, 416 ORGANIC). The

lasagnes and mozzarella-stuffed rice balls are also the real deal, made from the recipe of the owner's Italian mama.

Throughout the week, afternoon farmers' markets pop up in parks around town. On Tuesdays, there is **Riverdale Park** (Winchester and Sumach Streets, 416 961 8787, 3-7pm, early May to late October); on, Wednesdays check out **Nathan Phillips Square** (Bay and Queen Streets, 416 338 0338, 10am-2.30pm, June-Oct) and on Thursdays try **Dufferin Grove Park** (875 Dufferin Street, 416 392 0913, 3-7pm, year-round). Dufferin and Riverdale, with their own brick ovens, offer pizza slices and warm breads.

Gourmet goods are found at **Pusateri's** in Yorkville (57 Yorkville Avenue, 416 785 9100). Check out the crab cakes – and ask for a side of dipping sauce. Across the street at **Dinah's Cupboard** (50 Cumberland Street, 416 921 8112, *photo below*), you can peruse a smörgåsborg of fusion salads, perfect samosas and spring rolls plus soups and sandwiches for your picnic basket. Dig in.

Gourmet grocers

Dinah's Cupboard

50 Cumberland Street, at Bay Street, Yorkville (416 921 8112). Subway Bay or Bloor-Yonge. **Open** 9am-7pm Mon-Fri; 9am-6pm Sat. **Credit** AmEx, MC, V. **Map** p274 F4.

Though small, this foodie boîte is stocked with treasures for the discerning palate. In addition to the delicious prepared foods – from cheesy lasagne to fragrant Asian salads – the deli counter packs foie gras, fine terrines and artisan cheeses. There's a good selection of spices, teas, coffees and oils.

Pusateri's

57 Yorkville Avenue, at Bay Street, Yorkville (416 785 9100/www.pusateris.com). Bus 6/subway Bay. **Open** 10am-8pm Mon-Wed; 10am-9pm Thur, Fri; 8am-8pm Sat; 10am-7pm Sun. **Credit** AmEx, MC, V. **Map** p274 F4.

Uptown society matrons send their nannies here for groceries, or pop by themselves for gourmet takeaways. It's a pricey one-stop for folk who value time over money, but the downtown location's sleek new design and outstanding imported foods, plus ready-made food service, make it a favourite for everyone, even those who can't regularly afford to shop here. **Other locations:** 1539 Avenue Road, North Toronto (416 785 9100).

Grocers

Dominion

89 Gould Street, at Church Street, Dundas Square (416 862 7171/www.freshobsessed.com). Streetcar 505/subway Dundas. **Open** 24hrs daily. **Credit** AmEx, MC, V. **Map** p272 G6.

Dominion's motto proclaims they're fresh obsessed, but the store is neither as pretty nor as big as its yuppie competitor, Loblaws. At some locations you'll queue for a cashier or get lost in the labyrinth and odd organisation, but the flexible hours (some outlets are open 24 hours) make it a favourite among students, shift workers and night owls. **Other locations:** throughout the city.

Loblaws

650 Dupont Street, at Christie Street, West End (416 588 4881/www.loblaws.ca). Bus 26/subway Christie or Dupont. **Open** 8am-10pm Mon-Sat; 9am-8pm Sun. **Credit** MC, V.

It's been around since 1919, but until recently Loblaws was just your average grocer. Then the stores began a clean-up process and expanded into veritable mini malls: well lit, with in-house cafés, culinary classes, kids' cookery programmes, wine depots, exotic fresh fish, sushi chefs, dry-cleaners and chemists. Service is swift and, despite its gilded appearance, Loblaws manages to keep its prices competitive.

Other locations: 10 Lower Jarvis Street, at Queen's Key, St Lawrence (416 304 0611); 396 St Clair Avenue W, at Bathurst Street, Casa Loma (416 651 5166).

Health food

The Big Carrot

348 Danforth Avenue, at Hampton Avenue, East Toronto (416 466 2129/www.thebigcarrot.ca). Subway Chester. **Open** *Shop* 9.30am-8pm Mon-Wed; 9.30am-9pm Thur, Fri; 9am-7pm Sat; 11am-6pm Sun. *Juice bar* 9am-8pm Mon-Wed; 9am-9pm Thur, Fri; 9am-7pm Sat; 10.30am-6pm Sun. **Credit** MC, V.

Social consciousness and groceries didn't mix back when this worker-owned cooperative opened 20 years ago. Today, even though prices are what you'd expect in a niche market, it's near impossible to squeeze in here – especially at weekends – even though it's the biggest natural-food store in the city. Expect to find free-range chicken and eggs, sustainably harvested fish, supplements, organic meat, and just about anything else you can imagine.

Noah's Natural Foods

322 Bloor Street W, at Spadina Avenue, The Annex (416 968 7930). Streetcar 510/subway Spadina. **Open** 10am-8pm Mon-Wed; 10am-9pm Thur, Fri; 10am-7pm Sat; 11am-6pm Sun. **Credit** AmEx, MC, V. **Map** p274 D4.

A favourite pit stop for Annex dwellers on their way home from yoga, Noah's is Toronto's longest-running health-food store. The growing obsession with organic and all-natural foods has spurred its recent growth, and now you can find your alfalfa sprouts, carob chips and oatmeal cleansers at several handy points in the city. There's also a vegan café. **Other locations:** 667 Yonge Street, at Wellesley Street, Church & Wellesley (416 969 0220); 2395 Yonge Street, at Eglinton Avenue, North Toronto (416 488 0904).

Whole Foods Market

Hazelton Lanes, 55 Avenue Road, at Bloor Street, Yorkville (416 944 0500/www.wholefoods.com). Bus 6/subway Bay. **Open** 9am-10pm Mon-Fri; 9am-9pm Sat, Sun. **Credit** AmEx, MC, V. **Map** p274 F3/4.

This Texas-based health-food conglomerate has more than 130 stores in North America. To date, this is the only Canadian outpost, offering a rainbow of fresh produce, striking seafood displays, a sushi bar, preservative-free baked goods, natural meats, international cheeses and a gourmet deli. The prices are high but so is the quality.

Speciality

Greg's Ice Cream

750 Bloor Street W, at Spadina Avenue, The Annex (416 962 4734). Subway Spadina. **Open** 11.30am-10pm Mon-Thur, Sun; 11.30am-11pm Fri, Sat. **No credit cards**. **Map** p274 D4/E4.

Toronto's favourite ice-cream parlour attracts queues in the summer. The draw is the evocative and unusual handmade flavours. The palate-pleasing roasted marshmallow is famous far and wide, and the coffee toffee is made with real cream, real coffee and chunks of bittersweet brittle. Divine.

Eat, Drink, Shop

Kristapsons

*1095 Queen Street E, at Winnifred Avenue, East
End (416 466 5152). Bus 72/streetcar 501.* **Open**
by appointment only Mon; 9am-4pm Tue-Thur;
9am-noon Sat. **Credit** V.

In this age of diversification, it's hard to find a shop
that specialises in just one thing. Andris Grinbergs
continues Adolph Kristapson's tradition, selling
cold-smoked British Columbia salmon. Order ahead
and your catch will be smoked on the premises.

La Paloma Gelateria

*1357 St Clair Avenue W, at Lonsdale Avenue, Forest
Hill (416 656 2340). Subway St Clair West.* **Open**
7am-11.30pm daily. **No credit cards.**

With 200 flavours of authentic Italian ice-cream in
its repertoire, and about 50 on hand at any given
time, this classic *gelateria* is the choice of local
Italians. Though the prices are higher than
competitors, so is the quality. Chestnut or fig, per-
simmon or strawberry cheesecake, Ferrero Rocher
or traditional zabaglione… the list is deliciously and
deliriously overwhelming. If you don't do dairy,
there's a range of soy flavours. For savoury treats,
there's a traditional panino counter out back.

Sanko Trading Co

*730 Queen Street W, at Niagara Street, West End
(416 703 4550). Streetcar 501, 511.* **Open** 10am-
7pm Mon, Wed-Sun. **Credit** V. **Map** p270 C7.

It keeps a veritable library of Japanese mags and
weird-looking videos, but you're more likely to leave
Sanko with a jar of miso soup or a wad of seaweed.
Kids are kept enthralled by confectionery, cookies
and drinks imported from the Far East, while health-
conscious shoppers head for the macha powder.

Gay & lesbian

See p195.

Gifts & specialist

Art Interiors

*Unit 205, 446 Spadina Road, at Lonsdale Avenue,
Forest Hill (416 488 3157). Subway St Clair West.*
Open 10am-5pm Mon-Sat. **Credit** MC, V.

It takes an experienced eye to spot quality artwork,
but the owners of Art Interiors scout around. They
celebrate the finest new artists in town, selling their
pieces at this loft boutique in Forest Hill village.

Japanese Paper Place

*887 Queen Street W, at Walnut Avenue, West End
(416 703 0089/www.japanesepaperplace.com).
Streetcar 501.* **Open** 10am-6pm Mon-Wed, Sat;
10am-8pm Thur, Fri. **Credit** AmEx, MC, V.
Map p270 C7.

For those who take paper seriously, there are origa-
mi classes, invitation workshops and lectures at
weekends. But this is really just a pretty place to
wander, feeling paper samples, filling Christmas
stockings and getting whiffs of inspiration.

Health & beauty

Beauty shops

Iodine + Arsenic

*867 Queen Street W, at Niagara Street, West End
(416 681 0577/www.iodineandarsenic.com).
Streetcar 501.* **Open** 11am-7pm Mon-Fri; 11am-6pm
Sat; noon-5pm Sun. **Credit** MC, V. **Map** p270 C7.

The vibe here is playfully medicinal, from the hair
studio (called the OR) to the Arsenic 'Anti-Spa' at
the back. There are clinical white walls and pre-
scription-inspired fare, and the products (hand-
crafted bath salts, massage oils) are packaged in IV
bags. Choose from inexpensive novelty items like
red devil rubber duckies, or lotions and potions with
attitude (the Bitch line is especially popular).

PIR Cosmetics

*25 Bellair Street, at Cumberland Avenue, Yorkville
(416 513 1603/www.pircosmetics.com). Bus
6/subway Bay.* **Open** 11am-6pm Mon, Tue, Sat;
11am-6.30pm Wed-Fri; 1-5pm Sun. **Credit** AmEx,
MC, V. **Map** p274 F4.

This boutique is a hub for talked-about and hard-to-
find Japanese, Italian and French brands. Also on
offer are make-up application lessons, eyebrow
shaping, nail treatments and the requisite coif stuff.
Other locations: 77 Front Street E, at Jarvis Street,
St Lawrence Market (416 703 2480).

Complementary medicine

Toronto is an established haven of alternative
medicine. The **Toronto Healing Arts
Centre** (717 Bloor Street W, West End, 416 535
8777) enlists licensed homeopaths, hypnotists
and other holistic professionals for a range of
therapies. Or you can regroup, rebalance and
rejuvenate at the **Centre for Life Essentials**
in Forest Hill (416 238 7213, 705 742 7475,
www.life-essentials.com; phone for an
appointment), specialising in stress-, pain-
and fatigue-management through a variety of
therapies, including reflexology, aromatherapy
and meditation. Find your way to the **Yellow
Brick Road** (258 Dupont Street, at Spadina
Avenue, The Annex, 416 926 1101) to cleanse
your system and get a bout of aromatherapy,
reflexology, ear candling and other therapies.

Hairdressers

First Choice Haircutters

*1730 Bloor Street W, at Indian Grove, West End
(416 766 7222/www.firstchoice.com). Subway Keele.*
Open 9am-9pm Mon-Fri; 8am-6pm Sat; 11am-5pm
Sun. **Credit** MC, V.

The $11 snip may not be ideal for some of the girls
who brush through town, but to others it means a
competent cut that leaves you enough cash for a

night out afterwards. And the first-come, first-served policy will suit those on the fly.
Other locations: throughout the city.

John Steinberg & Associates Salon
585 King Street W, at Portland Street, Entertainment District (416 506 0268/www. johnsteinberghair.com). Streetcar 501, 504, 510.
Open 11am-4pm Mon; 10am-6pm Tue; 10am-4pm Wed; 10am-6pm Thur, Fri; 10am-3pm Sat. **Credit** MC, V. **Map** p271 D8.
This salon was a fixture on King Street West before the area became trendy, so the snippers have a loyal following among actors and media types. While you're getting a new, stylish look, check out the art exhibits, which change every six weeks.

Nail bars

Lux Spa
25 Bellair Street, at Cumberland Street, Yorkville (416 921 1680/www.lux-spa.com). Subway Bay.
Open 10am-6pm Tue, Wed; 10am-8pm Thur, Fri; 9am-5pm Sat. **Credit** MC, V. **Map** p274 F4.
This posh Manhattan-style nail bar is no-nonsense – both speed and hygiene are paramount. The decor is crisp, cool white, with a single treatment room for reflexology and massage and elegant potted orchids along the gleaming manicure table. A white banquette for pedicures can accommodate several customers at once. Brands used include (from Monaco) Ecrinal, Akileine, OPI and the house label. Prices start at $28 for a mani-LUX and $48 for a pedi-LUX. The spa also does a full range of waxing (for him and her), as well as brow-shaping and lash-tinting.

Opticians

Josephson Opticians
60 Bloor Street W, at Bay Street, Yorkville (416 964 7070/www.josephsonopt.com). Bus 6/subway Bay.
Open 9.30am-6pm Mon-Wed, Fri, Sat; 9.30am-8pm Thur. **Credit** AmEx, MC, V. **Map** p274 F4.
This family operation has been around since the '30s. Never a stodgy mom-and-pop outfit, it stocks the cream of Lacroix, Chanel, Mikli and Prada, along with funkier styles from LA Eyeworks. Turnaround on glasses is between two and four days, but emergency lenses are available in less than a day.
Other locations: throughout the city.

Pharmacies

Shoppers Drug Mart (360 Bloor Street W, The Annex, 416 961 2121) is the most prevalent of Toronto's pharmacies, with many locations open until midnight. **Pharma Plus** (concourse level, 55 Bloor Street W, University, 416 923 0570) is slightly less ubiquitous, and hours are less flexible. The same is true for another chain, **IDA** (66 Avenue Road, The Annex, 416 922 5555). For more information, *see p252.*

Spas

Hammam Spa
602 King Street W, at Portland Street, West End (416 366 4772/www.hammamspa.ca). Streetcar 504.
Open 11am-9pm Mon-Fri; 10am-8pm Sat; 11am-5pm Sun. **Credit** AmEx MC V. **Map** p271 D7.
Lying on a warm marble slab is what hammams are all about in the old country, and this New World version mixes such Turkish delights as vigorous body scrubs with New Age hot stone and craniosacral treatments. If you want to get squeaky clean, start by loosening up in the large co-ed steam room before being pummelled into a state of blissful relaxation.

The Oasis Wellness Centre & Spa
55 Mill Street, Building 36, Distillery District (416 364 2626/www.experienceoasis.ca). Streetcar 504.
Open 10am-7pm Mon-Thur; 10am-9pm Fri-Sat; 11am-6pm Sun. **Credit** AmEx, MC, V. **Map** p273 J8.
The country's largest day spa opened with a splash in early 2007 – by flooding the store below it. Things have calmed down since. The 19th-century industrial setting has been beautifully revamped to keep the 63 treatment rooms humming.

The Stillwater Spa at the Park Hyatt
4 Avenue Road, at Bloor Street W, Yorkville (416 926 2389/www.stillwaterspa.com). Subway Bay or Museum. **Open** 9am-10pm Mon-Fri; 8am-10pm Sat; 10am-5.30pm Sun. **Credit** AmEx, MC, V. **Map** p274 F4.
Both locals and visitors flock to this subterranean oasis of pampering and white noise (an underfoot stream beneath glass). After a hot stone massage or a wrap (choose from detoxifying seaweed or mud), linger in the steam room and sauna, or relax in front of the fire in the Asian-inspired tea lounge. The boutique carries cult cosmetics and new discoveries.

Windsor Arms Spa
18 St Thomas Street W, at Bloor Street, Yorkville (416 934 6031/http://www.windsorarmshotel. com/spa). Subway Bay or Bloor-Yonge. **Open** 10am-6pm Mon-Wed, Sat; 10am-8pm Thur, Fri; noon-6pm Sun. **Credit** AmEx, MC, V. **Map** p274 F4.
Tucked on the top floor of a luxe hotel, this cosy spa pampers like no other in town. Change into a fuzzy robe and kick back for treatments handled by skilled aestheticians using fancy European skin products. The pace is relaxed: depending on the season, take the time to lounge on the sunny terrace or poolside by the gas fireplace. If spas are meant to make commoners feel like emperors, this one takes the cake.

Home

Du Verre
188 Strachan Avenue, at Queen Street W, West End (416 593 4784/www.duverre.com). Streetcar 501.
Open 11am-6pm Tue-Sat; 1-5pm Sun. **Credit** AmEx, MC, V. **Map** p270 B7.

Eat, Drink, Shop

In an old coach house off Queen West, Du Verre sells tribal imports characterised by clean, contemporary lines. Japanese screens shield tables from Tibet and accessories from India. Brand-new metal hardware from home-grown artists offers a mod sheen.

L'Atelier

1224 Yonge Street, at Alcorn Avenue, Rosedale (416 966 0200). Subway St Clair or Summerhill. **Open** 10.30am-6pm Mon-Sat. **Credit** AmEx, MC, V. **Map** p275 G2.

Part bachelor pad, part French château, with a garden of delights thrown in, L'Atelier has plenty of gems in store, whether gilded Italian birdcages, Lucite loungers, hurricane lamps or thick marble mantels. Dramatic dressers and lighting set the scene, and smaller knick-knacks are also sold. Explore this stretch of Yonge, between Rosedale and Summerhill stations, for a slew of French antiques and modern lookalikes.

MADE

867 Dundas Street W, at Euclid Avenue, West End (416 607 6384/www.madedesign.ca). Streetcar 505. **Open** 11am-7pm Tue-Fri; 11am-6pm Sat. **Credit** MC, V. **Map** p270 C6.

Hip Canadian design – in furniture, lighting, ceramic, glass, textile and accessories – is on display in this new showroom. The carefully curated collection is practical, innovative and designed with a sense of humour. How about a pair of USB ports built into elk bookends or a portable sauna? Flexible Paper Soft Walls and honeycombed stools, both by Molo, are a staple of trendy lofts.

Teatro Verde

Hazelton Lanes, 55 Avenue Road, at Bloor Street, Yorkville (416 966 2227/www.teatroverde.com). Bus 6/subway Bay. **Open** 10am-6pm Mon-Wed, Fri, Sat; 10am-7pm Thur; noon-5pm Sun. **Credit** AmEx, MC, V. **Map** p274 F3.

Once a fashionable florist, this Hazelton Lanes boutique now does everything for the home, from sari-covered cushions and throws, to kitchen gear, cookbooks and a few boudoir accessories. You'll still find the odd vase, planter and recliner for the garden. Fresh, the New York home and fragrance line, is also sold here.

William Ashley

55 Bloor Street W, at Bay Street, Yorkville (416 964 2900/www.williamashley.com). Bus 6/subway Bay. **Open** 10am-6pm Mon-Wed, Sat; 10am-7.30pm Thur, Fri. **Credit** AmEx, MC, V. **Map** p274 F4.

Sooner or later, everyone comes through the door of Ashley's, whether buying gifts, contemplating the purchase of gourmet necessities, or creating wedding lists (stressed-out couples by the dozen wander around the maze of china). Staff are well informed, and seem to enjoy discussing the finer points of white bone china and crystal goblets, and helping select from the daunting array of patterns. Styles range from formal – Wedgwood, Worcester – to fashionable (Kate Spade, Jasper Conran).

Home accessories **MADE** good.

Music

HMV

333 Yonge Street, at Gould Street, Dundas Square (416 586 9668/www.hmv.ca). Streetcar 505/subway Dundas. **Open** 9am-10pm Mon-Thur; 9am-midnight Fri, Sat; 11am-7pm Sun. **Credit** AmEx, MC, V. **Map** p272 G6.

This flagship carries everything in audio and video entertainment and offers the occasional deal. **Other locations**: throughout the city.

Play de Record

357A Yonge Street, at Dundas Street, Dundas Square (416 586 0380/www.playderecord.com). Streetcar 505/subway Dundas. **Open** noon-8pm Mon-Wed; noon-10pm Thur, Fri; noon-9pm Sat; 1-6pm Sun. **Credit** AmEx, MC, V. **Map** p272 G6.

Squeeze past shelves of video tack to the vinyl haven at the back, where DJs and hooded club kids spin rare editions and the latest releases in hip hop, rap, Latin, electronica and jazz.

Rotate This

620 Queen Street W, at Markham Street, Entertainment District (416 504 8447/www. rotate.com). Streetcar 501. **Open** 11am-7pm Mon-Thur, Sat; 11am-8pm Fri; noon-6pm Sun. **Credit** MC, V. **Map** p270 C7.

Though the staff have attitude, there is an abundance of good indie vinyl here. The CD selection is also good, though prices are higher than average, even for used stuff. Obscure comics are also sold.

Sam the Record Man

347 Yonge Street, at Gould Street, Dundas Square (416 646 2775/www.samtherecordman.com). **Open** 9am-10pm Mon-Thur; 9am-midnight Fri, Sat; 11am-7pm Sun. **Credit** AmEx, MC, V. **Map** p272 G6.

You can't miss the giant, neon spinning platters. Known for the encyclopaedic staff, good classical and jazz sections and low prices, this rambling shop is a Toronto institution. This whole stretch of Yonge offers the best CD prices in the city.

Sonic Boom

512 Bloor Street W, at Bathurst Street, The Annex (416 532 0334). Subway Bathurst. **Open** 10am-midnight daily. **Credit** MC, V. **Map** p274 D3.

This massive secondhand CD emporium does not echo with the sound of music, but of plastic jewel cases being flipped madly. There are 20,000 CDs spanning every musical style and the pile is being constantly refreshed. The freshest tunes are at the front, where discs are grouped by day of arrival.

Soundscapes

572 College Street, at Manning Avenue, Little Italy (416 537 1620). Streetcar 506, 511. **Open** 10.30am-11pm Mon-Thur; 10.30am-midnight Fri, Sat; 10am-11pm Sun. **Credit** AmEx, MC, V. **Map** p270 C5.

The speciality here is good music, pure and simple. A former accountant and passionate listener, Greg Davis started this venture to promote new local talent and obscure classic rock, electronica and international beats. Concert tickets are sold; employee favourites are listed at the front. Local indie labels (like Paper Bag Records) are at the back, where you might discover the next Broken Social Scene.

Second-hand

Second Spin

386 Bloor Street W, at Spadina Avenue, The Annex (416 961 7746). Streetcar 510/subway Spadina. **Open** 11am-11pm Mon-Fri; 10am-11pm Sat; 11am-9pm Sun. **Credit** MC, V. **Map** p274 D4.

If you're selling, you stand to make a decent sum at Second Spin: staff offer as much as $7 for a well-kept CD. If you're buying, there's a remarkably extensive dance collection, or a rock classic.

Photography

For developing holiday snaps on the quick and cheap, the best deals are at the supermarkets. For better quality, stick with the specialists, the most prominent of which are **Black's** (20 Dundas Street W, Dundas Square, 416 595 0326; and other locations), **Japan Camera** (48 Front Street W, St Lawrence, 416 363 7476; and other locations) and **Henry's** (119 Church Street, St Lawrence, 416 868 0872). They can be pricey, but offer extras such as border options and custom alterations. Professional or aspiring photographers tend towards **West Camera** (514 Queen Street W, Entertainment District, 416 504 9432) and **Vistek** (496 Queen Street E, Moss Park, 416 365 1777), where you can also buy new or used equipment (Henry's also offers a good range). Self-service computers offer easy printing from digital.

Sex shops

In the '60s, when Toronto was young and naive, there was only one sex shop. **Lovecraft** (27 Yorkville Avenue, Yorkville, 416 923 7331) was (and still is) disconcertingly open-concept, with romantic rose-coloured walls and brazen dildo displays. Now the city has grown up, and it's easy to find… well, almost anything you require. **Condom Shack** (729 Yonge Street, Yorkville, 416 966 4226; 231 Queen Street W, Entertainment District, 416 596 7515) is the McDonald's of pleasure and protection, with a bright, scrubbed feel; **Come As You Are** (701 Queen Street W, Entertainment District, 416 504 7934) is more modern, with 'get-to-know-yourself' manuals, oils and toys geared towards same-sex partners. Across the street, get your bondage gear and trampy undergarments at **Miss Behav'n** (650 Queen Street W, Entertainment District, 416 866 7979).

Sport & outdoor

Mountain Equipment Co-op (MEC)
400 King Street W, at Peter Street, Entertainment District (416 340 2667/www.mec.ca). Streetcar 504, 510/subway St Andrew. **Open** 10am-7pm Mon-Wed; 10am-9pm Thur, Fri; 9am-6pm Sat; 11am-5pm Sun. **Credit** MC, V. **Map** p270 C8.
Renowned for its outdoor gear (tents, sleeping bags) and hiking wear (fleeces galore). A co-op (you must pay a small joining fee), it has a motivated staff and a family feel (there's even a climbing wall for kids).

Sporting Life
2665 Yonge Street, at Lytton Boulevard, North Toronto (416 485 1611). Subway Eglinton or Lawrence. **Open** 9am-9pm Mon-Fri; 9am-6pm Sat; 10am-6pm Sun. **Credit** AmEx, MC, V.
Designer kit for a broad selection of sports, and a destination for trendy sportswear. Range Rovers queue for the parking lot; inside it's madness – shoes, jackets and bathing suits piled everywhere.

Tobacconists

Thomas Hinds Tobacconist
8 Cumberland Street, at Yonge Street, Yorkville (416 927 0797/www.thomashinds.ca). Subway Bloor, Yonge. **Open** 9am-7pm Mon-Wed; 9am-9pm Thur, Fri; 9am-6pm Sat; noon-5pm Sun. **Credit** AmEx, MC, V. **Map** p275 G4.

Rock solid: **Mountain Equipment Co-op.**

This 19th-century Yorkville shop stocks the finest pipe tobacco and cigars, and attracts the occasional celebrity puffer. Most of the 150 brands of cigars are Cuban (which Americans can't buy at home).

Toys & gadgets

See also p143 **Pacific Mall**, *p147* **The Silver Snail** *and p147* **Clandestino**.

Kidding Awound
91 Cumberland Street, at Bay Street, Yorkville (416 926 8996). Subway Bloor-Yonge. **Open** *Summer* 10.30am-6pm Mon-Wed; 10.30am-7pm Thur-Sat; noon-5pm Sun. *Winter* 10.30am-6pm Mon-Sat; noon-5pm Sun. **Credit** AmEx, MC, V. **Map** p274 F4.
One-of-a-kind trinket shopping. You'll find things to be wound, spun, coloured and laughed at, and a selection of antique toys for big kids.

Science City
Holt Renfrew, 50 Bloor Street W, at Bay Street, Yorkville (416 968 2627/www.sciencecity.ca). Subway Bloor-Yonge. **Open** 10am-6pm Mon-Wed, Sat; 10am-8pm Thur, Fri; 1-5pm Sun. **Credit** AmEx, MC, V. **Map** p274 F4.
From telescopes to gyroscopes, brain-teasers to insect tweezers, this is paradise for junior geeks.

Travellers' needs

Photocopying/scanning

With all the expats in town, it's likely you'll come across a corner store with a mini office for faxing, scanning and copying. Or you could opt for **Kinko's**, which has branches in the Annex (459 Bloor Street W, 416 928 0110), the Financial District and Yonge Street (at several junctions), or **Alicos Digital Copy Centre** (66 Gerrard Street E, at Church Street, 416 977 6868), which also has outlets around town.

Shipping

Shippers will collect your purchases, pack, crate and haul them overseas – to your door – quicker than you'd think. **Alliance Services International** (416 469 5252) and **Worldwide Shipping & Forwarding** (1-905 673 9244) are both tried and tested.

Travel agents

Flight Centre
55 Yonge Street, at King Street, St Lawrence (416 304 6170/www.flightcentre.ca). Streetcar 504/subway King. **Open** 9am-6pm Mon-Fri; 10am-4pm Sat. **Credit** AmEx, MC, V. **Map** p272 G8.
Flight Centre tries to undercut any price you've been quoted for international and internal flights.
Other locations: throughout the city.

Arts & Entertainment

Features

Rockwood. *See p207.*

Festivals & Events

From big names to big beer tents, Toronto's calendar is chock-a-block.

At certain times of the year it seems you can't move for festivals in Toronto. At other times you wonder where everyone is, it's so quiet (tip: they've all gone off to their holiday cottages). But whatever month it is, there will always be something going on, and taking part in one or more of the festivities is a good way to get a feel for the city. It's certainly true that because the summer is short, locals make the most of it, filling the calendar with large- and small-scale events from Victoria Day (late May) through Labour Day (September). The biggies of the summer include Pride in late June and Caribana in late July, when the downtown core comes alive. But the rest of the year isn't neglected: autumn and winter play host to many indoor pursuits.

Below we review our favourites, but it pays to keep an eye out in the local press too, or go online (for a range of useful websites, *see p258*). It's also wise to book hotels well in advance of any major events, such as the renowned **Toronto International Film Festival** (*see p169*).

Arts & Entertainment

Top five Festivals

Beaches International Jazz Festival
Kick back and enjoy those lazy, hazy days of summer. *See p169*.

Contact Photography Festival
Get in the picture at this citywide celebration of photographic art. *See p167*.

International Festival of Authors
Your chance to eavesdrop as the big names gather for a natter. *See p170*.

Pride Week
A week-long extravaganza culminates with the splashiest parade of the year celebrating gay and lesbian life. *See p171*.

Toronto International Film Festival
Stargaze in a cinematic haze at this celebrity-driven spectacle. *See p170*.

Spring

Canada Blooms
South Building, Metro Toronto Convention Centre, 222 Bremner Boulevard, at Simcoe Street, Entertainment District (416 447 8655/www. canadablooms.com). Subway St Andrew or Union. **Map** p271 E8. **Date** Mar.
A massive flower and garden show running from Wednesday to Sunday, this floral wonderland attracts hordes of local green-fingered fans desperate for a first glimpse of spring. The main attractions are the display gardens and the prize-winning flower arrangements.

Good Friday Parade
College Street/Little Italy. Streetcar 506, 511. **Map** p270 C5. **Date** Good Fri.
Flagellating Roman centurions, candle-bearing worshippers, even the odd donkey, take to the streets of Little Italy for this sombre re-enactment of Christ on his way to the Crucifixion.

Images Festival of Independent Film & Video
Various venues (416 971 8405/www.images festival.com). **Date** Apr.
The most adventurous of the mini film fests, the week-long Images is characterised by dazzling innovation, though sometimes this comes with a price: a lack of narrative coherence.

Hot Docs International Documentary Festival
Various venues (416 203 2155/www.hotdocs.ca). **Date** mid Apr-early May.
North America's biggest documentary festival lasts ten days and features more than 100 films from around the world, from classics to the best of the current scene. Workshops and masterclasses are available. Monthly Doc Soup screenings and discussions run from October to April.

National Hockey League Play-offs
Date mid Apr-mid June.
This rite of spring whips the city into a frenzy. Bars and cafés do brisk business as long as the Maple Leafs are still in the running. They haven't won the Stanley Cup since 1967, a drought that's sated each year by plenty of beer and consternation. Despite this decades-long drought, tickets are impossible to get, except through scalpers.

Contact Photography Festival
Various venues (416 539 9595/www.contact photo.com). **Date** May.

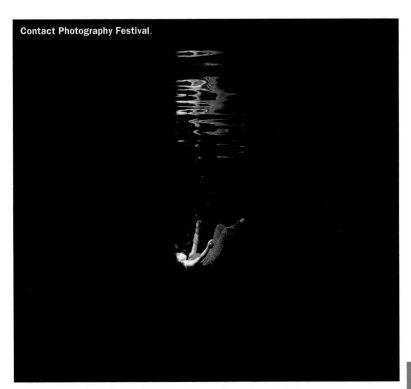

Contact Photography Festival.

A month-long festival of Canadian and international photography exhibited in galleries, bars and restaurants across the city. Photographers discuss their craft in workshops and seminars.

Inside Out Toronto Lesbian & Gay Film & Video Festival
Various venues (416 977 6847/www.insideout.on.ca).
Date May.
A social occasion as much as a cinematic experience, this popular ten-day event brings out the lesbian and gay community's arty elite. Up and running since 1990, Inside Out plays everything from commercial material to obscure documentaries.

Toronto Jewish Film Festival
Various venues (416 324 9121/www.tjff.com).
Date May.
The largest event of its kind in North America, this ten-day festival features Jewish films, shorts and documentaries from around the world.

Victoria Day Long Weekend
Date Mon closest to 24 May.
Victoria Day weekend is a national holiday and the unofficial launch of summer. Gardeners get busy, people head off to their cottages, and crowds gather for firework displays, all in honour of a queen who might well have disapproved. The date recognises the royal birthday, but also (coincidentally) the mode of celebration, the 'two-four,' or case of 24 beers, the largest you can buy.

Doors Open Toronto
Various venues (416 338 3888/www.doorsopen.org).
Date last weekend in May.
Many of the 100-plus sites on this two-day tour are normally off-limits to the public, so this is a good chance for both locals and tourists to discover Toronto's history and architecture. There is no formal tour: participating buildings simply hang out a welcoming blue banner (check local papers for a map). Best of all, it's free.

Summer

Luminato
Various venues (416 368 3100/www.luminato.ca).
Date early June.
This new annual arts festival, launching in 2007, celebrates diversity. Born out of the post-SARS slump to kick-start tourism, this collective pat on the back of local talent and international guests features

a multidisciplinary approach with theatre, music, dance and visual arts. Eric Idle premieres *Not the Messiah*, a musical based on *Life of Brian*, to be conducted by his cousin, Peter Oundjian, music director of the Toronto Symphony Orchestra.

North by Northeast Music & Film Festival

Various venues (416 863 6963/www.nxne.com). **Date** early June.

The sounds of independent music, the kind unfettered by those big record-label contract obligations, tear up the city centre during this popular three-day event. Tens of thousands of music fans prowl dozens of clubs, catching talent from Canada, the US and around the world. You can bet the musicians treat the whole thing as an audition for the ears of all those record-company execs who trawl the festival in search of the next big sound.

World Roots Festival

Harbourfront Centre, 235 Queens Quay W, Waterfront (416 973 4000/www.harbour frontcentre.com). Streetcar 509, 510. **Map** p271/p272 F9. **Date** June-Sept.

This summer-long series of weekend festivals spotlights different cultures through food, dance, art, film and music, and most importantly, music. The (mainly free) concerts are surprising, intriguing, offbeat and of an amazingly high quality, and they often feature internationally known stars such as Sao Jorge and the Neville Brothers, while the open-air lakeside venue makes this one of the best places in town to hear music on a hot summer's evening.

Pride Week

Various venues (416 927 7433/www.pride toronto.com). **Date** late June.

What started out as a small political picnic in 1970 has turned into a brash commercial success that lasts a week and is more celebration than march. There are beer gardens and entertainment on several stages in Church & Wellesley throughout the weekend – everything from disco to alterna-queer to lesbian folk. Late-night events are adult-oriented, but the big parade itself (always on the last Sunday in June) is increasingly family-friendly, with up to a million people ogling the drag queens and muscle boys and cheering the activists and politicians. The parade is long, the weather hot and the crowds enormous – so bring water. The smaller Dyke March takes place the day before. For details, check out *Xtra!*'s stand-alone guide, usually published in early June. **Photo** *p171*.

Queen's Plate

Woodbine Race Track, 555 Rexdale Boulevard, at Highway 427 (416 675 7223/www.woodbine entertainment.com). Bus 37A, 191. **Date** late June.

Three-year-old Canadian-bred thoroughbreds compete in the country's oldest horse races at Woodbine Race Track. Royalty – or at least their stand-ins – usually put in an appearance.

Toronto International Dragon Boat Race Festival

Centre Island (416 595 1739/www. dragonboats.com). **Date** late June.

The colourful dragon boats are the centrepiece of this Chinese festival, which takes place over a weekend. With food, games, music and dance, it attracts more than 100,000 people to the sylvan shores of the Toronto Islands. Across the water from the city, they offer a cool respite from the heat.

Toronto Downtown Jazz Festival

Various venues (416 928 2033/www.tojazz.com). **Date** late June-early July.

During this fest, hundreds of artists perform all styles of jazz at dozens of clubs, theatres and outdoor stages throughout the downtown area.

Canada Day

Downsview Park
John Drury Drive, at Sheppard Avenue, North Toronto (416 952 2222/www.pdp.ca). Subway Downsview.
Mel Lastman Square
5100 Yonge Street, at Sheppard Avenue, North Toronto (416 338 0338/www.city.toronto. on.ca/special_events). Subway North York Centre.
Nathan Phillips Square
100 Queen Street W, at Bay Street, Chinatown (416 338 0338/www.city.toronto.on.ca/special_events). Streetcar 501/subway Queen. **Map** p271/p272 F7.
York Quay Centre
235 Queens Quay W, at York Street, Waterfront (416 973 4000/www.harbourfrontcentre.com). Streetcar 509, 510. **Map** p271/p272 F9.
All Date 1 July.

Torontonians celebrate Canada's birthday (1 July 1867) with a Canadian mixture of deference and pride, usually by leaving town for the long weekend. Best bets for fun are Nathan Phillips Square, Mel Lastman Square, Harbourfront Centre and Downsview Park; most events feature Canuck entertainers and night-time fireworks displays. The Harbourfront festivities have the added bonus of a lake view and a cool breeze.

Toronto Fringe Theatre Festival

Various venues (416 966 1062/www.fringe toronto.com). **Date** early July.

At the Toronto Fringe, the trick is to see the hit shows before they're over. Venues are tiny and the grapevine is quick, so getting in can be tricky, but with more than 100 troupes from both Canada and abroad on hand over the 12 days, there's plenty of choice, and high quality. The Annex home base for the festival has a beer tent, where you can pick up the buzz on the hits and misses.

Grand Prix of Toronto

Exhibition Place, Lake Shore Boulevard W, between Strachan Avenue & Dufferin Street, Waterfront (416 872 4639/www.grandprixtoronto.com). Bus 29/streetcar 509, 511. **Map** p270 B9. **Date** early July.

Over a weekend in July, drivers burn rubber on the streets through Exhibition Place. Expect lots of testosterone-driven music and street parties.

Toronto Outdoor Art Exhibition

Nathan Phillips Square, 100 Queen Street W, at Bay Street, Chinatown (416 408 2754/www.toronto outdoorart.org). Streetcar 501/subway Queen. **Map** p270/272 F7. **Date** early July.

It's the largest outdoor art exhibition in Canada, so there's plenty to gaze upon at this free weekend-long expo. Artists range from established to students.

Beaches International Jazz Festival

Queen Street E, east of Woodbine Avenue, East Toronto (416 698 2152/www.beachesjazz.com). Streetcar 501. **Date** 3rd wk in July.

More than 50 bands perform from street corners, rooftops and parks in one of Toronto's most bucolic neighbourhoods. The main stage is located in Kew Gardens and, with its beach and boardwalk, it's worth going for the ambience alone.

Celebrate Toronto Street Festival

Various venues (416 338 3338/www.toronto.ca/ special_events). **Date** July.

Locals hate the traffic jams, but visitors love the free entertainment at this weekend-long event – everything from world to classical to hip-hop, on a series of stages situated at key intersections on Toronto's main drag (Dundas Street, Bloor Street, St Clair Avenue, Eglinton Avenue and Lawrence Avenue). It's good, cheap fun, with carnival rides for the kids and beer gardens for the adults.

Rogers Cup

Rexall Centre, York University, 1 Shoreham Drive (416 665 9777, ext 4333/www.tenniscanada.com). Subway Downsview then bus 106/subway Keele then bus 41. **Date** late July-early Aug.

Top international tennis players battle at the viewer-friendly Rexall Centre (11,500 seats), in the city's northern suburbs. Men and women play in alternate years with Montreal hosting the opposite sex. In the evening, bring a jacket as it gets breezy.

Caribana

Various venues (905 799 1630/www.caribana.com). **Date** Simcoe Day long weekend, late July-early Aug.

North America's largest Caribbean festival attracts a million-plus tourists and sends what little remains of Toronto's stodgy Anglo past into a happy tailspin. Thousands of colourfully costumed revellers participate in events like the King and Queen of the Bands competition, usually held at Lamport Stadium (1155 King Street W, West End) and the climactic parade that sees dozens of 'mas' (masquerade) bands floating west on Lake Shore Boulevard. For the next two days a cool-down-cum-arts festival takes place on Olympic Island, across the harbour. You can't miss the parade (or the thumping car stereos on Yonge Street at night), but the many spin-off events are sometimes hard to find. Check the local weeklies for last-minute details.

Fringe Festival of Independent Dance Artists

Distillery District (416 410 4291/www.ffida.org). Bus 65. **Map** p273 J8. **Date** Aug.

This ten-day festival features short works by experienced and emerging choreographers, with some site-specific works. It's a gamble, but worth it for the variety alone. Styles run the gamut from modern dance through ballet to belly dancing.

Taste of the Danforth

Various locations along Danforth Avenue, East Toronto (416 469 5634/www.tasteofthe danforth.com). Subway Broadview, Chester or Pape. **Date** early Aug.

During this weekend event up to a million people sample all kinds of food provided by the restaurants in this Greek neighbourhood. Top entertainers perform on three stages. All in all, a big, bustling people-friendly event.

SummerWorks Theatre Festival

Various venues (416 410 1048/www. summerworks.ca). **Date** Aug.

A ten-day event featuring a mix of established and emerging theatre companies presenting 40-odd plays. New work is encouraged.

Canadian National Exhibition

Exhibition Place, Lake Shore Boulevard W, between Strachan Avenue & Dufferin Street, Waterfront (416 263 3800/www.theex.com). Bus 29/streetcar 509, 511. **Map** p270 B9. **Date** mid Aug-early Sept.

A cross between an old-fashioned agricultural fair and a modern-day expo, the CNE (or the Ex, as it's known locally) mixes sheep-shearing and milking demonstrations with fun rides and theme days devoted to Toronto's ethnic communities. Some folks come just for the sideshows, but the real thrill is the nostalgia. Stick around for the last three days of the two-week fair, when high-flying acrobats take to the skies on Labour Day Weekend for the Canadian International Air Show. It's a blue-sky wonder, with Canada's own performing poodles of the sky, the Snowbirds aeronautic squad, always drawing plenty of cheers.

Autumn

Cabbagetown Festival

Various locations around Carlton & Parliament Streets, Cabbagetown (416 921 0857/www.old cabbagetown.com). Streetcar 506. **Map** p272/p273 H/J 5/6. **Date** early Sept.

A tribute to a working-class neighbourhood turned affluent enclave, this weekend-long fest offers corn roasts, street dances, pancake breakfasts, an arts and crafts fair, a parade and tours of some of the neighbourhood's unique bay and gable houses.

Toronto International Film Festival

Various venues (416 967 7371/www.bell.ca/filmfest). **Date** early Sept.

Arts & Entertainment

This ten-day film orgy now rivals Cannes and Sundance for PR power, and that means loads of celebrities and miles of celluloid – everything from Hollywood blockbusters to obscure Eastern European angst-fests. Even work-obsessed Torontonians take time off for this one. The giddiness is pervasive. Public screenings start at 9am, and go past midnight at some venues. With 300-plus features showing, there's always something to see, but popular items sell out quickly. The complete schedule doesn't usually appear until late August, but avid fans start buying passes and tickets in mid July. *See also p180.*

Word on the Street

Queen's Park, north of Ontario Parliament Buildings, University (416 504 7241/www. thewordonthestreet.ca). Subway Museum or Queen's Park. **Map** p274 F5. **Date** late Sept.
More than 100,000 people stroll beneath the oaks and elms of Queen's Park during a Sunday celebration of literacy. Publishers and writers promote their wares with readings and signings. Kids get their own special tent.

Nuit Blanche

Various venues throughout downtown (416 338 0338/http://nuitblanche.livewithculture.ca). **Date** last Sat in Sept.
After a stunning debut in 2006, when half a million people stayed out all night to take in fanciful art installations in parks, swimming pools, car washes and art galleries, Torontonians are hooked on the all-night arts idea. Patterned after – and scheduled to coincide with – other 'white nights' in Paris, among other cities, this 12-hour, free art party is destined to become a key event in the calendar.

International Festival of Authors

Harbourfront Centre, 235 Queens Quay W, at Spadina Avenue, Waterfront (416 973 4000/ www.readings.org). Streetcar 509, 510. **Map** p271/p272 F9. **Date** late Oct.
From the four corners of the world they come, trailing their Bookers, Pulitzers and Nobels – novelists, poets and biographers from the top tiers of the literary firmament. The ten-day event started in 1980 and quickly became a prestigious affair, but despite the glitter factor, the readings, talks and on-stage interviews have remained surprisingly intimate. The venues are usually the Harbourfront Centre's Premiere Dance Theatre and York Quay Centre, but check nearer the time. If you can't make it to the big event, there are other readings at Harbourfront, generally on Wednesday nights, from September to December, and February to June.

Toronto International Art Fair

South Building, Metro Toronto Convention Centre, 222 Bremner Boulevard, at Simcoe Street, Entertainment District (information 1-800 663 4173/604 925 0330/booking 416 872 1212/1-800 461 3333/www.tiafair.com). Subway St Andrew or Union. **Map** p271 E8. **Date** late Oct-early Nov.

It's not Basel or Venice but this four-day art binge gets stronger with each outing and is proving to be a must-see event on the contemporary art scene.

Canadian Aboriginal Festival

Rogers Centre (SkyDome), 1 Blue Jays Way, at Front Street, Entertainment District (519 751 0040/www .canab.com). Streetcar 504/subway Union. **Map** p271 E8. **Date** mid Nov.
North America's largest aboriginal arts event is a three-day affair featuring fashion, films, lacrosse, music awards and a giant powwow.

Santa Claus Parade

Bloor Street & University Avenue, Entertainment & Financial Districts (416 249 7833/www.thesanta clausparade.com). Streetcar 501, 504, 505/subway King, Museum, Osgoode, Queen's Park, St Andrew, St Patrick or Union. **Date** late Nov.
Started more than a century ago as a publicity stunt for a local department store, the Santa Claus Parade is now a Toronto institution. More than 500,000 people – mostly parents with kids on their shoulders – watch dozens of floats, storybook characters, marching bands and, of course, Santa and his sleigh, as they parade through the city centre.

Cavalcade of Lights

Nathan Phillips Square, 100 Queen Street W, at Bay Street, Chinatown (416 338 0338/www.toronto.ca/ special_events). Streetcar 501/subway Queen. **Map** p271/p272 F7. **Date** late Nov-late Dec.
A hundred thousand lights illuminate the city's central square, kicking off a month of skating parties and other events that culminate in a televised New Year's Eve party with top Canadian acts.

Winter

New World Stage

Harbourfront Centre 235 Queens Quay W, Waterfront (416 973 4000/www.harbour frontcentre.com). Streetcar 509, 510. **Map** p271/p272 F9. **Date** Jan-May.
This new, annual festival of theatre and dance showcases troupes from across the country and around the world. The programming promises to be edgy. For the launch in 2007, *Mabou Mines Doll House* cast male dwarves and towering women in a deconstructed retelling of Ibsen's *A Doll's House*.

WinterCity

100 Queen Street W, at Bay Street, Chinatown (416 338 0338/www.toronto.ca/special_events). Streetcar 501/subway Queen. **Map** p271/p272 F7. **Date** late Jan-early Feb.
Toronto in the depths of winter can be harsh. Hence this city-sponsored attempt to make a cold month cool – two weeks of flashy outdoor entertainment (mostly at Nathan Phillips Square), discounted admission to local landmarks (check the website for details) and discounted prices at local restaurants via the popular Winterlicious promotion. Find out how many ways ice and snow can be turned into art.

Pride Week. *See p168.*

Children

Small pleasures in the big city.

Wet and wild at **Ontario Place**. *See p173.*

Toronto is kid-friendly all year round, from the water park of Ontario Place to the free ice rinks at Harbourfront and Nathan Phillips Square. While hipsters may decry the city's lack of urban edginess, parents can relax in an environment of cleanliness and safety in a big-city setting. An easy-to-navigate streetscape and transport system make most outings straightforward, and those behind a pram will be relieved to see that most major subway stops have lifts, and that all significant destinations have ramp access.

An obvious first stop is an orienting visit to the **CN Tower** (*see p63*), followed by souvenir hunting at the consumer's paradise that is the **Toronto Eaton Centre** (*see p69*) or, for a shift in gears, a ferry ride to the bucolic **Toronto Islands** (*see p76* **Bike on**).

Babysitting & daycare

Any number of websites (www.helpwevegot kids.com is a good one) will provide a list of daycare centres in the Toronto area – many, such as **It's Playtime** (416 465 6688), provide drop-in babysitting services, some up to six hours. Visit the above website for more information about supervised playgrounds, community centres that cater for single parents and emergency services. For a directory of

downtown drop-ins and times, call **Community Information Toronto** (416 397 4636). Otherwise, the **YMCA** (Family Development Centre, 416 928 9622), is open from dawn till dusk and will take kids from 18 months to 12 years. Major hotels will be able to arrange babysitting (services are listed under individual hotels; alternatively, call a reputable agency such as **Christopher Robin** (416 483 4744, $65 for first three hours, then $15 per hour thereafter).

Indoor attractions

Art Gallery of Ontario

For full listings, *see p73*.

The current construction-site appearance of Frank Gehry's AGO makeover, due to be completed in 2008, may appeal to kids as much as the art programmes on offer inside. All the same, AGO works on a scale that is well suited to families – not too big to exhaust you, but with enough quirky material to satisfy neophyte art critics (handy tip: head for the giant hamburger).

CBC Broadcasting Centre

250 Front Street W, at John Street, Entertainment District (museum 416 205 5574/www.cbc.ca/ museum). Streetcar 504/subway St Andrew or Union. **Open** *9am-5pm Mon-Fri; noon-4pm Sat.* **Admission** *free.* **Map** *p271 E8.*

Admittedly Canadian TV history isn't going to mean much to visitors from abroad, but the CBC Broadcasting Centre's big-box architecture, giant atrium and main-floor museum are well worth a look. Interactive stations feature newsreels, children's shows and sports trivia.

Hockey Hall of Fame

For full listings, *see p66.*

How many museums have their own ice rink where you can test your slap-shot skills? This impressive building houses the world's greatest hockey memories and lets you record your own broadcast and pose beside the Stanley Cup.

Lorraine Kimsa Theatre for Young People

165 Front Street E, at Sherbourne Street, St Lawrence (416 862 2222/www.lktyp.ca). Streetcar 504. **Open** *Box office* 9am-5pm Mon-Fri. *Shows* Sat, Sun. **Tickets** $19-$29. **Credit** AmEx, MC, V. **Map** p272 H8.

Toronto's premier venue for children's theatre offers productions that are aimed at kids but will also appeal to their adult escorts. Shows are tailored for specific age groups, so call ahead or check the website.

Ontario Science Centre

For full listings, *see p91.*

Following a revamp, this shrine to fun with science and technology is more kid-friendly than ever. Kids like the hands-on approach in the countless interactive exhibits. The OSC also features an Omnimax Cinema (for big close-ups in science and nature films). And you can touch practically everything – except the liquid nitrogen. **Photo** *p174.*

Paramount Toronto

For full listings, *see p181.*

If cinema is on your offspring's agenda, this movie madhouse is the place to go. Small children may feel overwhelmed, but with more than 12 screens, including an IMAX, there's bound to be something suitable. Be warned: the 'waiting lounge' is a noisy video arcade surrounded by pricey junk-food kiosks. If your film buffs are old enough to be left alone, take refuge in the giant Chapters bookstore below.

Royal Ontario Museum

For full listings, *see p78.*

Now that the ROM's dramatic enlargement is complete, the entire museum is once again open for an exploration through the millennia, from dinosaur bones and mummies to every child's favourite, the bat cave. There are also improved eating facilities. The permanent collection offers 'Hands-on Biodiversity' rooms with interactive displays.

Outdoor fun

Toronto has several large parks where restless young legs can run wild. The Toronto Islands provide the largest getaway (with a fun ferry ride to boot) and, from May to September, the **Centreville Amusement Park** (*see p76*) offers tyke-friendly pony and train rides. **High Park** (*see p92*) over in the West End features bicycle and inline skating paths, forest walks, a large pond, a small zoo, a tractor-train and a huge children's play castle that's a must for the 4-12 set. **Riverdale Park** is smaller, but has a petting zoo and various barnyard demonstrations. **Harbourfront Centre** (*p60*) on the city's lakeshore always has something going on, from tall ships to craft fairs. Catch a blown-glass demonstration in the craft studio.

For something simple and handy, check out the Yorkville rock (Cumberland Avenue between Avenue Road and Bay Street), a giant chunk of Canadian shield granite plonked down in the centre of the city. Kids love climbing it, and parents love the nearby shopping.

If your kids are sporty, the city has many public swimming pools and beaches, as well as tennis courts and golf courses. In winter public ice-skating rinks, indoor and outdoor, abound. There are also two ski runs in Earl Bales and Centennial Parks (*see p217*).

Ice skating in Nathan Phillips Square

For full listings, *see p215.*

If you want to do something very Toronto, grab some skates and take a twirl before the landmark City Hall towers. Weekdays, when the coast is clear, are best for beginners. Rentals and sharpening services are positioned by the snack bar. Open from late November to late March, weather permitting.

Ontario Place

For full listings, *see p61.*

This is the mega playground kids dream about. Water activities include slides and bumper boats, and a huge concrete field where massive features spray water and serve as jungle gyms. Dry delight can be had with the indoor maze funhouse, fast food and various amphitheatres (including an IMAX that is built out over the water). **Photo** *p172.*

Paramount Canada's Wonderland

9580 Jane Street, at MacKenzie Drive, Vaughan (905 832 7000/www.canadas-wonderland.com). Yorkdale or York Mills subway then GO bus/Highway 400, exit Rutherford Road (just north of Highway 401). **Open** *Late May-mid June* 10am-6pm daily. *Mid June-Aug* 10am-10pm daily. *Sept-mid Oct* 10am-8pm Sat, Sun. Closed mid Oct-late May. **Admission** $50; $25 3-6s, concessions. **Credit** AmEx, MC, V.

Situated out of town but well worth a family visit, this does all the things giant amusement parks do, from stomach-churning roller coasters to inhabited cartoon characters. For a more authentic experience, the Canadian National Exhibition (*see p169*) operates for three weeks up to Labour Day (first Monday in September) at Exhibition Place.

Arts & Entertainment

Ontario Science Centre. *See p173.*

Speaker's Corner

ChumCity Building, 299 Queen Street W, at John Street, Entertainment District (416 591 5757/www.citytv.com). Streetcar 501/subway Osgoode. **Open** 24hrs daily. **Admission** $1. **No credit cards. Map** p271 E7.
Speaker's Corner is named after its London counterpart, though it's more high tech. A video soapbox ensconced in the Citytv building encourages passers-by of all ages to speak their minds. Depositing a dollar triggers the video camera; pull back the curtain, and you're a pundit. Citytv (Channel 7) airs the best comments on a show called *Speaker's Corner*; the money goes to local charities.

Toronto Hippo Tours

416 703 4476/www.torontohippotours.com. Tours leave from 151 Front Street W, at Simcoe Street, Entertainment District. Subway St Andrew or Union. **Tours** *May-Oct* hourly 11am-6pm daily. **Admission** $38; $33 students 13-17; $25 3-12s; $3 under-3s; $110 family. **Credit** AmEx, MC, V. **Map** p272 F8.
This amphibious tour bus morphs into a raft at the Toronto harbour. Meet the crew at the south-east corner of Front and Simcoe Streets for a street tour followed by a view from the harbour.

Toronto Zoo

361A Old Finch Avenue, Meadowvale Road, north of Highway 401, North Toronto (416 392 5900/ www.torontozoo.com). Bus 85/GO Rouge Hill Station (weekends only). **Open** *Jan-early Mar, early Oct-Dec* 9.30am-4.30pm daily. *Early Mar-late May, early Sept-early Oct* 9am-6pm daily. *Late May-early Sept* 9am-7.30pm daily. **Admission** $19; $12 concessions; $11 4-12s; free under-4s. **Credit** AmEx, MC, V.
This zoo gives animals – and human interlopers – plenty of room to roam. There's enough outdoor fun and adventure to make a day of it; call ahead for

feeding times, particularly for the polar bears, whose giant enclosure features an underwater observatory. All the big beasts are here, plus their littl'uns – this zoo's inhabitants are remarkably fecund. Hop on to the Zoomobile when energy begins to wane. A safari simulator ride makes a nice treat as you leave.

Eating out

There's no shortage of fast-food joints, but you'll be missing out on ethnic flavours, from Lebanese *shwarmas* to Chilean empanadas. Chinatown offers great dim sum, and the finger-friendly delicacies are good value; after a visit to the Royal Ontario Museum, try **Dynasty** (131 Bloor Street W, 416 923 3323).
If the kids insist on the tried but true, **Planet Hollywood** (277 Front Street W, 416 596 7827) is located between the two major tourist spots, the CN Tower and Rogers Centre. The Entertainment District is lined with bustling eateries catering to large groups. **Wayne Gretzky's** (99 Blue Jays Way, 416 979 7825), named after Canada's greatest hockey player, makes a child-friendly detour after a visit to the Hockey Hall of Fame. **Alice Fazooli's** (294 Adelaide Street W, 416 979 1910) serves wings, burgers and bottomless Cokes.

Keg Steakhouse & Bar

12 Church Street, at Front Street, St Lawrence (416 367 0685/www.kegsteakhouse.com). Streetcar 504/subway Union. **Open** 4pm-1am Mon-Sat; 4-11pm Sun. **Main courses** $14-$32. **Credit** AmEx, DC, MC, V. **Map** p272 G8.
Steak and chicken, steak and ribs, steak and lobster – you get the picture. Burgers are also good. Quality is high, and service smiley, American-style.

Old Spaghetti Factory

54 The Esplanade, at Yonge Street, St Lawrence (416 864 9761/www.oldspaghettifactory.ca). Streetcar 504/subway Union. **Open** 11.30am -11pm Mon-Thur, Sun; 11.30am-midnight Fri, Sat. **Main courses** $9-$18. **Credit** AmEx, DC, MC, V. **Map** p272 G8.
Toronto's answer to Chuck-E-Cheez has been filling kids with 'pasghetti and meat bulbs' for yonks. Near the Hockey Hall of Fame (*see p66*).

Shopping

The 'Kids' suffix is catching on everywhere, from Gap to Pottery Barn, but if you don't want your children looking like walking billboards, there are some decent alternatives, such as **Misdemeanours** (*see p148*), which does playful girls' outfits. For brand names at a discount, check out **Chocky's** (*see p148*). For outdoor gear for the entire family, try **Mountain Equipment Co-op** (*see p159*). For shops selling toys and gadgets, *see p160*.

Comedy

Where to tickle your funny bone.

Comedy is Canada's number one cultural export after hockey and Toronto, the hometown of Mike Myers and Jim Carrey, has always been a fertile ground for funny men and women. Beginning in the silent-movie era, when actress Mary Pickford and *Keystone Cops*' creator Mack Sennett blew down to Hollywood, northern yuksters have made an enormous impact on the worldwide comedy industry. The average Torontonian can reel off a list of home-grown greats. In addition to Myers and Carrey, there's Dan Aykroyd, Rich Little, Michael J Fox, Eric McCormack, the *SCTV* crew of Martin Short, John Candy, Eugene Levy, Catherine O'Hara, Joe Flaherty, Andrea Martin, Rick Moranis, Dave Thomas and Harold Ramis and the *Kids in the Hall* gang, including Scott Thompson. *Saturday Night Live* producer Lorne Michaels is also from Toronto (Tom Green, thankfully, is from Ottawa, as is Matthew Perry).

Toronto was the launching pad for these comedians' careers, and ranks as one of the three most important comedy centres in North America (New York and San Francisco being the other two). On any given night you can see seasoned stand-ups practising their craft at **Yuk Yuk's** or the legendary sketch comedy of **Second City**. If you're feeling more adventurous, seek out some experimental laughs at venues like the **AltdotComedy Lounge** (*see below*) and **Bad Dog Theatre Company** (*see below*), but brace yourself for some off-colour comedy. In 2003, for instance, at the height of the SARS scare, an alternative comedy troupe staged *Sarsical*, a musical comedy complete with doo-wop ditties about the virus and surgical masks for the audience. Which just goes to show that, beneath Toronto's grey, Calvinist surface beats a bawdy, mischievous heart – a natural reaction that finds expression in dozens of comedy venues.

For details of comedy shows, pick up a copy of *eye* or *NOW*, the city's free listings rags. Comedy shows are always hit and miss, but the venues listed below should provide a few guaranteed laughs and are bound to offend a few people too. Touchy Americans have been known to walk out of clubs: making fun of the Yanks is a national pastime in Canada, just as the reverse is true south of the border.

Venues

ALTdotCOMedy Lounge

The Rivoli, 332-334 Queen Street W, at Spadina Avenue, Entertainment District (416 596 1908/ www.altcomedylounge.com). Streetcar 501, 510. **Show** 8.30pm Mon, 1st & 3rd Tue/mth. **Admission** pay what you can. **Credit** AmEx, MC, V. **Map** p271 E7.

Every Monday night the back room at the Rivoli (*see also p134, p203 and p216*) is transformed into a cabaret, where Toronto's alternative comedians come out to play. On some nights it seems 'alternative' is a euphemism for 'poorly rehearsed', but admission is on a 'pay what you can' basis, which means it's normally good value for money. If you're lucky, you'll catch a visiting celebrity blowing off some steam. Scott Thompson, Janeane Garofalo, Will Ferrell and Tom Green have all made appearances here. The first and third Tuesday of each month are now devoted to sketch comedy.

Bad Dog Theatre Company

138 Danforth Avenue, at Broadview Avenue, East Toronto (416 491 3115/www.baddogtheatre.com). Subway Broadview. **Shows** 8pm Wed-Fri; 8pm, 10pm Sat. **Tickets** prices vary. **Credit** MC, V.

Toronto is known for its comedic improvisers, the most famous being Mike Myers, the Kids in the Hall, Colin Mochrie and improv guru Bruce Hunter. The breeding ground for this talent was Theatresports, which, after a turbulent run at Toronto's Poor Alex Theatre, went under to be replaced by Bad Dog Theatre. This full-time improvisational venue presents an eclectic range of shows – everything from Harry Potter parodies ('Hairy Patter & the Improvisers Stone') to an open comedy jam such as Midweek Mayhem. They offer a weekly free 'drop-in' one-hour improv class, so adventurous types can try their hand. The atmosphere is warm and friendly, tinged with a bit of inventive agitation.

Diesel Playhouse

56 Blue Jays Way, at King Street W, Entertainment District (416 971 5656/www.dieselplayhouse.com). Streetcar 504/subway St Andrew. **Shows** times vary. **Tickets** average $10. **Credit** AmEx, MC, V. **Map** p271 E8.

This roadhouse took over the digs from Second City when the latter moved across the street in 2005, and, in doing so, boosted the comedy content in the Entertainment District. Touring shows take the main stage, and most are in a comic vein. Sunday Night Live features The Sketchpersons troupe, with well-known local hosts Ryan Malcolm (from

Laugh school

So you want to be the next Mike Myers? Well, comedy costs, and right here is where you start paying (in the form of a couple of grand a year). In 1999, Toronto's **Humber College** started the world's first degree-granting comedy school. Aspiring cut-ups can enrol in the two-year undergraduate diploma programme. Each spring thousands of hopefuls audition for the school, and from this pool of prospective talent 75 students are chosen. But they have to be serious about being funny: courses cost upwards of $2,500 a year.

The school is located at Humber's Lake Shore campus, which is (appropriately) housed in an old insane asylum. The curriculum is a class clown's dream. A typical schedule might include a morning class in sketch comedy followed by a few hours of stand-up, improv and bit of shtick. It boasts a faculty that has plenty of industry experience. Instructors include television producer Lorne Frohman, who in the 1970s won eight Emmy awards for his work with the likes of Richard Pryor and Lily Tomlin; SCTV alumnus Joe Flaherty; Yuk Yuk's (see p176) owner Mark Breslin and veteran Canadian stand-up Larry Horowitz. Humber also brings in guest speakers. In past semesters luminaries such as *Seinfeld* producer George Shapiro, Chevy Chase, Steve Allen, Joan Rivers and the Smothers Brothers have all spoken to Humber students.

When it opened, the school was greeted with disdain by the comedy community. 'You can't teach funny,' went the refrain. The idea of getting a degree in comedy seemed to contradict everything that being a comedian entailed – a rebellious personality with an anti-establishment streak. The school's dean, author Joe Kertes, argued that Humber's goal was to help 'funny people get funnier'.

To his credit, it seems to be working. Humber graduates such as stand-up Levi McDougall and sketch comedian Ryan Belleville are making waves both north and south of the border, and each night Toronto's comedy clubs are full of Humber grads plying their trade. Comedy fans wishing to see what Humber has to offer can check out Yuk Yuk's Tuesday night shows, which feature sets from current comedy-programme students.

Humber School of Comedy

Humber Lakeshore Campus, 3199 Lake Shore Blvd W, at 23rd Street, West End (416 675 6622/www.humber.ca). Subway Kipling then bus 44.

Canadian Idol), Barenaked Ladies guitarist/keyboardist Kevin Hearn, *Puppets Who Kill* star Dan Redican, comedian Teresa Pavelinek, Toronto Argonaut John Avery and Don Ferguson of CBC's *Royal Canadian Air Farce*.

Laugh Resort

Holiday Inn Hotel, 370 King Street W, at Peter Street, Entertainment District (416 364 5233/ www.laughresort.com). Streetcar 504/subway St Andrew. Shows 8.30pm Wed, Thur; 8.30pm, 10.45pm Fri, Sat. Tickets $7-$15. Credit MC, V. Map p271 E8.

This cosy 100-seat theatre is in the basement of a Holiday Inn, but it feels like the basement of someone's house. The club moved to this smaller venue a few years ago, and now you can get within spitting distance of some of comedy's finest. The intimate setting means the heckling can be fast and furious, and there's no place to hide if a performer sets their satirical sights on you. In addition to hosting local stars, the venue has traditionally been a good spot to see international acts just before they hit the big time. Adam Sandler, David Spade and Ellen DeGeneres all performed here shortly before they became household names.

Second City

99 Blue Jays Way, at King Street W, Entertainment District (416 343 0011/www.secondcity.com). Streetcar 504/subway St Andrew. Shows times vary. Tickets $12-$28. Credit AmEx, DC, MC, V. Map p271 E8.

Toronto's oldest and most famous comedy venue is still the best place in town to take in an evening of sketch comedy. A venue change in 2006 took the venerable establishment back to its 1973 roots: it is now a smaller, more casual 300-seat club where you can dress casually. The main productions are loosely linked sketches with an underlying theme, packaged under pithy titles like *Bird Flu Over the Cuckoo's Nest*. Shows run seven nights a week and members of the audience can stick around to watch the same performers hone their improvisation skills. The resident comedians use these free improv sets, which start around 10pm, to develop material for the next big show. Robin Williams has been known to stop by to keep his stand-up chops in shape. Photos of Second City alumni, including Dan Aykroyd, Eugene Levy, Dave Thomas, Martin Short, Gilda Radner and John Candy, line the halls. Those early greats created the seminal TV show *SCTV*, a popular spoof from the early 1980s.

Spirits Bar & Grill
*642 Church Street, at Hayden Street, Church
& Wellesley (416 967 0001/www.spiritsbar
andgrill.com). Subway Bloor-Yonge.* **Shows**
9pm Wed. **Admission** free. **Credit** AmEx,
DC, MC, V. **Map** p275 G4.

Hosted by the irrepressible stand-up comedian Jo-
Anna Downey, Spirits is the funniest spot in
Boyztown, though it's not officially a gay pub. It is
homo-friendly, though, which perhaps explains why
it is the city's longest-running showcase for
independent new material. Every Wednesday it
offers a mix of beginners trying to find their feet and
seasoned comics testing out new bits. The
atmosphere is warm and wacky, and the emphasis
is on experimentation. Admission is free, so don't
even think about asking for your money back.

Yuk Yuk's
*224 Richmond Street W, at Simcoe Street,
Entertainment District (416 967 6425/www.
yukyuks.com). Streetcar 501/subway Osgoode.*
Shows 8.30pm Wed, Thur, Sun; 8pm, 10pm
Fri, Sat; phone for details Tue. **Tickets** $3-$18.
Credit AmEx, MC, V **Map** p271/p272 F7.

Yuk Yuk's, the world's largest chain of comedy
clubs, was founded in 1976 by Mark Breslin, whose
manic artistic vision created a launching pad for the
likes of Jim Carrey, Howie Mandel and Norm
Macdonald. Alternative American comedians like
Bill Hicks and Sam Kinison also found refuge here
when US clubs wouldn't book them. Tuesday nights
feature amateurs, including Humber students (*see
p176* **Laugh school**). The rest of the week, the club
offers the best stand-up Canada has to offer.

Yuk Yuk's.

Film

Reel time.

Star quality: **Royal Cinema.** *See p180.*

Toronto is a movie-mad city. Though sceptics claim Toronto cinemagoers are undiscerning – that they'll see anything, anywhere, at any time – others insist that local audiences are passionate, educated cineastes. Either way, scores of fans haul themselves off to cinemas weekly – come rain, sleet or snow.

Torontonians get to see the latest Hollywood hits before most Americans do. The big studios launch most of their offerings in New York, Los Angeles and Toronto. The city is also home to a few significant firsts in film, including the world's first multiplex shoebox built in the 1970s, an 18-screen warren now relegated to the dustbin of cinema lore. But like some mutating alien, it spawned the monsterplex that is today's industry standard.

Another innovation that predates the glut of giant home-entertainment centres is the **Varsity Cinema**'s VIP screening rooms. With just 30 comfy seats and concession-stand wait staff, it's popular with serious movie-goers, who pay a premium for the pleasure of seeing current flicks in an exclusive setting. And then there is the eye-popping phenomenon of IMAX, the giant-screen format that was invented and launched in Toronto in the 1970s and that has since circumnavigated the globe with its spectacular nature docs.

To keep appetites sated, there are a hundred or so film festivals (*see p166-169*), including the greatly hyped **Toronto International Film Festival** (*see p180*) in September. There's also an excellent cinematheque (**Cinematheque Ontario**, *see p179*), a waterfront drive-in (The Docks, *see p181*), a number of outdoor screenings and a guy with two rooms and a projector who has become a local legend (CineForum, *see p179*).

Any week of the year, the lights dim for Bollywood excesses, retro romances, avant-garde films, documentaries and kids' classics. One thing you probably won't see is a Canadian movie: each year home-grown fare racks up as little as 0.02 per cent of screen time. You have to be quick to catch a Canadian flick; they rarely last more than a week at the cinema.

Although film content is abundant in Toronto, the great old movie houses are gone, and the lights recently went out at a number of rep houses. Even in the heart of the city, it's usually a choice between going to a small-or big-box cinema – places where people with limited attention spans and unlimited mobile-phone time struggle with pizza and other foods not meant to be eaten in the dark. Still, there are a few gems, and plenty of cinephiles, to keep up Toronto's glorious cinematic tradition.

TICKETS AND INFORMATION

Tickets at a first-run cinema vary but average about $10; the best deals are to be had on Tuesdays (when discounts are offered) and on weekday matinées. Rep circuit and Cinematheque Ontario tickets are also $10. There are free screenings in the summer in Nathan Phillips Square, at the CHUM/Citytv parking lot on Queen Street West and in various parks.

For details of these, as well as weekly film listings, check the local press. The daily papers publish movie sections on Fridays, while the two free weeklies – *eye* and *NOW* – both have reviews and listings and come out on Thursday.

Art-house & rep

Bloor Cinema

*506 Bloor Street W, at Bathurst Street, The Annex
(416 516 2330/www.bloorcinema.com). Streetcar
511/subway Bathurst.* **Admission** $6-$8; $3.50-$4
concessions. **No credit cards. Map** p274 D4.
As the last single-screen venue downtown, the Bloor
has history – and a few stains – written all over it.
Expect a mix of classics, foreign titles and first-run
releases on their last stop before DVD. The cinema
is also home to many a mini fest, including the One-
Minute Film Festival and the Jewish Festival.

Carlton

*20 Carlton Street, at Yonge Street, Church
& Wellesley (416 598 2309/www.cineplex.com).
Streetcar 506/subway College.* **Admission** $10;
$6 concessions; $6 before 4pm Mon-Fri, all day Tue.
Credit AmEx, MC, V. **Map** p275 G5.
This art-house multiplex shows the latest indie and
foreign films. The nine theatres are small, but if you
want to see the latest Godard this is your best bet.

CineForum

*463 Bathurst Street, at College Street, Kensington
Market (416 603 6643). Streetcar 506, 511.*
Admission $20; $10 concessions. **No credit
cards. Map** p271 D6.
Owner Reg Hartt claims he was the first to screen
the porn classic *Deep Throat* (admission was free if
you showed up naked). His 'theatre' is actually his
modest home. Hartt revels in the weird, but cartoons

are his speciality: his Animation series highlights
obscure gems from the likes of Tex Avery, Bob
Clampett and Friz Freleng.

Cinematheque Ontario

Advance ticket box office: *Manulife Centre,
55 Bloor Street W, at Bay Street, Yorkville (416
968 3456/www.e.bell.ca/filmfest/cinematheque).
Bus 6/subway Bay.* **Open** noon-6pm Mon-Sat.
Admission $11-$12.50. **Credit** AmEx, MC, V
Map p274 F4. **Screenings**: *Jackman Hall, Art
Gallery of Ontario, 317 Dundas Street W, at
McCaul Street, Chinatown. Streetcar 505/subway
St Patrick.* **Map** p271 E6.
Housed in the Art Gallery of Ontario, this cine-
matheque offers movie masterpieces, children's
classics and foreign rarities.

Fox Theatre

*2236 Queen Street E, at Beech Avenue, East
Toronto (416 691 7330/www.festivalcinemas.
com). Streetcar 501.* **Admission** $8; $3.50-$4
concessions. **No credit cards.**
This old rep house has seen better days, but it's a
Beaches classic. Expect recent and foreign releases.

Mount Pleasant Theatre

*675 Mount Pleasant Road, at Davisville Avenue,
North Toronto (416 489 8484 www.frontrow
centre.com/cinema/Ontario/Toronto). Subway
Davisville then bus 28.* **Admission** $9.50; $5
concessions. **No credit cards.**
Old-school, family-run theatre screens current
releases that are on their last commercial legs.

Double bills with a difference

Predictions that monster home-entertainment
systems would spell the end of cinemas have
been greatly exaggerated. While it's true
the lights have gone out on the old movie
palaces, most rep houses and movie theatres
are expanding their horizons to keep bums in
the seats.

Metropolis (*see p181*), a new megaplex,
will see double duty as a lecture hall for
nearby Ryerson University students when
it opens in late 2007. The 24 screens
and 5,000 seats address two problems:
overcrowded campus facilities and who to
sell popcorn to on weekdays at 9am.

The oddest combination is found at The
Docks (*see p181*), which is a golf driving
range by day and drive-in cinema by night.
On the waterfront with a cinematic view of
the downtown skyline, these retro pursuits
take on a surreal quality.

Can't get tickets to the Leafs hockey
games? Catch the action on high-definition
giant screens and hear the bone-crunching

bodychecks in Dolby Digital Surround Sound.
Between November and March, Cineplex
Odeon transforms 25 Toronto cinemas
into hockey rinks – without that distinctive
ice-and- sweat aroma. The $12 price is a
fraction of what tickets cost for the real
thing at the Air Canada Centre (*see p62*).
And you won't have to sit in the cold.

As more theatres go digital, opportunities
for simulcasts of everything from rock
concerts to religious revivals are being
explored. The Scotiabank Theatre (*see
p181*) is beaming in live broadcasts from
New York City's Metropolitan Opera House
on Saturday afternoons to packed houses.

And two beloved rep houses were saved
from a final curtain by a post-production
company. The Royal Cinema (*see p180*)
and the Regent (*see p180*) now see
double-duty as audio mixing studios by
day and neighbourhood cinemas by night
(during the scary scenes, be careful not
to spill your drink on the soundboard).

The Toronto Film Festival

If you haven't heard of the Toronto International Film Festival (TIFF) by now, congratulations, you've managed to ignore one of the most aggressive publicity machines on the planet. Either that, or you have been living under a rock. This bloated extravaganza brings out the star-crazed and the cineastes every September. Hollywood flies north to unspool its Oscar hopefuls and indie gems. World cinema gets its due with (often brilliant) movies that disappear once the circus rolls out of town. Fans trip over the celebs in Yorkville, while the press go into overdrive with breathless accounts of who ate where, who was seen with whom, and who was wearing what.

Amid all the celebrity hype, it's easy to forget about the business side. Buyers and sellers come to see titles tested in front of the public and the critics. Film-industry types also come to schmooze and make deals. As for the artistic side, Cannes had better watch out. While the French festival wins for glamorous location and Gallic sophistication, Toronto gets a stronger selection of movies. Oscar contenders, especially foreign-language winners such as *No Man's Land* (2002) and *Antonia's Line* (1995), are often seen first at the festival. And sometimes major hits are unearthed here, most famously *Shine* (1996), *American Beauty* (1999) and *Sideways* (2004).

To accommodate the growing number of films and crowds, the festival is looking for more space. And, like the rest of the city, it is getting into the condominium business. The new Festival Centre, in the heart of the Entertainment District, will be topped by 37 storeys of luxury condos, the sale of which will help pay fund the new project, scheduled to open in 2009.

Film buffs could do worse than to plan a holiday in Toronto for September, but book your hotel room early and also book tickets. Contact the box office at 416 968 3456 from mid July or go to www.toronto internationalfilmfestival.ca. You can also buy rush tickets on the same day.

Ontario Place Cinesphere

Ontario Place, 955 Lake Shore Boulevard West, at Dufferin Street, Harbourfront (416 314 9900/www. ontarioplace.com/en/Cinesphere). Bus 29/streetcar 509, 511/subway Union. **Admission** $8-$10; $6 concessions. **Credit** AmEx, MC, V. **Map** p270 B10.
The world's first permanent IMAX theatre is inside a geodesic lake-side dome at Ontario Place (*see also p61*). A year-round schedule mixes purpose-made IMAX thrillers with Hollywood blockbusters.

Regent Theatre

551 Mount Pleasant Road, at Davisville Avenue, Davisville (416 480 9884). Subway Davisville then bus 28. **Admission** $10; $5 concessions. **No credit cards**.
This indie theatre screens beyond-first-run releases for a loyal neighbourhood crowd.

Royal Cinema

606 College Street W, at Clinton Street, Little Italy (416 516 4845/www.festivalcinemas.com). Streetcar 506, 511. **Admission** $10; concessions $4. **No credit cards**. **Map** p270 C5.
This single-screen cinema has a great location on College. Expect arty offerings along with second-run new releases and small festivals. **Photo** *p178*.

Mainstream & first-run

Canada Square

2190 Yonge Street, at Eglinton Avenue, Davisville (416 646 0444/www.cineplex.com). Subway Eglinton. **Admission** $10; $7.50 concessions; $7.75 before 6pm Mon-Fri, all day Tue; $8.75 before 6pm Sat, Sun. **Credit** AmEx, MC, V.

This 13-screen theatre offers an appealing mix of foreign films and first-run mainstream pictures. As multiplexes go, it is pleasant and spacious.

Colossus

3555 Highway 7 W, at Weston Road, Woodbridge (905 851 1001/www.cineplex.com). Subway Wilson then bus 165. **Admission** $10; $8.50 concessions; free under-3s; $8.25 before 6pm Mon-Fri; $9.25 all day Tue. **Credit** AmEx, MC, V.

During the 1990s, movie houses got bigger and bigger. This 18-screen emporium, owned by Famous Players, lives up to its name.

Cumberland Four Cinemas

159 Cumberland Street, at Avenue Road, Yorkville (416 646 0444/www.allianceatlantiscinemas.com). Subway Bay. **Admission** $12.75; $7.75 concessions; free under-3s; $9.50 before 6pm Mon-Fri; $10 before 6pm Sat, Sun.* **Credit** MC, V. **Map** p274 F4.

This midtown art house screens Euro and indie flicks with the odd Hollywood movie thrown in. **Other locations** Alliance Atlantis Beach Cinemas, 1651 Queen Street E, East Toronto (416 646 0444); Alliance Atlantis Bayview Village Cinemas, 2901 Bayview Avenue, North Toronto (416 646 0444).

The Docks Drive-In

11 Polson Street, at Cherry Street, East Toronto (416 461 3625/www.thedocks.com). Bus 72. **Open** *Late Apr-Sept* Tue, Fri, Sat; phone for details. **Admission** $13; $4 concessions; $6.50 all day Tue. **Credit** AmEx, MC, V.

This waterfront theme park shows double bills of mainstream movies to 500 cars three times a week in summer, on what's billed as the largest drive-in screen in North America.

Metropolis

Dundas Square (888 440 8457/www.movie watcher.com). Subway Dundas. **Admission** TBA. **Credit** AmEx, MC, V. **Map** p272 G6.

The first new multiplex to open downtown in a decade. It boasts 24 screens, 5,000 seats and a giant video billboard. Scheduled to open in autumn 2007.

NFB Mediatheque

150 John Street, at Richmond Street W, Entertainment District (416 973 3012/ www.nfb.ca). Streetcar 501, 504. **Open** 1-7pm Mon, Tue; 10am-7pm Wed; 10am-10pm Thur-Sat; noon-5pm Sun. **Admission** free. **Map** p271 E7.

Slide into an 'interactive personal viewing station' and choose from more than 3,500 movies by the National Film Board (including classic documentaries and bizarre animation).

Scotiabank Theatre (formerly the Paramount)

259 Richmond Street W, at John Street, Entertainment District (416 368 5600/ www.cineplex.ca). Streetcar 501, 504. **Admission** $10; $7.50 concessions; free under-3s; $8.50 before 6pm Mon-Fri, all day Tue. **Credit** MC, V. **Map** p271 E7.

This theatre complex delivers a bruising assault on the senses. Among the midway atmosphere of video games and concessions stands, there are 13 screens, plus an IMAX 3D theatre. Expect blockbusters.

SilverCity Yonge-Eglinton Centre

2300 Yonge Street, at Eglinton Avenue, Davisville (416 544 236/www.cineplex.ca). Subway Eglinton. **Admission** $10; $8.50 concessions; free under-3s; $9.25 before 6pm Mon-Fri, all day Tue. **Credit** MC, V.

There is a collection of SilverCity cinemas around town: multiplexes with all the noise, bright lights, games and junk food you'll (n)ever want. **Other locations**: SilverCity Yorkdale, 3401 Dufferin Street, North Toronto (416 787 2052); SilverCity North York, 5095 Yonge Street, North Toronto (416 223 9550).

Varsity Cinemas

Manulife Centre, 55 Bloor Street W, at Bay Street, Yorkville (416 961 6303/www.cineplex. com). Subway Bay. **Admission** *Main theatre* $10; $8.50 concessions; $9.25 before 6pm Mon-Fri, all day Tue; $11.50 before 6pm Sat, Sun. *VIP theatres* $16.95; $12.25 before 6pm Mon-Fri; $14.50 before 6pm Sat, Sun. **Credit** AmEx, MC, V. **Map** p274 F4.

This eight-screen multiplex on the 'mink mile' boasts top facilities and a good mix of mainstream, independent and foreign fare. In addition, the four VIP screening rooms offer some of the most intimate viewing experiences outside a home theatre system.

Scotiabank Theatre: blockbuster central.

Galleries

The lowdown on local colour.

If the two key ingredients for a thriving art scene are an enthusiastic public and patrons willing to spend the big bucks, then Toronto is sitting pretty in the first decade of the 21st century. The enthusiasm is clear: in September 2006, more than 400,000 people poured into the streets for an all-night art party called Nuit Blanche, in which galleries opened their doors into the wee hours and artists displayed their work on the streets. The occasion signalled a new dawn for the Toronto art scene; the event will hopefully become an annual fixture on the cultural calendar. The street-level enthusiasm is matched by the big-league buyers. The moneyed crowd continues to drive the value of Canadian art through the roof. New records were set in 2006 for works by Canadian artists Alex Colville, Jean-Paul Lemieux, Henrietta Mabel May, Jack Shadbolt and Robert Pilot. With the Frank Gehry addition to the **Art Gallery of Ontario** (AGO; *see p73*) scheduled to open in 2008, art will be in the spotlight.

The gallery scene is also booming, as West Queen West gains popularity as a key destination for art lovers in search of the new and offbeat. Storefront galleries beckon with eye-catching art: the **Casuccio Gallery** (972 Queen Street W, 416 913 7603), featuring work from Cuba, is typical of the new breed, as are galleries with no names and kitschy curios displayed in their windows. A new addition to the street, the **Ontario Crafts Council** (990 Queen Street W, 416 925 4222), brings the fine crafts movement to a new audience. Then there's **MOCCA** (Museum of Contemporary Canadian Art; *see p96*), which acts as an anchor for the collective of galleries sprouting around it. But the neighbourhood is at risk of becoming the victim of its own success. Developers are circling, looking to capitalise on – and tarnish – the artsy, bohemian vibe.

Street traffic picks up along Queen West on Thursday and Friday evenings, when many exhibition openings are in full gear; trendies spill on to the streets and posses of artists gallery hop. Refreshment is never far away on the strip, and the ultra-hip **Drake Hotel** (*see p52*) and the more earthy **Gladstone Hotel** (*see p52*) both cater to the art crowd; they have artists-in-residence and event spaces that are constantly occupied with arty gatherings, from indie film festivals to burlesque shows.

Dark arts: **Nuit Blanche** keeps culture vultures on the streets all night long.

Power Plant.

While the Queen scene is taking hold in the west, across town an arts scene is flourishing in the Distillery District (*see p185*), where several high-end galleries fill the vast warehouse spaces left from a Victorian-era booze factory. The area has quickly become touristy, with bars, coffee shops and designer-furniture stores bringing a crowd that is slightly more well-heeled than the hipsters along Queen West. Likewise, the galleries are upscale and housed in some of the most beautiful industrial spaces in the city. **Monte Clark** and **Sandra Ainsley** (Building 32, 55 Mill Street, 416 214 9490) galleries were among the first to arrive (the latter shows fabulous glass art) and have recently been joined by **Artcore/ Fabrice Marcolini** and the **Corkin Gallery**. The district's galleries comprise a labyrinth of viewing areas under a high ceiling with skylights that cast atmospheric shafts of light.

In the 1980s, the gallery scene was focused around the posh Yorkville area, and there are still a number of galleries around Hazelton Avenue. Many of them, however, are beginning to show the conservatism and inertia that comes with age.

One project on the horizon will bring an artsy edge to midtown by providing a new live/work space for artists in converted TTC streetcar sheds. The **Green Arts Barns** (76 Wychwood Avenue), just south-west of Forest Hill, will house studios and a community gallery. Funded by the city, it will help Toronto retain its creative edge.

Despite the established scenes, art can happen anywhere. The new trend is for artists to take over private spaces for a temporary exhibit or screening. Dan Browne opens his doors in Kensington Market every Sunday for his Free Radicals film programme of local and

experimental works and moves the show out of doors for summertime projection on nearby buildings (647 267 4373). Betty White, a Cabbagetown artist, holds exhibits in her home, where she displays work in pencil and chalk pastels (416 469 2008 ext. 231). **Alley Jaunt** (www.alleyjaunt.com) takes over the garages in the characterful back alleys around Trinity-Bellwoods Park for an annual treasure hunt that showcases local artists. The weekend festival takes place each year in early August.

Two mainstays of the art calendar are the **Toronto International Art Fair**, *see p170*, and the **Toronto Outdoor Art Exhibition**, *see p168*. Each November, the TIAF brings galleries and audiences together in the hangar-like Toronto Convention Centre for a weekend of exhibits that present a good cross-section of trends both at home and abroad. The free outdoor art fair is held in July in Nathan Phillips Square and is one of the largest of its kind in North America, with more than 100,000 people passing stalls of work that ranges from crafts to the avant-garde. Also notable is the **Queen West Art Crawl** (www.torontoart scape.on.ca), a weekend-long art festival held on Queen Street West each September.

While the city awaits the reopening of the Art Gallery of Ontario in 2008 following a revamp by Frank Gehry, other venues are stepping up to the plate. New leadership at The **Power Plant** at Harbourfront Centre (*see p60*) is broadening its mandate as a cultural force in the city, with lectures and innovative programming. In the suburbs, the **Art Gallery of York University** (416 736 5169, www.yorku.ca/agyu) is one to watch. It recently re-opened under the stewardship of art critic Philip Monk with a promising inaugural exhibition that included work by Stan Douglas, Fiona Tan and Jeremy Deller.

FURTHER INFORMATION

The listings in this chapter are a broad sample of the galleries to be found around the city. For comprehensive listings of current exhibitions, read *NOW* (www.nowtoronto.com; out on Thursdays) and the monthly *Slate* art guide, free in most galleries or online at www.slate artguide.com. For reviews, check out the Saturday editions of the *Globe and Mail*, the *Star* and the *National Post*.

Apart from Ydessa Hendeles Art Foundation, all of the following galleries have free entry.

Entertainment District

Prefix Institute of Contemporary Art

Suite 124, 401 Richmond Street W, at Spadina Avenue (416 591 0357). Streetcar 501, 510. **Open** noon-5pm Wed-Sat. **Credit** MC, V. **Map** p271 D7.
Prefix Photo started out in 2000 as a contemporary art-photography magazine. Now it's an institution for edgy photo-based art by the likes of Stan Douglas and China's Wang Qingsong. Like the mag, the gallery is sleek and up to date on new media. There's even a soundproof room for audio works.

Wynick/Tuck Gallery

Suite 128, 401 Richmond Street W, at Spadina Avenue (416 504 8716/www.wynicktuckgallery.ca). Streetcar 501, 510. **Open** 11am-5pm Tue-Sat. **Credit** AmEx, MC, V. **Map** p271 D7.

The style at this veteran gallery is contemporary with a pop-culture slant. Canvases by conceptual painter Gerald Ferguson are created with a rope dipped in black paint, and Angela Leach's paintings of bright wavy stripes can baffle your eyes.

YYZ Artists' Outlet

Suite 140, 401 Richmond Street W, at Spadina Avenue (416 598 4546/www.yyzartistsoutlet.org). Streetcar 504, 510/subway Osgoode. **Open** 11am-5pm Tue-Sat. **Credit** MC, V. **Map** p271 D7.
An artist-run centre that's open to all genres, from film, video and photography to painting, sculpture and installation by both local and international contemporary artists. YYZBOOKS publishes glossy catalogues and critical writing.

St Lawrence

Archive Gallery

56 Berkely Street, at King Street E (416 703 6564/ www.archivegallery.com). Streetcar 504. **Open** 10-6pm Mon-Fri; by appointment Sat. **No credit cards**. **Map** p271 D7.
The Archive Gallery has a large exhibit space, but the main attraction is a sizeable computer database of artists, mostly from Toronto and Montreal. Clients from the worlds of film, television and business use it to rent contemporary art, but there are also exhibitions. Among notable Toronto contributors are painter Jaga Jarosiewicz, sculptor John Dickson and photographer Katherine Knight.

Warrior of the wasteland

Edward Burtynsky photographs some of the most hellish places on earth and makes them captivating. The detritus of the industrial landscape is his raw material for unblinking portraits of strip mines, ship-breaking sites and dumps. The power of these huge colour images draws you in like a voyeur, looking for an explanation, some sense of how we have allowed the planet to be so defaced, and who is to blame. Burtynsky offers no simple answers and by this ambiguity, his photography moves from mere documentary to conceptual art.

Toronto-based Burtynsky has been photographing scenes of industrial incursion for two decades. Now that the environmental movement has gone mainstream, Burtynsky is a greatly sought-after artist, and his work is exhibited around the world. This popularity casts him in a new role of eco-champion, but he is ambivalent about being seen as an environmental propagandist. Still, he doesn't need to be: his striking work speaks for itself.

The documentary film *Manufactured Landscapes* (2006) follows Burtynsky from old quarries in Vermont to the polluted wasteland of the Bangladeshi coast. In China he photographed the construction of the Three Gorges Dam and that country's rapid industrialisation. His images are both staggeringly beautiful in their composition and astonishingly bleak in their content. And the film is as much a meditation on an artist at work as it is a comment on the modern practice of disposing industrial waste from one continent to the next.

A montage of images can be viewed on his website (www.edwardburtynsky.com). In Toronto Burtynsky runs a commercial dark room, Toronto Image Works (80 Spadina Avenue, 416 703 1999), where some of his photography is on display in a small exhibition space. His work is available through Nicholas Metivier Gallery (451 King Street West, 416 205 9000) and in a growing collection of coffee-table books.

Warehouse chic is the backdrop for the edgy **Corkin Gallery**.

Goodwater Gallery
234 Queen Street E, at Sherbourne Street (647 406 5052/www.goodwatergallery.com). Streetcar 501. **Open** 6-9pm Fri; 1-5pm Sat. **No credit cards.** **Map** p270 F7.
This conceptual-art gallery has been eliciting curious looks from passers-by since 2001. And it's bound to create more of a stir in its new storefront location on a down-at-heel stretch of Queen Street East (one that will surely become gentrified soon). All work is created specifically for the space. It includes Roderick Buchanan's fanciful photo series about soccer, Garry Neill Kennedy's bold graphics and Steven Shearer's text-heavy wall displays.

Distillery District

Artcore/Fabrice Marcolini
Building 62, 55 Mill Street, at Parliament Street (416 920 3820/www.artcoregallery.com). Bus 65. **Open** 10am-6pm Tue-Sat; noon-5pm Sun. **Credit** MC, V. **Map** p272 H8.
Artcore/Fabrice Marcolini is one of a handful of galleries in the city with an international scope, showing both Canadian artists such as Medrie MacPhee, and international talents like Joseph Beuys, Hans Broek and Stephan Reusse.

Corkin Gallery
Building 61, 55 Mill Street, at Parliament Street (416 304 1050/www.corkingallery.com). Bus 65. **Open** 10am-6pm Tue-Sat. **Credit** MC, V. **Map** p272 H8.
This large converted industrial space in the Distillery District has five exhibit halls. This allows Jane Corkin to programme simultaneous exhibits by contemporary photographers, painters and video-based installations. Artists represented include the likes of Robert Rauschenberg, David Urban, Barbara Astman and Nan Goldin. It's worth a trip for the location alone.

Gibsone Jessop Gallery
Building 4, 55 Mill Street, at Parliament Street (416 360 6800/www.gibsonejessop.com). Bus 65. **Open** 10am-6pm daily. **Credit** V. **Map** p272 H8.
Devoted solely to international artists who have not shown before in Canada, Gibsone Jessop displays a keen eye for trend-spotting in painting, mixed media and digital art.

Monte Clark Gallery
Building 2, 55 Mill Street, at Parliament Street (416 703 1700/www.monteclarkgallery.com). Bus 65. **Open** 10am-6pm Tue-Sat; noon-5.30pm Sun. **Credit** V. **Map** p272 H8.
The style of this gallery is cool, wry and luscious to the eye. The artists are mainly drawn from the original Monte Clark Gallery in Vancouver and the prevailing school of concept photography. Artists represented include Roy Arden, Scott McFarland, and author-artist Douglas Coupland.

Yorkville

Beckett Fine Art
120 Scollard Street, at Hazelton Avenue (416 922 5582/www.beckettfineart.com). Subway Bay. **Open** 10.30am-5pm Wed-Sat. **Credit** V. **Map** p274 F3.
This gallery keeps a fresh perspective on contemporary art, showing works by local painter and sculptor John Coburn and First Nations' artists David General and Arthur and Travis Shilling, and it exhibits emerging and established artists from Japan, the UK and the US.

Mira Godard Gallery
22 Hazelton Avenue, at Scollard Street (416 964 8197/www.godardgallery.com). Subway Bay. **Open** 10am-5pm Tue-Sat. **Credit** MC, V. **Map** p274.
This venerable Yorkville institution has mounted shows by top contemporary artists from Canada and around the world. Artists shown in the past have

Arts & Entertainment

included Picasso, Lucian Freud, Alex Colville and Christopher Pratt. With three floors of exhibit space it is one of the largest commercial galleries in the city and easily located on the street: just look for the life-size bronze bull.

West End

For the **Museum of Contemporary Canadian Art** (MOCCA), *see p96*.

Angell Gallery

890 Queen Street W, at Crawford Street (416 530 0444/www.angellgallery.com). Streetcar 501. **Open** noon-5pm Wed-Sat & by appointment. **Credit** V. **Map** p270 B7.

Angell was one of the first galleries on West Queen West, which makes the flamboyant proprietor, Jamie Angell, something of an elder statesman on the scene. Angell has mentored rising talent such as Kim Dorland, who paints wild, goofy clichés of cattlemen and pin-up girls, and Kristine Moran, whose enamel paintings of cars flying through buildings sell out faster than she can paint them. Also look for Jakub Dolejs' photographs; mounted on painted backdrops, they challenge the veracity of the photographic image.

Art Metropole

2nd Floor, 788 King Street W, at Bathurst Street (416 703 4400/www.artmetropole.com). Streetcar 504, 511. **Open** 11am-6pm Tue-Fri; noon-5pm Sat. **Credit** MC, V. **Map** p270 B7.

This gallery and art bookstore was created in 1974 by the celebrated General Idea collective. There is usually an installation with a conceptual bent here and always a lot of clever publications on display. Exhibitions delve into video, audio and electronic media. Watch for works by Martin Creed, David Shrigley, Yoko Ono and Lawrence Weiner.

Birch Libralato Gallery

129 Tecumseth Street, at Queen Street W. (416 365 3003/www.birchlibralato.com). Streetcar 501, 511. **Open** 11am-5pm Wed-Sat; **Credit** MC, V. **Map** p272 H8.

Installed in a garage space just south of Queen Street West, Robert Birch has brought together an excellent band of mostly local artists – Lee Goreas, Eric Glavin and Euan Macdonald – who share a postmodern sensibility. Also look out for work by Wanda Koop, a Winnipeg painter whom *Time* magazine called one of the best in Canada, Gina Rorai, who specialises in large, abstract canvases, and Will Gorlitz, whose sensual nature paintings examine the relationship between art and photography. The playful conceptual sculptures by Micah Lexier, a New York-based Winnipeg artist, are another highlight.

Christopher Cutts Gallery

21 Morrow Avenue, at Dundas Street W (416 532 5566/www.cuttsgallery.com). Streetcar 505/subway Dundas West or Lansdowne. **Open** 11am-6pm Tue-Sat. **No credit cards**.

This immaculate establishment is worth the time it will take you to find it. It's located off the beaten track in a small complex of West End galleries that also includes the Olga Korper Gallery (*see below*). It exhibits work by pioneers of modern Canadian painting such as Kazuo Nakamura and Ray Mead, founding members of Painters Eleven from the 1950s, as well as an excellent bunch of younger artists including the likes of Janieta Eyre, Richard Stipl and David Acheson.

Clint Roenisch Gallery

944 Queen Street W, at Shaw Street (416 516 8593/www.clintroenisch.com). Streetcar 501. **Open** noon-6pm Thur-Sat; 1-5pm Sun. **Credit** AmEx, MC, V. **Map** p270 B7.

Clint Roenisch was a curator before becoming a dealer, so his exhibitions always feature interesting groupings. You might find delicate, Renaissance-inspired landscape paintings by Douglas Walk juxtaposed with photography by Nan Goldin and weird little drawings and dolls made from wool socks by local artist Seth Scriver.

DeLeon White Gallery

1139 College Street, at Dufferin Street (416 597 9466/www.eco-art.com). Streetcar 506. **Open** noon-5 pm Wed-Sun. **No credit cards**.

SPIN Gallery. *See p187.*

This gallery is a little off the beaten path both in location and content. Its mandate is to show artists who explore environmental or ecological themes. There is performance art once a month and an emphasis on new media and interactive media.

Edward Day Gallery

952 Queen Street W, at Shaw Street (416 921 6540/www.edwarddaygallery.com). Streetcar 501. **Open** By appointment Mon; 10am-6pm Tue-Thur, Sat; 10am-7pm Fri; noon-5pm Sun. **Credit** AmEx, MC, V. **Map** p270 B7.

Edward Day used to be ensconced in the blue-chip Yorkville district. But when the gallery moved to Queen West it doubled its floor space and widened its scope. The new venue has room for large-scale sculptures and installations. And it's a buffet-style gallery – a wealth of different tastes in close proximity. The styles and artistic temperaments range from the high to the low, with everything in between. And, just like a buffet, it leaves you feeling full and (sometimes) satisfied.

Katharine Mulherin Contemporary Art Projects

1080 & 1086 Queen Street W, at Brookfield Street (416 537 8827/www.katharinemulherin.com). Bus 63/streetcar 501. **Open** noon-5pm Thur-Sat & by appointment. **Credit** V. **Map** p270 B7.

Katharine Mulherin works with a large number of young and mid-career artists and shows their work in two neighbouring galleries. She has played a large role in cultivating West Queen West and is therefore a large figure on the scene. Watch for work by Lisa Griffiths, Mike Bayne and Dana Holst.

Mercer Union

37 Lisgar Street, at Queen Street W (416 536 1519/ www.mercerunion.org). Streetcar 501. **Open** 11am-6pm Tue-Sat. **Credit** V. **Map** p270 A7.

An ideologically and theoretically driven artist-run space, Mercer Union is more fun than it sounds, having seen many of Canada's best contemporary artists pass through. The exhibition space is divided into three distinct areas, allowing for concurrent exhibitions, lectures, video screenings, readings and performances. Recent shows have featured Turner Prize winners Jeremy Deller and Martin Creed and local talent Kelly Mark and Derek Sullivan. Expect the abstract and the avant-garde.

Olga Korper Gallery

17 Morrow Avenue, at Dundas Street W (416 538 8220/www.olgakorpergallery.com). Streetcar 505/ subway Dundas West or Lansdowne. **Open** 10am-6pm Tue-Sat. **Credit** AmEx, V.

This is one of most beautiful galleries in the city – a cavernous and well-lit space that was once a foundry, then a garbage repository for a mattress factory. Established in 1973, the gallery has become something of an institution on the scene and has a strong group of artists, including Lynn Cohen, Marcel Dzama, Paterson Ewen and Tim Whiten. The gritty area has become a magnet for artists.

Paul Petro Contemporary Art

980 Queen Street W, at Ossington Avenue (416 979 7874/www.paulpetro.com). Bus 63/streetcar 501. **Open** 11am-5pm Wed-Sat. **No credit cards.** **Map** p270 B7.

There is a tiny, easy-to-miss sign outside this gallery; there may be art in the window to clue you in, but if there isn't, you could easily walk straight past it. Go inside and find intimate artwork that centres on personal identity and identity politics by the likes of Paul P, Julie Voyce and Stephen Andrews.

SPIN Gallery

2nd Floor, 1100 Queen Street W, at Dovercourt Road (416 530 7656/www.spingallery.ca). Bus 29, 63/streetcar 501. **Open** noon-6pm Wed-Sat; 1-5pm Sun. **No credit cards.** **Map** p270 A7.

Located in an old industrial building, SPIN is charmingly rugged, with creaky wooden floors, exposed brick and arching windows looking out to the lake. The speciality here is local artists, but national and international artists also get a look-in. Well-known names who have had exhibitions here include Michael Stipe, photographer and filmmaker Floria Sigismondi, and fashion photographer George Whiteside. **Photo** *p186.*

Stephen Bulger Gallery

1026 Queen Street W, at Ossington Avenue (416 504 0575/www.bulgergallery.com). Streetcar 501. **Open** 11am-6pm Tue-Sat. **Credit** AmEx, MC, V. **Map** p270 A6.

This photography gallery focuses on documentary work by masters like Ansel Adams and André Kertész also exhibits established contemporary lens-meisters. The adjoining Camera Bar opens on Saturday afternoons for screenings of photography-related films. The gallery is a driving force behind the CONTACT photography festival (*see p166*).

Susan Hobbs Gallery

137 Tecumseth Street, at Richmond Street W (416 504 3699/www.susanhobbs.com). Streetcar 501, 504, 511. **Open** 1-5pm Thur-Sat & by appointment. **No credit cards.** **Map** p270 C7.

On a side street off the main Queen Street strip, Susan Hobbs exhibits mostly sculpture and installation pieces by established Canadian artists such as Ian Carr-Harris, Robin Collyer and Liz Maor.

Ydessa Hendeles Art Foundation

778 King Street W, between Niagara & Tecumseth Streets (416 413 9400). Streetcar 504, 511. **Open** noon-5pm Sat & by appointment. **Admission** $4. **No credit cards.** **Map** p270 C8.

Described by *Art News* as one of the 50 most influential people in the art world, Ydessa Hendeles has helped put Toronto on the international art map. When Hendeles was a dealer, representing artists like Jeff Wall and Jana Sterbak, she began collecting art herself and later went public. She has showed artists like Cindy Sherman or Louise Bourgeois before they became famous and her 1,000-strong collection contains the best in contemporary art.

Gay & Lesbian

Introducing the village people.

Despite its varied ethnic make-up, the Toronto gay scene is a Waspy mixture of respectability and raunch. Unlike most American cities, for instance, Toronto never closed its bathhouses, even at the height of the AIDS epidemic. And to the surprise of locals, the city has gradually developed a vaguely sexy reputation. There are now at least eight bathhouses, not to mention a strip joint where the boys bare all. At the same time, the city's gay scene sometimes feels like a sleeper cell for domesticated gay couples. A 2003 judicial decision legalised gay marriage in the province of Ontario, and in many quarters gays are no longer regarded as sexual outlaws or rabid activists, but simply folk with the same concerns as everybody else – getting a big-screen TV and a mortgage-free home in which to put it.

The community came of age during the legendary bath raids of the early 1980s and still cherishes its activist past, but in-your-face antics have largely been exchanged for establishment clout. Prosperous queer couples have colonised the left-liberal neighbourhood of Riverdale (east of downtown), the formerly raunchy Queen West area of Parkdale and the up-and-coming artsy enclave of Leslieville (near Queen Street East and Pape). If the core of gay life around Church and Wellesley streets seems less vital of late, many point to this migration to other parts of the city as the reason why. A new generation of young gay men and women don't feel the same need to stick together. While there's still some friction with the police, the local community has political push and a very visible presence. An openly gay councillor represents the local ghetto at City Hall, the mayor sometimes joins the **Pride Week** parade, and the public library keeps a section of queer books at its Yorkville branch (22 Yorkville Avenue, 416 393 7660).

As for 'flaunting' your gayness, most Torontonians are pretty blasé about homos. Gay couples hold hands openly in the village, but are more circumspect in the 'old suburbs' of Etobicoke or Scarborough, or even in the straight part of the Entertainment District–Richmond–Adelaide, where testosterone can get in the way of tolerance.

The bar action is concentrated on Church Street, one block east of Yonge Street, and on the side streets in between. It's a small, compact scene that's close to the subway (both College and Wellesley stations, on the Yonge Street line) and easily toured on foot. So if you don't like one bar, you can walk to another.

Not everyone enjoys the bar and bath scene, of course, and many local gays organise their social lives around volunteer organisations or the city's many active sports leagues. For information about gay social and political groups, drop in on the **519 Community Centre** (519 Church Street, 416 392 6874, www.the519.org) in the heart of the gay neighbourhood. Next to it is **Cawthra Park**, which is a hive of activity during Pride Week and home to the city's **AIDS Memorial** (**photo** *p189*) a series of modernist concrete slabs set amongst greenery. The memorial is inscribed with the names of those in the city who have succumbed to the disease (more than 2,300 people); a candlelight vigil is held here every June in the week before Pride Day.

Women often prefer to socialise outside the bars, either through sports leagues or in trendy, gay-friendly neighbourhoods. Both the studenty Annex and Queen Street West of Bathurst Street, including Parkdale, are popular. Lesbians have been more visible on Church Street in recent years, but the action is still hard to find. There are only a couple of dedicated lesbian bars, and though many mainstream and gay male bars host women's nights, the events come and go with the speed of a press release. For further details, check out the **Lesbian Social and Business Network** (www.lsbntoronto.com) or the bulletin board at the **Good For Her** sex shop (*see p195*).

Note: unless otherwise stated, venues in this chapter are in the Church & Wellesley district.

MEDIA

The key local paper is *Xtra!*, 'Toronto's Lesbian & Gay Biweekly' (www.xtra.ca). A direct descendant of an influential activist paper called *The Body Politic* that flourished in the 1970s, *Xtra!* has a political pedigree that makes it the local paper of record. It focuses on art, entertainment and politics and runs listings of local events, both clubby and cultural. For a lighter, more hedonistic guide to the scene, try *fab* (www.fabmagazine.com). It's the one with cute boys on the cover and loads of party dish inside. Both papers are distributed free in bars, shops and restaurants within the ghetto, as well

Arts & Entertainment

as further afield. *Xtra!* has its own pink
newspaper boxes on street corners across
the city. Online, Gay Guide Toronto (www.
gayguidetoronto.com) offers listings, plus
tips on upcoming events. Features are
updated monthly.

Bars & clubs

In recent years, the bar scene has grown both
more specialised (leather, bears, twinks) and
more diffuse. Young dance queens in particular
tend to head out to one-night-only events at
otherwise straight clubs like the **Guvernment**
(132 Queens Quay E, Harbourfront; *see also
p206*) and various venues on what's being
called Queer Street West. But don't believe
all the guff about life outside the ghetto. Sure,
there are all kinds of gay events at West End
hotspots such as the **Drake** (*see p52, p140
and p202*) and the **Gladstone** (*see p46, p141*),
but finding them can be tricky. Plus, many of
them are gay-friendly without being gay-
cruisey; it's hard to feel raunchy with an artsy
crowd. Check the gay media for new venues or
nights, or stand around Church Street and wait
for a young 'un to give you a promo flyer.

Licensing laws dictate that bars officially
close at 2am, and all alcohol must be 'off the
tables' within half an hour. Therefore after-
hours partying tends to be limited, except at
weekends, when **Fly** keeps thumping and
bumping to the wee hours.

As well as the following, *see also p194*
Byzantium and *p209* **El Convento Rico**.

Alibi

*529 Yonge Street, at Maitland Street (416 964
9869/www.alibitoronto.com). Bus 94/subway
Wellesley.* **Open** noon-3am daily. **Credit** AmEx,
MC, V. **Map** p275 G5.

This Yonge Street gay bar has changed its name
(Trax, Cube) and look several times. Under its new
moniker, there is a come-all approach with two dance
floors, licensed patio and cruise maze. It hosts a fetish
night on the first Friday of the month.

The Black Eagle

*457 Church Street, at Alexander Street (416 413
1219/www.blackeagletoronto.com). Bus 94/subway
Wellesley.* **Open** 2pm-2am daily. **No credit cards.**
Map p275 G5.

A leather-and-denim cruise joint with dress codes
(and porn) to match, this two-storey bar varies from
casual to intense, depending on the day of the week.
Watch the signs at the door: it can be disconcerting
to walk in on a watersports night when you just
wanted some boot lickin'. The second-floor deck is
a pleasant oasis of quiet during the summer and
offers a change from the dungeon-like back room.

Ciao Edie

*489 College Street, at Bathurst Street, Little Italy
(416 927 7774/www.ciaoedie.com). Streetcar 506,
511.* **Open** 8pm-2am Mon-Sat; 9pm-2am Sun. **Credit**
AmEx, MC, V. **Map** p270 D6.

If you get tired of the gay ghetto, venture west to
this funky and gay-friendly College Street bar. The
decor is pleasingly kitsch, with retro furniture and
old-school lamps, and the cocktail list is groovy. On
a Sunday, it hosts Here, Kitty, Kitty, the longest-
running women's night in town; it attracts a
fashionable young crowd and girl-heavy bands.

Aids Memorial. *See p188.*

Arts & Entertainment

Where the boys are: **Woody's/Sailor** is gay central station in Toronto. *See p191.*

Arts & Entertainment

Crews, Tango & The Zone
508-510 Church Street, at Alexander Street
(416 972 1662/www.crews-tango.com). Streetcar
506/subway Wellesley. **Open** noon-2am daily.
Credit AmEx, MC, V. **Map** p275 G5.
A motley crowd of dykes and queens mingles in
these Victorian houses. Entertainment ranges from
drag to dancing to karaoke, and the vibe is down to
earth. Expect queues on weekends.

Fly
8 Gloucester Street, at Yonge Street (416 925 6222/
www.flynightclub.com). Bus 94/subway Wellesley.
Open 10pm-7am Sat. **Credit** AmEx, MC, V.
Map p275 G5.
Once a week the boys turn up in droves, eager to
shed their shirts in honour of top DJs. Cover charges
can be high, but the party goes on till morning at the
biggest dance club in the ghetto.

George's Play
504 Church Street, at Alexander Street (416 963
8251). Streetcar 506/subway Wellesley. **Open** 11am-
2am daily. **Credit** AmEx, MC, V. **Map** p275 G5.
In the week, this unpretentious bar draws an older
crowd with its catchy '80s-heavy tunes. On the
weekend, there are Latin nights with lots of drag,
dancing and hip-swivelling enthusiasm.

Hair of the Dog
425 Church Street, at Wood Street (416 964 2708).
Streetcar 506/subway Wellesley. **Open** 11.30am-2am
daily. **Credit** MC, V. **Map** p275 G5.
A smart and cosy pub with a quiet patio (in
summer), a decent menu and a good selection of beer.
Men and women, gay and straight.

Lo'La
7 Maitland Street, at Yonge Street (416 920 0946).
Bus 94/streetcar 506/subway Wellesley. **Open** 4pm-
2am Wed-Fri; 11am-2am Sat; 11am-midnight Sun.
Credit MC, V. **Map** p275 G5.
A small bar with a larger patio whose purpose is to
lubricate the boys before a night of partying.

Lüb Lounge
487 Church Street, at Wellesley Street E (416 323
1489/www.lub.ca). Bus 94/subway Wellesley. **Open**
4pm-midnight Mon-Wed; 4pm-2am Thur, Fri; noon-
2am Sat; noon-1am Sun. **Credit** AmEx, MC, V.
Map p275 G5.
Everything at this trendy bar has changed except
the name, which is especially unappealing now that
there is a dining room. The decor is swanky – white
chairs and wood and stone walls – but the upstairs
lounge is still party central, where the disco boys
and DJs come out to play after the dishes are cleared.

Pegasus Bar
489B Church Street, at Wellesley Street E (416 927
8832/www.pegasusonchurch.com). Bus 94/subway
Wellesley. **Open** noon-2am daily. **Credit** AmEx,
MC, V. **Map** p275 G5.
Comfortable, well-lit, second-floor pool hall attract-
ing both men and women.

Remington's
379 Yonge Street, at Gerrard Street, Dundas Square
(416 977 2160/www.remingtons.com). Streetcar
505/subway Dundas. **Open** 5pm-2am daily. **Credit**
AmEx, MC, V. **Map** p272 G6.
The infamous Sperm Attack on Mondays is no more,
but numerous hunky strippers continue to bare all
on two stages and in private sessions. Get your fun
in early; the cover starts at 7pm.

Slack's
562 Church Street, at Wellesley Street E (416 969
8742). Bus 94/subway Wellesley. **Open** 2pm-2am
Mon-Fri; 11am-2am Sat, Sun. **Credit** AmEx, MC, V.
Map p275 G5.
Smart lesbians dominate this bar-restaurant on
weekends, but the rest of the time it's a real mix, not
to mention a hoot. Formerly known as Slack Alice.

Sneakers
502A Yonge Street, at Grosvenor Street, University
(416 961 5808). Subway Wellesley. **Open** 11am-2am
daily. **Credit** AmEx, MC, V. **Map** p275 G5.
Skinny young guys, hefty older men.

Statlers
471 Church Street, at Alexander Street (416 925
0341). Streetcar 506/subway College. **Open** 4pm-
2am daily. **Credit** AmEx, MC, V. **Map** p275 G5.
A tiny piano bar with an older but lively clientele.

Tallulah's Cabaret
Buddies in Bad Times Theatre, 12 Alexander Street,
at Yonge Street (416 975 9130/www.buddiesin
badtimestheatre.com/tallulahs/index.cfm). Streetcar
506/subway Wellesley. **Open** 10.30pm-2am Fri, Sat.
Credit MC, V. **Map** p275 G5.
Hip kids in graphic Ts dance to chart and
alternative hits every weekend. They probably
learned their moves from a Britney video, but that's
half the appeal. A 70/30 split of men and women.

Vibe
501 Church Street, at Wellesley Street E (no phone).
Bus 94/subway Wellesley. **Open** 8pm-2:45am daily.
No credit cards. Map p275 G5.
In place of the old Bar 501 comes a stripped down
bar with a sizeable dance floor. DJs spin lounge
music from Sunday to Tuesday, and pop gets the
young crowd bopping the rest of the week.

Woody's/Sailor
465-467 Church Street, at Maitland Street (416
972 0887/www.woodystoronto.com). Bus 94/
subway Wellesley. **Open** 2pm-2am daily.
Credit AmEx, MC, V. **Map** p275 G5.
One of the most popular bars in the city, but don't
let the dual name fool you. Everyone calls it
Woody's, and everyone goes there sooner or later.
The bar was famous long before it was featured on
the American *Queer as Folk* and, in a fickle market,
it has demonstrated an astonishing longevity.
Patrons tend to cower in cliques, making it difficult
for newcomers to make their entrance, but guys turn
out in droves, especially on weekends and Thursday

Arts & Entertainment

nights, when the Best Chest Contest draws some of the cutest specimens in town. On Fridays, it's the best ass competition. Be warned: it's usually the out-of-towners who show off their stuff. **Photo** *p190*.

Zipperz

72 Carlton Street, at Church Street (416 921 0066/ www.zipperz-cellblock.ca). Streetcar 506/subway College. **Open** noon-2am daily. **Credit** AmEx, MC, V. **Map** p275 G5.

Sedate types settle at the piano bar in the front, while beat-mongers bop to retro tunes in the dance club in the back. No attitude, all ages, lots of fun.

Bathhouses

Barracks

56 Widmer Street, at Richmond Street W, Entertainment District (416 593 0499/www. barracks.com). Streetcar 504/subway St Andrew. **Open** 24hrs daily. **Credit** AmEx, MC, V. **Map** p271 D7.

In the Entertainment District, this small townhouse provides plenty of it, in the form of edgy sex with leather accessories. Now that's entertainment.

Bijou

370 Church Street, at Gerrard Street E (416 971 9985). Bus 94/subway Wellesley. **Open** 9pm-4am Wed, Thur, Sun; 9pm-5am Fri, Sat. **No credit cards. Map** p275 G6.

Home of the infamous 'slurp ramp' (don't ask), this former backroom bar is now a cross between a porno palace and a stand-up bathhouse. It's dimly lit, which helps patrons get into a frisky mood, and full of dark nooks and crannies. Most of the 'rooms' are too narrow for true horizontal action.

Cellar

78 Wellesley Street E, at Church Street (416 975 1799). Bus 94/subway Wellesley. **Open** 24hrs daily. **No credit cards. Map** p275 G5.

The darkest bathhouse in town, this is where you go when you don't want to meet anyone you know. It doesn't even have a sign, just a black door.

Good times at Bad Times

Theatre is too stuffy a word for an institution as salacious as Buddies in Bad Times. A theatre-cum-social centre, Buddies offers everything from a serious subscription series to dance, queer comedy and lesbian cabaret. But whatever form it takes, it's always tinged with a colourful queer vibe.

Co-founded by controversial local playwright Sky Gilbert, it still bears the stamp of his outrageous personality. A prolific playwright, Gilbert has written a string of plays with titles like *Suzie Goo: Private Secretary* and *Drag Queens in Outer Space*, and he has maintained a high profile in the local media as an outspoken proponent of sex-positive gay chauvinism. Woe betide anyone who suggests gays are just like anyone else – Sky just won't have it. A scourge of the gay middle class, he inveighs against sexual hypocrisy and often appears as his drag alter ego, a busty, big-haired blonde named Jane.

So that's Sky, and that, for most of his 18-year tenure as artistic director of the theatre, was Buddies. In the years since his resignation in 1997, Buddies has moved a little closer to the mainstream, emphasising the provocative as much as the sexual, but most productions still feature some kind of queer angle.

A women's festival called Hysteria appeared for the first time in 2003, and Rhubarb! (February), the theatre's long-running festival

of shorter works, continues to be one of Toronto's most avid promoters of young, dramatic talent. It's also just giddy, good fun. Most of the plays are so short and produced so fast – lickety-split, one after another – that you can get high just from the sense of creative freefall. Quality varies, but the best of these dramatic short stories give you the sense of being there at the moment of creation.

Buddies moved to its present location in 1994, and instantly became a centre of local society. The theatre attracts a young, hip crowd late on Friday and Saturday nights, when the smaller of its two spaces, Tallulah's Cabaret, turns into an intimate dance club (*see p191*). In addition, Buddies hosts even larger dance events on most of the major gay holidays – Pride, Halloween and New Year's Eve. For Pride, Buddies usually programmes a week to ten days of queer comedy, staged readings and other performances, with an extra heavy dash of parties. On the Pride weekend (*see p168*), the small park beside the theatre often turns into a mini festival for queer youth.

Buddies in Bad Times Theatre

12 Alexander Street, at Yonge Street, Church & Wellesley (box office 416 975 8555/www. buddiesinbadtimestheatre.com). Streetcar 506/subway Wellesley. **Open** Box office noon-5pm Tue-Sat. **Credit** MC, V. **Map** p275 G5.

Club Toronto Mansion

231 Mutual Street, at Carlton Street (416 977 4629/ www.clubtoronto.com). Subway Wellesley. **Open** 24hrs daily. **No credit cards. Map** p272 G6.

This Victorian mansion boasts stained-glass windows and ornate details, but it's the rambling corridors that really matter: they are perfect for cruising. It has a whirlpool and a tiny outdoor pool. It sometimes hosts a women's night (Pussy Palace).

GI Joe

4th Floor, 543 Yonge Street, at Wellesley Street E (416 927 0210). Subway Wellesley. **Open** 24hrs daily. **Credit** MC V. **Map** p275 G5.

Once a government office building, this top-floor spa is a lot sexier these days. There's a whirlpool, sauna, cinema and 120 private rooms.

Spa Excess

105 Carlton Street, at Jarvis Street (416 260 2363/ www.spaexcess.com). Streetcar 506. **Open** 24hrs daily. **Credit** AmEx, DC, MC, V. **Map** p272 G6.

A maze of dark corners and cubicles provides room for groping on part of the top floor. Elsewhere there are private rooms, a licensed lounge and a deck.

Steamworks

2nd Floor, 540 Church Street, at Wellesley Street E (416 925 1571/www.steamworks.ca). Bus 94/subway Wellesley. **Open** 24hrs daily. **Credit** AmEx, MC, V. **Map** p275 G5.

With high ceilings, glass-walled showers and industrial-chic decor, this bathhouse feels more boutique hotel than erotic emporium. The entrance is so discreet you may have to ask for directions (hint: it's directly across from Zelda's patio).

Cafés

Beaver Café

1192 Queen Street W, at Beaconsfield Avenue (416 537 2768). Streetcar 501. **Open** 10am-2am daily. **Credit** MC, V. **Map** p270 A7.

Legendary queer club promoter Will Munro has resurfaced after his Vazaleen rave days with this cute café. Though it's essentially a diner, call to ask about evening events, when the place gets hopping to everything from punk to electro to disco for a mixed crowd of artsy queers. The licensed patio in the back gets busy in the summer.

Bull Dog Coffee

89 Granby Street, at Church Street (416 606 2275/ www.bulldogtoronto.com). Subway College. **Open** 7am-7pm daily. **No credit cards. Map** p272 G6.

A coffee shop with a subtle leather vibe and decent signature drinks. The side-street location boasts a pleasant tree-shaded patio.

Lettieri Espresso Bar & Café

77 Wellesley Street E, at Church Street (416 944 3944/www.lettiericafe.com). Bus 94/subway Wellesley. **Open** 7am-11pm Mon-Thur, Sun; 7am-2am Fri, Sat. **Credit** MC, V. **Map** p275 G5.

The prettiest coffee chain on the block, with outdoor tables and views of the busiest corner in the village. Grab a panini and watch the world go by.

7 West Café

7 Charles Street W, at Yonge Street, University (416 928 9041). Subway Bloor-Yonge. **Open** 24hrs daily. **Credit** MC, V. **Map** p275 G4.

A rambling three-storey hotspot where students, film-lovers and bohemian types nurse coffees into the wee hours. Known for its desserts and salads.

Timothy's World Coffee

500 Church Street, at Alexander Street (416 925 8550/www.timothys.ca). Streetcar 506. **Open** 7pm-12.30am daily. **No credit cards. Map** p275 G5.

Bears, deaf gays and older guys make this one of the busiest rendezvous on Church Street. In summer, the small patio overflows.

Cruising

Cruising is best done Downtown, and can happen anywhere from clothing shops to the appropriately named Queen's Park, but a few spots retain a hold on the popular imagination, notably **Hanlan's Point** (*see p76*) on the Toronto Islands, where there's a 'clothing optional' beach with a great view; the wooded ravines of **David Balfour Park**, in posh Rosedale, where legends of late-night orgies linger on; **Riverdale Park** on the eastern edge of the Don Valley, where there's a spectacular view and dazzling outdoor pool favoured by homos in the summer; the bike trails around **Cherry Beach** on the Toronto waterfront, where the action starts as early as 8am; and **High Park** in the West End. Cruise at your own risk: visits from the police are a possibility.

Culture

Queer culture is found in many mainstream venues, from established alternative theatres like the **Factory** (*see p221*) and the **Tarragon** (*see p221*) to the local art house **Carlton** multiplex (*see p178*).

But it's the queer-run venues that set the pace for cutting-edge culture. In addition to the following, the **Metropolitan Community Church of Toronto** (115 Simpson Avenue, 416 406 6228) is very vocal on the gay scene, organising events for the community.

See also p192 **Good times at Bad Times**, *and p167* **Inside Out Toronto Lesbian & Gay Film & Video Festival**.

Canadian Lesbian & Gay Archives

Suite 202, 65 Wellesley Street E, at Church St (416 777 2755/www.clga.ca). Subway Wellesley. **Open** 7.30-10pm Tue-Thur; also by appointment. **Admission** free. **Map** p275 G5.

Arts & Entertainment

The second-largest queer archive in the world, set in the heart of the gay village. It boasts a huge collection of books and periodicals documenting the history of gay rights. In March 2008, it will move to 34 Isabella Street. Call before you come.

We're Funny That Way
Buddies in Bad Times Theatre, 12 Alexander Street, at Yonge Street, Church & Wellesley (416 975 8555). **Date** May. **Map** p275 G5.
Queer comedy so good it's been filmed for TV.

Gyms

Bally Total Fitness
80 Bloor Street W, at Bay Street, Yorkville (416 960 2434/www.ballyfitness.com). Subway Bay. **Open** 6am-11pm Mon-Fri; 8am-7pm Sat, Sun. **Credit** AmEx, MC, V. **Map** p274 F4.
Brutal lighting doesn't dissuade the gay clientele. Maybe it's because it's next to Banana Republic.
Other locations: throughout the city.

Metro-Central YMCA
20 Grosvenor Street, at Yonge Street, University (416 975 9622/www.ymcatoronto.org). Streetcar 506/subway Wellesley. **Open** 6am-11pm Mon-Fri; 7am-8pm Sat, Sun. **Credit** AmEx, MC, V. **Map** p275 G5.
A gay favourite, even though most of its 11,000 members are straight. A $4-million renovation has enlarged the conditioning room. It's friendly and relaxed, with a beautiful indoor pool and a lovely rooftop running track.

Restaurants

Byzantium
499 Church Street, at Wellesley Street E (416 922 3859). Bus 94/subway Wellesley. **Open** 5.30-11pm Mon-Sat; 11am-3pm, 5.30-11pm Sun. **Main courses** $25. **Credit** AmEx, MC, V. **Map** p275 G5.
The swankiest spot on the strip, this pale green room serves upscale bistro-style fare early in the evening, then morphs into a loud bar, complete with mirror ball and excellent martinis. It attracts a well-heeled crowd, and offers a great view of the strip.

Churchmouse & Firkin
475 Church Street, at Maitland Street (416 927 1735/ www.firkinpubs.com). **Main courses** $6-$18. **Open** 11am-1am daily. **Credit** AmEx, DC, MC, V. **Map** p275 G5.
Standard pub grub – pasta, curry and so forth – plus lots of draught beer and a great patio facing north (so you get a view of who's coming into the ghetto – as opposed to who's leaving in despair).

Fire on the East Side
6 Gloucester Street, at Yonge Street (416 960 3473/ www.fireontheeastside.ca). Bus 94/subway Wellesley. **Open** noon-1am Tue-Fri; 10am-midnight Sat, Sun. **Main courses** $10-$28. **Credit** AmEx, MC V. **Map** p275 G5.

This casual eatery takes its culinary cue from the Deep South: jambalaya, spicy bayou wings and Louisiana crab cakes. Set on a leafy side street, the patio is pleasant, especially at brunch.

Garage Sandwich Co at Pusateri's
497 Church Street, at Alexander Street (416 929 7575). Bus 94/subway Wellesley. **Open** 11am-7pm Mon-Sat. **Main courses** $5-$10. **Credit** AmEx MC V. **Map** p275 G5.
A tiny, funky sandwich place that's best known for its vegetarian and meat-based chilli con carne.

Il Fornello
491 Church Street, at Wellesley Street E (416 944 9052/www.ilfornello.com). Bus 94/subway Wellesley. **Open** 5-11pm Mon-Fri; 10.30am-3pm, 5-11pm Sat, Sun. **Main courses** $7-$25. **Credit** AmEx, DC, MC, V. **Map** p275 G5.
This trendy Italian eatery has branches around town, and its winning formula – comforting food (pizza, pasta, caesar salads) and good prices has stood the test of time. Though competition is not stiff, it is the ghetto's culinary 'it spot'.
Other locations: throughout the city.

Mitzi's Café
100 Sorauren Avenue, at Pearson Avenue, West End (416 588 1234). Streetcar 501. **Open** 7.30am-5pm Tue-Fri; 9am-4pm Sat, Sun. **Main courses** $7-$11. **No credit cards.**
In trendy Parkdale on the west side, this retro '50s diner is big on brunch and popular with women.

Mitzi's Sister
1554 Queen Street W, at Dowling Avenue, West End (416 532 2570). Streetcar 501. **Open** 3pm-midnight Mon; 3pm-2am Tue-Fri; 10am-2am Sat; 10am-midnight Sun. **Main courses** $7-$12. **Credit** V.
A bigger version of Mitzi's Café, with a licence, lots of local artwork and a big female following.

Arts & Entertainment

Zelda's.

O'Grady's Tap & Grill

518 Church Street, at Maitland Street (416 323 2822). Bus 94/subway Wellesley. **Open** 11am-2am daily. **Main courses** $10-$16. **Credit** AmEx, MC, V. **Map** p275 G5.

Skip the food, go for the street scene. The gigantic patio offers the best people-watching on the strip.

Zelda's Restaurant Bar Patio

542 Church Street, at Maitland Street (416 922 2526/www.zeldas.ca). Bus 94/subway Wellesley. **Open** 11am-2am Mon-Sat; 10am-2am Sun. **Main courses** $7-$14. **Credit** AmEx, MC, V. **Map** p275 G5.

With zany atmosphere, cute waiters and kitsch decor, lively Zelda's is a must-see. It's a tongue-in-cheek tribute to trailer-park trash (complete with pink flamingos). The patio is buzzing.

Shops

Glad Day Bookshop

598A Yonge Street, at Dundonald Street (416 961 4161/www.gladdaybookshop.com). Bus 94/subway Wellesley. **Open** 10am-6.30pm Mon-Wed; 10am-9pm Thur, Fri; 10am-7pm Sat; noon-6pm Sun. **Credit** AmEx, MC, V. **Map** p275 G5.

The second-oldest gay and lesbian book store in the world (established 1970), Glad Day is a pain to find and no fun to browse (the second-floor space is quite cramped), but it does have an astonishing range of queer titles – everything from fiction to parenting and transgender issues, plus a good selection of queer videos and DVDs, both arty and mainstream. There's often a selection of vintage porn mags.

Good For Her

175 Harbord Street, at Bathurst Street, Harbord (416 588 0900/www.goodforher.com). Bus 94/ streetcar 511. **Open** 11am-7pm Mon-Thur; 11am-8pm Fri; 11am-6pm Sat; noon-5pm Sun. *Women & trans only* 11am-2pm Thur; noon-5pm Sun. **Credit** MC, V. **Map** p274 D4.

Known for educational workshops on everything from G-spots to female ejaculation, this women-centred sex shop is also a good source of info on local lesbian events. Some periods of the week are set aside for women and transsexuals only.

Out on the Street

551 Church Street, at Gloucester Street (416 967 2759). Bus 94/subway Wellesley. **Open** 10am-8pm Mon-Wed, Sun; 10am-9pm Thur-Sat. **Credit** AmEx, MC, V. **Map** p275 G5.

Aimed squarely at gay men, this three-level shop carries casual clothing, plus a broad selection (over 100) of T-shirts with catchy queer slogans.

Priape

2nd Floor, 465 Church Street, at Maitland Street (416 586 9914/www.priape.com). Bus 94/subway Wellesley. **Open** 10am-9pm Mon-Sat; noon-6pm Sun. **Credit** AmEx, DC, MC, V. **Map** p275 G5.

A squeaky-clean sex store, Priape stocks everything from huge dildos to leather harnesses, but some people come just for the sexy streetwear or new porn releases. Tickets for local events are also sold.

Where to stay

The major hotels know the value of the pink dollar and, as a result, are gay-friendly. But for a specifically queer ambience, try a B&B in the ghetto. Good picks include **Dundonald House** (35 Dundonald Street, 416 961 9888, www.dundonaldhouse.com), **10 Cawthra Square** (10 Cawthra Square, 416 966 3074, www.cawthrasquare.com) and **Victoria's Mansion** (68 Gloucester Street, 416 921 4625, www.victoriasmansion.com).

Music

Strike up the band.

Latin lovers: Brazilian beats and tropical rhythms fill the air at **Lula Lounge**. *See p202*.

Classical

There's nothing like a new concert stage to liven up the music scene. The debut of the **Four Seasons Centre for the Performing Arts** (see *p198* **The curtain rises**) in 2006 was met with standing ovations. Though it's no architectural jewel – it looks more IKEA than La Scala – the intimate 2,000-seat venue is better than the old barn of a building that housed the Canadian Opera Company and the National Ballet of Canada. Tickets are selling quickly so book ahead. The **Toronto Symphony Orchestra**, the other top draw for classical music, has trouble filling its hall, but its new programme of more approachable music is finding new audiences. In choral music, the **Toronto Mendelssohn Choir** is a good bet as is the **Tafelmusik Baroque Orchestra and Chamber Choir**.

More first-class rooms for music are on the horizon for autumn 2007, when the **Royal**

Conservatory of Music opens the **TELUS Centre for Performance & Learning**. This mammoth arts and education venue will feature an acoustically perfect 1,000-seat concert hall.

Performing groups

Canadian Opera Company

416 363 8231/www.coc.ca.

Opera is hot in Toronto. With near sold-out performances all season long, the largest producer of opera in Canada is riding high. In its shiny new home (*see p198* **The curtain rises**), the COC hopes to attract more international stars and, with greater backstage space, mount more repertory productions at the same time as the big shows.

Part of opera's appeal has come from director Richard Bradshaw's policy of enlisting top Canadian talent from outside the world of opera. Local filmmaker Atom Egoyan directed *Die Walküre* and Quebec film-maker François Gerard took the reigns for *Siegfried* for the inaugural production of Wagner's Ring Cycle at the Four Seasons.

For the 2007/08 season, the COC has added two more productions, bringing the seasonal total to eight operas. These will include *Don Carlos*, *Eugene Onegin* and *The Barber of Seville*. The only thing missing is a range of home-grown operas, but now that the COC has settled into its new digs, perhaps it can turn next to cultivating Canadian scores and librettos. There is a series of free concerts held from October to June at the Four Seasons Centre for the Performing Arts (*see below*) on Tuesdays and Thursdays at noon and the first Wednesday of the month at 5pm. These feature emerging artists in classical, jazz, world music and modern dance.

Tafelmusik Baroque Orchestra & Chamber Choir

416 964 6337/www.tafelmusik.org.
This choir and ensemble manages the unthinkable: it makes baroque chamber music sexy, using witty, entertaining and technically superb shows. Since forming in 1970, it has earned popular and critical acclaim both at home and abroad. When not touring internationally, Tafelmusik presents more than 40 concerts a year in the atmospheric environs of Trinity-St Paul's Centre (*see p200*), as well as performing at such venues as the George Weston Recital Hall and Royal Ontario Museum. The leadership of musical director and award-winning violinist Jeanne Lamon has been crucial to their success.

Toronto Mendelssohn Choir

416 598 0422/www.tmchoir.org.
With a core of about 20 professional singers, this respected ensemble has been a Toronto mainstay since 1894, performing in venues all over the city. Under artistic director Noel Edison, it continues to seek innovative ways to present choral music. The ensemble is highly respected: it is a regular companion of the Toronto Symphony Orchestra, Les Grands Ballets Canadiens and the National Arts Centre Orchestra. TMC concerts are frequently heard on CBC Radio, and the ensemble has recorded on EMI and Naxos.

Toronto Symphony Orchestra

416 598 3375/www.tso.on.ca.
Canada's most prominent philharmonic ensemble is getting its groove back after years of dwindling audiences and red ink. Thanks to increased private and federal government support, the TSO is in much happier shape these days under the baton of music director Peter Oundjian, with increased ticket sales (over 400,000 annually) and a significant improvement in the acoustics of its home base, Roy Thomson Hall. The orchestra has a reputation for diversity and accessibility, having brought in such famous guests as Yo-Yo Ma, Kathleen Battle and Jessye Norman. Renowned composers Henri Dutilleux, R Murray Schafer and the late Sir Michael Tippett have all attended the orchestra's presentations of their music, and Igor Stravinsky once guest-conducted his own work.

Smaller performing groups

The **Royal Conservatory of Music** (416 408 2824, www.rcmusic.ca) organises symphonic and small ensemble recitals (as well as world-music events) at various venues around town. Its 2007 move into the TELUS Centre for Performance & Learning will boost its profile significantly. Founded in 1974, the **Toronto Symphony Youth Orchestra** (416 593 7769 ext 372, www.tso.on.ca/season/youth/youth02.cfm) has alumni performing all over the world. The large **Orpheus Choir of Toronto** (416 530 4428, www.orpheus.on.ca) was founded in 1964 and has a reputation for accomplished and adventurous performances of choral work. Its themed concerts are always popular. The **Nathaniel Dett Chorale** (416 340 7000, www.nathanieldettchorale.org) was founded in 1998 by artistic director and conductor Brainerd Blyden-Taylor. Inspired by early 20th century African-Canadian composer Dett, the chorale explores Afrocentric styles, including classical, spiritual, gospel, jazz and blues. Its infrequent performances are worth investigating. The **Amici Chamber Ensemble** (416 368 8743, www.amiciensemble.com) has become one of the city's most popular small classical ensembles. Together since 1985, it has an annual series at the Glenn Gould Studio (*see below*), with the four core members bringing in distinguished guests. Founded in 1968, the **Toronto Chamber Choir** (416 699 8121, www.geocities.com/torontochamberchoir) is a 40-voice ensemble with a repertoire that originally covered only Renaissance music, but now ranges from medieval to modern.

Venues

Four Seasons Centre for the Performing Arts

145 Queen Street W, at University Avenue (416 363 6671/www.fourseasonscentre.ca). Streetcar 501/ subway Osgoode. **Open** *Box office* 11am-7pm Mon-Sat; 11am-performance time Sun. **Credit** AmEx, MC, V. **Map** P271 E7.
For review, *see p198* **The curtain rises**.

George Weston Recital Hall

Toronto Centre for the Arts, 5040 Yonge Street, at Hillcrest Avenue, North Toronto (416 733 9388/www.tocentre.com). Subway North York Centre or Sheppard. **Open** *Box office* 11am-6pm Mon-Sat; noon-4pm Sun. **Tickets** prices vary. **Credit** AmEx, MC, V.
Loved by performers and concert-goers alike, this hall is one of Canada's finest. Located far from the city centre, in the Toronto Centre for the Arts in North York, the elegant 1,032-seat theatre is

Arts & Entertainment

The curtain rises

An opera house can assume a larger-than-life presence and become a symbol of a city. Think of Milan's La Scala, the swooping sail architecture of Sydney or the stunning 21st-century opera houses in Copenhagen and Oslo. These theatres become a point of pride for citizens, even if they never went to the opera, because they placed the city on the cultural map.

Toronto has wanted to join the big leagues for a long time. Since 1960, the Canadian Opera Company and the National Ballet of Canada bunked together at what is now called the Hummingbird Centre for the Performing Arts, a multi-purpose hall that also endured circus acts and, when the Clash came to town, seat-tossing antics. With a sloped floor and a capacity of 3,000, the setting was anything but intimate for those in the cheap seats.

In the 1980s, plans were launched for a dedicated opera house. After a quarter-century of infighting and political dithering, the Four Seasons Centre for the Performing

the Erik Bruhn Prize
March 3, 2007

The Taming of the Shrew
March 10–18, 2007 presented by: A5er HARRY WINSTON

A Footstep of Air &
Opus 19/The Dreamer &
March 21–25, 2007

The Four Seasons & Pol
& New Work by Matjash

modelled on European concert halls like Amsterdam's Concertgebouw, and has outstanding acoustics and sight lines. In addition to many outstanding international performers, the Canadian Opera Company and Tafelmusik perform here.

Glenn Gould Studio

Canadian Broadcasting Centre, 250 Front Street W, at John Street, Entertainment District (ticketline 416 205 5555/www.glenngouldstudio.cbc.ca). Streetcar 504/subway St Andrew. **Open** *Box office 11am-6pm Mon-Fri.* **Tickets** *prices vary.* **Credit** *AmEx, MC, V.* **Map** *p271 E8.*

Named after the Canadian piano virtuoso, this theatre continues to be one of Toronto's favourite concert venues. It is home to many of CBC Radio's broadcasts, which cover classical, jazz and world music. The 340-seat auditorium has a pleasingly intimate atmosphere and pristine sound.

Harbourfront Centre Concert Stage

235 Queens Quay W, at Lower Simcoe Street, Waterfront (416 973 4000/www.harbourfront centre.com). Streetcar 509, 510. **Open** *Box office 1-8pm Tue-Sat.* **Tickets** *$20-$60.* **Credit** *AmEx, Disc, MC, V.* **Map** *p271/p272 F9.*

The fan-shaped outdoor summer stage looks out on to Lake Ontario and the Toronto Islands. It usually hosts world music concerts, but you can sometimes catch the Canadian Opera Company or other classical ensembles here. The view makes this a memorable place to watch a show, although noise

Arts opened in 2006. At long last, Toronto got the first purpose-built opera house in Canada.

Designed by Toronto architect Jack Diamond, the $180-million music box has a prominent location on the corner of University Avenue and Queen Street West. A high glass curtain across the main lobby connects the streetlife to the rarefied world of opera within.

And yet Toronto is not satisfied: this is not the picture-postcard icon many had hoped for. The Four Seasons didn't even make it on to the *Toronto Star*'s 'Ten projects that changed Toronto in 2006'. Architecture critic Christopher Hume called it 'a generic box that looks no further than its own black-brick walls'. When hopes are pinned on a building to vault a city's reputation, disappointment is often the end result.

But settle into a seat in the intimate, multi-tiered auditorium and forget the naysayers. With perfect sight-lines and vastly improved acoustics, a night at the opera – or the ballet, which also performs here – is worth the price of admission (if you can get a ticket).

laws mean that the fun has to end by 11pm so the condo-dwellers can get some shut-eye. The seats are notoriously uncomfortable, so bring a cushion.

Hummingbird Centre for the Performing Arts

1 Front Street E, at Yonge Street, St Lawrence (416 393 7469/www.hummingbirdcentre.com). Streetcar 504/subway King or Union. **Open** *Box office* 10am-6pm Mon-Fri; 10am-5pm Sat. **Tickets** $20-$150. **Credit** AmEx, MC, V. **Map** p272 G8.

With the COC and ballet gone, this 3,000-seat theatre is will continue to act as a roadhouse for touring Broadway-style shows, and a wide range of pop and classical performers. The stage has been graced by such diverse stars as the Clash and Björk.

Massey Hall

178 Victoria Street, at Shuter Street, Dundas Square (416 872 4255/www.masseyhall.com). Streetcar 501/subway Queen. **Open** *Ticketline* 9am-8pm Mon-Fri; noon-5pm Sat. **Tickets** $20-$100. **Credit** AmEx, MC, V. **Map** p272 G7.

The first concert at this historic auditorium took place in 1894 and featured Handel's *Messiah*, performed by a 500-member choir and 70-piece orchestra. Today the 2,765-seat hall is still one of the most rewarding places in the city to hear classical music. Sight lines vary, and the upper seats are hard and cramped, but the acoustics and intimacy compensate. Before Roy Thomson Hall was opened, this was home to the Toronto Symphony Orchestra.

Classical concerts are not as common now at Massey Hall, but you can still see great folk, blues, country and jazz. There is no better place to catch such acts as Wynton Marsalis, Alison Krauss and BB King.

Roy Thomson Hall

60 Simcoe Street, at King Street W, Entertainment District (416 872 4255/www.roythomson.com). Streetcar 504/subway St Andrew. **Open** *Ticketline* 9am-8pm Mon-Fri; noon-5pm Sat. *Box office (in person)* 10am-6pm Mon-Fri; noon-5pm Sat. **Tickets** $29-$135. **Credit** AmEx, MC, V. **Map** p271 E8.

In the shape of a snare drum, this striking glass building is hard to miss. The home of the Toronto Symphony Orchestra, the 2,812-seat theatre also hosts many other classical ensembles, along with occasional visits from the likes of Bonnie Raitt and Tony Bennett, to name but two. Opened in 1982, the hall was supposed to be acoustically perfect, but it didn't live up to expectations. However, the acoustics improved vastly following major renovations in 2002, when the austere concrete interior was replaced by warm wood.

Trinity-St Paul's Centre

427 Bloor Street W, at Robert Street, Harbord (416 964 6337/www.tspucc.org). Streetcar 510/subway Spadina. **Open** *Box office* 10am-1pm, 2-6pm Mon-Fri. **Tickets** $18-$69. **Credit** MC, V. **Map** p274 D4.

Intimate, sacred and mellow: with those qualities, it's no surprise that this has been Tafelmusik's main stage for almost 25 years. It is also the favourite venue of local roots heroes Cowboy Junkies. Musicians say the acoustics are good, but audiences say they're great, and the deep horseshoe layout means that everyone gets close to the stage. The church is also used by many other chamber-music ensembles, as well as by such contemporary artists as Rufus Wainwright.

Rock, Roots & Jazz

The Toronto music community defies being pigeonholed with one identifiable sound: it is simply too large, diverse and vibrant to be so easily commodified, packaged and sold.

At times guilty of ignoring the talent within, while fawning over imported flavours of the month, Toronto's media and audiences alike are now rightfully brimming with pride that the rest of the world has been catching on to the city's near-embarrassment of musical riches. The thriving live scene gives emerging talents the opportunity to show their stuff in public, and though the Toronto-based branches of the multinational record labels are dwindling, adventurous and creative independent labels (Maple, Arts & Crafts, Paper Bag, True North) have stepped into the void.

On any given night in Toronto, there is live music to be found in at least 30 different clubs,

many on the lively Queen West and College Street strips. New additions to the scene are frequent, with existing venues constantly rebranding. Every March Toronto hosts **Canadian Music Week** (CMW), while **North by Northeast** (NXNE; *see p168*) takes place every June. The former is more industry-oriented, while NXNE is a little more populist. Each event brings in hundreds of bands from across the country and beyond, as well as music-industry execs scouting the next big (or at least interesting) thing.

TICKETS AND INFORMATION

The city's two major free entertainment weeklies, *eye* and *NOW*, feature extensive listings sections. The information is generally the same, although *NOW*'s listings are marginally easier to use for those unfamiliar with particular venues or acts. The monthly *Toronto Life* magazine has good listings for classical and jazz concerts, as well as significant rock concerts.

Expect most club shows to get under way at 10pm or later, even on a weeknight. Most are pay-at-the-door, but expect club shows with popular acts to sell out in advance. It is prudent to book ahead, or at least show up early. Most stadium and arena shows, as well as some events at smaller venues, are handled by **Ticketmaster** (416 870 8000, www.ticket master.ca), which has outlets at most **Sunrise** record stores (336 Yonge Street, Dundas Square; call 416 498 6601 for branches) and at the **Rogers Centre** box office (*see p201*), among other locations. Tickets for many of the club shows can be found at two of the city's best record shops, **Soundscapes** (572 College Street; *see also p163*) and **Rotate This** (620 Queen Street W; *see also p162*).

Venues

Arenas/stadiums

Phone or check the local press for ticket prices and opening times for the following.

Air Canada Centre

40 Bay Street, at Front Street W, Entertainment District (416 815 5500/ticketline 416 870 8000/ www.theaircanadacentre.com). Subway Union. **Credit** AmEx, DC, MC, V. **Map** p271 E8.

This modern 21,000-seat arena alternates between major-name concerts and hockey and basketball games. This is where you're likely to find Madonna, Elton John or Justin Timberlake when they're playing in town; Babs Streisand gave a memorable show here in 2006. The centre can be reconfigured (by pulling a giant curtain across the auditorium) into a comparatively intimate 5,200-seat venue.

Molson Amphitheatre

909 Lake Shore Boulevard W, at Dufferin Street,
West End (416 260 5600/www.hob.com/venues/
concerts/molsonamp). Bus 29/streetcar 509, 511.
Credit AmEx, MC, V. **Map** p270 B10.
Many locals still sing the blues over the demolition
of their beloved revolving stage at Ontario Place, but
its larger replacement remains the city's best
outdoor venue for the big names in rock and pop.
The amphitheatre has 9,000 seats, while another
7,000 can sprawl on the hillside grass. The venue is
open in summer (May to September), and on a warm
evening this is a wonderful place to be. Be aware,
though, that the lakeside setting occasionally brings
a chill, so bring a jacket or jumper.

Rogers Centre (formerly SkyDome)

1 Blue Jays Way, at Front Street W, Entertainment
District (416 341 3663/ticketline 416 870 8000/
www.rogerscentre.com). Streetcar 504/subway St
Andrew or Union. **Credit** AmEx, DC, MC, V.
Map p271 E8.

With the arrival of the Air Canada Centre, the
cavernous, oft-maligned Rogers Centre now hosts
fewer concerts, but it's the one place in town for
stadium shows, and remains an occasional
stomping ground for such dinosaurs as Rod Stewart
and the Rolling Stones. Baseball, football, monster
truck rallies and wrestling events are its clients now.

Mid-sized venues & clubs

Horseshoe Tavern

370 Queen Street W, at Spadina Avenue,
Entertainment District (416 598 4226/
www.horseshoetavern.com). Streetcar 501, 510.
Open 9pm-1am Mon-Thur; 9pm-2.30am Fri-Sun.
Admission free-$25. **Credit** MC, V. **Map** p271 E7.
A Toronto legend, the rough-and-ready Horseshoe
has been serving up pints and kick-ass tunes since
1947. It has had colourful incarnations as a country
and punk bar, and now it books rock and roots acts.
In the middle of Queen Street's trendy strip, the

Northern star

Recognised as the brightest and most
charismatic star to emerge from Toronto in
the past five years, Emily Haines has other
cities fighting to claim her as their own.

That's understandable, given that Metric,
the band she fronts, is one highly nomadic
ensemble. Comprising both Canadians and
Americans, Metric formed in Brooklyn in
1998, recorded an aborted debut disc in
London with Stephen Hague (New Order),
and was based in Los Angeles for a spell.

Haines is quick to pledge allegiance to
her Toronto hometown, and it was this city's
independent record label, Last Gang (Death
From Above 1979) that kick-started Metric's
then-stagnant career. The band's official
debut album, 2003's *Old World Underground,*
Where Are You Now?, fused a melodic new-
wave vibe, modern rock energy and Emily's
sexy femme fatale aura.

The result was a band that appealed equally
to ageing male rock scribes and teenage girls
seeking a powerful role model, and success
came quickly. The disc went gold in Canada
and gave Metric an international profile. *Live*
It Out (2005) was equally strong, prompting
the Rolling Stones to invite them to open two
shows at Madison Square Garden.

Haines has revealed a warmer, more
relaxed side in her role as a contributor
(along with Canadian comrades Amy Millan
and Leslie Feist) to Toronto's freewheeling
musical collective, Broken Social Scene,

who took the indie world by storm in 2002.
The outfit also features her Metric co-
conspirator, guitarist/producer Jimmy Shaw.

The extent of Emily's creative ambition and
musical talent was revealed in her 2006 solo
debut, *Knives Don't Have Your Back*. Though
recorded over a five year period, the album
has a consistent feel, spotlighting Haines as
a piano-playing chanteuse. It features
allusive, eloquent lyrics delivered with
subtle vocal inflections.

Eliciting a positive critical response, it
confirmed Haines as an artist of real depth,
not just a flash-in-the-pan mini-skirted rocker.
That shouldn't come as a surprise, given that
she cites the likes of Carla Bley and Robert
Wyatt (both friends of her father, the late poet
Paul Haines) as more important influences
than Debbie Harry or Chrissie Hynde.

She is a proud ambassador for the local
music scene and the city in general. 'I get
very sentimental about the great education I
got here (she attended the Etobicoke School
of Art). My friends in New York or LA just can't
believe our luck in the things we had access
to and the generosity of the grants system.'

Metric now has its own Toronto studio,
something Emily calls 'a real measure of
success' and a 'huge ten-year dream. It
feels great to be back in Canada to do
this work here, having established ourselves
out in the world. That was always our plan.'
Watch this space.

unpretentious 'Shoe keeps its feet firmly on the ground. It can hold 520 people, and has regularly featured such major acts as Wilco and Los Lobos; it even hosted a secret Stones gig in 1997. The no-cover Tuesday New Music nights show up-and-coming bands from across Canada and abroad.

Hugh's Room

2261 Dundas Street W, at Bloor Street W, West End (416 531 6604/www.hughsroom.com). Streetcar 504, 505/subway Dundas West. **Open** 6pm-2am Tue-Sun. **Admission** $10-$25. **Credit** AmEx, MC, V.

This classy folk club was a dream of Richard and Hugh Carson. Hugh died before the dream was realised, but his name and spirit lives on in this West End venue. Hugh's Room attracts attentive, if sometimes slightly uptight, audiences, many of whom come for dinner plus the show. The booking policy includes world beat, blues and singer-songwriters, alongside traditional artists in its broad definition of folk. Such big draws as the McGarrigle Sisters and the Strawbs have played here.

Lee's Palace & the Dance Cave

529 Bloor Street W, at Bathurst Street, Harbord (416 532 1598/www.leespalace.com). Streetcar 511/subway Bathurst. **Open** 9pm-2am Thur-Sat; phone for details Mon-Wed, Sun. **Admission** $2-$20. **No credit cards. Map** p274 D4.

Helped by its proximity to the University of Toronto, this has long been one of the city's premier rock clubs. The high, wide stage, rockin' bartenders and good sight-lines are other assets of the 600-capacity venue. Nirvana played their first Toronto gig here, and it remains a great place to see those climbing the rock 'n' roll ladder. On the second floor, the 250-capacity Dance Cave hosts DJs spinning alternative rock, retro new wave, and dance hits.

Lula Lounge

1585 Dundas Street W, at Dufferin Street, West End (416 538 7405/www.lula.ca). Bus 29/streetcar 505. **Open** 7pm-2am Fri, Sat; phone for details Mon-Thur, Sun. **Admission** free-$25. **Credit** AmEx, MC, V. **Map** p270 A6.

A refreshing addition to the scene, Lula's is on the edge of Little Brazil, and has a Latin vibe to its drinks (fine Mojitos), food (tasty tapas) and decor. It looks like an old-style banquet hall, but has a top-notch sound system and great sight-lines. Regular bookings stress Latin and world music, but veteran local promoter Gary Topp has also brought in cult heroes like Jonathan Richman and James Hunter; Norah Jones and Jason Mraz have also performed in the 250-capacity room. **Photo** *see p196.*

Mod Club Theatre

722 College Street, at Shaw Street, Little Italy (416 588 4663/www.themodclub.com). Streetcar 506. **Open** phone for details. **Admission** free-$25. **Credit** AmEx, MC, V. **Map** p270 B5.

Further confirmation of Toronto's long-standing Anglophilia is provided by this new club, which was named after and founded on the success of the long-

running Mod Club series previously held at other local clubs. Boasting good sight-lines, excellent sound and a location on the edge of the busy College strip, it has rapidly become one of the city's leading mid-sized club venues. Such big-name English acts as Jamie Cullum, the Stranglers and Dizzee Rascal have packed the joint, while American acts (Blues Explosion, Matthew Sweet) have also been hosted.

Opera House

735 Queen Street E, at Broadview Avenue, East Toronto (416 466 0313/www.theoperahouse toronto.com). Streetcar 501, 504, 505. **Open** phone for details. **Admission** $8-$40. **Credit** AmEx, MC, V. **Map** p273 K7.

This former vaudeville theatre, built in the early 1900s, was converted into a multi-level, multi-purpose venue in 1990. On a run-down section of Queen East, it has had to work hard to compete with more central venues. And it has, hosting sell-out gigs from the likes of Björk, Blur and Radiohead.

Phoenix Concert Theatre

410 Sherbourne Street, at Carlton Street, Church & Wellesley (416 323 1251). Streetcar 506/subway Wellesley. **Open** 8pm-2.30am Fri-Sun; phone for details Mon-Thur. **Admission** $5-$50. **Credit** MC, V. **Map** p275 H5.

Part nightclub, part concert venue, the Phoenix boasts impressive sight-lines and sound, and has a more opulent feel than many of its peers. It regularly hosts top Canadian and international pop and rock acts, plus occasional 'all ages' shows.

Bars

Cadillac Lounge

1296 Queen Street W, at Brock Street, West End (416 536 7717). Streetcar 501. **Open** 11am-2am daily. **Admission** free-$10. **Credit** MC, V.

Yes, that really is a Cadillac embedded in the wall above this bar's front entrance. Inside you'll find more vintage in the form of Elvis memorabilia and old country-music posters, complemented by better-than-average bar food and brews. It's really a cosy neighbourhood bar with a diverse clientele that just happens to have reliably high-quality music. The huge, heated patio out back occasionally hosts bands, but it is the intimate indoor lounge (holds 120) that regularly features rock, blues and country acts from right across Canada. The occasional big name, like American rockabilly legend Robert Gordon, will pack the joint. Every third Sunday of the month features a matinée show with honky-tonk troubadour Scotty Campbell.

Cameron House

408 Queen Street W, at Cameron Street, Chinatown (416 703 0811/www.thecameron.com). Streetcar 501, 510/subway Osgoode. **Open** 4pm-2am daily. Performances 6-8pm Sat, Sun. **Admission** *Front room* pay what you can. *Back room* $5-$10. **Credit** V. **Map** p271 D7.

Red hot **Opal Jazz Lounge.** *See p204.*

After 20-plus years, the Cameron remains a favourite with Queen West bohemian hipsters. The eclectic booking policy meanders through cabaret, country, jazz, swing, folk and rock territory, but experimental theatre troupes, poets and spoken-word artists are also hosted. In the front bar, Kevin Quain's Mad Bastards holds court on Sunday nights and the Cameron Family Singers throw down some ol' country on Saturdays (6-8pm); the other gigs are in the back room. There's no cover in the front room, but be ready when they pass the hat around.

Drake Underground

1150 Queen Street W, at Beaconsfield Avenue, West End (416 531 5042/www.thedrakehotel.ca). Streetcar 501. **Open** 8pm/9pm-2am daily. **Admission** free-$15. **Credit** AmEx, DC, MC, V. **Map** p270 A7.
The basement of the hip Drake Hotel possesses an underground artistic sensibility. Local artists and musicians have taken to this intimate, well-designed

space, which features superior sound and a fun video jukebox. The vibe is suited to cabaret-styled or maverick acts, and the room has hosted memorable performances from the likes of Broken Social Scene and Juana Molina. It is also used for performance art, comedy, film, spoken word and board-game nights. *See also p52 and p140.*

El Mocambo

464 Spadina Avenue, at College Street, Harbord (416 777 1777/www.elmocambo.ca). Streetcar 506, 510. **Open** phone for details. **Admission** free-$15. **No credit cards. Map** p274 D5.
For decades, the Elmo was the city's most internationally famous live music club. The Rolling Stones played an infamous gig here in the '70s (Margaret Trudeau in tow), and the likes of Elvis Costello, Talking Heads and U2 have also graced the stage. It fell on hard times and briefly closed, but a major renovation brought it back, albeit with lesser stature. Most of the action takes place on the more spacious ground level, which sports a Moroccan vibe, expanded stage, improved sound, and room for 250 clubgoers. An eclectic booking policy ranges from rock to hip hop to roots (Billy Bragg, Alejandro Escovedo and Jet have all appeared here). It's good to have music back under the neon palms.

Jeff Healey's Roadhouse

56 Blue Jays Way, at King Street W, Entertainment District (416 593 2626/www.jeffhealeysroadhouse. com). Streetcar 504. **Open** 5pm-2am Mon-Fri; 3pm-2am Sat. **Admission** $5-$20. **Credit** MC, V. **Map** p271 D9.
The venue is new, but the same name is still above the door. The blues-rock guitar ace has outgrown his basement digs and has a bigger house to play in, along with guests in rock, jazz and blues. Healey's Jazz Wizards house band do a credible version of New Orleans jazz from the '30s.

Orbit Room

580 College Street, at Manning Avenue, Little Italy (416 535 0613). Streetcar 506, 511. **Open** 10.30pm-1.30am daily. **Admission** free-$35. **Credit** AmEx, MC, V. **Map** p270 C5.
This small, second-floor bar is a happy place to hear upbeat Hammond-organ funk and jazz. It occasionally brings in stars like Brian Auger and Joey DeFrancesco, but mostly relies on shining local talents (guitar wizard Kevin Breit's Sisters Euclid and Doug Riley, for instance). It can get crowded even on Sunday nights, so be prepared to wriggle. In fact, it's so cosy you have to walk through the band to get to the washrooms and small terrace out back. Retro decor and friendly staff keep things real.

Rivoli

332-334 Queen Street W, at Spadina Avenue, Entertainment District (416 596 1908/http:// rivoli.ca/2003). Streetcar 501, 510. **Open** *Bar/restaurant* 11.30am-1am daily. *Back room* phone for details. **Admission** $5-$10. **Credit** AmEx, MC, V. **Map** p271 E7.

Arts & Entertainment

The back room at the Riv has been a key spot on the Queen scene since the late '70s, and is a favoured venue for all things alternative, whether it's rock, comedy, jazz, funk or punk. The club is often used by record labels for industry parties. The spacious pool hall upstairs also hosts the Maple Lounge series every Wednesday, featuring top Canadian singer/songwriters. *See also p134, p175 and p216.*

Jazz & blues

With full-on support from the local radio station JAZZ.FM91, Toronto's jazz scene is climbing out of a slump. Following the closure of the Montreal Bistro and Top o' the Senator, two clubs have stepped up to the plate: **Opal Jazz Lounge**, opened in late 2006, and **Live at the Courthouse**, scheduled to open in 2007. The jazz festival scene continues unabated with the **Toronto Downtown Jazz Festival** (*see p168*) which brings in top names to perform in in Nathan Phillips Square and various clubs. The **Beaches International Jazz Festival** (*see p169*) literally stops traffic in the east end, as thousands check out the free and eclectic musical fare on the street and in Kew Gardens.

Toronto is blessed with many fine female jazz vocalists (Molly Johnson, Alex Pangman, Sophie Milman, Heather Bambrick) and talented instrumental ensembles traverse classic be-bop, contemporary and avant-garde territory. The blues is a style better heard live than on disc, and it has long been a key component of the city's music scene. Local heroes like Downchild, Jack DeKeyzer and Paul Reddick are always worth catching.

Grossman's Tavern
379 Spadina Avenue, at Cecil Street, Chinatown (416 977 7000/www.grossmanstavern.com). Streetcar 506, 510. **Open** 11am-2am Mon-Sat; noon-2am Sun. **Admission** free. **Credit** V. **Map** p271 D6.
Opened in 1949, this Chinatown tavern features a cast of seasoned regulars who look as though they came with the original furniture. Beery and a little grimy, the bar has a perfect soundtrack: loud blues played by locals and visiting dignitaries. The likes of Jeff Healey and Downchild (the inspiration for the Blues Brothers) paid their proverbial dues here. It can also be a good place for Dixieland.

Live @ Courthouse
57 Adelaide Street E., at Church Street (416 214 9379, www.liveatcourthouse.com.ca). Streetcar 504/subway King. **Open** 5pm-2am Mon-Sat. **Admission** Varies with performance. **Credit** AmEx, MC, V. **Map** p272 G7.
With the backing of a solid club impresario, booking by the head of the Toronto Jazz Festival and a historic room with balconies, fireplaces and oodles of atmosphere, this new jazz club promises to become a hot destination for jazz fans and stars.

Opal Jazz Lounge
472 Queen Street W, at Spadina Avenue (416 646 6725/www.opaljazzlounge.com). Streetcar 501, 510. **Open** 5.30pm-2am Tue-Sat. **Admission** No cover Tue, Wed; varies Thu-Sat. **Credit** AmEx MC V. **Map** p271 D7.
The mood at this cool, intimate club is set by the exposed brick walls, soft candlelight and nostalgic photos of jazz legends (including a giant portrait of Miles Davis) along the walls. Washington Savage tinkles the ivories on Tuesday and Wednesday and legends like David 'Fathead' Newman and Benny Green have played on weekends. The bar list is pure Rat Pack, and if you like tenderloin with your tenor sax, the dinner menu offers melodies for the mouth. *Photo p203.*

Reservoir Lounge
52 Wellington Street E, at Church Street, St Lawrence (416 955 0887/www.reservoirlounge.com). Streetcar 504/subway King. **Open** 8pm-2am Mon-Thu; 7.30pm-2am, Fri-Sat. **Admission** free-$10. **Credit** AmEx, DC, MC, V. **Map** p272 G8.
The swing revival may be dead as a doornail in most places, but it lives on in this basement lounge, underneath the eye-catching Flatiron building. Close to the St Lawrence Centre for the Performing Arts and the Hummingbird Centre, it is an ideal place to kick back with a post-theatre Martini and listen to Toronto's best swing bands and such fine singers as Tory Cassis and Alex Pangman. Low ceilings and brick pillars, high tables and long, velvet couches set the scene. The food's a tad pricey, but worth it. The place gets packed at weekends, but there's always a couple or two who find space to dance.

Rex Hotel Jazz & Blues Bar
194 Queen Street W, at University Avenue, Entertainment District (416 598 2475). Streetcar 501/subway Osgoode. **Open** 6.30pm-1.30am Mon-Fri; noon-1.30am Sat, Sun. **Admission** free-$12. **No credit cards. Map** p271 E7.
If you're tired of the elitist and snobbish atmosphere of some jazz clubs, then the Rex is a refreshingly low-key alternative. The casual atmosphere, friendly regulars and a wide range of beers on tap make this a social place to hear the best local jazz artists. Two, sometimes three, acts play daily, and stars such as Harry Connick Jr have also been known to jam here. A great budget venue.

Silver Dollar Room
486 Spadina Avenue, at College Street, Chinatown (416 763 9139/www.silverdollarroom.com). Streetcar 506, 510. **Open** 10pm-1.30am daily. **Admission** free-$15. **No credit cards. Map** p274 D5.
Look for the large backlit silver dollar over the door and then step back in time. This legendary dive has seen better days, but it still draws top-notch blues acts from Chicago and the cream of the local crop. The High Lonesome Wednesdays series helped spark a bluegrass revival in Toronto, while garage rock bands from Canada and the US occasionally hit the stage too.

Nightlife

Canadian frisky.

Republik. *See p207.*

The smoking ban was supposed to put a dent in club owners' pockets. It didn't. Then gun crime brought tension to the scene, but it couldn't kill it. In fact, the punters are still coming – in droves. Clubland in the Entertainment District is one of the most concentrated party scenes in the world, keeping the city jumping till past dawn (though visitors should be aware of the 2am last call for booze). Warehouses converted into cavernous clubs attract the after-work set, then rev up on weekends when the suburban kids descend.

The **Entertainment District** – the area roughly bordered by Queen Street, Spadina Avenue, King Street and University Avenue – is ground zero for the party scene, drawing upwards of 30,000 clubbers on any given Saturday night. This means heavy traffic, outlandish parking fees, promotional litter, public drunkenness and relentless thumping bass emanating from clubs. Queues are a given at most spots after 11pm on Thursdays to Saturdays, regardless of the size of the crowd within; the velvet rope is all about illusion, and behind it may lie a club packed with revellers or one that is still struggling to find its groove. Advance planning (surfing the club's website) may get you on the VIP list, allowing you to swagger past the crowds outside. Alternatively, just show up looking glam; the days when jeans were acceptable are largely gone; clubland

attracts a young, dressy crowd. The scene is cut-throat, so a favourite haunt may be here one day, gone the next, and back again later.

In terms of tunes, in Toronto anything goes: the city's numerous DJs vie for residencies, constantly inventing new speciality nights. On most days of the week you can find old school, classic, progressive and deep house, or hip hop, R&B, techno and drum 'n' bass. Stray from deepest downtown and you'll also find clubs and lounges playing world sounds, from Latin and African to Caribbean beats.

Club owners concentrate their holdings in a few key neighbourhoods. Next after Clubland is **College Street**, the main artery through the city's oldest Italian and Portuguese neighbourhoods. For several giddy blocks you can effortlessly slide from drink to food and back again, as lounges and restaurants and hybrids (some with dancefloors) compete for your attention. **West Queen West** is also building momentum as a nightlife destination, with the Drake Hotel (*see p140*) and the Gladstone Hotel (*see p141*) spawning bars and clubs that draw indie-music scenesters, the alt-art crowd and even swingers to the trendiest stretch in town.

The diversity of Toronto's clubland is due in part to the fact that the city lies on the flight path between Chicago, home of house, and New York, with techno centre Detroit just a few

Rockwood. *See p207*.

hours' drive away. With a drinking age two years lower than border states and a still-friendly exchange rate, Toronto has become a popular destination for American party-goers, as well as high-profile DJs.

To find out what's on, grab a copy of free weeklies *NOW* or *eye* a sidewalk box. They're both published on a Thursday.

Waterfront

The Guvernment
132 Queens Quay E, at Lower Jarvis Street (416 869 0045/www.theguvernment.com). Streetcar 509/subway Union then 15 mins walk. **Open** 10pm-3am Thur, Fri; 10pm-6am Sat. **Admission** $10-$15. **Credit** AmEx, MC, V. **Map** p272 G9.

While its current clientele was still crawling, this venue – as the celebrated RPM – held marathon parties for mods, goths and punks. It eventually morphed into this equally enduring clubbing complex that attracts Toronto's top house DJs, alongside international turntable royalty. Bouncers won't turn away the shabbily dressed, but they will make you wait: it's a rare night that the queue is not wrapped around the block. On Saturday nights, 3,000 clubbers cram the venue, dancing to the house beats of DJ Mark Oliver on the main floor, getting psychedelic in the Orange Room or gazing at the skyline in the Skybar. The hangar-like space is also home to concert venue Kool Haus, which attracts international DJs and eclectic acts (Kruder and Dorfmeister, Tenacious D), as well as bands that play good old-fashioned instruments. There is lounge space galore, plus two rooftop patios.

Entertainment District

CiRCA

126 John Street, at Richmond Street W (416 979 0044/www.circatoronto.com). Streetcar 501. **Open** call for details. **Admission** $10-$20. **Credit** call for details. **Map** p271 E7.

Peter Gatien, the Canadian impresario behind New York's Limelight and Tunnel nightclubs, is back home and looking to make a comeback with a club that has been tantalisingly slow in opening its doors. A legal tangle over a liquor licence is the latest snag. When it does open, watch out for one of the biggest clubs (it was formerly Lucid) to make its mark. Weekend nights are for clubbers, with concerts held in the mammoth four-storey space on weeknights.

C Lounge

456 Wellington Street W, at Spadina Avenue (416 260 9393). Streetcar 510. **Open** 10pm-2am Mon-Wed, Fri; 5pm-2am Thur; 9pm-2am Sat. **Admission** $5-$10. **Credit** AmEx, MC, V. **Map** p271 D8.

Liberty Group, a nightlife conglomerate, specialises in clubs that mix decadence with elegance. The 'C' gives a nod to Miami: the multiple water features include waterfalls and a wading pool in summer, an ice lounge in winter, plus bottle service (the price of two bottles of spirits or champagne for a group of friends gets you a private enclave to lounge in). These attractions attract both Beamer types and young wannabes. The unisex loo isn't a great idea, however: boys have been known to hog the mirrors.

Crocodile Rock

240 Adelaide Street W, at Duncan Street (416 599 9751/www.crockrock.ca). Streetcar 501/subway Queen. **Open** 4pm-2am Wed-Fri; 7pm-2am Sat. **Admission** $5. **Credit** AmEx, MC, V. **Map** p271 D8.

You want to party like the kids but feeling a little past your clubbing prime? This safe, blue-collar club is where firemen and nurses go for 911 Nights on Wednesdays. Ball caps and jeans suffice as a fashion statement, and the music is pure pop.

Footwork

425 Adelaide Street W, at Brandt Street (416 913 3488). Streetcar 501, 510. **Open** 10pm-4am Fri, Sat. **Admission** $10-$20. **Credit** AmEx, MC, V. **Map** p271 D7.

Fancy footwork is on display at this intimate club, with house and techno keeping some 400 dancers packed on the floor in pared-down surroundings.

Lot 332

332 Richmond Street W, at Peter Street (416 599 5332). Streetcar 501. **Open** 9pm-3am Thur-Sat. **Admission** $15-$20. **Credit** AmEx, MC, V. **Map** p271 E7.

The retractable roof gives this dance palace a breath of fresh air – at carefully calculated intervals – to keep the steamy dancefloor from boiling over. Dress to impress – the competition from the scantily clad staffers raises the bar.

Republik

261 Richmond Street W, at Peter Street (416 598 1632/www.republiknightclub.com). Streetcar 501. **Open** 10pm-6am Thur-Sat. **Admission** $20-$40. **Credit** AmEx, MC, V. **Map** p271 E7.

This party palace deals in attitude and ham-fisted bouncers. But coloured lights can hypnotise, as the Guess Who sang, and if it's three rooms of dazzling lights you're after – each with its own music and look (fibre-optic curtains, indoor waterfalls, strobes) – join the line of bright young things. **Photo** *p205*.

Rockwood

31 Mercer Street, at Blue Jays Way (416 979 7373). Streetcar 504. **Open** 10pm-3am Mon, Thur-Sat. **Admission** $15-$20. **Credit** AmEx, MC, V. **Map** p271 D8.

For a natural clubbing high, this earth-toned venue is decked out in rock, wood and grass on three levels (including a rooftop deck). The music is mostly house, with a crowd edging into their 30s. It's typical of the current trend for smaller spaces, which makes mingling easy. **Photo** *p206*.

Schmooze

15 Mercer Street, at King Street W (416 341 8777/www.schmooze.ca). Streetcar 504. **Open** *Restaurant* 4-9pm Fri; 7-9pm Sat. *Club* 9pm-2am Fri; 10pm-2am Sat. **Admission** $10-$25. **Credit** AmEx, MC, V. **Map** p271 E8.

In the early evenings a crowd of lawyers and bankers descends (the club's 'over-25' policy makes this inevitable), which means a little dancing and a lot of schmoozing. If you stay late enough, the romance of the place (1930s cathedral ceilings, chandeliers) may encourage you to take to the floor. There is a good-looking crowd, who clearly follows the club's suggestion: 'Dress as if you're expecting to meet someone, because chances are you will.'

This is London

364 Richmond Street W, at Peter Street (416 351 1100/www.thisislondonclub.com). Streetcar 501. **Open** 10pm-3am Fri, Sat. **Admission** $20. **Credit** AmEx, MC, V. **Map** p271 E7.

Styled after a velvet-roped Soho palace, this hidden club projects a refined brand of hedonism. Sophisticates sip Veuve or premium vodka in the upstairs lounge, while bouncers oversee the lower-level party with military tenacity. The women's bathroom has beauticians on hand. DJs Dimitri from Paris and Benny Benassi stop here on the circuit.

Ultra Supper Club

314 Queen Street W, at Peter Street (416 263 0330/www.ultrasupperclub.com). Streetcar 501, 510. **Open** 5.30pm-midnight Mon-Wed; 5.30pm-2am Thur-Sat. **Credit** AmEx, DC, MC, V. **Map** p271 E7.

The city's original hybrid resto-lounge is a lavish affair, with silk curtains, ottomans and Roman columns. Earlier in the evening, it offers sophisticated dining. The drinking and dancing (on tables, wherever) gets going later at night. They try to push bottle service on you (buying a whole bottle of spirits in return for a table and a server), but won't hold it against you if just feel like a beer. The rooftop deck in summer is superb.

Up & Down Lounge

270 Adelaide Street W, at John Street (416 977 4038). Streetcar 501, 504. **Open** 9pm-3am Wed-Sat. **Admission** free. **Credit** AmEx, MC, V. **Map** p271 E7.

This perennially cool, intimate two-level club is more of a cocktail lounge than a dance club, but it nonetheless has a clubby vibe. Go fashionably late.

Chinatown

Sonic

270 Spadina Avenue, at Dundas Avenue (416 977 1111/www.sonicnightclubcom). Streetcar 510. **Open** 1am-9am Sat. **Admission** $20 before 3am; $30 after 3am. **No credit cards**. **Map** p271 D6.

This old Chinatown porn theatre has a massive sound system to keep ravers going all night. The catch? This non-licensed venue doesn't get going until last call, so you'll be drinking juice and water. International DJs play house, tribal and progressive.

Supermarket

260 Augusta Avenue, at College Street (416 840 0501/www.supermarkettoronto.com). **Open** 5.30pm-2am daily. **Admission** free-$5. **Credit** AmEx, MC, V. **Map** p271 D6.

This evening restaurant morphs into a club with entertainment as eclectic as its Kensington neighbourhood. Melting Pot Friday has DJ Andrew Allsgood, while Do Right Saturday brings DJ John Kong and Fase to spin funk, hip hop and disco.

University

Comfort Zone

486 Spadina Avenue, at College Street (416 763 9139). Streetcar 501, 510. **Open** 11pm-6am Thur, Fri; 3am-2pm Sat; 6am Sun-4am Mon. **Admission** prices vary. **Credit** MC, V. **Map** p271 D5.

Comfort is the last thing you'll find at this party after the after-party. It's essentially a dingy basement where people crash on the pool tables – but it is nonetheless a favourite with great house DJs.

Yorkville

Babalúu

136 Yorkville Avenue, at Avenue Road (416 515 0587/www.babaluu.com). Bus 6/subway Bay. **Open** 6pm-2am Tue-Sun. **Admission** $5-$12. **Credit** AmEx, DC, MC, V. **Map** p274 F4.

Babalúu is an upscale gem of a Latin club, ensconced down a flight of stairs in the heart of Yorkville, land of pretty (and pretty loaded) people. Expect to see sexy dancing to salsa, merengue and cumbia, as well as clumsier moves from well-heeled, Moët-sipping amateurs. Dance moves are taught earlier in the evening (classes at 9pm).

West End

Andy Poolhall

489 College Street, at Markham Street (416 923 5300/www.andypoolhall.com). Streetcar 506, 511. **Open** 6pm-2am Mon, Sat; 7pm-2am Tue-Fri. **Admission** varies; call for details. **Credit** AmEx, MC, V. **Map** p270 C5.

Kitsch white plastic bubble chairs and red pool tables create a groovy atmosphere, which draws a funky clientele. The Andy refers to Warhol, and he would surely approve of this subterranean alt cocktail bar. A popular lesbian dance night packs the place on the second to last Saturday of every month. Music covers the gamut: soul, house, hip hop, electro and new wave spun by local faves Denise Benson on Fridays and Fase on Tuesdays.

Cervejaria Downtown Bar & Grill

842 College Street, at Ossington Avenue, Little Italy (416 588 0162). Streetcar 506. **Open** *Restaurant* noon-2am daily. *Club/music* 10pm-2am Fri, Sat. **Admission** $8. **Credit** MC, V. **Map** p270 B5.

Timing is key at this hybrid beer hall/dance haven. On Fridays the Cuban band Son Ache heats up the place with salsa, while Saturdays can bring Brazilian beats, fado or rock. Either way the crowd will be on its feet. Otherwise, it's Euro disco mixed with overplayed Latin pop. Still, there are always cheap Portuguese eats, football on the big screen and pitchers of beer in the front bar.

El Convento Rico

750 College Street, at Crawford Street, Little Italy (416 588 7800/www.elconventorico.com). Streetcar 506, 511. **Open** 10pm-3am Thur; 8pm-4am Fri, Sat. **Admission** $10. **No credit cards**. **Map** p270 B5.

Ultra. See p207.

On weekends you'll find a mixed bunch here: singles, married folk, gay and straight couples. They've all come for one thing: the heady mayhem leading up to the midnight drag show. Before and after, Latin music and Euro dance tunes are the order of the day. It's kitsch, but it's a ball.

Matador Club Country Music

466 Dovercourt Road, at College Street (416 533 9311). Streetcar 506, 511. **Open** 2am-5am Fri, Sat. **Admission** prices vary. **No credit cards**. **Map** p270 A5.

While the rest of the city is running out of gas, this old barn is revving up for a marathon hoedown. The country music is sometimes proffered by amateur musicians, occasionally by stars. The rowdy vibe and late opening have made Matador a cult classic.

Octapus

293 Palmerston Avenue, at College Street (416 929 7214). Streetcar 506. **Open** 9pm-2am Wed-Sat. **Admission** free-$5. **Credit cards** AmEx, MC, V.

This revamped garage cultivates a Caribbean feel with billowing curtains and a relaxed vibe. DJs spin house, soul, reggae and hip hop. Survey the scene from the balcony or step on to the (unlicensed) patio.

Revival

783 College Street, at Shaw Street (416 535 7888/www.revivalbar.com). Streetcar 506. **Open** 9.30pm-2am Sat; otherwise phone for details. **Admission** $5-$10. **Credit** AmEx, MC, V. **Map** p270 B5.

This party palace in Little Italy has been going strong for five years, with its mixed programme of DJs, concerts and the occasional surprise event, such as performances from the Black Eyed Peas and

Justin Timberlake. DJs play sets that tend towards soul, funk and newly mixed Brazilian beats.

The Social

1100 Queen Street W, at Dovercourt Road (416 532 4474/www.thesocial.ca). Streetcar 501. **Open** 5pm-2am Mon, Wed-Sat. **Admission** free. **Credit** AmEx, MC, V.

With a long bar, brick walls and a concrete floor, this room is really whatever the crowd makes of it. The disco ball drops around 11pm; DJs spin a mix of '80s old school, new wave and rock. There's no sign – just look for the crowds smoking on the steps.

Vogue

1032 Queen Street W, at Ossington Avenue (416 414 9334/www.voguebar.ca). Streetcar 501. **Open** 10pm-3am Fri, Sat. **Admission** varies; call for details. **Credit** AmEx, MC, V. **Map** p270 B7.

This slightly salacious newcomer is all about exploring your wild side. Theme nights like naughty co-eds and belly-dancing set the mood, and the sexy staff keep shaking on the long bar till late. There are drag shows and Madonna wannabe dancers; upstairs is Wicked, a new swingers club.

East Toronto

The Docks

11 Polson Street, at Cherry Street (416 469 5655/ www.thedocks.com). Bus 72. **Open** 9pm-3am Fri, Sat. **Admission** $10-$15. **Credit** AmEx, MC, V. **Map** p273 J10.

This waterfront playground is a bit out of the way, but it throws some huge parties, with international DJ crews spinning house, techno, trance and jungle. The lakeside location adds a bit of romance.

Arts & Entertainment

Sport & Fitness

Sports-mad Toronto provides plenty to get pumped about.

In 2007 a sixth Torontonian pro sports franchise joined the ranks of hockey, baseball, basketball, football and lacrosse. As we went to press, Toronto FC was poised to bring soccer to town, along with a brand-new stadium to play in (*see p214*). This all adds up to year-round action for the city's sports fans, who cling to the hope of cheering on a winner, even though – aside from lacrosse's Toronto Rock – championship wins have eluded the city for longer than most care to remember. It's been 40 years since the Maple Leafs last hoisted hockey's Stanley Cup, and still die-hard fans insist it's the only game in town. Just about every activity – from badminton to horse racing to cricket and windsurfing – can be enjoyed and observed at a highly competitive level. And if you're willing to spend up to 90 minutes on the road, terrific golf courses and what passes for downhill skiing in southern Ontario are yours for the taking.

Staying fit is easy in Toronto – whether you run the forest trails of High Park, hit the ice at Harbourfront's outdoor rink or swim in the lake off a sandy beach on the islands. Cyclists pedal throughout the year and jostle with rollerbladers and joggers for space on well-marked trails that cross the city through the network of ravines. The city's well-maintained recreation system boasts dozens of free tennis courts, pools, tracks, skating rinks, playing fields and basketball hoops, and the plethora of gyms and exercise studios is a testament to a populace obsessed with fitness.

One unlamented loss to the city's sportscape was the closure in 2006 of the Olympic-themed entertainment complex Olympic Spirit Toronto. What was touted as a beacon to amateur athletics, with interactive and multimedia displays, in the end proved to be a reminder of Toronto's failed bid to host the 2008 Olympic Games. On that particular global playing field, Toronto – it seemed – didn't stand a chance.

Spectator sports

American football

Football, as it is played in Canada, is a far cry from the high-priced glamour sport seen south of the border. With three downs (instead of four

as in the US game), and fields that are both wider and longer, the Canadian game is arguably faster and more dramatic than its American cousin. But salaries are closer to that of a supply teacher than a CEO, and player ranks are studded with has- and never-beens from the NFL. The missing glamour of the American game might account for the locals' general indifference to the **Toronto Argos** through most of the '90s, but the perseverance of former player, one-time president and current coach of the team, Mike 'Pinball' Clemons, has turned things around. After considering a move from the cavernous Rogers Centre to a smaller venue in the suburbs, the Argos are staying put for now. The profile of the game should get a boost when Toronto hosts the Grey Cup – the oldest professional championship game in North America – in November 2007. But even with a distinguished past, the future of the Canadian Football League seems tenuous. The biggest threat is talk of a Toronto franchise in the US National Football League, something that Maple Leaf Sports & Entertainment Ltd, owners of the Leafs, Raptors and Toronto FC teams, seems determined to secure.

Toronto Argonauts

Rogers Centre (formerly SkyDome), 1 Blue Jays Way, at Front Street W, Entertainment District (information 416 341 2700/tickets 416 341 2746/ www.argonauts.on.ca). Streetcar 504/subway St Andrew or Union. **Season** June-Nov. **Tickets** $18-$65; $15-$60 concessions. **Credit** AmEx, MC, V. **Map** p271 E8/E9.

Baseball

Toronto has joyously embraced America's pastime since the **Toronto Blue Jays** played their first snow-blanketed game back in 1977 at the old Exhibition stadium. Fan fervour grew through the late 1980s and exploded during the World Series-winning seasons of '92 and '93, but since the strike-shortened season of 1994 attendance has been in decline. Coming off a strong second-place season in 2006, hope springs eternal that talent, and owner Ted Rogers's pocketbook, can carry the Jays to renewed glory. Either way, there's no more relaxing way to spend a sunny afternoon or a steamy summer night than at an open-roof game at the Rogers Centre. **Photo** *p211.*

Toronto Blue Jays

Rogers Centre (formerly SkyDome), 1 Blue Jays Way, at Front Street W, Entertainment District (information 416 341 1000/tickets 416 341 3000/www.bluejays.com). Streetcar 504/subway St Andrew or Union. **Season** May-Sept. **Tickets** $26-$37. **Credit** AmEx, MC, V. **Map** p271 E8/E9.

Basketball

The **Raptors** (**photo** *p212*) continue to be niche players in a crowded sports market. The games sell well at home, but often the results come up short in terms of inspiring citywide support. However, the 2006/7 season may have signalled a turn for the better as the Raptors build a strong international roster, including Andrea Bargnani, who was acquired as the NBA's first draft pick. He is the first European player to be so honoured and the only Italian-born player currently in the league. The team's Italian connection extends to Maurizio Gherardini, the assistant general manager, who is keeping an eye on developing European talent for the NBA. Other team players pumping the spirits of the Raptors are Chris Bosh, José Calderón and Jorge Garbajosa.

Toronto Raptors

Air Canada Centre, 40 Bay Street, at Front Street W, Entertainment District (info 416 815 5600/ tickets 416 872 5000/www.nba.com/raptors). Subway Union. **Season** Oct-June. **Tickets** $36-$665. **Credit** AmEx, DC, MC, V. **Map** p271/p272 F8/F9.

Cricket

Cricket is certainly the oldest organised sport played in Toronto, although it's fair to say many of the game's participants and observers are among the city's newest arrivals. Beloved by Commonwealth expats, the game in many ways exemplifies Toronto's multiculturalism, with over 100 clubs bringing together members of the Asian, West Indian, British and Australian communities in particular. The **Toronto & District Cricket Association** (www.cricketstar.net) is the largest league in North America, and regularly supplies upwards of 80 per cent of the players on the Canadian national team. The city is also a regular host to international tests, providing neutral ground (and sell-out crowds) for matches.

There are several dozen cricket pitches throughout the Toronto parks system, with at least 20 devoted exclusively to the game. One of the most idyllic locations to enjoy a match is at **Sunnybrook Park** (Eglinton Avenue E, at Leslie Street) in North Toronto, which is home pitch for the West Indian Cricket Club of Toronto. The **Canada Cricket Online** website (www.canadacricket.com) also has information on current tours and tournaments, as well as details of Canada's cricketing history.

Horse racing

Located out by the airport in the north-west corner of the city, **Woodbine Racetrack** is a bit far-flung but, when it comes to racing, it's the only game in Toronto. It's also the only racetrack in North America that can offer both thoroughbred and standard-bred horse racing on the same day, as well as providing video links to several other major racetracks, including Churchill Downs and Aqueduct. The track is also home to a number of $1

Toronto Blue Jays.

Arts & Entertainment

Slam dunk: **the Toronto Raptors** score well with Toronto crowds.

million-plus races, including North America's oldest stakes race, the **Queen's Plate** (which has been run without interruption since 1860; *see also p168*), the **ATTO Mile** and harness racing's **North America Cup**. Slot machines have been added to the mix, so you can really work on your gambling. There are a couple of out-of-town alternatives at **Mohawk** (a 45-minute drive away in Campbellville, near Guelph, for harness racing) and **Fort Erie** (just over an hour's drive from the city).

Fort Erie Racetrack

230 Catherine Street, Fort Erie (1-800 295 3770/905 871 3200/www.forterieracetrack.ca).
Open *Racetrack* May-Oct; phone for details.
Slots 9am-3am Mon-Thur; 24hrs Fri-Sun.
Admission free. **Credit** AmEx, MC, V.

Mohawk Racetrack

9430 Guelph Line, Campbellville (416 675 7223/www.woodbineentertainment.com).
Open *Racetrack* June-Oct; phone for details.
Slots 9am-3am Mon-Thur; 24hrs Fri-Sun.
Admission free. **Credit** AmEx, MC, V.

Woodbine Racetrack

555 Rexdale Boulevard, at Highway 427, Rexdale (416 675 7223/www.woodbineentertainment.com).
Subway Islington. **Open** *Racetrack* phone for details. *Slots* 24hrs daily. **Admission** free.
Credit MC, V.

Ice hockey

Win or lose, Toronto loves its **Leafs (photo** *p215*) almost as much as everyone else in the country hates them. They are the most watched, analysed, adored and reviled team in NHL history. They have won more league championships than any team aside from their long-standing rivals the Montreal Canadiens, but sadly, all the wins were prior to 1967, the last time Lord Stanley's Cup was hoisted in victory by a Leaf (the Cup lives at the Hockey Hall of Fame *see p66*, just up the road from the Air Canada Centre). Oddly enough, the decades-long absence of a championship team is about equal to the length of time you'd have to wait to get a decent season ticket – the Leaf's legendary waiting list is more easily measured in generations than in years. Virtually every game is sold out. Attendance remains constant even after the team moved from the grotty, nostalgic old Maple Leaf Gardens to the sanitised confines of the high-tech, antiseptic Air Canada Centre in 1999. The best tickets for games are generally only attainable through ticket agencies and scalpers at inflated prices. Quite why fans pay through the roof to watch a losing team is a mystery; the national obsession with hockey probably explains it.

Toronto Maple Leafs

Air Canada Centre, 40 Bay Street, at Front Street W, Entertainment District (information 416 815 5700/tickets 416 872 5000/www.torontomaple leafs.com). Subway Union. **Season** Oct-Apr. **Tickets** $24-$390. **Credit** AmEx, DC, MC, V. **Map** p271/p272 F8.

Lacrosse

Lacrosse is the official national sport of Canada, protestations from hockey enthusiasts aside. But for a city that adores champions, Toronto has inexplicably ignored its winning pro lacrosse team, the Toronto Rock (who deserve far more attention than the losing Maple Leafs). Since its inception in 1998, the team has won three league titles, yet its triumphs have gone largely unnoticed by the masses. Perhaps it's the difficulty of the game. It's an extremely rough-and-tumble sport with little glamour, but also one of the most exciting and physically challenging contests a human can endure.

Toronto Rock

Air Canada Centre, 40 Bay Street, at Front Street W, Entertainment District (information 416 596 3075/tickets 416 872 5000/www.torontorock.com). Subway Union. **Season** Jan-Apr. **Tickets** $10-$53. **Credit** AmEx, DC, MC, V. **Map** p271/p272 F8.

Soccer

See p214 **A new game in town**.

Active sports & fitness

Beach volleyball

A flat sandy expanse at Ashbridge's Bay Park is home to one of the largest collections of beach-volleyball courts in North America, a place where thousands of recreational players and those with Olympic dreams pursue their passion. As a spectator sport, what's not to like about watching buff bods in skimpy clothing take face plants in the sand? Beach volleyball is as much fun to play as it is to watch. The **Toronto East Sport & Social Club** runs the programme at Ashbridge's Bay, where 85 permanent courts are marked in the sand for 690 teams and close to 6,000 players. To catch some tournament action or get in on a game of pick-up – dating is a big draw for participants – see www.tessc.com.

Cycling

Toronto is a fantastic city for cycling. Most major thoroughfares have bike lanes and, on the whole, drivers respect them. There are, of course, exceptions, but generally speaking you can cross the entire city by bike without a scratch. Travel east–west (most spectacularly along the often scenic lakeshore), and the ride is mostly flat. Head north, and things start getting hilly, but at least that means the ride back is downhill. For route maps check out

On yer bike: rain or shine, sleet or snow, Torontonians cycle to get around.

Arts & Entertainment

A new game in town

Soccer has always been a popular amateur sport in Toronto, but turning that passion into a professional (which is to say profitable) pursuit has always eluded the city. Past attempts to field a team in fledgling North American leagues were met with indifferent fans, non-committal media and a dearth of sponsors. It has been argued that the continuous nature of the game prevents broadcasters from selling advert time. Add to this the low scores inherent in soccer, and you have a recipe that many say will fail to persuade North American fans to support a league of their own – even though spectactor interest in the beautiful game is high, with sports bars and local fan clubs screening international matches.

In the spring of 2007 Toronto took on the local soccer challenge once again. Only this time the money was in place, a new stadium had been built and perhaps, in the aftermath of the World Cup (always a big party in Toronto), the zeitgeist was right to take soccer to the next level. Enter Toronto FC. Backed by the sports company that owns the Leafs, Raptors and Toronto Rock, the team is poised to turn Torontonians into footie fans during the April to October season. BMO Field, the new purpose-built stadium, is a tiered, European-style pitch at Exhibition Place, able to hold 20,000 fans. The inaugural season squad is not the stuff of headlines – players plucked from among the 12 other teams in Major League Soccer and a handful of newbies. As more of a publicity stunt than proper scouting, Toronto FC held an open call for wannabes four months before the season opener.

Toronto enters the league in its 11th season and, by happy coincidence, arrives just in time to be able to shout about David Beckham's defection from Real Madrid to Los Angeles Galaxy. Following news of his move, Toronto FC sold 2,600 season tickets the next day. BMO Field is also hosting the FIFA U-20 World Cup Championship in July 2007, which is set to raise the profile of soccer in the city. Now, if only Toronto FC could lure Ontario-born David Edgar back from Newcastle United...

Toronto FC

170 Princes Boulevard, Exhibition Place (416 360 4625/http://toronto.fc.mlsnet. com). Streetcar 511. **Fees** *$15-$60.* **Credit** *AmEx, MC, V.*

www.city.toronto.on.ca/parks/maps.htm or visit a bike shop. And, before you set off, keep in mind that it is illegal to cycle on the sidewalks.

Try the **Martin Goodman Trail** along the lakeshore, or head over to the **Toronto Islands** (*see p76*) for fresh air and spectacular views of the city; rental is available on Centre Island (call 416 203 0009 for details). If you think you'll want a bike for more than a day, you might want to investigate **Bikeshare** at 761 Queen Street W in the West End (416 504 2918, www.bikeshare.org), the yellow bike-lending programme, which has hubs around the city. **Wheel Excitement** (249 Queens Quay W, 416 260 9000, www.wheelexcitement.ca) is another reputable bike-rental outfit.

Golf

A round of inner city golf has its devotees, as queues to play the city-run Don Valley Golf Course will attest (4200 Yonge Street, at Wilson Avenue, North Toronto, 416 392 2465). Other links accessible by subway include the par 3 Dentonia Park Golf Course (416 392 2558) and Humber Valley Golf Course (40 Beattie Ave,

West End, 416 392 2488). For details about all three, visit www.city.toronto.on.ca/parks/golf. With green fees from $10 to $60, you can't beat the price, but be prepared to play alongside absolute beginners or possibly a star of the next generation.

For a more serious swing of the clubs, head for the countryside and an almost embarrassing assortment of options that has turned southern Ontario into Canada's golf heaven. Ontario-born Mike Weir, who won the Masters Tournament in Augusta, Georgia, a few years ago, calls **Taboo** (800 461 0236, www.tabooresort.com), the lavish Muskoka resort, his home course. The club offers a helicopter service from downtown for high-fliers. The most famous local course is **Glen Abbey** (1-800 288 0388/905 844 1811, www.glenabbey.com): designed by Jack Nicklaus, it was host to the Canadian Open when Tiger Woods made his dramatic winning shot to take the title in 2000. It's a short drive west of town (in Oakville) and open to all. *ScoreGolf* magazine, Canada's golf bible, rates the much more affordable **St George's Golf & Country Club** (1668 Islington Avenue, at Eglinton Avenue W,

Etobicoke 416 231 9350, www.stgeorges.org) in the West End as the country's No.1 (Glen Abbey came in at No.13). You'll need a letter of reference from your home club, but non-members are welcome by advance arrangement.

If checking out the occasional celebrity duffer is to your liking, the coolest course in the neighbourhood is **Wooden Sticks** (905 853 4379, www.woodensticks.com), just outside of town in Uxbridge. Said to be owned by several hockey players, this is where sport freaks go to see and be seen. Wooden Sticks has been hailed because it has several holes inspired by classic courses like Augusta National and the Old Course at St Andrews.

Closer to downtown, the big entertainment complex at the **Docks** (11 Polson Street, at Cherry Street, East Toronto, 416 469 5655, www.thedocks.com) includes several golf activities, such as sand traps, a chipping green and an 18-hole Pro Putt course, as well as 75 hitting stations at the driving range (which doubles as a drive-in cinema at night).

For more information on local courses, call **Toronto Parks & Recreation** on 416 392 8186 or visit www.city.toronto.on. ca/parks/golf. Note that the golf season runs from mid April to mid November, and that fees tend to be higher at weekends.

Gyms

From Pilates to spinning, yoga to stretching, you can choose pretty much any form of sweat extraction in Toronto. Good-value daily rates are available at several excellent gyms in the heart of downtown. The **YMCA** (*see p194*) and **Bally Total Fitness** (*see p194*) both have locations within easy walking distance of many centrally located hotels. The University of Toronto's massive **Athletic & Physical Education Centre** (55 Harbord Street, at Spadina Avenue, 416 978 3437, www. utoronto.ca/physical) also has a day rate. Known as the AC, it has several gyms, pools, a strength and conditioning centre, and an indoor running track. Bally also has personal trainers available.

Ice-skating/'shinny'

In addition to many indoor rinks with designated skating hours at affordable prices, the city also boasts 50 well-maintained free outdoor rinks, including two that are especially popular. You can fall around to your heart's content in the dramatic shadow of City Hall at **Nathan Phillips Square**, or down by the lake at the **Harbourfront Centre** (**photo** *p216*). Skate rental is available at both. The outdoor

skating season runs from roughly December through to the beginning of March.

Hockey enthusiasts don't have to look far to find a game of 'shinny' (the informal, non contact, 'be nice' version of the game) at any public rink. All you need is a stick and skates.

Harbourfront Centre
235 Queens Quay W, at York Street, Harbourfront (416 973 4866/www.harbourfrontcentre.com). Streetcar 509, 510. **Open** 10am-10pm daily. **Rentals** $5-$7. **No credit cards**. **Map** p271/ p272 F9.

Nathan Phillips Square
100 Queen Street W, at York Street, Chinatown (416 338 7465/www.city.toronto.on.ca/parks). Bus 6/streetcar 501/subway Osgoode or Queen. **Open** 9am-10pm daily. **Rental** $9; $7 concessions/ 2hrs (deposit ID or $40). **No credit cards**. **Map** p271/p272 F7.

On thin ice: **Toronto Maple Leafs**. *See p212.*

In-line skating

Not surprisingly for a hockey-mad town like Toronto, in-line skating is also hugely popular. During rush-hour cyclists have to share their bike lanes with all manner of skaters gliding to and from work. The city's hiking and bike trails are perfect for the sport – the boardwalk in the Beach is always full of bladers, as is Toronto Island – and rental skates are available at many bike-hire outfits, including **Wheel Excitement** (*see p214*), which also offers training. Rates for skates start at $12 for the first hour; $3 for each additional hour.

Pool/billiards

Pool playing is well loved and readily available throughout Toronto. An array of specialised pool halls has sprouted up for the more practised player, the most exotic establishment being the luxurious **Academy of Spherical Arts**, located in the former Brunswick Billiards factory. The Academy boasts 15 sumptuous antique billiard tables, some valued at over $100,000. Fast-forward a century or so and you'll find a modern counterpart at the pool hall at the **Rivoli**, upstairs from one of Queen Street's trendiest nightspots. It's stocked with 13 vintage pool tables (smaller for faster games). The **Charlotte Room** boasts some of the last of the Dufferin Challengers, 2.7-metre (nine-foot) tables built in Toronto, it draws the after-work crowd, as well as serious snooker types.

Academy of Spherical Arts

38 Hanna Avenue, at King Street W, West End (416 532 2782/www.sphericalarts.com). Streetcar 504. **Open** noon-2am Mon-Fri; 5pm-2am Sat. **Credit** AmEx, DC, MC, V. **Map** p270 A8.

Charlotte Room

19 Charlotte Street, at King Street W, Entertainment District (416 598 2882). Streetcar 504. **Open** 3pm-1am Mon-Thur; 3pm-2am Fri; 6pm-2am Sat. **Credit** AmEx, MC, V. **Map** p271 E8.
For full review, *see p134*.

Rivoli

332-334 Queen Street W, at Spadina Avenue, Entertainment District (416 596 1501/www.rivoli.ca). Streetcar 501, 510. **Open** 4pm-1am Thur-Sun. **Credit** AmEx, MC, V. **Map** p271 D7.
For full review, *see p134*.

Rock climbing

Joe Rockhead's, Canada's largest indoor climbing facility, with over 50 ropes and 278 square metres (3,000 square feet) of bouldering, is deep in the heart of Toronto. **Toronto**

Harbourfront Centre. *See p215.*

Climbing Academy in the east of the city has ten different climbing areas, which include caves and overhangs; instruction is available. For the real thing, travel west of town to the Niagara Escarpment. **Mountain Equipment Co-op** (*see p163*) is the city's best resource for both climbing equipment and information.

Joe Rockhead's Indoor Rock Climbing

29 Fraser Avenue, at Liberty Street, West End (416 538 7670/www.joerockheads.com). Streetcar 504. **Open** 10am-9pm Sat; 10am-7pm Sun. **Admission** $9-$15. **Credit** MC, V.

Toronto Climbing Academy

100A Broadview Avenue, at Queen Street, East Toronto (416 406 5900/www.climbingacademy.com). Streetcar 501, 504. **Open** noon-11pm Mon-Fri; 10am-10pm Sat, Sun. **Admission** $14; $12 concessions. **Credit** V.

Skiing

A mild winter can really spoil dreams of snowy pursuits in the city. In 2007 Toronto's two public ski runs (one stops short of calling them hills) didn't open until the end of January. Families and learners can pick up the basics (downhill, cross-country and snowboarding) at two parks, **Earl Bales** (4169 Bathurst Street, 416 395 7934) and **Centennial** (256 Centennial Park Road, 416 394 8750). Call 416 338 6754 for information on public skiing or visit www.city. toronto.on.ca/parks/recreation. Cross-country enthusiasts can choose from a wealth of trails across the city (weather permitting).

For longer runs, there are many downhill resorts to choose from once you leave town and head north. Less than an hour's drive from the city centre, near Barrie, is the **Horseshoe Resort** (1-800 461 5627, www.horseshoe resort.com), a well-maintained facility with seven lifts and 22 runs. The resort also has 35 kilometres (22 miles) of cross-country trails, as well as snowboarding areas and lessons. It would be worth it, though, to drive an hour further, to Collingwood, to hit Ontario's largest resort, **Blue Mountain** (705 445 0231, www. bluemountain.ca). Here you'll find 34 trails and 12 lifts that accommodate skiing for beginners, as well as challenging double black diamond runs for experts, three half-pipes for snowboarding and a snowtubing park. For the first time in its history, Blue Mountain was forced to close for two weeks in January 2007, due to lack of snow.

Swimming

The City of Toronto operates more than 30 public pools in just the central core alone; more than half of those are indoors and open all year round. Of the many outdoor pools, the most significant one is the **Gus Ryder Sunnyside Pool**, next to Budapest Park on the lakeshore. Originally built as part of a vast amusement complex in the 1920s, Sunnyside was the city's most popular destination for outdoor summer fun for decades. If you'd rather not deal with the general public, both the **YMCA** (*see p194*) and U of T's **Athletic & Physical Education Centre** have pools (*see p215*). For more information on public pools call 416 392 8189 or visit www.city.toronto.on.ca/parks.

Gus Ryder Sunnyside Pool

1 Faustina Drive, West End (416 394 8726). Streetcar 501. **Open** phone for details. **Admission** $1. **No credit cards**.

Tennis

The pro tennis circuit comes to town annually for the Rogers Cup (*see p169*), hosting the men's tournament one year and the women's the next. The **Rexall Centre** at York University makes watching the matches a pleasure, with its

comfortable 3,000-seat grandstand court (bring a jacket in the evening). The tournament usually takes place in early- to mid-August.

While there are many private tennis clubs in Toronto (you'll need a member to get you in), there are also over 30 courts in public parks, some of them covered in the winter (for example, **Eglinton Flats Park** in the West End), which have slots available to one and all. Generally from 9am to 5pm on weekdays you can use these courts at will, while at weekends and in the evenings they become semi-private – which means if a club member shows up, you have to relinquish your court. As for the free courts, the best-maintained ones are in the more upmarket neighbourhoods, such as Rosedale and Forest Hill. Moore Park, at Bayview and St Clair Avenues, also has particularly nice courts.

If the club life is what you desire, then among the best are the **Toronto Lawn Tennis Club** and the **Boulevard Club**.

For a list of public courts, call 416 392 1111 or see www.city.toronto.on.ca/parks/recreation.

Boulevard Club

1491 Lake Shore Boulevard W, at Dowling Avenue, West End (416 532 3341/www.boulevardclub.com). Streetcar 501. **Open** 7am-11pm Mon-Fri; 7am-10pm Sat, Sun. **Membership** phone for details. **Credit** MC, V.

Toronto Lawn Tennis Club

44 Price Street, east of Yonge Street, Rosedale (416 922 1105/www.torontolawn.com). Subway Rosedale or Summerhill. **Open** 8am-10pm Mon-Fri; 8am-8pm Sat, Sun. **Membership** phone for details. **Credit** MC, V.

Watersports

The city's public-health department insists that Lake Ontario is safe to swim in most days during the summer and hoists the blue flag to prove it when the bacterial content is acceptable. There are days when it is not – typically after a rainstorm. Though the lake water never warms up until late summer, thousands of people take to the beaches across the waterfront and on the islands. There are other ways to enjoy the lake that don't involve getting wet. Marinas dot the entire lakeshore, and there are several places where visitors can rent canoes, kayaks and sailboards. For family fun head over to Centreville on the Toronto Islands for rowing and pedal boats (*see p76* **Bike on**). For a list of local windsurfing sites consult the website www.torontowindsurfing club.com. The **Harbourfront Canoe & Kayak Centre** (283A Queens Quay W, 1 800 960 8886, 416 203 2277, www.paddle toronto.com) provides rentals and lessons.

Arts & Entertainment

Theatre & Dance

Making a song and dance.

Theatre

For the past 20 years Toronto has been passing itself off as the third-largest theatre centre in the English-speaking world, after London and New York. This holds true in terms of the number of venues and independent theatre companies in the city, but is debatable in terms of quality or government support. Yet, while the local tourist office and other civic boosters still pull the 'North Broadway' tag out of the hat to impress foreigners, locals scratch their heads trying to remember the last time they even went to the theatre. Thankfully, though, the scene is no longer just about quantity, and theatres have plenty to shout about without having to brag about the busloads of Americans that once came for *Phantom* (it ran for ten years solid in Toronto) and other Broadway standards.

What's giving the theatre scene a boost these days is seeing shows that began life as fringe productions in Toronto go on to wider acclaim in New York and London. Leading the charge is *The Drowsy Chaperone*, an old-style Broadway musical by composers Lisa Lambert and Greg Morrison, with a book by Bob Martin and Don McKellar. It got its start in the back room of the Rivoli as a sketch for a bachelorette party in 1999, played the fringe festival the next year and was mounted by Toronto's reigning theatre impresario, David Mirvish, before capturing Broadway to win a fistful of Tonys. The musical opened in London in the spring of 2007, but not before Lambert and Morrison sent London mayor Ken Livingstone a singing telegram, in the form of a song called 'A Breadcrumb Now and Then', hoping to persuade him to rescind his ban on feeding pigeons in Trafalgar Square. Other notable productions that got their start at Toronto's fringe include *Da Kink in My Hair*, *Pond Life* and *Top Gun! – The Musical*. Michael Healey's *Drawer Boy*, which started at Theatre Passe Muraille and spawned many touring productions, plus John Mighton's *Half Life*, are also successful Canadian stage exports.

Toronto audiences have shown they won't always flock to a show just because it happens to première here or bring to the stage the most expensive production of all time – as was the case with *The Lord of the Rings*, the show that distilled a thousand pages of literature and three feature films into a three-hour stage extravaganza. The producer blamed Toronto audiences for not 'getting it' when the $28-million show closed in the autumn of 2006 after just six months, and withdrew back to London for some recrafting before a second debut. *Blue Man Group* suffered a similar fate when audiences decided that opening a ten-year-old show for an indefinite run in a sophisticated theatre city wasn't such a great idea after all. It lasted a little over a year, leaving the future of the retro-fitted Panasonic Theatre on Yonge Street up for rejigging by Live Nation, the American juggernaut that owns it and produces theatre around the world.

The sizeable independent theatre scene in Toronto is highly competitive, fuelled by the city's concentration of artists and cultural institutions. There are five theatre schools in the Greater Toronto Area alone, turning out hundreds of aspiring actors, playwrights, directors and designers. Many new theatre companies have been started over the past two decades by these graduates. **Soulpepper Theatre** (*see p222* **Spicing up the scene**) and **Canadian Stage Company** (*see p222*) vie for the hearts, minds and wallets of those who enjoy the indie theatrical middle ground between the experimental and the blockbuster.

Canadian theatre as an identifiable movement is a relatively new phenomenon that can be traced back to the late 1960s. Until then, Toronto played host to touring companies from the UK and the US, and a repertoire of musicals, variety shows and middle-brow fair was the norm. The opening of **Theatre Passe Muraille** in 1967, the oldest alternative theatre in Toronto, marked a turning point in what can be safely termed Canadian-themed theatre. The 1970s saw an explosion of other local companies (**Tarragon Theatre**, **Factory Theatre**, **Buddies in Bad Times Theatre**); the busy scene today is a direct result of those formative years. For these theatres, commercialism is a dirty word.

All this translates into some very lively, sometimes groundbreaking, sometimes insufferably sophomoric efforts. When theatre in Toronto is good, it can be thrillingly so. But quality varies wildly, so check local newspapers for reviews (see the list below). Bigger theatres do not mean better plays, and the best of Toronto theatre is found in smaller venues dotted around town, where creativity abounds – even if money is in short supply.

TICKETS AND INFORMATION

Most performances are at 8pm Tuesday to Saturday, with Sunday matinées at 2.30pm, for which many small and mid-sized theatres run a 'pay what you can' (PWYC) policy. Larger theatres also have shows on Monday, plus Wednesday and Saturday matinées. Prices range from $10 in the independent sector to up to $125 for the Broadway-style shows (tickets for most mid-sized theatres average $30). For all theatre bookings, call the box office directly to reserve seats and, for mid-sized theatres, arrive early (most don't have numbered seating). You can also buy tickets to big shows from **TicketKing** (416 872 1212, www.ticket king.com) and **Ticketmaster** (416 870 8000, www.ticketmaster.ca).

TO TIX (416 536 6468 ext 40, www.totix.ca), located in Yonge-Dundas Square, across from the Toronto Eaton Centre, sells day-of-performance tickets (usually discounted by 50 per cent), Tuesdays to Saturdays, noon-6.30pm (and also online, noon-5pm).

A bi-monthly magazine called *Theatre Guide*, with reviews, listings and maps, is distributed free at many hotels and tourist outlets. As well as the free listings magazines *eye* and *NOW*, there is an excellent website for theatre information: www.scenechanges.com has both reviews and previews of current plays.

FESTIVALS

Toronto's theatre scene is supplemented by serious contributions from the classical repertoires of two out-of-town festivals: the **Shaw Festival** in Niagara-on-the-Lake (*see p238*) and the **Stratford Festival** (*see p242*), both of which have a wide appeal.

If you're in Toronto in July, don't miss the **Toronto Fringe Theatre Festival** (*see p168*). This ten-day festival runs 130 different productions chosen by lottery from more than 500 submissions. Attendance continues to grow and now hovers around 50,000 for the 19th season in 2007. The smaller but more rewarding **SummerWorks** (*see p169*) is held in the first week of August at a number of theatres across the city.

Venues

With the exception of the Young Centre for the Performing Arts, which welcomed Soulpepper (*see p222* **Spicing up the scene**) in the autumn of 2006, none of Toronto's theatres

Elgin & Winter Garden Theatre. *See p221*.

has a resident company as such. Every season (September to May), each venue offers a selection of plays, some of which are co-productions with local or regional theatre companies, some produced individually in-house, and some touring. Quality can vary.

Berkeley Street Theatre

26 Berkeley Street, at Front Street E, St Lawrence (416 368 3110/www.canstage.com). Streetcar 504. **Open** *Box office* 10am-6pm Mon-Sat. **Tickets** $20-$55. **Credit** AmEx, MC, V. **Map** p280 H8.

Canadian Stage Company (*see p222*) sends its edgier work to this 240-seater. Edward Albee's *The Goat or Who is Sylvia?* played here, as well as American 9/11 polemic *Omnium Gatherum*.

Bluma Appel Theatre

St Lawrence Centre, 27 Front Street East, St Lawrence (416 368 3110/www.canstage.com). Streetcar 504/subway King or Union. **Open** *Box office* 10am-6pm Mon-Sat. **Tickets** $20-$95. **Credit** AmEx, MC, V. **Map** p272 G8.

This 875-seater is where CanStage's (*see p222*) flashier productions are mounted. It's a relatively large space, but excellent sight-lines make it feel quite intimate. New Canadian drama is mixed with international theatre and classic musicals along the lines of *Hair, Ain't Misbehavin'* and the *Rocky Horror Picture Show*.

Buddies in Bad Times Theatre

12 Alexander Street, at Yonge Street, Church & Wellesley (416 975 8555/www.buddiesin badtimestheatre.com). Streetcar 506/subway Wellesley. **Open** *Box office* noon-5pm Tue-Sat. **Tickets** $18-$25. **Credit** MC, V. **Map** p275 G5.

North America's largest queer theatre (call it gay and lesbian at your peril) dates back to 1979 and is a focal point for the gay community. Its heyday was the 1980s, when its then artistic director Sky Gilbert made it home to grungy, postmodern gay-themed plays that had edge but insufficient audience appeal. After a few years in the artistic wilderness of gay lowbrow fare, the company has changed its focus, offering risk-taking theatre that is straight, gay and in-between. There's a small cabaret theatre too. *See also p192* **Good times at Bad Times**.

Canon Theatre

244 Victoria Street, at Dundas Street, Dundas Square (416 872 1212/www.mirvish.com). Streetcar 505/subway Dundas. **Open** *Box office* 10.30am-6pm Mon, Tue; 10.30am-8.30pm Wed-Sat; 11am-3pm Sun. **Tickets** $44-$94. **Credit** AmEx, DC, MC, V. **Map** p272 G7.

This exquisitely restored theatre (which was previously known as the Pantages) is the location of choice for box-and-truck touring shows like *Spamalot* and *Wicked*. The tribute show *We Will Rock You* takes over in 2007.

Royal Alexandra Theatre: the grand dame of the scene. *See p221.*

Elgin & Winter Garden Theatre

189 Yonge Street, at Shuter Street, Dundas Square (416 314 2884/www.ticketmaster.ca). Streetcar 505/subway Dundas or Queen. **Open** *Box office* 11am-5pm Mon-Sat. **Tickets** from $25. **Credit** AmEx, DC, MC, V. **Map** p272 G7.

North America's only remaining double-decker theatre complex (a popular design in the early 1900s), the Elgin and the Winter Garden were both restored in the 1980s after decades of neglect. The larger Elgin is richly appointed, with ornate fabrics and gilt cherubs. The Winter Garden sits above, festooned in Arcadian watercolour scenes and hanging garlands. The theatres are now home to productions that vary from baroque opera in the grand Elgin, to one-woman shows in the Winter Garden. It draws international touring productions, such as *Umoja*, and well-to-do North Toronto crowds for whom theatre is a diversion after dinner. The Elgin also doubles as a cinema during the Toronto International Film Festival (*see p169*). Photo *p219*.

Factory Theatre

125 Bathurst Street, at King Street W, Entertainment District (416 504 9971/www. factorytheatre.ca). Streetcar 501, 511. **Open** *Box office* noon-4pm Mon; 1-8pm Tue-Sat. **Tickets** $20-$34. **Credit** AmEx, MC, V. **Map** p271 D8.

The Factory is the quintessential Canadian theatre. Established in 1970 by Ken Gass, who returned in 1997 as artistic director, it was the first in Canada to focus exclusively on works by indigenous playwrights, who have a soft spot for the venue since many got their first break here. A Victorian building on the edge of the Garment District, it defines shabby genteel. Historical significance aside, approach the Factory with care: each season plays host to a clunker or two in the name of national pride. Its studio theatre brings to life edgier material like *SARSical*, a musical comedy based on the SARS scare that traumatised the city in 2003.

Harbourfront Centre

235 Queen's Quay W, Waterfront (416 973 4000/www.harbourfrontcentre.com). Streetcar 509, 510/subway Union. **Open** *Box office* 1-8pm Tue-Sat. **Tickets** $25-$75. **Credit** AmEx, MC, V. **Map** p271/p272 F9.

This cultural centre by the lake is reviving its festival of international theatre for 2007. An annual event from January through May, New World Stage hosts a choice selection of theatre and dance companies from around the world. The centre also rents out its three performing-arts venues – Enwave Theatre, Premiere Dance Theatre and Studio Theatre – when they're not in use for its own programming.

Hummingbird Centre for the Performing Arts

1 Front Street E, at Yonge Street, St Lawrence (416 393 7469/www.hummingbirdcentre.com). Streetcar 504/subway King or Union. **Open** *Box office* 10am-6pm Mon-Fri; 10am-5pm Sat. **Tickets** $20-$150. **Credit** AmEx, MC, V. **Map** p272 G8.

Named after a sponsoring Toronto software firm, this barn-like (3,000-seat) theatre is in search of a purpose now that the opera and ballet have decamped across town to new digs (*see p198* **The curtain rises**). Expect to see a mishmash of shows: everything from *Tap Dogs Rebooted* and performances by the likes of Dionne Warwick and Morrissey, to the umpteenth tour of *Grease*.

Panasonic Theatre

651 Yonge Street, at Isabella Street, Church & Wellesley (Ticketmaster 416 872 1111). Subway Bloor-Yonge. **Open** *Box office* phone for details. **Tickets** average $60. **Credit** AmEx, DC, MC, V. **Map** p275 G4.

After being kitted out for the short-lived performance-art ensemble Blue Man Group, this 700-seater is now a roadhouse. The sleeper hit *Menopause the Musical* moved in for a spell in 2007.

Princess of Wales Theatre

300 King Street W, at John Street, Entertainment District (416 872 1212/www.mirvish.com). Streetcar 504/subway St Andrew. **Open** *Box office* 10.30am-6pm Mon, Tue; 10.30am-8.30pm Wed-Sat; 11am-3pm Sun. **Tickets** $26-$94. **Credit** AmEx, DC, MC, V. **Map** p271 E8.

This venue in the Entertainment District is the first privately owned theatre built in Canada since 1907. With Peter Smith as its architect, Yabu-Pushelberg as its interior-design firm and Frank Stella responsible for its murals, this place is noted as much for its looks as its productions. It opened in 1993 with *Miss Saigon* and is part of the Mirvish subscription season, which runs safe, middlebrow fare.

Royal Alexandra Theatre

260 King Street W, at University Avenue, Entertainment District (416 872 1212/www. mirvish.com). Streetcar 504/subway St Andrew. **Open** *Box office* 10.30am-6.30pm Tue-Sat; noon-7pm Sun. **Tickets** $44-$86. **Credit** AmEx, DC, MC, V. **Map** p271 E8.

This 'Edwardian jewel box' turns 100 in 2007, and its legacy is rich. It is where John Gielgud and Ralph Richardson performed, and where Piaf belted and Fred Astaire put on the Ritz. In 1962 it was bought by Ed Mirvish and now it is used for road shows. A stage version of *Dirty Dancing* saunters onto its stage in the autumn of 2007. Photo *p220*.

Tarragon Theatre

30 Bridgman Avenue, at Howland Avenue, Casa Loma (416 531 1827/www.tarragontheatre.com). Bus 7/subway Dupont. **Open** *Box office* 10am-5pm Mon; 10am-7pm Tue-Sat. **Tickets** $15-$33. **Credit** MC, V. **Map** p274 D2.

Artistically and financially, the Tarragon is the most reliable theatre in Toronto and, probably, Canada. Here you're likely to see Canadian theatre at its best, as well as some fine productions by, say, David Hare, David Mamet or Tony Kushner. English translations of major works from Quebec are a house speciality. The programming emphasis remains on

Spicing up the scene

There's a double meaning in the name of the Young Centre for the Performing Arts, the new home of Toronto's much-lauded **Soulpepper Theatre Company**. The name refers to a patron who coughed up $3 million to kick-start the $14 million project, which was inaugurated in 2006. But it could also refer to the educational programme that is at the heart of this spicy theatre troupe, the scene's hottest indie company. While searching for a permanent home, Soulpepper partnered with George Brown College Theatre School and together they built a unique performance and education space.

Soulpepper was founded in 1998 by 12 actors who wanted to immerse themselves in theatre classics of the 20th century (chiefly Samuel Beckett, Harold Pinter and other Absurdist playwrights). Every theatre company dreams of having a home, and artistic director Albert Shultz proved to be as deft in the boardroom as on the boards. He managed to secure a venue in the Distillery District that needed some night-time activity; he hired a top Toronto architect firm to transform the industrial space; and he established a mentoring programme, all in the space of a few years. The founding artists had themselves benefited from tutoring at Ontario's established theatres, as well as at the Stratford Festival and the Shaw Festival, and decided to make youth outreach and theatre education an integral part of the house that Soulpepper built.

Soulpepper Theatre Company
416 203 6264/www.soulpepper.ca.

well-established Canadian playwrights. Tarragon has two auditoriums: the main theatre, a 205-seater for works of wider appeal, and the Extra Space, one of the best small venues in town, where experimental or small-scale plays are staged.

Theatre Passe Muraille
16 Ryerson Avenue, at Wolseley Street, Entertainment District (416 504 7529/www.passemuraille.on.ca). Streetcar 501, 511. **Open** *Box office* noon-5pm Mon-Fri; later hours & also weekends during performances. **Tickets** $16-$38. **Credit** AmEx, MC, V. **Map** p271 D7.
The who's who of Canadian theatre started here. Some of them, like Ann-Marie MacDonald a nd Michael Ondaatje, have since become internationally renowned novelists. The main stage has a jazz-bar feel, with an open balcony and well-stocked bar; the small Backspace is notoriously uncomfortable (patrons are provided with cushions) but has seen some important independent productions.

Young Centre for the Performing Arts
Building 49, 55 Mill Street, the Distillery District (416 866 8666/www.youngcentre.ca). Streetcar 504. **Open** *Box office* 1-8pm Tue-Sat; 1hr prior to performance on Mon, Sun. **Tickets** $28-$95. **Credit** AmEx, MC, V. **Map** p273 J8.
The latest venue to open for theatre is a showstopper in itself: 19th-century tank houses in the Distillery District were converted into three stages, a spacious foyer, a bookstore, and a café and cosy nook with a fireplace. Local architect firm KPMB kept the exposed beams and rough brick walls for aesthetics, though the acoustics suffer as a result in some seats. Soulpepper Theatre (*see above* **Spicing**

up the scene) stages performances year-round. Combine the show with dinner at nearby Perigee (*see p118*). **Photo** *p223.*

Companies

On current estimates, Toronto has 250 theatre companies of all stripes and sizes. Below is a select list of those tested by time and critics.

Note that in 2007, **Da Da Kamera** (416 586 1503, www.dadakamera.com), one of Canada's best and most original theatre companies, winds up a 20-year run, during which time artistic director Daniel MacIvor has dazzled audiences with a heightened sense of theatricality and deceptive simplicity in his approach to writing and acting. Keep an eye out for the return of MacIvor's trademark performance-art-meets-theatre style.

Bluemouth Inc
www.bluemouthinc.com.
Preferring to put on site-specific pieces, this inventive troupe has staged performances in funeral homes, barbershops and city parks, and has even been known to bus the audience from one venue to the next all in the course of an evening. The themes tend to mix history and psychoanalysis, dance and text, theatre and anti-theatre in a powerful package. They don't perform often, but are well worth seeking out when they do.

Canadian Stage Company
416 368 3110/www.canstage.com.
CanStage operates two auditoriums, with its main roster in the Bluma Appel (*see p219*) and edgier stuff

in the Berkeley Street (*see p219*). Canadian plays get their due, along with some fine productions by the likes of Stephen Sondheim, David Hare, David Mamet and Tony Kushner. CanStage offers 'pay what you can' (PWYC) performances on Monday nights at both theatres. Quality varies, but this is usually a safe bet if you want to avoid mainstream theatrical fare.

Modern Times Stage Company

416 790 1016/www.moderntimesstage.com.
Artistic director Soheil Parsa's company fuses Middle Eastern theatrical traditions with Western ones to create a unique bi-cultural experience. Emphasis on movement and imagistic theatre results in an evocative show – even if the work can suffer from overstylisation. Expect to be dazzled.

Native Earth Performing Arts

416 531 1402/www.nativeearth.ca.
The first theatre company dedicated to developing and creating works that express the aboriginal experience in Canada. Its most famous alumnus is Tomson Highway, whose *The Rez Sisters* and *Dry Lips Oughta Move to Kapuskasing* are Canadian (not just Native) classics. The company continues to support a number of playwrights and performers with various degrees of success.

Necessary Angel Theatre Company

416 703 0406/www.necessaryangel.com.
Artistic director Daniel Brooks collaborates with some of the best in the business to produce intellectually stimulating theatre. John Mighton's *Half Life* enjoyed a national tour following its Toronto debut, and cheeky shows like *Bigger than Jesus* enjoy well-deserved reruns.

Nightwood Theatre

416 944 1740/www.nightwoodtheatre.net.
Nightwood focuses on work by women writers and has a strong feminist bent but it has emerged over the last 20 years as a home of good theatre, period. Sonja Mills' *The Danish Play*, remounted in 2007, is a good example. Staged readings of new work by female playwrights are part of a series called Extreme Women.

Theatre Smith-Gilmour

416 504 1277/www.theatresmithgilmour.com.
Since 1980, artistic directors Dean Gilmour and Michele Smith have been creating original, improvisational theatre inspired by sources as various as clown theatre and Dante. But they really made their mark with inventive interpretations of Chekhov. A European influence pervades, but the talent is wholly Canadian.

Old building, new talent: **Young Centre for the Performing Arts.** *See p222.*

Arts & Entertainment

Dance

In terms of size and cultural significance, Toronto's contemporary dance scene is small fry compared to the one in Montreal, the dance capital of Canada. The biggest event to hit the dance scene was Mikhail Baryshnikov's defection from the USSR while performing in Toronto in 1974. The National Ballet of Canada may have its headquarters in Toronto, but dance in general (and contemporary dance in particular) is an elite art form here. Those who remain active work on the edge of creative and financial anxieties, which lends a compelling roughness to the scene. This, combined with visits from touring groups, means there is plenty here for the dance-loving traveller. For ticket information, *see p218*.

Venues

Buddies in Bad Times Theatre (*see p192*) is another major dance-friendly venue. Every August it hosts **fFida**, Fringe Festival of Independent Dance Artists (www.ffida.org).

Betty Oliphant Theatre
404 Jarvis Street, at Wellesley Street, Church & Wellesley (416 964 5148/www.nbs-enb.on.ca). Subway Wellesley. **Open** phone for details. **Map** p275 G5.
Part of the newly expanded National Ballet School of Canada, this 300-seat space was designed with dance performance (in particular, ballet) in mind – which explains why local and touring dance companies return to it year after year. On the downside, its massive stage can overwhelm more minimalist choreography.

Premiere Dance Theatre
Harbourfront Centre, 235 Queens Quay W, Waterfront (416 973 4000/www.harbourfrontcentre.com). Streetcar 509, 510. **Open** Box office 1-8pm Tue-Sat. **Tickets** $21-$38. **Credit** AmEx, MC, V. **Map** p271/p272 F9.
Home to the New World Stage International Performance series, which features the best in contemporary dance from around the world. The curated series runs from January to May, and always has spots showcasing Canadian companies, as well as international troupes.

Theatre Centre
1087 Queen Street W, at Dovercourt Road, West Toronto (416 538 0988/www.theatrecentre.org). Streetcar 501. **Open** Box office noon-5pm Mon-Fri. **Tickets** $10-$20. **Credit** MC, V. **Map** p270 A7.
This funky Queen West space supports multidisciplinary creations, many relying on movement and choreography. *Uqquaq, The Shelter* is typical of the productions on show: a performance piece that literally wraps the audience in cotton string to the sound of drum dance, a type of dance from Nunavut, in Canada's far north.

Winchester Street Theatre
80 Winchester Street, at Parliament Street, Cabbagetown (416 967 1365/www.tdt.org). Bus 65/streetcar 506. **Open** Box office 10am-5pm Mon-Fri. **Tickets** $15-$35. **Credit** MC, V. **Map** p275 J5.
This Cabbagetown theatre is operated jointly by Toronto Dance Theatre (*see below*) and the School of Toronto Dance Theatre. With 115 seats, it may be a small venue, but its medium-sized stage is ideal for a mixture of choreographic styles.

Companies

Dancemakers
416 367 1800/www.dancemakers.org.
Toronto's most challenging dance company, physically and intellectually, continues a 20-year tradition with new artistic director Michael Trent, a highly regarded dancer and choreographer.

Danny Grossman Dance Company
416 408 4543/www.dannygrossman.com.
Physical storytelling is the best description of the politicised work by this legend in the dance world. The company is currently making its way through a three-year retrospective of ten of the choreographer's best-known works from a long career that will be documented and archived as part of a legacy project for the preservation of dance.

National Ballet of Canada
416 345 9595/www.national.ballet.ca.
The standards may be international, but artistic director James Kudelka has been infusing his programming with works by local choreographers. Yes, expect to see the standard (but lavish) interpretations of *Swan Lake* or *Giselle*, but keep an eye out for the groundbreaking choreography he sneaks up on his blue-rinse audiences.

Peggy Baker Dance Projects
416 804 4164.
The grande dame of contemporary dance has previously worked with the Lar Lubovitch Dance Company and Mikhail Baryshnikov's White Oak Dance Project. Recent productions include *The Disappearance of Right and Left*, based on landmark moments in Baker's life.

Toronto Dance Theatre
416 967 1365/www.tdt.org.
Formed in 1968, TDT has been part of the evolution of dance culture in Toronto. Current artistic director Christopher House adds wit, as well as visual and dramatic appeal, to a controversial company that has as many hard-core fans as it has detractors. In addition to its regular season, TDT mounts Four at the Winch, a showcase for emerging choreographers.

Trips Out of Town

Getting Started

Gear up for the great outdoors.

Maps pp266-267

With close to 13 million people, Ontario may be the most populous province in Canada, but, like the rest of the country, around 85 per cent of its inhabitants live within 150 kilometres (100 miles) of the US border, which leaves a lot of space for uninhabited wilderness. Attractions include rugged campsites, provincial parks, luxury tennis retreats, family resorts, fly-in fishing camps, winter ski hills, miles of quiet cross-country trails and 20 per cent of the world's freshwater supply dispersed among half a million lakes.

The province is also both the geographical and the political centre of the nation (separating the constant and often fractious 'east–west' national positions), the country's main base for industry and trade, and home of two capital cities: Toronto is the capital of Ontario, while Ottawa is the capital of Canada (though the 'Capital City Region' does extend into Quebec to appease the Anglo-French rivalry).

It seems that the province's name, given by the native tribes, was a reference to water. The word comes either from the Huron (meaning 'beautiful or sparkling water') or from an Iroquois term meaning 'rocks standing near the water', which referred to the Falls of the Niagara Escarpment. Either way, the word describes Ontario's original transport system.

The province is too big to experience in one weekend, with an area of approximately 1,000,000 square kilometres (400,000 square miles; you could fit France, Germany and Italy within its borders). If you decided to spend the weekend driving north from Toronto to Thunder Bay, on the north shore of Lake Superior, it would take you, well, all weekend, just to get there. And then, if you really wanted to drive north to the province's furthest border – forget it, there are no roads. Destinations in the following chapters, then, are a manageable distance away from town, covering the nearby Niagara area and the choicest day trips. Visitors should keep in mind that half the urban population seems to have a summer cottage, so there's a mass exodus from the city on summer Fridays, and major roads can get clogged, especially out towards the Muskokas and Haliburton Cottage Country. Niagara Falls is heaving from Friday to Sunday. So if you can, plan your getaways during the week.

GETTING AROUND

Public transport is patchy, and a car is the only option for many trips out of town. For rental offices, *see p249*. However, **VIA Rail** (65 Front Street W, 1-888 842 7245, www.viarail.ca) provides an excellent service along the well-travelled 'corridor' route from Windsor through Toronto, Kingston, Ottawa, Montreal and Quebec City (it also covers the Toronto–Niagara Falls route, though neither the train or the bus station at the latter are especially convenient for the Falls themselves).

Greyhound buses (1-800 661 8747/416 594 1010, www.greyhound.ca) are more likely to serve the smaller places on the map, and will be cheaper as well. They are the cheapest public transport to Niagara Falls. Greyhound's main Toronto terminal is centrally located at 610 Bay Street, at Edward Street (*see p246*).

Camper vans are a good way of exploring the Ontarian vastness. **CanaDream Campers** hire out all kinds of moving accommodation. The office is near Pearson International Airport at 5315 General Road, Mississauga (1-800 461 7368/416 243 3232, www.canadream.com).

TOURIST INFORMATION

Information on the province is available from **Ontario Travel Information Centre** (*see p256*). Particularly useful are its tours and accommodation brochures. **Ontario Tourism Marketing Partnership** (1-800 668 2746, www.ontariotravel.net) and **Resorts Ontario** (1-800 363 7227/705 325 9115, www.resorts-ontario.com) also offer information on travel and destinations in the province.

For information on parks and camping, contact the **Ministry of Natural Resources** (1-800 667 1940) or **Ontario Parks** (1-888 668 7275, www.ontarioparks.com); for information on Ontario's many heritage sites, contact the **Ontario Heritage Foundation** (416 325 5000, www.heritagefdn.on.ca).

TELEPHONE CODES

When calling long distance from Toronto, you will need to dial 1 before the area code. This goes for the Niagara region's 905 code, although some 905 numbers in the Greater Toronto area have the same prefix and are local calls.

Niagara River.

Niagara Falls & Around

Water, water everywhere – and plenty of wine to drink.

Many Torontonians are blasé about Niagara Falls, seeing them as a convenient way of getting rid of houseguests for the day. But watching 750,000 gallons of water a second slide off a cliff right in front of you is pretty impressive by any standards, and if you're in Toronto, you should make the trip. Cynical though the surrounding town's exploitation might be, hell, some people *like* viewing towers, sightseeing 'experiences' and unashamed tourist attractions. Millions certainly come; 12 to 14 million a year, in fact, to the Canadian side alone. If you're not expecting to commune with nature, it can be, well, fun.

The first European to witness the spectacle was Jesuit Louis Hennepin, who was introduced to the then-sacred site in 1678 by local native tribes. The missionary was awestruck by what he saw and immediately sent word of this wonder back to Europe, effectively launching a form of eco-tourism. But it wasn't long before the tacky trappings that have long been associated with the Falls kicked in. The first record of a couple spending their honeymoon at this site was in 1801; in 1803 Jérôme Bonaparte, Napoleon's little brother, brought his bride here, starting something of a fad: the city of Niagara Falls now issues 13,000 honeymoon certificates a year. Oscar Wilde famously summarised the visit to Niagara by newlyweds as 'a bride's second great disappointment'. Border skirmishes in the early 19th century deterred visitors, but by 1827, when the three hotels of the time combined to float a boatful of animals over the Horseshoe Falls, 10,000 people turned up to watch. When the railway arrived in 1840, tourists swarmed in, and the sideshow culture started to evolve. In 1859 Blondin made the first of his nine tightrope crossings; ever since then a rash of the rash have jumped, plunged and barrelled over, across or into the Falls and rapids (*see p232* **Over the edge**).

With 'experiences' rather than stunts taking over in the later 20th century (the *Maid of the Mist*, Journey Behind the Falls, IMAX, cable cars) and death-defying plunges firmly outlawed (though not altogether knocked on the head), Niagara has became increasingly sanitised. Recently the region has undergone a transformation, expanding from purely Falls-oriented attractions into more general tourist activity – shopping, golf, gambling, miscellaneous mainstream sights – in an attempt to keep visitors overnight (Niagara Falls is Canada's number one tourist attraction).

THE FALLS

The Niagara river is the border between Canada and the US. It is effectively a drainage channel between Lake Erie and Lake Ontario, transporting 5,500 cubic metres (200,000 cubic feet) of water per second for 55 kilometres (34 miles), with a total drop of 108 metres (350 feet). It runs over the Niagara Escarpment, in which sedimentary layers of hard and soft rock from the ancient Michigan Sea are tilted at an angle. The Falls occur at a bend in the river about halfway along its length, where its total width is about a mile. Goat Island sits on the US side,

Top five Wineries

Cave Spring Cellars

Like many of Niagara's best wineries, this is a family affair. The finest wines are the Estate Bottled; the Cave Spring Vineyard chardonnays and rieslings are popular. *See p236.*

Château des Charmes

One of Canada's oldest winemakers is winning praise for its chardonnay and Bordeaux-type reds. Look for the late-harvest rieslings and viognier. *See p236.*

Henry of Pelham Family Estate Winery

Known for fine vintages, including a delicious bubbly called Cuvée Catherine. Don't miss the riesling icewine. *See p236.*

Inniskillin

Set Canada's ice-wine industry in motion when it won top honours at the 1991 VinExpo Bordeaux – and never looked back. *See p237.*

Tawse Winery

A newcomer that has wine-lovers praising its signature chardonnays. It's a small estate, so call ahead to book an appointment. *See p237.*

Trips Out of Town

dividing the two main attractions: the American Falls (56 metres/184 feet) and the smaller Bridal Veil Falls on one one side; and the more impressive Canadian (Horseshoe) Falls (54 metres/177 feet), which link the island to the Canadian bank in a 675-metre (2,125-foot) arc. The geology here is in a continual state of flux: turbulence at the foot of the Falls erodes the soft rock layer, digging out a deeper drop; periodically, the increasingly unsupported upper, heavier layer breaks off. As a result, the Falls retreat gradually upstream, at a rate of about a foot every ten years. At the end of the last Ice Age, 10,000 years ago, the Niagara Falls were 11 kilometres (seven miles) closer to Lake Ontario, as high cliffs testify.

A couple of kilometres downstream (and visible as you look at the Falls) is the Niagara Power Project. This joint Canadian/US enterprise generates 2.4 million kilowatts by diverting part of the flow through its turbines. A hard-argued 1950 pact requires it to leave at least 300 cubic metres (100,000 cubic feet) per second in the original river during daylight hours in the visitor season, half the average total flow (thus helping to limit erosion). Take time to imagine how the Falls would be naturally without any intervention: twice as much crashing water (and 24 million fewer light bulbs).

ORIENTATION

Falls activity centres on two spots on the river, the Falls area itself and the Whirlpool Basin area five kilometres (three miles) down river. A road and a strip of parkland with a railed walkway and viewing platforms built along the cliffs link the two. The town of Niagara Falls and its tourist attractions are set on a rise above the river, with a hotel hinterland stretching west; you could walk between the two, but people seldom do. There's a funicular (the Falls Incline Railway) near the Horseshoe Falls; hotels run shuttle buses, and most tours take you straight to the Falls. In summer the city wheels out its 'people-movers', frequent shuttle buses run between the Falls and various points in town; out of season you'll have to take normal city buses. The train and Greyhound stations are at the far end of town and a five-minute walk from the nearest bus stop, which is at the corner of Bridge and Erie Streets.

The Niagara Parkway runs the whole length of the river on the Canadian side. North and

Tacky tourists go wild at **Clifton Hill**, Niagara's boulevard of garish dreams. See p231.

south of the Falls are, yes, more attractions, plus parks, picnic areas and viewpoints. It's pretty, in a regulated sort of a way.

You can cross over to the US side of the river on foot or by car on either the Rainbow Bridge (near the Falls) or the Whirlpool Rapids Bridge. Take your passport and any visa documents (*see p247* **US passport regulations**) and be prepared for security checks and body searches. Queues have been longer since 9/11. Given that the views are less impressive from the American side, it's not really worth it.

WHAT TO SEE

First – and quite possibly only – the Falls themselves. There are always crowds, often dozens deep, at the main Table Rock site, where you can stand (behind a strong stone and metal railing) a mere metre away from the edge of the Horseshoe Falls. There is a spot where you are literally at the peak of the cascade as it rushes by your toes, plummeting 54 metres (177 feet) down into the foaming, misty gorge. In high season you may have to jostle to get into position by the railing, but it's worth the wait.

The Table Rock Complex has a restaurant, a snack bar and souvenir shops filled with tacky trinkets. It is also the entry point for the **Journey Behind the Falls**. Visitors take a lift down 38 metres (125 feet) through solid rock, don yellow macs and then walk through a tunnel behind the curtain of water plunging over the Horseshoe Falls. There is also an outdoor observation deck at the side, where you can watch the thundering waters hit the gorge and turn into white mist. Pretty dramatic stuff.

Half a mile north is the departure point for the *Maid of the Mist*, at the bottom of Clifton Hill, opposite the American Falls. There's a direct road from town, or you can take the crowded, scenic and invariably damp riverside walk through Queen Victoria Park. There's no advance booking, so prepare for a lengthy queue at busy times, or get there early – the first cruise leaves at 9.45am – but this is one water ride that is well worth the wait. At the bottom of the cliffs you get suited up in blue slickers. The little ship chugs past the American Falls and Cave of the Winds before it charges straight for the horseshoe of water. Passengers aboard the bucking boat will find the world turns totally white as they disappear into the mists of Niagara. Make no mistake, you will get wet. But it's worth it for the thrill.

Three more river-centric attractions are based in the Whirlpool Basin area, a couple of miles downstream. The **Great Gorge Adventure** (905 371 0254, closed Nov-late April) takes you down in a lift to a boardwalk beside the seething rapids; the **Niagara**

Whirlpool Aero Car, built in 1913, spans the dramatic whirlpool (subject to weather conditions) – the ride is lovely, but pretty tame. For a real thrill, book a flight over the Falls with **Niagara Helicopters** (905 357 5672).

Many people prefer to visit Niagara during the frigid, white winters. For one thing, there are no crowds. But the main reason is that the entire area around the Horseshoe Falls turns into a stunning winter tableau of ice and snow. The mist covers buildings, trees, railings and coats everything with layers of ice. It is a beautiful spectacle, especially at night, when the **Niagara Light Show** (year-round after dusk) bathes the water, mist and ice in startling white, red and blue. Note that many attractions (and restaurants) will be closed, though, or operating on reduced opening hours.

In the town itself you can pretty much take your pick of international tourist franchises, viewing towers and assorted attractions. The **Skylon Tower** is not hard to find. Take one of the little 'yellow bug' exterior lifts for a ride to the indoor or outdoor observation deck. This will give you another view of the Falls – and it is breathtaking – from some 236 metres (775 feet) above ground level. You can see the perfect horseshoe shape of the Canadian Falls and the plume of mist spilling up from the rolling waters of the Niagara river. It's also fun to watch the toytown-tiny *Maid of the Mist* fight its way towards the Horseshoe Falls.

Clifton Hill (**photo** *p230*), the steep street that runs up from the *Maid of the Mist* dock, is a glorious concentration of tacky attractions. Here you will find Dracula's Haunted Castle, the Mystery Maze, the Movieland Wax Museum of Stars, Ripley's Believe It or Not, the Great Canadian Midway, the House of Frankenstein and the Dinosaur Park putting course.

The **IMAX Theatre Niagara Falls & Daredevil Gallery** showcases the largest collection of barrels and home-made contraptions used to challenge the Falls, successfully and otherwise. To save you making the leap yourself, there is some incredible video footage filmed by a daredevil through the reinforced window of his barrel. Don't miss the photos of Blondin as he crossed the gorge on the high wire. The stunning IMAX film *Niagara: Miracles, Myths and Magic*, plays regularly.

The **Sky Wheel** (photo *p234*) is the newest attraction to the strip, a London Eye-type wheel that rises 55 metres (175 feet) above the tack factor to take in views of the Falls at a gentle pace. One revolution takes about ten minutes.

If looking at all that water makes you want to take a dip, head for **Fallview Indoor Water Park**, which boasts an array of slides, fountains, a 1,000-gallon tipping bucket and tidal pool. At $45 a head, you may feel your wallet is getting soaked, but discounts are offered when staying at the adjoining Sheraton on the Falls, Brock Plaza and Skyline Inn hotels. **MarineLand** is one of the town's most popular attractions. The show features killer whales, sea lions and leaping dolphins; there's also a zoo with elks, bears and buffalos.

When Niagara's city fathers looked for ways to boost tourism, gambling was the obvious way to go. The town has always had the ersatz vibe of an Atlantic City or Las Vegas, so gambling has become as much a part of Niagara culture as fudge factories and trinkets.

Casino Niagara has a massive 9,000 square metres (96,000 square feet) of gaming space, but it was eclipsed in 2004 by the **Niagara Fallsview Casino Resort** (*see p234*), a huge hotel/casino that is twice the size. Both establishments are open daily, round the clock.

At the opposite end of the tourist spectrum is **Niagara Parks Butterfly Conservatory**, about eight kilometres (five miles) north along the Niagara Parkway and just south of the Floral Clock (a free attraction that is exactly what it sounds like). This living museum features more than 2,000 butterflies from around the globe. It's an explosion of hues in a lush, climate-controlled rainforest setting. Wear colourful clothing, and the butterflies will land on you for the perfect photo op. The Butterfly Conservatory is part of the **Niagara Parks Botanical Gardens** (905 371 0254). Nature lovers also flock to **Bird Kingdom**, formerly Niagara Falls Aviary, where free-flying toucans, hornbills and some 350 other species of birds reside in a faux jungle temple ruin.

Niagara has some gorgeous green spaces. One is the **Niagara Glen Nature Reserve**, a tranquil antidote to some of the more raucous Niagara attractions. Located on the Niagara Parkway, the Glen is a haven mostly missed by tourists who are put off by the steep, rugged paths. Those willing to make the effort are rewarded with rare wild flowers, ferns and mosses that grow on boulders, a centuries-old stand of rare tulip trees and close-up views of the surging Niagara river. Maps are available from the Niagara Glen gift shop (905 371 0254).

Bird Kingdom

5561 River Road (866 994 0090/905 356 8888/ www.niagarafallsaviary.com). **Open** *Apr-June, Sept, Oct* 9am-5pm daily. *July, Aug* 9am-7pm daily. *Nov-Mar* 10am-5pm daily. **Admission** $17.50; $11.65 concessions. **Credit** AmEx, MC, V.

Over the edge

The fact that it's illegal hasn't stopped numerous 'daredevils' from attempting to cross Niagara Falls or plunge over the edge. There have been 16 known attempts (only ten people have survived). And whichever method they choose – in a barrel, on a tightrope, or simply in the clothes they stand up in – they have all been memorable.

The first person to have survived a plunge was Sam Patch (aka the Yankee Leaper), who in October 1829 jumped over Horseshoe Falls and lived. But perhaps the most famous crosser was the Great Blondin, a French tightrope walker, who in 1859 crossed the gorge on a specially made rope. Such was his confidence that he made the crossing several times – once with his manager on his back, and once with a small stove that, halfway across, he used to cook an omelette.

The first successful 'barrel-crossing' was back in 1901, when Annie Taylor climbed into an air-tight wooden barrel. She survived (albeit a little bruised and battered), hoping to make some hard cash from her fame. She died in poverty. Then there was Bobby Leach, who in 1911 plunged over the Falls in a steel barrel. He broke both kneecaps but survived – only to die 15 years later from gangrene after slipping on an orange peel. In 1920 Charles G Stephens thought that the way to go was to tie himself to an anvil (which he was using as ballast) within his barrel. Unfortunately, when the barrel 'hit the deck' the anvil (with Stephens attached) kept going. No trace of him was ever found... unless you count his right arm, which was still in the barrel. In 1930 poor George L Stathakis, a Greek waiter, suffocated after his barrel was trapped in the current behind the Falls for 14 hours. George's pet turtle, Sonny Boy, who'd come along for the ride, survived.

The most recent attempt was in October 2003, when Kirk Jones from Michigan made the jump – and survived – wearing only the clothes on his back. He was fined $2,300 dollars for the offence and banned from entering Canada ever again. He and a friend had bought a video camera to record the event. Unfortunately, the pair were so inebriated at the time that Kirk's friend couldn't work out how to operate the camera; the entire stunt went unrecorded.

Casino Niagara

5705 Falls Avenue (1-888 946 3255/905 374 3598/www.casinoniagara.com). **Open** 24hrs daily. **Admission** free. **Credit** AmEx, MC, V.

Fallsview Indoor Water Park

5685 Falls Avenue (888 234 8408/905 374 4444/www.fallsviewwaterpark.com). **Open** 10am-10pm daily. **Admission** $44.95 per person; no concessions. **Credit** AmEx, MC, V.

IMAX Theatre Niagara Falls & Daredevil Gallery

6170 Fallsview Boulevard (905 374 4629/www. imaxniagara.com). **Open** 11am-8pm daily. **Admission** $13.92; $9.86 concessions. **Credit** MC, V.

Journey Behind the Falls

6650 Niagara River Parkway (1-877 642 7275/ 905 371 0254/www.niagaraparks.com). **Open** *Summer* 9am-5.30pm daily; 9am-6.30pm Sat. *Winter* call for details. **Admission** $11; $6.50 concessions; free under-6s. **Credit** AmEx, MC, V.

Maid of the Mist

5920 River Road (905 358 5781/www.maidof themist.com). **Departures** vary; call for details. Closed Nov-Mar. **Admission** $14; $8.60 concessions; free under-6s. **Credit** AmEx, MC, V.

MarineLand

7657 Portage Road, Niagara Falls (905 356 9565/www.marinelandcanada.com). **Open** *Late May-late June* 10am-5pm Mon-Fri; 10am-6pm Sat, Sun. *Late June-early Sept* 9am-6pm daily. *Early Sept-early Oct* 10am-5pm daily. Closed early Oct-late May. **Admission** $18.95-$26.95; $13.95-$23.95 concessions; free under-4s. **Credit** AmEx, MC, V.

Niagara Glen Nature Reserve

Niagara River Parkway (905 371 0254/www. niagaraparks.com). **Open** phone for details. **Admission** free.

Niagara Parks Butterfly Conservatory

2405 Niagara River Parkway (905 358 0025/ www.niagaraparks.com). **Open** *Jan-early Mar* 9am-5pm daily. *Early Mar-June, early Sept-Dec* 9am-6pm daily. *June-early Sept* 9am-9pm daily. **Admission** $11; $6.50 concessions; free under-6s. **Credit** AmEx, MC, V.

Niagara SkyWheel

4950 Clifton Hill (905 358 4793/www.cliftonhill. com). **Open** *Summer* 9am-2am daily. *Winter* 9am-11pm daily. **Admission** $9.99; $5.99 concessions. **Credit** AmEx, MC, V.

Niagara Whirlpool Aero Car

3850 Niagara River Parkway (905 262 4274/ www.niagaraparks.com). **Open** 10am-5pm Mon-Fri; 9am-5pm Sat, Sun. Closed late Nov-early Mar. **Admission** $11; $6.50 concessions; free under-6s. **No credit cards.**

Skylon Tower

5200 Robinson Street (1-877 475 9566/905 356 2651/www.skylon.com). **Open** Observation deck: *May-Aug* 8am-midnight daily. *Sept-Apr* 11am-9pm daily. **Admission** $10.95; $6.45-$9.95 concessions. **Credit** AmEx, MC, V.

Where to eat

Niagara Falls isn't known for its fine dining. Fast and theme food is the order for the day (here you will find Denny's and the Hard Rock Café, plus all the other usual suspects). There are, however, two places that are always busy, if not for the food, then for the views. The **Table Rock Restaurant** serves decent casual meals and snacks at fair prices, but it has a constant queue because it is only 100 metres from the Horseshoe Falls (hence you are not encouraged to linger over coffee). You can reserve a table, but not a window seat.

The **Skylon Tower** (*see p231*) has two eateries, the best of which is the revolving **Skylon Tower Restaurant**. The food is of the rich, international type that aims to impress, and is fairly pricey; the views are the attraction.

Skylon Tower Restaurant

Skylon Tower, 5200 Robinson Street (1-877 475 9566/905 356 2651/www.skylon.com). **Open** *May-Sept* 11.30am-2pm, 4.30-9pm daily. *Oct-Apr* 11.30am-2pm, 4.30-10pm Mon-Sat; 11.30am-3pm, 4.30-10pm Sun. **Main courses** $42-$70. **Credit** AmEx, MC, V.

Table Rock Restaurant

6650 Niagara Parkway (905 354 3631/www. niagaraparks.com). **Open** phone for details. **Main courses** $30-$35. **Credit** AmEx, MC, V.

Where to stay

If you want a lovely place to stay, **Niagara-on-the-Lake** (*see p237*) is more pleasant than Niagara town. It's a 30-minute, scenic drive from the Falls, and the antithesis to its honky-tonk neighbour, characterised by quaint gingerbread houses and quiet, shaded streets. However, if you're playing tourist and want the full Niagara experience, you can choose between the many uniform chain hotels, the down and dirty 'no-tell motel' strip above Clifton Hill or the opulence of a palatial suite overlooking the Falls – with, perhaps, a fireplace and a heart-shaped jacuzzi (such things are almost *de rigueur* in the honeymoon suites). Downtown, try one of the period B&Bs lining the road towards the Falls, such as the **Lion's Head B&B**, a lovely Arts and Crafts house with stylish rooms. Contact **Niagara Falls Tourism** (*see p234*) for comprehensive suggestions. Always ask about deals and packages, particularly off season.

Trips Out of Town

Two of the most prominent hotels in the city are the **Brock Plaza Hotel** and the adjacent **Sheraton on the Falls**. They stand side by side a block from the Niagara Parkway in the giant Falls Avenue complex (along with the casino and various theme restaurants), and both have views of the American Falls. For a room in the shadow of the Skylon Tower, check out the **Holiday Inn by the Falls**, or if you want a less anonymous location, try the **Travelodge Clifton Hill** in the colourful carnival atmosphere of Clifton Hill. If you have kids in tow, try the new **Great Wolf Lodge**, four kilometres (2.5 miles) north of the city across from the Whirlpool; it has a faux log-cabin setting and a huge waterpark. If gambling's your thing, consider the **Niagara Fallsview Casino Resort** (*see below*), which contains various restaurants, plus shopping and gambling amenities. Many of its 368 guest rooms command stunning views of the Falls.

Brock Plaza Hotel

5685 Falls Avenue, ON L2E 6W7 (1-800 263 7135/905 374 4444/www.niagarafallshotels.com). **Rates** $89-$329. **Credit** AmEx, DC, MC, V.

Great Wolf Lodge

3950 Victoria Avenue, ON L2E 7M8 (1-800 605 9653/www.greatwolf.com). **Rates** $199-$800. **Credit** AmEx, MC, V.

Holiday Inn by the Falls

5339 Murray Street, ON L2G 2J3 (1-800 263 9393/905 356 1333/www.holidayinn.com). **Rates** $69-$265. **Credit** AmEx, DC, MC, V.

Lion's Head B&B

5239 River Road, ON L2E 3G9 (905 374 1681/ www.lionsheadbb.com). **Rates** $95-$165. **Credit** MC, V.

Niagara Fallsview Casino Resort

6380 Fallsview Blvd, ON L2G 7X5 (1-888 325 5788/www.fallsviewcasinoresort.com). **Rates** $119-$529. **Credit** AmEx, MC, V.

Sheraton on the Falls

5875 Falls Avenue, ON L2G 3K7 (1-888 229 9961/905 374 4444/www.niagarafallshotels.com). **Rates** $99-$329. **Credit** AmEx, DC, MC, V.

Travelodge Clifton Hill

4943 Clifton Hill, ON L2G 3N5 (1-800 668 8840/905 357 4330/www.falls.com). **Rates** *Sept-June* $99-$299. *July, Aug* $99-$329. **Credit** AmEx, DC, MC, V.

Tourist information

Hotel concierges tend to be the best sources of information, but there are signs everywhere. To save money when visiting attractions, it's worth investing in an all-in-one pass.

Niagara Falls Tourism

5705 Falls Avenue, PO Box 300, Niagara Falls, ON L2E 6T3 (1-800 563 2557/905 356 6061/ www.niagarafallstourism.com). **Open** *Mid May-Aug* 8am-8pm daily. *Sept-mid May* 8am-6pm Mon-Fri; 10am-6pm Sat; 10am-4pm Sun.

Niagara Parks Commission

Table Rock Complex, 6650 Niagara Parkway, Niagara Falls (1-877 642 7275/905 371 0254/ www.niagaraparks.com). **Open** phone for details.

Tourism Niagara

424 South Service Road, Casablanca Boulevard exit on the QEW, Grimsby (1-800 263 2988/ 905 945 5444/www.tourismniagara.com). **Open** 9am-6pm daily.
Busy tourist centre off the highway; provides information on the whole region. Hotel reservations can be made through this office at a discount.

Getting there

By car

When traffic co-operates (avoid the afternoon rush hour), Niagara is a 90-minute drive on one highway, the Queen Elizabeth Way from the city, rounding Lake Ontario. Take the well-signed Highway 420 to drive the last few miles into town.

By public bus

Greyhound buses (1-800 661 8747/416 594 1010, www.greyhound.ca) run throughout the day from Toronto. But at $59 return ($61 on weekends) they're not much cheaper than a tour bus, and less convenient at both ends.

Bus tours/day trips

Several companies run scheduled tours from Toronto to Niagara. Their literature is ubiquitous, their packages manifold (from transport only to the full excursion/attraction monty) and their differences negligible. Ask at your hotel; staff should know which are the most convenient and may have deals going. Standard operators include Gray Line (416 594 0343, www.grayline.ca) and Niagara & Toronto Tours (416 868 0400, www.torontotours.com).

The Magic Bus Company (416 516 7433, www.magicbuscompany.com) sends a funky, brightly coloured school bus round the hostels before trundling down to Niagara, where it stops at a winery, gives the trippers three to five hours at the Falls and stops at the whirlpool and other attractions before heading back ($40). Casino Niagara (*see p233*) and Niagara Fallsview Casino Resort (*see above*) both have contracts with several companies.

By train

There are two VIA Rail (1-888 842 7245, www. viarail.ca) trains a day in either direction, taking under two hours to make the journey. One-way fares are $33 for adults, $17-$30 concessions. You can book a cheaper fare with five days' advance reservation for as little as $21 each way.

Getting around

By bus

The green-and-white people-movers (available to those buying all-in-one visitors' passes; *see p234*), are sometimes hard to spot among the numerous tour buses. They're convenient, however, dropping off visitors at the different sights around town.

Wine Country

The fertile southern part of the Golden Horseshoe that wraps around Lake Ontario from Toronto to Niagara is home to one of the largest wine industries in Canada (the other being the interior of British Columbia), with more than 70 wineries and counting. The extent of the monoculture becomes evident along the QEW highway, where the rows of vineyards are so dense and uniform as to be potentially hypnotising to the sleepy driver. But, in spite of appearances, all is not equal – far from it.

Niagara, which has rather loftily become known as the 'Napa of the North', does indeed bear some resemblance to its Californian cousin. It's a popular destination for gastronomy tours, biking and sipping excursions, and has plenty

of pretty hotels. Celebrities are getting in on the act as well, with the likes of Dan Aykroyd and golfer Mike Weir putting their names and faces (and a lot of dosh) on bottles from Niagara. The next big thing is set to be a winery designed by architect Frank Gehry for **Le Clos Jordan**.

Like Napa, the Niagara region is dominated by giants that tend to pump out passable plonk, while an increasing number of craftspeople are producing truly glorious wine. Even British wine guru Jancis Robinson has turned her attention to Niagara. Number one of her top ten Canadian wine list, published in the *Financial Times*, was a syrah from Niagara's Daniel Lenko winery. This small estate reflects the region's rise. In the 1970s Lenko senior (Bill) planted some of the first chardonnay vines from Europe in the area, replacing the traditional concord grapes that were used to make sweet, generally hideous but ubiquitous wines. Lenko was ahead of his time, as the concord continued to rule until the late 1970s, later to be replaced almost entirely by European varietals. Bill Lenko supplied the big producers with grapes but did not sell wine; when son Daniel took over in the '90s, though, the small operation joined a groundswell of serious winemakers.

You say you want a revolution: **Sky Wheel**. *See p231.*

The climate, moderated by the lake and protected by the Niagara Escarpment, has allowed for winemaking here for more than 200 years. The most successful transplant to date is the riesling, which does well in northern climes. Wines made from pinot noir and chardonnay are also worth seeking out, as are some reds such as baco noir.

The Vintners Quality Alliance (VQA; www.vqaontario.com) was established in 1989 to control standards of wine production in the province. One of the best services this producer-led group offers is to distinguish between Ontario wines and the so-called 'cellared in Canada' bottles which use as little as one per cent of local grapes. The growing conditions are often harsh, and Ontario yields can be small, so some producers haul in foreign juice. VQA, on the other hand, is 100 per cent Ontario-grown.

The first to experiment and to achieve global recognition for its blends was **Inniskillin**. This winery is particularly renowned for its ice wines, which are made from grapes that are pressed while still frozen, producing a very sweet, intense and fairly expensive wine. You can sample it at the historic Brae Burn Barn on the Inniskillin estate, as well as at local restaurants. **Château des Charmes** was also important in the development of Niagara winemaking. It is a great place to visit, located in the nearby village of St David's. The **Henry of Pelham Family Estate Winery** has some excellent VQA products in its cellars. The highlight of its winery and vineyard tours is wine tasting on its patio, next to Short Hills Provincial Park.

There are many other fine wineries and winery restaurants in the region, known as 'the Bench'. The main wineries to visit in Niagara-on-the-Lake are **Peller Estates**, for its elegant old-world-style chateau with vaulted cellars, and **Jackson-Triggs**, a sleek modern winery, where huge industrial doors roll up in fine weather to reveal an expansive view – right through the winery – of the vineyards. A classical-style amphitheatre seats up to 500 people for summer concerts. Next door is a popular newcomer, **Stratus Vineyards**, notable for its wines, as well as its environmentally friendly operation and dazzling architecture.

Away from Niagara-on-the-Lake, it's worth making the 40-kilometre (25-mile) trip to the **Cave Spring Cellars** in the village of Jordan, in the Bench. The winery has its own sumptuous 26-room hotel, **Inn on the Twenty**, with jacuzzis and fireplaces in each suite, as well as one of the area's best dining spots, **On the Twenty**. Here you'll also find

smaller wineries that sell direct at the farmgate, such as the **Thirteenth Street Wine Corp**. If your taste runs to more adventure, get a map of the area and seek out the smaller estates: often you won't find these goods in any shops.

The recommended time to go wine touring is from May to October, though if you visit in January you can catch the annual **Icewine Festival**, where the liquid gold is served outdoors at a bar made of – you guessed it – carved ice. For more information, see www.niagarawinefestival.com. The major event of the year is the annual late September celebration of the harvest, the **Niagara Grape & Wine Festival** (905 688 0212, www.grapeandwine.com). Over 100 events include tours, tastings, concerts and seminars, and food samplings, set off by the autumn foliage. Also look out for the **Niagara New Vintage Festival** in June.

Wineries are good places to eat in Niagara. **Jackson-Triggs** serves light, bistro-style cheese and fruit plates in a tasting room overlooking the vineyard. **Peller Estates** offers a formal dining room (with prices to match). It, too, has a great patio overlooking the vineyard. **Hillebrand Estates** winery has the **Vineyard Café**, known for its summer jazz and blues concerts held in the vineyard. Also very pleasant is **Strewn Winery**, with its restaurant **Terroir La Cachette**. In Vineland, **Vineland Estates Winery** (*see p237*) boasts an award-winning restaurant and top-notch accommodation. Call ahead to book a tasting at **Tawse Winery**, a newcomer that is earning praise for its small-yield pinot noirs and signature chardonnays.

Cave Spring Cellars

3836 Main Street, Jordan (905 562 3581/www. cavespringcellars.com). **Open** *Tours July-Oct 3pm daily. Nov-June 3pm Sat, Sun. Shop May-Oct 10am-6pm Mon-Sat; 11am-6pm Sun. Nov-Apr 10am-5pm Mon-Thur; 10am-6pm Fri, Sat; 11am-5pm Sun. Restaurant 11.30am-3pm, 5pm-late daily.* **Admission** *Tours* $5. **Main courses** $10-$16. **Hotel rates** $149-$355. **Credit** AmEx, MC, V.

Château des Charmes

1025 York Road, Niagara-on-the-Lake (905 262 4219/www.chateaudescharmes.com). **Open** 10am-6pm daily. *Tours* 11am, 3pm daily. **Admission** *Tours* $2. **Credit** AmEx, MC, V.

Henry of Pelham Family Estate Winery

1469 Pelham Road, St Catharines (905 684 8423/ www.henryofpelham.com). **Open** *Tours* May-Oct 1.30pm daily. Nov-Apr phone for details. *Shop* May-Oct 10am-6pm daily. Nov-Apr 10am-5pm Mon-Sat; 11am-5pm Sun. **Admission** *May-Oct* free. *Nov-Apr* phone for details. **Credit** AmEx, MC, V.

Hillebrand Estates

Niagara Stone Road, off York Road, Niagara-on-the-Lake (1-800 582 8412/905 468 7123/www.hillebrand.com). **Open** *Tours* 10am-6pm daily. *Tasting tours* phone for details. *Restaurant* phone for details. **Admission** *Tours* free. *Tasting tours* $8-$10. **Main courses** $13-$24. **Credit** MC, V.

Inniskillin

RR 1, Niagara Parkway, south of Niagara-on-the-Lake (1-888 466 4754/905 468 3554/www.inniskillin.com). **Open** *Tours* May-Oct 10.30am, 2.30pm daily. Nov-Apr 10.30am, 2.30pm Sat, Sun. *Shop* May-Oct 10am-6pm daily. Nov-Apr 10am-5pm daily. *Tasting bar* May-Oct 11am-5.30pm daily. Nov-Apr 11am-4.30pm daily. **Admission** *Tours* free. *Tastings* $5-$11. **Credit** AmEx, MC, V.

Jackson-Triggs

2145 RR 55, Niagara-on-the-Lake (1-866 589 4637/905 468 4637/www.jacksontriggswinery.com). **Open** *May-Oct* 10.30am-5.30pm daily. Nov-Apr 10.30am-5.30pm Mon-Fri, Sun; 10.30am-6.30pm Sat. *Tours* May-Oct 10.30am-5.30pm daily. Nov-Apr 10.30am-4.30pm Mon-Fri; 10.30am-5.30pm Sat, Sun. **Admission** $5. **Credit** MC, V.

Peller Estates

290 John Street E, Niagara-on-the-Lake (1-888 673 5537/905 468 4678/www.peller.com). **Open** 11.30am-5.30pm daily. *Tours* 11.30am-5.30pm daily. *Restaurant* noon-3pm, 5.30-8.30pm Mon-Thur, Sun; noon-3pm, 5-9pm Fri, Sat. **Admission** *Tours* free. **Main courses** $25-$38. **Credit** MC, V.

Stratus Vineyards

2059 Niagara Stone Road, Niagara-on-the-Lake (905 468 1806/www.stratuswines.com). **Open** *May-Oct* 11am-5pm daily. *Nov-Apr* Wed-Sun. **Admission** free. *Tasting flights* $10. **Credit** MC, V.

Strewn Winery

1339 Lakeshore Road, Niagara-on-the-Lake (905 468 1229/www.strewnwinery.com). **Open** 10am-6pm daily. *Tours* 1pm daily. *Private tours* phone for details. *Restaurant* phone for details. **Admission** free. *Private tours* $4-$25. **Main courses** $21-$35. **Credit** AmEx, MC, V.

Tawse Winery

3955 Cherry Avenue, RR 1, Vineland (905 562 9500/www.tawsewinery.ca). **Open** 10am-5pm daily. **Credit** MC, V.

Thirteenth Street Wine Corp

3983 Thirteenth Street, Jordan Station (905 562 9463/www.13thstreetwines.com). **Open** *Mar-Dec* 10.30am-5pm; otherwise by appointment. *Tours* phone for details. **Credit** MC, V.

Vineland Estates Winery

3620 Moyer Road, Vineland (1-888 846 3526/905 562 7088/www.vineland.com). **Open** phone for details. *Tours* late May-Oct 11am, 3pm daily. Nov-late May 3pm Sat, Sun. *Restaurant* phone for details. **Main courses** $15-$36. **Hotel rates** $145. **Credit** AmEx, MC, V.

Wine tours

Both scheduled and custom wine tours are available; they usually include a meal, as well as several winery visits and a knowledgeable guide. You will normally need to arrange a pick-up in the Wine Country or Niagara-on-the-Lake area, though sometimes transport from Toronto or elsewhere can be provided. Tour companies include **Crush on Niagara Wine Tours** (1-866 408 9463, www.crush tours.com); **Wine Country Tours** (905 892 9770, www.winecountrytours.ca) and **Niagara Nature Tours** (1-888 889 8296, www.niagara naturetours.ca), which has an eco slant and can also cover regional cooking, history, agriculture and gardens. For something a little more challenging, sign up for the bike tours of Niagara wineries with **Steve Bauer** (905 563 8687, www.stevebauer.com).

Tourist information

The tourist offices in Niagara Falls and particularly Niagara-on-the-Lake also have information on Wine Country.

Wine Council of Ontario

110 Hannover Drive, St Catharines (1-888 594 6379/905 684 8070/www.winesofontario.org).

Getting there

You can't properly experience Wine Country without your own transport, though several Niagara tours (*see p234*) include a winery stop as part of their itinerary.

Niagara-on-the-Lake

This quaint village at the mouth of the Niagara River, where it empties into Lake Ontario, is the yin to Niagara Falls' yang. After the garish sights and sounds of the falls, NOTL provides a soothing antidote, with charming old houses and plenty of history. Besides, the journey from Niagara Falls along the precipice of the Niagara Gorge is one of the most scenic routes in the country. The towering cliff faces reveal the extent of the erosion that has seen the Falls steadily carve their way backwards through this dramatic setting.

The Niagara Parks Commission has controlled development and growth along the Canadian side of the river since 1885. The result is the Niagara Parkway, a verdant green belt through which a leisurely winding drive brings you to the perfectly preserved 19th-century village of Niagara-on-the-Lake.

In 1792 Niagara-on-the-Lake became the first capital of Upper Canada, later the Province of

Take a hike

Niagara Falls marks the southern end of one of Ontario's most-loved protected areas, the Niagara Escarpment. Niagara Falls may be the largest, but it is only one of dozens of waterfalls that tumble over these limestone cliffs stretching north some 2,300 kilometres (1,430 miles) towards Georgian Bay and beyond. In 1990 it was designated a UNESCO World Biosphere Reserve. Although urban sprawl has encroached somewhat in recent years, the Niagara Escarpment is still home to interesting wild flora and fauna, including 1,000-year-old gnarly, cliff-clinging cedars and rare ferns.

The best way to explore the scenic vistas is to hike a section of the Bruce Trail, which traces the escarpment from Queenston (just north of Niagara Falls) to Tobermory and Bruce Peninsula National Park. Local clubs each maintain a section of the 900-kilometre (497-mile) trail, marking the route with white-paint blazes. Along the route are assorted conservation areas and parks.

Highlights include **Balls Falls Conservation Area**, where Twenty Mile Creek tumbles over the escarpment into the verdant Jordan Valley. The creek takes its name from the distance Loyalists travelled from the border when fleeing the United States during the Revolutionary War. They looked for waterfalls like these to establish mills and settlements, the remains of which have been preserved in this historic park.

Dundas Valley, on the outskirts of Hamilton, is situated in a corner of the escarpment, where it bends around the western end of Lake Ontario. A network of over 40 kilometres (25 miles) of interconnecting trails wind through the valley, past moss-covered rocks that have tumbled from the cliffs.

At **Crawford Lake Conservation Area**, near Milton, the trail skirts a reconstructed Iroquoian longhouse and winds down a canyon where turkey vultures nest.

For dramatic scenery, the northernmost section of the trail near Tobermory can't be beaten. It undulates along white limestone cliffs overlooking the sky-blue waters of Georgian Bay, past gravel beaches, caves and towering islands that have broken away from the cliffs. Some of Ontario's best hiking is found in **Bruce Peninsula National Park** (www.pc.gc.ca).

Copies of the official Bruce Trail guide are available through the **Bruce Trail Association** (PO Box 857, Hamilton L8N 3N9, 905 529 6821, www.brucetrail.org).

Ontario, and was a major site in the occasional conflicts with the American forces just across the river. Just south of the town, **Historic Fort George** national park is a restored version of the original fort (1797), where costumed staff provide the history lessons.

Upon leaving the fort, you will find yourself in the village. The first major building you pass, on the left, is the Shaw Festival Theatre, one of the province's most important (the season runs from April to November). The company's mandate is to present plays written by George Bernard Shaw 'and his contemporaries'. But the company has performed such varied fare as Shaw's *Caesar and Cleopatra*, Noël Coward's *Hay Fever* and a revival of Stephen Sondheim's musical *Merrily We Roll Along*. The **Shaw Festival** has turned this sleepy hamlet into one of the province's most popular tourist and theatre destinations. After you have picked up your tickets (best to order some months in advance or check www.totix.ca for last-minute seats), park your car anywhere you can find a space and then stroll around town. It isn't very big, and the Clock Tower, in the middle of the main road (Queen Street), marks the centre.

On the corner opposite the clock is the **Niagara Apothecary Museum** (5 Queen Street, 905 468 3845), a perfectly preserved 'drugstore' from 1866, operated and maintained by the Ontario College of Pharmacists. Note the original walnut and butternut fixtures, and the rare collection of apothecary glass.

The town provides shopping and browsing galore; think fudge, chocolate, wine, candles, deli goods, antiques and paintings. Visit **Greaves Jams & Marmalades** (55 Queen Street, 905 468 3608, www.greavesjams.com) for jams made with local fruit. After you tire of shopping, wander the picturesque backstreets to the lakefront park, a popular picnic spot from which you can see the US.

The area's history is explained in detail at the **Niagara Historical Society Museum** (43 Castlereagh Street, 905 468 3912, www.niagarahistorical.museum). Founded in 1907, it contains over 20,000 artefacts from the periods of the Loyalists, the War of 1812 and the Victorian age, including some gripping first-hand accounts of the American occupation of 1812, and virtual Canadian icons such as Laura Secord's beaded Iroquoian purse.

Historic Fort George

905 468 4257/www.niagara.com/~parkscan. **Open** *May-Nov* 10am-5pm daily. *Dec-Mar* by appointment only. *Tours* by appointment. **Admission** $11; $5.50-$9.25 concessions; free under-6s. *Tours* $7. **No credit cards**.

Where to eat

This little town is a diner's delight – the culinary antithesis to Niagara Falls. Forget the conventional wisdom that the restaurant in your hotel is there just as a promotional exercise; the inns of NOTL are known nationally for their cuisine and service. Some of the best places to eat are also the best places to stay. Prime examples include the Prince of Wales Hotel, where you can have dinner in the gorgeous **Escabèche** restaurant or lunch in its Churchill Bar. Pub fare is served all day in the bar of the **Olde Angel Inn** (*see p239*), which features plenty of draught beer and local wines. If there's no time for a leisurely lunch, grab a sandwich or salad at the **Shaw Café & Wine Bar**, across from the Royal George Theatre.

Other than the winery restaurants (*see p237*), one of the best choices is the dining room at the **Charles Inn** (*see below*), an elegant 1832 former residence with tables on the verandah during summer.

Escabèche

6 Picton Street (1-888 669 5566/905 468 3246/ www.vintageinns.com). **Open** noon-2pm, 5-9pm Mon-Fri; noon-2pm, 5-10pm Sat, Sun. **Main courses** $15-$24. **Credit** AmEx, DC, MC, V.

Shaw Café & Wine Bar

92 Queen Street (905 468 4772). **Open** phone for details. **Main courses** phone for details. **Credit** AmEx, MC, V.

Where to stay

The quaintness of this 18th-century village makes NOTL a favourite weekend getaway. Billed as one of the world's finest heritage hotels, the **Prince of Wales Hotel** is the first choice for deluxe spa accommodation right in the middle of town. The **Olde Angel Inn** is the town's oldest inn, with colonial-style guest rooms above the bar (complete with wandering ghost) and two rental cottages. The **Moffat Inn** is an affordable 22-room, two-storey historic inn just off the main street, with an elegant penthouse suite. The **Charles Inn** has 12 guest rooms furnished with antiques. The **Harbour House** is a 31-room boutique

hotel featuring feather beds, plush Frette bathrobes and oversized whirlpool tubs.

Niagara-on-the-Lake has more B&Bs than any other village in Ontario. Check with the local tourism office and the Shaw Festival office (*see below*) for more information.

Charles Inn

209 Queen Street, ON L0S 1J0 (905 468 4588/ www.charlesinn.ca). **Rates** *Winter* $99-$270. *Summer* $199-$365. **Credit** AmEx, MC, V.

Harbour House

85 Melville Street, ON L0S 1J0 (1-866 277 6677/ www.harbourhousehotel.ca). **Rates** *Winter* $199-$370. *Summer* $295-$445. **Credit** AmEx, MC, V.

Moffat Inn

60 Picton Street, ON L0S 1J0 (905 468 4116/ www.moffatinn.com). **Rates** *Nov-Apr* $79-$179. *May-Oct* $109-$189. **Credit** AmEx, DC, MC, V.

Olde Angel Inn

224 Regent Street, ON L0S 1J0 (905 468 3411/ www.angel-inn.com). **Rates** *Nov-Apr* $79-$169. *May-Oct* $119-$229. **Credit** AmEx, DC, MC, V.

Prince of Wales Hotel

6 Picton Street, ON L0S 1J0 (1-888 669 5566/ 905 468 3246/www.vintageinns.com). **Rates** *Nov-Mar* $170-$295 single/double; $320 suites. *Apr-Oct* $255-$400 single/double; $495 suites. **Credit** AmEx, MC, V.

Tourist information

Niagara-on-the-Lake Chamber of Commerce and Visitor & Convention Bureau

26 Queen Street, PO Box 1043, ON L0S 1J0 (905 468 1950/www.niagaraonthelake.com). **Open** *Nov-Mar* 10am-5pm daily. *Apr-Oct* 10am-7.30pm daily.

Shaw Festival

10 Queen's Parade (1-800 511 7429/905 468 2172/ www.shawfest.com). **Open** *Box office* 9am-5pm Mon-Sat. *Season* Apr-Nov 9am-8pm daily. **Tickets** $45-$95; $25-$30 concessions. **Credit** AmEx, MC, V.

Getting there

By bus

Niagara-on-the-Lake is poorly served by public transport, but if you take the bus or train to Niagara Falls, there is a shuttle-bus service (905 359 3232/800 667 0256) to Niagara-on-the-Lake that runs twice a day in each direction from some of the larger hotels. The schedule changes, so it's best to call ahead.

By car

NOTL drive is 129 kilometres (80 miles) from Toronto. Follow the same directions as for Niagara Falls, but turn off the QEW on to Highway 55 just past the St Catharines turn-off.

Quick Trips

Head for the hills... and galleries, theatres and restaurants.

Destinations in this chapter are recommended as the best local day trips, but if you want to spend the night, the tourist offices listed can recommend a variety of places to stay.

For theme-park fun at **Paramount Canada's Wonderland**, *see p173*; for skiing and snowboarding at **Barrie** and **Collingwood**, *see p217*; for **Black Creek Pioneer Village**, *see p96*.

Woodbridge & Kleinburg

Although the former farming village is now more of a suburban bedroom community, the town of Kleinburg is still a favourite day trip for Torontonians. It is best known for the **McMichael Canadian Art Collection** (photo *p241*), an impressive gallery situated in a forest on the edge of a valley, a setting that blends perfectly with the principal theme of its permanent collection: the Canadian landscape. Philanthropists Robert and Signe McMichael constructed an immense building of rough stone and raw timber to showcase their collection of paintings by Tom Thomson and the Group of Seven. These early 20th-century artists spent years in the wilderness capturing the majestic scenery and brilliant colours of a country few of their contemporaries had ever experienced. More recently, landscapes by Doris McCarthy, a pre-eminent Toronto-based painter who studied with Group of Seven member Arthur Lismer, have been added to the gallery's collections. There are also Inuit and Native Canadian artworks, including paintings and soapstone sculptures; most notable are the bold designs of Norvel Morriseau, who captured the ancient legends of warriors and gods on canvas.

Join in a guided tour, then take a hike down into the woods to refresh the senses for a slice of real Canadiana. And before you leave, pay homage to six members of this famed group of painters at their burial sites, which are marked by jagged, pink and grey boulders.

As you head out of town, the **Kortright Centre** in Woodbridge is a must for nature-lovers. It features 16 kilometres (ten miles) of hiking trails, plus many outdoor attractions and seasonal programmes from dog-sledding to autumn colour walks. There's an information centre where you can get trail maps and watch films, plus a gift shop and café.

Kortright Centre

9550 Pine Valley Drive, Woodbridge (416 661 6600/ www.kortright.org). **Open** 9am-4pm Mon-Fri; 10am-4pm Sat, Sun. **Admission** $6; $5 concessions; free under-5s. **Credit** MC, V.

McMichael Canadian Art Collection

10365 Islington Avenue, Kleinburg (905 893 1121/ www.mcmichael.com). **Open** 10am-4pm daily. **Admission** $15; $12 concessions; free under-5s. **Credit** AmEx, MC, V.

Where to eat & drink

The **Doctor's House** is Kleinburg's most historic building, dating from 1867. It's now a classy venue for banquets and weddings, with a restaurant (Sunday brunch is a speciality). If tea time with country cuisine and fresh desserts is in order, drop into **Mr McGregor's House** (10503 Islington Avenue, 905 893 2508).

The Doctor's House

21 Nashville Road (905 893 1615/416 234 8080/ www.thedoctorshouse.ca). **Meals served** noon-3pm, 5.30-11pm Mon-Sat; 10.30am-3.30pm, 5.30-11pm Sun. **Main courses** $30-$40. **Credit** AmEx, MC, V.

Getting there

By car

For Kortright, drive north from the city on Highway 400, exit west at Major MacKenzie Drive and south on Pine Valley. For Kleinburg, continue on Major MacKenzie Drive to Islington Avenue. For more information, see www.kleinburgvillage.com.

Elora & St Jacobs

With its scenic gorge and historic stone buildings, the village of Elora – on the Grand River 90 minutes north-west of Toronto – is a favourite destination for a Sunday drive and swim in the old quarry or in the gorge. A century and a half ago mills sprang up alongside the waterfalls and limestone cliffs in the area now known as the **Elora Gorge Conservation Area** (www.grandriver.ca). Today the fast-flowing waters attract tourists and fishermen. In summer, inflatable tubes can be rented for a bouncy ride down the rapids. Every spring the river is stocked with brown trout; **Grand River Troutfitters Ltd** (519 787 4359) offers guiding services.

The busiest time of year is mid July to early August, when the **Elora Festival** (519 846 0331, 1-800 265 8977, www.elorafestival.com) of choral, classical and contemporary music is staged in some striking venues, including St John's Anglican Church. Florence Nightingale, was said to be romantically attached to the man who became a pastor here. Sadly, he was her first cousin, so marriage was impossible, and she headed off to the Crimea.

A free walking-tour map is available from the information centre in the nearby town of Fergus. It directs visitors to many of the historic buildings, including an 1856 former school, now the **Elora Centre for the Arts** (519 846 9698, www.eloracentreforthearts.ca). One of the best ways to enjoy the scenery is from the seat of a horse-drawn carriage, similar to those used by many of the local Mennonite farmers. From March to October schoolteacher Jacque Dion (519 638 5079) offers 30-minute jaunts around town.

The area to the west is dotted with Mennonite farms. Many of the regional roads have extra-wide shoulders to accommodate their black, horse-drawn buggies. **St Jacobs**, with its shops selling quilting supplies, scented candles and crafts, has become a popular bus-tour destination, but anyone interested in authentic Mennonite culture can learn about it on one of the horse-drawn trolley rides offered by **Country Livery Services & Heritage**

Harvest Farm (519 888 0302). It takes passengers to a Mennonite farm to see a maple-syrup bush, while describing how the Mennonites came to settle here in the early 1800s. Alternatively, visit **Telling the Mennonite Story**, a multimedia museum in **St Jacobs Visitor Centre** (*see below*).

Where to eat & drink

The **Desert Rose Café** is known for its vegetarian menu. The Penstock Lounge in the **Elora Mill Country Inn** serves up a sense of history with its ploughman's lunches; there's an elegant dining room for more formal meals.

Desert Rose Café
130 Metcalfe Street, Elora (519 846 0433). **Open** hours vary. **Main courses** $5-$15. **Credit** MC, V.

Elora Mill Country Inn
77 Mill Street W, Elora (519 846 9118/1-866 713 5672/www.eloramill.com). **Open** 8-10am, 11am-4pm, 5-9.30pm daily. **Main courses** $23-$49. **Credit** AmEx, MC, V.

Tourist information

Centre Wellington Chamber of Commerce
400 Tower Street S, Fergus (519 846 9841/1-877 242 6353/www.ferguselora.com). **Open** 10am-5pm Mon-Fri; noon-4pm Sat, Sun.

St Jacobs Tourism Office
1-800 265 3353/519 664 1133/www.stjacobs.com. **Answerphone** 24hrs daily.

St Jacobs Visitor Centre
1408 King Street N, St Jacobs (519 664 3518/ www.stjacobs.com). **Open** 11am-4.30pm Sat; 2-4.30pm Sun.

Getting there

By car
Elora and St Jacobs are about 90 minutes west of Toronto by car (the only option). Take Highway 401 for about 95 kilometres (60 miles), turn north on to Highway 6, then take Wellington County Road 7 right to Elora. St Jacobs is a lovely meandering 24-kilometre (15-mile) country drive away, south on County Road 18, which turns into CR 22, then west on CR 17. Just follow the signs.

Stratford & St Marys

One of Toronto's main attractions is its diverse theatre scene. Rural Ontario also has its own network of more than 30 summer-stock theatres, **ASTRO** (Association of Summer Theatre's 'Round Ontario, www.summer theatre.org), but it is the town of **Stratford**

McMichael Canadian Art Collection. *See p240.*

that draws theatregoers in droves. Since 1953, when Alec Guinness starred in *Richard III* in a sweltering tent, the **Stratford Festival** has grown huge. Each season, from April to November, a stellar cast (which has included the likes of Peter Ustinov, Christopher Plummer and Maggie Smith) performs more than a dozen plays, ranging from Shakespeare to high-kicking Broadway musicals. There are Monday evening concerts too.

With its 19th-century main drag (Ontario Street), its distinctive yellow-brick churches and numerous parks, Stratford is one of the most picturesque small towns in Ontario, with parkland lining the swan-dotted Avon River.

While wandering east through the park, stop at the little 1833 **Gallery Stratford**, which offers contemporary and traditional Canadian art (hours vary, so phone ahead). Free heritage walks and garden tours depart from the

Spa trek

You've left the city behind, so relax! The Ontario countryside is full of luxurious spas, where the soothing delights of massage and hydrotherapy meet the comforts of fine food and gracious grounds. For the energetic, there are walking trails through woods and clean country air. For those who want pampering and nothing else, there are relaxing mud wraps, soothing massages and skin-softening facials.

The rolling Caledon Hills, a one-hour drive north-west of Toronto, are full of bucolic scenery. And the **Millcroft Inn & Spa** is a picturesque retreat. The stone-and-timber architecture of the historic mill is echoed in the new spa facility. Guests enjoy a full range of services including *ofuro*, a Japanese bath ritual that begins with an exfoliating body polish and is followed by a relaxing herb-scented session in a Japanese soaking tub or an al fresco massage on the private patio.

Just outside Cambridge, an hour west of Toronto, is the august **Langdon Hall Country House Hotel & Spa**, a Federalist Revival mansion. Meticulously groomed grounds and elegant rooms are topped off with all the spa comforts. Try the hot-stone therapy for the ultimate in stress relief. And book a meal here: the sophisticated dining room is one of the province's best and boasts a superb wine list.

Cottage Country's newest spa is **Avalon**, in the Inn at Christie's Mill in Port Severn. Guests float in the indoor mineral-salts pool with picture windows overlooking the Trent Severn waterway.

Ontario's largest destination spa **Ste Anne's Country Inn & Spa** seems to undergo constant redevelopment in order to bring in the latest luxuries. Its 30 treatment rooms offer everything from full-immersion mud baths to Thai massage. And its old-fashioned stone buildings are set idyllically on a sprawling country property with miles of

walking trails and undulating hills. It is about an hour north-east of Toronto by car.

Elemental Embrace Wellness Spa Retreat incorporates traditional practices from East India under the supervision of two Ayurvedic doctors. Start the day with meditation and yoga, followed by a woodland walk or *shirodhara* (oil-drip massage). It's located an hour and a half east of Toronto.

Our suggestions are simply a tasting: for a complete guide to spa facilities throughout the province, contact **Premier Spas of Ontario** (176 Napier Street, Barrie, ON L4M 1W8, 705 721 9969, 1-800 990 7702, www.premierspasofontario.ca).

Avalon, the Spa at Christie's Mill

263 Port Severn Road , Port Severn (1-800 465 9966/705 538 2354/www.christie smill.com). **Rates** $330-$390. **Credit** AmEx, MC, V.

Elemental Embrace Wellness Spa Retreat

255 Georgina Street, Brighton (613 475 9941/1-800 212 9355/www.elemental embrace.com). **Rates** $765-$3,070. **Credit** AmEx, MC, V.

Langdon Hall Country House Hotel & Spa

1 Langdon Drive, Cambridge (519 740 2100/ 1-800 268 1898/www.langdonhall.ca). **Rates** $259-$609. **Credit** AmEx, DC, MC, V.

Millcroft Inn & Spa

55 John Street, Alton (519 941 8111/1-800 383 3976/www.millcroft.com). **Rates** $240-$355. **Credit** AmEx, DC, MC, V.

Ste Anne's Country Inn & Spa

1009 Massey Road, north of Grafton (905 349 3704/1-888 346 6772/www.spa village.ca). **Rates** $375-$680. **Credit** AmEx, DC, MC, V.

riverside branch of the tourist office most summer mornings. The double-decker bus trip by Festival Tours (519 273 1652) is a hoot.

Just 15 minutes' drive west of Stratford is the sleepy town of **St Marys**, dubbed 'Stonetown' for its 19th-century limestone buildings. At the pretty **Westover Inn** (*see below*), the quarry that provided the stone is now Canada's largest outdoor swimming pool.

Gallery Stratford
54 Romeo Street S, Stratford (519 271 5271/ www.gallerystratford.on.ca). **Open** Tue-Sun; hours vary. Closed 2wks Dec/Jan. **Admission** $5; $4 concessions; free under-12s. **Credit** MC, V.

Where to eat & drink

Stratford boasts some excellent restaurants and its gastronomic reputation is bolstered by the Stratford Chefs School (68 Nile Street, 519 271 1414), which has trained many culinary stars.

Rundles always makes top ten lists of the best restaurants in Canada; it overlooks the park and river. **Church** serves up divine dishes in a deconsecrated building; eat under a vaulted ceiling or upstairs in the more casual Belfry. The cosy **Old Prune** is a favourite with theatre fans; those in the know ask for a table in the sun room. **Balzac's Coffee** has the best latte in Stratford, while sleek **Pazzo Ristorante** serves high-end Italian food upstairs and great pizza downstairs. Festival actors favour **Down the Street**, a friendly bar with good food. The budget-conscious opt for **York Street Kitchen** (take-out fare for riverside picnics) and **Boomers Gourmet Fries** (superior fish and chips). For all venues, always book ahead.

In St Marys, **Westover Inn** (*see above*) serves specialities using such local ingredients as cheese and pork in its attractive dining room.

Balzac's Coffee
149 Ontario Street, Stratford (519 273 7909/ www.balzacscoffee.com). **Open** Summer 7am-8pm daily. Winter 7am-9pm daily. **Credit** V.

Boomers Gourmet Fries
26 Erie Street, Stratford (519 275 3147). **Open** hours vary. **Main courses** $5-$10. **No credit cards**.

Church
70 Brunswick Street, Stratford (519 273 3424/ www.churchrestaurant.com). **Open** Mid Mar-Dec 11.30am-1am Tue-Sat; 11am-1.30pm, 5-8.30pm Sun. **Main courses** $29-$44. **Credit** AmEx, DC, MC, V.

Down the Street
30 Ontario Street, Stratford (519 273 5886). **Open** Summer 5pm-1am Mon; 11.30am-1am Tue-Sun. Winter 11.30am-1am Thur-Sat. **Main courses** $18-$25. **Credit** AmEx, MC, V.

Old Prune
151 Albert Street, Stratford (519 271 5052/www. oldprune.on.ca). **Open** Mid May-mid Oct 5-7.45pm Tue; 11.30am-1pm, 5-9pm Wed-Sat; 11.30am-1pm, 5-7.45pm Sun. **Main courses** Lunch $9.50-$30. **Set dinner** $68.50. **Credit** AmEx, MC, V.

Pazzo Ristorante
70 Ontario Street, Stratford (519 273 6666/www. pazzo.ca). **Open** Summer 11.30am-12.30pm daily. Winter 11.30am-10pm Tue-Thur; 11.30am-11pm Fri, Sat. **Main courses** $10-$27. **Credit** AmEx, MC, V.

Rundles
9 Cobourg Street, Stratford (519 271 6442). **Open** Late May-mid October 5-7pm Tue; 5-8.30pm Wed-Fri; 11.30am-1.15pm, 5-8.30pm Sat; 11.30am-1.15pm, 5-7pm Sun. **Set dinner** $67.50-$79.50. **Credit** AmEx, MC, V.

Westover Inn
300 Thomas Street, St Marys (519 284 2977). **Open** 7.30-10.30am, 11.30am-2pm, 5-8pm Mon-Thur, Sun; 7.30-10.30am, 11.30am-2pm, 5-8.30pm Fri, Sat. **Main courses** $19-$54. **Credit** AmEx, MC, V.

York Street Kitchen
41 York Street, Stratford (519 273 7041). **Open** Summer 8am-8pm daily. Winter 8am-3pm daily. **Main courses** $7-$14. **Credit** AmEx, MC, V.

Tourist information

St Marys Tourist Information
5 St James Street N, St Marys (1-800 769 7668/ www.townofstmarys.com). **Open** 8.30am-4.30pm Mon-Fri.

Stratford Festival
55 Queen Street, Stratford (1-800 567 1600/ 519 271 4040/www.stratfordfestival.ca). **Season** late Apr-early Nov. **Tours** year-round; phone for details. **Tickets** $45-$100; $24-$50 concessions. **Credit** AmEx, MC, V.

Tourism Stratford
47 Downie Street, Stratford (1-800 561 7926/ 519 271 5140/www.city.stratford.on.ca). **Open** 8.30am-4.30pm Mon-Fri.

Getting there

By bus
Greyhound bus service runs throughout the day from the main bus terminal in Toronto (610 Bay Street, 1-800 661 8747, 416 594 1010, www.greyhound.ca).

By car
From Toronto, drive west along Highway 401, turn north on Highway 8 to Kitchener-Waterloo, then follow signs west to Stratford along Highway 7/8.

By rail
VIA Rail trains to both Stratford and St Marys (1-888 842 7245, www.viarail.ca) operate from Toronto's Union Station.

DISCOVER MORE CITIES

Tell us what you think and you could win £100-worth of City Guides

Your opinions are important to us and we'd like to know what you like and what you don't like about the Time Out City Guides

For your chance to win, simply fill in our short survey at
timeout.com/guidesfeedback

Every month a reader will win £100 to spend on the Time Out City Guides of their choice – a great start to discovering new cities and you'll have extra cash to enjoy your trip!

Directory

Directory

Getting Around

By air

Lester B Pearson International Airport

Terminal 1 416 247 7678; Terminal 3 416 776 5100; www.gtaa.com.

Pearson, around 25 kilometres (16 miles) north-west of downtown, is in the middle of a massive $4.4 billion reconstruction project designed to improve the airport's ability to cope with the rising number of passengers (projected to increase from 31 million in 2007 to 50 million by 2020). The latest addition to this sprawling complex opened in January 2007. Terminal 1's Pier F replaces Terminal 2 (which is why Toronto has a terminal 1 and 3 but no longer a 2). The LINK shuttle connects the two terminals with a long-term parking lot. Terminal 1 is for Air Canada's domestic and international flights, and a number of foreign airlines. Terminal 3 is home to charters, some European airlines and some American carriers. All passengers are currently charged an airport improvement fee; the fee – $15 for passengers departing from the airport, $8 for passengers making connecting flights – is included in your ticket price.

The best way to get to Pearson by bus is the Pacific Western Airport Express (1-800 387 6787, www.torontoairportexpress.com). Buses and vans pick up and drop off passengers at many downtown hotels and the Greyhound bus terminal every 30 minutes from 4am to 2pm and 10pm to 1am, and every 20 minutes from 2pm to 10pm. The trip takes 20-40 minutes, depending on where you get on and the time of day, and costs $16.95 one way or $29.25 return. Seniors and students with valid ID get a ten per cent discount on one-way trips. Two children aged 11 and under per adult ride for free.

City buses also serve the airport, but the routes are long and circuitous, and there's nowhere to put your luggage. However, it is possible to get to the airport for the baseline TTC fare of $2.75. The designated 192 airport shuttle

runs from Kipling subway station between 5.20am and 2am; alternatively, take the No.58 from Lawrence subway station (departing every 15 minutes). The 307 Eglinton night bus will also get you to the airport and back; it runs between 1.30am and 5am.

If you want a quicker way to connect with the subway, the GO bus service runs between Terminals 1 and 3, and the Yorkdale and York Mills subway stations ($4.05 one-way).

Most taxi companies offer a flat rate to the airport of around $40. Confirm the price before you set off.

Toronto City Centre Airport

416 203 6942/www.torontoport.com. Map p270 C10/p271 D10.

Porter Airlines is the only commerical carrier operating from this downtown island airstrip, with services to Ottawa and Montreal, and some US cities in 2007. There is a free shuttle bus to and from Union Station to the foot of Bathurst Street, where passengers board a ferry for the two-minute crossing.

Major airlines

Air Canada *1-888 247 2262/ www.aircanada.ca.*
Air France *416 922 5024/ www.airfrance.com.*
American Airlines *1-800 433 7300/www.aa.com.*
America West Airlines *1-800 235 9292/www.americawest.com.*
British Airways *416 250 0880/ www.britishairways.com.*
Continental Airlines *1-800 784 4444/www.continental.com.*
Delta Air Lines *1-800 221 1212/ www.delta.com.*
Northwest Airlines *1-800 441 1818/www.nwa.com.*
Porter Airlines *1-888-619-8622/www.flyporter.com.*
United Airlines *1-800 241 6522/ www.united.com.*
US Airways *1-800 943 5436/ www.usairways.com.*

By bus

Greyhound Canada (416 594 1010, 1-800 661 8747, www.greyhound.ca) runs

many routes to Toronto from other parts of Canada and the US. The main terminal is located centrally at 610 Bay Street, at Dundas Street, Downtown, and is open from 5am to 1am daily. Note that arrivals come in to the smaller terminal directly across Elizabeth Street from the main terminal.

By rail

VIA Rail trains (general enquiries 1-888 842 7245, www.viarail.ca) operate from Union Station (65 Front Street W, at University Avenue), which is on the Yonge-University-Spadina subway line. The phone number for enquiries about VIA Rail trains from the station is 416 366 8411. In addition to setting off on the three-day journey westwards to Vancouver, you can board VIA trains for Ottawa, Montreal and the Maritimes. You can also get to New York City and Chicago (12hrs to both). Tickets are available at most travel agents in Canada or the US. In the UK, contact Thomas Cook Signature (0870 443 4442, www.tcsignature.com).

Toronto has an efficient and easy-to-use public transport service run by the Toronto Transit Commission (TTC) (www.toronto.ca/ttc). In the central Toronto area frequent subway services, buses and streetcars ply the major arteries.

Directory

Subway services generally start around 6am Monday to Saturday, and the last train runs at around 1.30am. On Sundays, service starts at about 9am and ends near 1am. Buses and streetcars generally run from 6am to midnight or 1am daily. The Blue Night Network of buses, identified by a blue stripe on the kerbside sign, takes over at night. The 320 Yonge Blue Night bus traces the route of the Yonge subway line and runs all night. It can often get rowdy with drunken passengers, and for this reason it is known by locals as 'the Vomit Comet', but the mood on board is generally friendly.

If you need to transfer from one mode of transport to another, be sure to obtain a transfer/proof of purchase when you start your trip. They're available from the red machines in subway stations or from the streetcar or bus driver. If you leave it too long before starting the second stage of your journey, TTC staff may not accept the transfer ticket, though it's a rather ad hoc system. You're supposed to take the next connecting vehicle, but locals often dash into a shop between legs of a commute.

The TTC takes safety seriously. Subway trains have alarms in every car,

and there is a Designated Waiting Area on each platform that is brightly lit and has a 'push for help' button. This is also the spot where the conductor's car always stops. On the platforms there is a lever that stops the power on the subway trains, in the event that someone falls onto the tracks. Women using buses between 9pm and 5am can ask to get off between stops to minimise the walk to their final destination.

TTC INFORMATION

Call 416 393 4636 or visit www.city.toronto.on.ca/ttc. Network maps are free from all subway-station offices.

FARES AND TICKETS

The cash fare for adults is $2.75. Travellers aged 65 and older, or students under 19 pay $1.85 (with photo ID); under-12s pay 70¢ for a one-way trip; kids aged two and under travel free. Subway fare collectors can give change, but it's exact fare only on streetcars and buses (pay on board for both).

Fares are cheaper if you buy tickets or tokens in bulk. Adults can buy five for $10.50 or ten for $21. Five senior or student tickets are $7 and ten $14 (again, take photo ID), and ten children's tickets are $4.70. Tokens are available only at

subway stations, while tickets are sold at convenience and other stores.

If you're going to be covering a lot of ground, your best bet is a day pass for $8.55, allowing unlimited travel from 9.30am Monday to Friday, and all day on Saturday and Sunday. The same pass, for the same price, can be used for groups of up to six, with no more than two adults, for unlimited travel on Sundays and public holidays.

A monthly pass gives you unlimited travel at any time. It's $99.75 for adults or $83.75 for seniors and students, but can only be purchased between the 24th of the month and the fourth business day of the following month.

Subway

There are four main subway lines. The Bloor–Danforth line runs from Kipling Station in the west to Kennedy Station in the east. The north–south line is divided into two parallel arms – the Yonge line, which runs from Union Station to Finch Station, and the University–Spadina line, which runs from Union Station to Downsview Station. The fourth line runs east–west along Sheppard Avenue, from Yonge-Sheppard Station to Don Mills Station on the north

US passport regulations

As part of the programme to tighten border security, the US now requires visitors who are nationals of Visa Waiver Program (VWP) countries to present a machine-readable passport in order to be admitted to the country. VWP countries include the UK, Australia and New Zealand. Machine-readable passports contain either a magnetic strip or barcode. The standard-issue EC/EU maroon passport is machine-readable. Each traveller needs their own passport, which must be valid for at least a further six months.

Passports issued to VWP travellers on or after 26 October 2005 must contain biometric data and, for the purposes of US border officials, index finger prints and a digital photo.

If you intend to make a trip across the US border once in Canada, check the situation before you travel at www.travel.state.gov/visa (click on 'temporary visas').

As of January 2007, Canadian citizens require a passport to enter the United States by air.

side. (Don't be fooled into thinking there is something to see up there just because there's a subway – aside from a nearby IKEA and a hospital, it's mostly suburban housing.)

The major transfer points between these east–west and north–south lines are Bloor-Yonge, St George and Yonge-Sheppard stations, where the lines connect, with platforms linked by stairs. You don't need a transfer to change subway trains.

Bus

Bus stops are marked by red- and-white poles or bus shelters, and are often just before an intersection. Many – but not all – shelters have route timetables posted. Generally, buses arrive every 10-30 minutes. Currently around ten per cent of Toronto's current fleet are so-called 'kneeling' buses, which allow for easier access for the elderly and disabled; all new buses introduced are of this type.

Streetcars

Toronto's streetcars are the best way to get around the city. Because many run on rail tracks in dedicated central lanes, they usually run to schedule. And they evoke a feeling of nostalgia – romance even. Conveniently for visitors, many of the main central arteries – Queen, College, Dundas, King and Spadina – are served by streetcars (whose numbers start with a 5). Most of the streetcars start downtown, but many journey into the outer edges of town. For visiting areas such as the Beaches, Roncesvalles Village, Parkdale, or Little India, you will almost certainly have to use the streetcar to get there, as they are not served by subway lines.

To take the streetcar, wait at the stop (they look the same as bus stops) and cross in front of stopped cars to board by the front door. Sometimes you'll need to look for a shelter in the middle of the road, especially along the 510 Spadina route. (Passengers who have a transfer or pass may board by the back door along the busy 501 Queen line only – you must use the front door on all other lines.) To disembark, step down into the stairwell and push open the doors using the bars. Cars are supposed to stop well behind streetcar doors but it's always a good idea to look right before getting out. Streetcars are not wheelchair accessible.

Rail

The Scarborough Rapid Transit line is a suburban above-ground extension of the Bloor–Danforth subway line that most visitors only see en route to the Toronto Zoo. GO Transit, the province-run company, runs a commuter rail network, but it's of little use to visitors.

Water transport

The city operates ferries from Harbourfront to Centre Island (summer only), Hanlan's Point and Wards Island. Call 416 392 8193 for schedule information or visit www.city.toronto. on.ca/parks/to_islands/ferry. htm. Return fares are $6 for adults; $3.50 for seniors (65 and older) and under-19 students; $2.50 for under-15s; kids aged two and under go free. The ferry terminal is at the foot of Bay Street, at Queens Quay W, by the Westin Harbour Castle. Ferries generally run from 6.30am to midnight daily at 30-minute to 2.5-hour intervals, but services change depending on the

season and the weather. In the summer, a trip on the ferry is a Toronto tradition and a wonderful way to cool off. Always call ahead, and be careful not to miss the last boat back.

Taxis

Toronto taxis operate under a standard system of fees and rights as set out by the city. The meter starts at $3 and increases by 25¢ for every 0.19km (0.12 miles) driven or 31 seconds of waiting. As in any city, check the meter has been reset when you get into the cab.

Drivers are not allowed to recommend restaurants or hotels to you unless you make a request, and they must follow any route you suggest or otherwise take the most direct route.

If you think you have left an item of property in a taxi, call the company directly.
Beck Taxi *416 751 5555.*
CO-OP Cabs *416 504 2667.*
Crown Taxi *416 750 7878.*
Diamond Taxicab *416 366 6868.*
Royal Taxi *416 777 9222.*
Yellow Cab *416 504 4141.*

The taxi complaints line is 1-877 868 2947 and it operates 24 hours daily.

Driving

As with most big North American cities, you should avoid having to drive in central Toronto if you can help it. During morning and afternoon rush hours especially, jams are long and tedious, and public transport or your own two feet will always get you where you're going quicker.

You need to be at least 16 years old and have a valid licence from your home country to drive in Toronto. The speed limit is generally 50kmph (about 31mph), while the major highways are 80kmph (50mph) to 100kmph (62mph). While you can drive close to 120kmph (75mph) on the major 400-series highways to keep up with the pace of traffic without getting a ticket, don't try that on city streets. Police enforce speed limits strictly, especially in marked school zones where the limit is reduced to 40kmph (24mph). In Toronto, it's legal to make a right turn on a red light (unless the signs say otherwise) if you first come to a full stop.

As in most cities, drivers are required to stop for school buses picking up and dropping off passengers. You must stop for a school bus on either side of the road unless you're on a divided highway, and you should also stop for streetcars picking up passengers. It's illegal to drive around one, and you'll not only get a ticket but also run the risk of getting an earful from disgruntled commuters.

Pedestrians always have the right of way at crosswalks, which have painted markings and a string of lights, but they can be tricky to spot in congested areas.

Breakdown services

Canadian Automobile Association

461 Yonge Street, at Carlton Street, Church & Wellesley (416 221 4300/ emergencies 416 222 5222/www. caa.ca). **Open** 8.30am-6pm Mon-Fri; 9.30am-4pm Sat. *Emergency line* 24hrs daily. **Map** p275 G5. Breakdown services for members and members of reciprocal organisations, depending on plan. **Other locations**: throughout the city.

Fuel stations

Esso

241 Church Street, at Dundas Street, Dundas Square (416 703 4556/1-800 567 3776/www.imperialoil.ca). **Open** 6am-midnight daily. **Credit** AmEx, MC, V. **Other locations**: throughout the city.

Petro-Canada

55 Spadina Avenue, at King Street W, Entertainment District (416 977 3653/1-800 668 0220/www.petro-canada.ca). **Open** 24hrs daily. **Credit** AmEx, MC, V. **Map** p271 D7. **Other locations**: throughout the city.

Parking

Parking rates are steep. You'll pay as much as $4 for half an hour or $20 for a day of parking in a privately run downtown lot. City-operated lots are a little less expensive at $3 an hour (look for the green 'P' emblem).

Parking on most major city streets is illegal without feeding a nearby meter (costing between $1 and $3 an hour), and parking enforcement officers are ever vigilant. Downtown streets have either single-space meters or pay-and-display machines that cover multiple spaces on one block. Meters and machines take take coins and many take credit cards, but keep a collection of loonies ($1), toonies ($2) and quarters handy. Street parking privileges are withdrawn during rush hour on busy roads, usually 7-9am and 3.30-6.30pm. On residential side streets uptown, one-hour parking is usually free, but even these streets are monitored by officers.

Vehicle hire

You must be 21 or over to rent a car in Ontario. Rental companies will offer you accident and collision insurance and, although it may seem expensive, you'd be wise to take it if not covered by your own policy.

Alamo

920 Yonge Street, at Davenport Road, Yorkville (416 935 1533/ 1-800 462 5266/www.alamo.com). Subway Bloor-Yonge. **Open** 7am-9pm Mon-Fri; 7am-6pm Sat; 9am-5pm Sun. **Credit** AmEx, MC, V. **Map** p275 G3.

Budget

556 St Clair Avenue W, at Bathurst Street, Forest Hill (416 651 0020/ 1-800 561 5212/www.budget toronto.com). Subway St Clair. **Open** 8am-6pm Mon-Fri; 8am-4pm Sat. **Credit** AmEx, MC, V. **Other locations**: throughout the city.

Discount Car & Truck Rentals

243 Danforth Avenue, at Broadview Avenue, East Side (416 465 8776/ 1-866 310 2277/www.discountcar. com). Streetcar 504, 505/subway Broadview. **Open** 8am-6pm Mon-Fri; 8am-4pm Sat. **Credit** AmEx, MC, V. **Other locations**: throughout the city.

Enterprise Rent-a-Car

700 Bay Street, at Gerrard Street, Chinatown (416 599 1375/1-800 736 8222/www.enterprise.com). Bus 6/streetcar 506/subway College. **Open** 7.30am-6pm Mon-Fri; 9am-noon Sat. **Credit** AmEx, MC, V. **Map** p271/p272 F6. **Other locations**: throughout the city.

Cycling

Experienced city cyclists will find Toronto a doddle, with easy navigation and about 59 kilometres (37 miles) of bike lanes. But you need street smarts, and accidents are a regular occurrence. For details of city bike programmes, call 416 392 9253 or go to www.toronto. ca/cycling. *See also p213.*

Walking

For off-street strolls, take a self-guided Discovery Walk through parks and points of interest – contact the Parks and Recreation department (www.toronto.ca/parks).

A useful map is 'The *OTHER* Map of Toronto', which guides you through green sights – available free at Tourism Toronto (*see p257*) and the TOTIX booth in Yonge-Dundas Square. We've also included street maps of central Toronto at the back of this book (*pp265-275*).

Directory

Resources A-Z

Addresses

Addresses in Toronto are pretty straightforward as most of the central city is arranged on a grid. Generally, street numbers start at 0 at Lake Ontario and increase as you head north. Even-numbered addresses are on the west side and odd numbers on the east side of all north–south streets. Similarly, even-numbered addresses are on the north side and odd numbers on the south side of east–west streets. The east and west designation of streets running east–west changes at Yonge Street.

Throughout this guide, we give the nearest cross street within each listing, though the venue is not always right on the corner itself.

Age restrictions

To drink and purchase alcohol in Ontario, and to buy tobacco products, you must be 19. Note that fines for buying tobacco for minors are steep. To drive a car or truck, you must be 16 or over (21 to hire one).

The age of consent for heterosexual sex, according to Canada's Criminal Code, is 14, or 18 if one party is in a position of legal authority over the other. The age of consent for gay sex in Ontario is also 14 (18 in most other parts of the country).
See also p252 **ID**.

Business

For copy shops, *see p164.*

Conventions & conferences

International Centre
6900 Airport Road, at Derry Road, North End (905 677 6131/www. internationalcentre.com). Subway Lawrence West then bus 58B.

Metro Toronto Convention Centre
255 Front Street W, at John Street, Entertainment District (416 585 8000/www.mtccc.com). Streetcar 504/subway St Andrew or Union. Map p271 E8.

Couriers & shippers

FedEx
215 Lake Shore Boulevard E, at Sherbourne Street, Waterfront (1-800 463 3339/www.fedex.ca). Bus 75. **Open** 9am-10pm Mon-Fri; noon-5pm Sat. **Credit** AmEx, MC, V. **Map** p272 H9.

Purolator Courier
335 Bay Street, at Adelaide Street, Financial District (1-888 744 7123/ www.purolator.com). Streetcar 504/Subway King. **Open** 8am-9pm Mon-Fri. **Credit** AmEx, MC, V. **Map** p271/p272 F7.

Quick Messenger Service
296 Richmond Street W, at John Street, Entertainment District (416 368 1623/www.qms-tor.com). Streetcar 501, 504. **Open** 7.30am-6.30pm Mon-Fri. **No credit cards**. **Map** 271 D7.

Secretarial services

BBW International
2336 Bloor Street W, at Windermere Avenue, West End (416 767 3036/ www.bbwinternational.com). **Enquiries** 9am-5pm Mon-Fri. **No credit cards**.
This is the mailing address only; call to make an appointment.

Translators & interpreters

ABCO International Translators & Interpreters
330 Bay Street, at Adelaide Street W, Financial District (416 359 0873). Streetcar 504. **Open** 9am-5pm Mon-Fri. **No credit cards**. **Map** p271/p272 F7.

Consumer

Ontario has strong consumer-protection laws. To lodge a complaint against a business, contact the Ontario Ministry of Consumer & Business Services, General Inquiry Unit (416 326 8800, www.cbs.gov. on.ca). Or call 211 on the phone or visit (www.211toronto.ca).

Customs

Canadian customs regulations allow you to bring the following into the country without paying tax: 200 cigarettes or 50 cigars, plus 1.5 litres of wine, 1.14 litres of liquor or 24 cans of beer.

You are prohibited from carrying firearms, weapons (including knives of any sort), drugs, endangered species (plant or animal) and cultural property (as in antiquities).

Contact Canada Customs & Immigration for details (1-204 983 3500 outside Canada; 1-800 461 9999 in Canada, www.ccra-adrc.gc.ca).

UK Customs & Excise (www.hmce.gov.uk) allows returning travellers to bring home £145 worth of gifts and goods and any sum of money they can prove is theirs. US Customs (www.customs. ustreas.gov) allows Americans to return home from Canada with US$800 worth of gifts and goods duty-free.

Disabled

Toronto is fairly well equipped for the disabled, with accessible buses and public buildings. Many restaurants and shops are also accessible, but it's best to call ahead. On the street, the vast majority of kerbs are dropped at an intersection, enabling easy wheelchair access.

Note that not all subway stations and city buses are wheelchair-equipped, and that streetcars are not wheelchair-accessible. **Wheel-Trans** (416 393 4111, www.toronto. ca/ttc) provides door-to-door services at normal TTC rates. VIA Rail (*see p246*) and most long-distance bus companies can accommodate wheelchair users with enough notice. Many car rental agencies

Directory

(*see p249*) have disabled-adapted cars, though you'll need to book well in advance. **Kino Mobility** (416 635 5873, 1-888 495 4455, www.kino mobility.com) has various specially adapted vehicles. Vans are available for able-bodied drivers at $125 a day. Discounts apply for longer than five-day rentals.

The website www.enable link.org is an online guide to accessible locations in Ontario.

Drugs

Drug offences are taken very seriously in Canada, so avoid the use of narcotics while in the country. Though the use of medicinal marijuana is legal for those individuals who have applied for access (see www.medicalmarihuana. ca), don't expect authorities to turn a blind eye if you light up.

Electricity

Just like the United States, Canada uses 110-volt electric power with two- or three-pin plugs. Visitors from the UK and Europe will need adaptors, available at most hotels and department stores, to use their appliances from home.

Embassies & consulates

American Consulate General
360 University Avenue, at Dundas St W, University (416 595 1700). Subway Osgoode or St Patrick. **Open** 8.30am-1pm Mon-Fri.
Australian Consulate General
Suite 1100, south tower, 175 Bloor Street E, at Jarvis Street, Church & Wellesley (416 323 1155). Subway Sherbourne. **Open** 9am-1pm, 2-4.30pm Mon-Fri. **Map** p275 G4.
British Consulate-General
777 Bay Street, at College Street, University (416 593 1290). Subway College/streetcar 506. **Open** 9am-4pm Mon-Fri. **Map** p271/p272 F5.
Consulate General of Ireland
20 Toronto Street, at King Street E, St Lawrence (416 366 9300). Streetcar 501. **Open** 10am-4pm Mon-Fri. **Map** p272 G7/G8.

New Zealand Consulate
Suite 2A, 225 MacPherson Avenue, at Avenue Road, Midtown (416 947 9696). Bus 5/subway St George. **Open** 8am-4.30pm Mon-Fri. **Map** p274 F2.
South African Consulate
2 Bloor Street W, at Yonge Street, Yorkville (416 944 8825). Subway Bloor-Yonge. **Open** 8am-4.30pm Mon-Fri. **Map** p275 G4.

Emergencies

If you require emergency assistance from police, firefighters or medical services, call 911. It's free from all phones.

For hospitals, *see p252* **Health**. For other emergency numbers, *see p252* **Helplines** and *p255* **Police stations**.
Poison Information Centre
416 813 5900.

Gay & lesbian

Toronto is a very gay-friendly city. You can freely hold hands or kiss your partner in the Church & Wellesley neighbourhood or even on Queen Street West, but play it cool elsewhere, especially in the suburbs. Toronto is a tolerant city, but gay-bashing is not unheard of. From a gay perspective, the best time to visit is during Pride Week, held the last week of June.

For details of gay-friendly accommodation, *see p195*.

Help & information

For HIV/AIDS information, *see p252* **Health**.
519 Church Street Community Centre
519 Church Street, at Dundonald Street, Church & Wellesley (416 392 6874/www.the519.org). Subway Wellesley. **Open** 9am-10pm Mon-Fri; 9am-5.30pm Sat; 10am-5pm Sun. **Map** p275 G5.
Gay Bashing Reporting Line
416 392 6878 ext 337.
Lesbian Gay Bi Trans Youth Line
416 962 9688. **Open** 4-9.30pm Sun-Fri.
Trained youth volunteers provide support for callers under the age of 27 and information on groups.

Health

Accident & emergency

If you need immediate medical attention, dial 911 (free) from any phone.

If you need medical information but it's not an emergency, call **Telehealth Ontario** on 1-866 797 0000. Registered nurses take calls 24 hours a day, seven days a week, and can help diagnose your problem over the phone.

Travel advice

For up-to-date information on travel to a specific country – including the latest news on safety and security, health issues, local laws and customs – contact your home country government's department of foreign affairs. Most have websites packed with useful advice for would-be travellers.

Australia
www.smartraveller.gov.au

New Zealand
www.safetravel.govt.nz

Canada
www.voyage.gc.ca

UK
www.fco.gov.uk/travel

Republic of Ireland
http://foreignaffairs.gov.ie

USA
http://travel.state.gov

Directory

They can't send out prescriptions but can refer you to a pharmacy and help decide if you need hospital attention. The service is free, and provides help in English and French, with translation for 110 other languages.

To contact the police in a non-emergency situation, call 416 808 2222.

See also below **Insurance**.

Contraception & abortion

Hassle Free Clinic
66 Gerrard Street E, at Church Street, Church & Wellesley (416 922 0566 women; 416 922 0603/www.hasslefreeclinic. org). Streetcar 505/subway Dundas. **Open** call for hours. **Map** p272 G6.
Planned Parenthood of Toronto
36B Prince Arthur Avenue, Yorkville (416 961 0113/www.ppt. on.ca). Subway Bay or Museum. **Open** 9am-4.30pm Mon, Tue, Thur, Fri; 9am-noon Wed. **Map** p272 D4.

Dentists

For emergency dental service, contact **Dental Emergency Clinic** (1650 Yonge Street, at St Clair Avenue, Midtown, 416 485 7121, 8am-noon daily).
Ontario Dental Association
416 922 3900/www.dental.oda.on.ca. This organisation can supply information about local dentists.

Doctors

College of Physicians & Surgeons of Ontario
416 967 2603/www.cpso.on.ca. For references to local doctors.

Hospitals

The hospitals listed below all have emergency wards open 24 hours daily.
Hospital for Sick Children
555 University Avenue, at Gerrard Street E, Chinatown (416 813 1500). Streetcar 506/subway St Patrick. **Map** p271/p272 F6.
Mount Sinai Hospital
600 University Avenue, at College Street, University (416 586 4800). Streetcar 506/subway Queen's Park. **Map** p271/p272 F5.
North York General Hospital

4001 Leslie Street, at Sheppard Avenue E, North Toronto (416 756 6000). Subway Leslie.
St Joseph's Health Centre
30 The Queensway, at Roncesvalles Avenue, West End (416 530 6000). Streetcar 504.
St Michael's Hospital
30 Bond Street, at Queen Street E, Dundas Square (416 360 4000). Streetcar 501/subway Dundas or Queen. **Map** p272 G7.
Sunnybrook Health Science Centre
2075 Bayview Avenue, at Lawrence Avenue E, Don Mills (416 480 4207/ www.sunnybrook.ca). Bus 11, 124.
Toronto East General Hospital
825 Coxwell Avenue, at Mortimer Avenue, East Side (416 461 8272). Subway Coxwell.
Toronto General Hospital
200 Elizabeth Street, at University Avenue, Chinatown (416 340 3111). Subway Queen's Park. **Map** p271/p272 F6.
Toronto Western Hospital
399 Bathurst Street, at Dundas Street W, Chinatown (416 603 2581). Streetcar 505, 511. **Map** p270 C6/p271 D6.

Opticians

See p161.

Pharmacies & prescriptions

Pharmacies are allowed to set their own dispensing fee, an extra $6 to $14 on top of your drugs cost. The cheapest drugs are available from department stores such as Zellers (www.hbc.com/zellers) or Wal-Mart (1-800 328 0402).

Pharmacies are ubiquitous in Toronto. Most open between 9am and 10am and close between 10pm and midnight, though some open 24 hours a day. For locations, contact Shoppers Drug Mart (1-800 746 7737, www.shoppersdrug mart.ca); *see also p161.*

STDs, HIV & AIDS

AIDS Committee of Toronto
4th Floor, 399 Church Street, at Carlton Street, Church & Wellesley (416 340 2437/www.actoronto.org). Streetcar 506/subway College. **Open** 10am-9pm Mon-Thur; 10am-5pm Fri. **Map** p272 G6.

Alcoholics Anonymous
416 487 5591/www.aatoronto.org.
Assaulted Women's Helpline
416 863 0511/www.awhl.org. Crisis counselling and support, shelter referrals, legal advice.
Distress Centres of Toronto
416 408 4357. Trained volunteers are available 24 hours daily for people who need to talk or are feeling suicidal.
Kids Help Phone
1-800 668 6868/ www.kidshelpphone.ca.
Narcotics Anonymous
416 236 8956/www.torontona.org.
Toronto Rape Crisis Centre
416 597 8808.
Victim Support Line
416 325 3265. Practical advice on what to do if you are the victim of a crime.

ID

You must be 19 or older to buy tobacco products, and most corner stores will ask for photo ID if you look 25 or younger.

Carding is rare in gay bars but more common in straight bars and (especially) clubs, so carry some photo ID with you.

Insurance

Canada does not provide health or medical services to visitors for free, so travel and health insurance is a must. Hospitals and walk-in clinics will want the name of your insurer and policy number, so be sure to keep them handy.

Internet

Toronto hotels usually provide sockets in rooms for laptop users (though speed varies, and at some a charge is levied); some rooms have wireless access. In cheaper hotels access may only be via consoles in the lobby. Public access is available at public libraries and many cafés. For library locations, contact the Toronto Reference Library (416 393 7131; *see also below*).

For a few useful Toronto websites, see p258 **Further reference**.

Bell Sympatico
416 310 7873/www.sympatico.ca. A reliable, reasonably priced internet service provider that offers dial-up or DSL connections.

Insomnia Internet Bar/Café
563 Bloor Street W, at Bathurst Street, The Annex (416 588 3907/www.insomniacafe.com). Streetcar 511/subway Bathurst. **Open** 4pm-2am Mon-Fri; 10am-2am Sat, Sun. **Credit** AmEx, DC, MC, V. **Map** p272 C3.

Language

English is the main language used in Toronto, although with such a multicultural population, you're likely to hear everything from Mandarin to Punjabi on the streets. Though Canada is officially a bilingual country, business and services are conducted largely in English.

Common expressions lean towards the US with a few UK remnants. You'd get in the line-up to order food to go (put the wrapper in the garbage), or ask for the bill. You may need to visit the washroom. You fill your car with gas at a gas station, put your luggage in the trunk and may need to look under the hood.

Left luggage

There are lockers at Terminals 1 and 3 at Lester B Pearson International Airport (see p246), and at the downtown Greyhound terminal (see p246), but there are none at City Centre Airport or Union Station (though if you're travelling via VIA Rail you can check bags in for same-day pick up).

Legal help

If you run into legal trouble, contact your insurers or your national consulate (see p251).

Libraries

Toronto Reference Library
789 Yonge Street, at Cumberland Street, Yorkville (416 393 7131/www.tpl.toronto.on.ca). Subway Bloor-Yonge. **Open** 9.30am-8.30pm Mon-Thur; 9.30am-5.30pm Fri; 9am-5pm Sat; 1.30-5pm Sun. Closed Sundays in summer. **Map** p275 G4. Unlike all the other branches in the city, you can't sign books out from the Reference Library. Check the website for other library branches.

Lost property

Airports

Report lost luggage claims to your airline immediately. If you've lost property in the airport itself, call 416 776 7750 (Terminal 1) or 416 776 4816 (Terminal 3). For City Centre Airport, call 416 203 6942.

Public transport

All lost property found on subways, buses and streetcars ends up at Bay Station, at Bloor Street West and Bay Street. You may visit the Lost & Found office in person 8am-5pm Mon-Fri or call 416 393 4100 (noon-5pm Mon-Fri).

Taxis

Call the company itself (for a list, see p247).

Media

Where many big cities in North America are now one-newspaper towns, Toronto boasts four big dailies: the Toronto Star, the Globe and Mail, the Toronto Sun and the National Post.

Newspapers & magazines

Dailies and monthlies
Globe and Mail
The Globe and Mail is considered the paper of record for the country, a sort of New York Times-lite. Strong arts and business coverage.

Metro/Toronto 24 Hours
Two freebie commuter tabloids that offer news in bite-sized bits.
National Post
A right-leaning rival to the Globe and Mail, launched by Conrad Black and now owned by Canwest Media.
Toronto Life
A monthly glossy catering to Toronto's expanding bourgeoisie. Its listings are good for planning ahead.
Toronto Star
The Star is Canada's biggest daily paper. It's small 'l' liberal in outlook, claims to defend the working stiff and covers city news well. The 'What's On' section on Thursdays is good for planning your weekend.
Toronto Sun
'The little paper that could' is a feisty, conservative tabloid rag.

Alternative papers
NOW and eye are free weeklies that come out on Thursday. NOW is more granola and eye hipper to the downtown music scene. Both have extensive entertainment listings. You'll find them in street boxes and pubs, cafés and stores.
Xtra! and Fab compete on the gay scene. They come out every two weeks on alternating Thursdays. Other freebies include Exclaim! (www.exclaim.ca), which covers the indie music scene every month and can be found in bars downtown. Slate (www.slateartguide.com) is a free monthly listings guide to art shows, available in most galleries. WholeNote (www.thewholenote.com) is a free bi-monthly about the classical scene, new music and jazz. Word (www.wordmag.com) covers the urban music scene and is available ten times a year at music and Caribbean shops.

Foreign-language press
Pick a country, and there's probably a Toronto-based publication that caters to its expat community. Weekly papers can be had in French, German, Greek, Spanish, Ukrainian, Hindi and Malaysian, to name a few. The Portuguese community is served by a bi-weekly and papers appear daily in Italian and Korean; there are three daily newspapers in Chinese.
Newsstands carry lots of UK and US press, or try **Book City** (see p145) or **Maison de la Presse Internationale** (124 Yorkville Ave, Yorkville, 416 928 2328).

Radio & television

Radio
There are 33 radio stations (AM frequencies are difficult to tune to downtown because of interference

from office towers). Talk rules – in many tongues – on AM with all sports (**The Fan 590**), all news (**CFTR 680**), more talk (**CFRB 1010**) and oldies (**AM 740**, **1050 CHUM** and **KCOC 1150**).

Flick over to FM, where you'll find adult contemporary dominates on barely distinguishable services: **Jack Radio 92.5**, **EasyRock 97.3**, **CHFI 98.1**, **CKFM 99.9** and **CHUM FM 104.5**. Urban culture can be found on **Flow 93.5**. Classic rock blares on **Q107**, while **The Edge 102.1** tries to be just that, playing alternative rock. One interesting newcomer is **Aboriginal Voices Radio** on 106.5.

The CBC, the taxpayer-funded national service, doesn't draw the numbers in Toronto that it commands elsewhere. **Radio One** (99.1) is predominantly talk, with national shows that go in search of the Canadian identity blended with local and regional programmes. It's about the only place you'll hear new radio drama. The flagship current-affairs programme, *As It Happens*, is a much-loved national institution. **Radio 2** (94.1) plays light classics mixed with Cape Breton fiddlers and weekend jazz and opera. **CJBC** (90.3) is CBC's French service, with superb classical, jazz and contemporary music content. More classics are on the commercial **CFMX** (96.3), which has a penchant for waltzes. **Jazz FM** (91.1) is finding its way now that it runs commercials (it was previously funded by donations).

As is often the case, it is left to campus radio to push the frontiers of programming. Their wildly eclectic tastes make them unlistenable over long stretches, but dropping in on **CKLN** (88.1), **CIUT** (89.5) and **CHRY** (105.5) is certain to refresh.

Television

Toronto has entered the 500-channel universe. Speciality channels cater to niche tastes and generalised topics – history, golf, hockey, news, more news, food, home decor. But if you want a dose of mainstream Canadian TV, here are the best options: **CBC** (Channel 5) keeps Canadian content upfront along with strong news and sports coverage. **CTV** (Channel 9) is the largest private broadcaster and relies heavily on US programming, as does **Global TV** (Channel 6,41). **Citytv** (Channel 57) has shaped cultural coverage with intelligent shows on film, media, fashion and music. If you're hooking up a TV and want a cable package, contact local conglomerate Rogers (1-888-ROGERS1, www.rogers.com).

Money

Each dollar is made up of 100 cents. Coin denominations include the one-cent penny (copper in colour), the five-cent nickel (silver, featuring a beaver) the ten-cent dime (silver, with the *Bluenose* schooner depicted), the 25-cent quarter (which usually features a caribou, the one-dollar loonie (gold-bronze in colour) and the two-dollar toonie (two-tone nickel and aluminium with a polar bear). Notes, or bills, come in denominations of $5 (blue), $10 (purple), $20 (green), $50 (pink) and $100 (brown). Shops have recently begun refusing $50 and $100 bills because of counterfeit worries. In the last few years the Bank of Canada has changed the design of its $5, $10 and $20 bills, and it's still common to use both designs.

ATMs/ABMs

Known in Canada as ABMs (automatic bank machines), bank machines are ubiquitous. Your best bet is to use one operated by a major bank. Privately owned and operated machines are popping up in bars and shops, and while they may be handy, most charge an additional user fee of $2-$3.

Most ABMs are part of the Interac, Plus or Cirrus network, so non-Canadians shouldn't have any trouble accessing their home account. But check in advance with your bank to find out what the charge bands are.

Banks

CIBC
2 Bloor Street W, at Yonge Street, Yorkville (416 980 4430/www.cibc. com). Subway Bloor-Yonge. **Open** 8am-4pm Mon-Wed; 8am-5pm Thur, Fri; 10am-3pm Sat. **Map** p275 G4.
Other locations: throughout the city.
Royal Bank
200 Bay Street, at King Street, Financial District (416 974 3940/

www.royalbank.ca). Streetcar 504/ subway King. **Open** 9am-5pm Mon-Fri. **Map** p271/p272 F8.
Other locations: throughout the city.
Scotiabank
222 Queen Street W, at McCaul Street, Entertainment District (416 866 6591/www.scotiabank.ca). Streetcar 501/subway Osgoode. **Open** 10am-4pm Mon-Thur; 10am-5pm Fri. **Map** p271 E7.
Other locations: throughout the city.
TD Canada Trust
65 Wellesley Street E, at Church Street, Church & Wellesley (416 944 4135/www.tdcanadatrust.com). Bus 94/subway Wellesley. **Open** 9.30am-4pm Mon-Thur; 9.30am-5pm Fri. **Map** p275 G5.
Other locations: throughout the city.

Bureaux de change

Most bank branches have foreign exchange services.
Calforex
170 Bloor Street W, at University Avenue, Yorkville (416 921 4872/www.calforex.com). Subway Museum or St George. **Open** 8.30am-7pm Mon-Fri; 9am-6pm Sat; 10am-5pm Sun. **Map** p274 E3.

Credit cards

Most businesses in Toronto take Visa, MasterCard and American Express. You can make toll-free calls to report lost or stolen cards at the numbers below 24 hours a day, seven days a week:
American Express
1-800 668 2639.
Discover
1-801 902 3100 (long-distance call).
MasterCard
1-800 307 7309.
Visa
1-800 847 2911.

Tax

Most goods and services bought in Ontario are subject to two taxes – the six per cent federal Goods and Services Tax and the eight per cent Provincial Sales Tax. Both taxes are levied on just about everything you can imagine, other than books and most groceries, and even those are PST exempt only.

Visitors are eligible for a GST refund on goods and short-term accommodation. You must have spent at least $200 to qualify. For more information, contact the Visitor Rebate Program at 1-800 668 4748 (within Canada) or 1-902 432 5608 (outside Canada), or visit the Canada Customs and Revenue Agency website at www.ccra-adrc.gc.ca/visitors. Major shops will have information and claim forms on hand. Present these at the tax-refund booth at the airport for an immediate refund.

Opening hours

Shops tend to open at around 10am and close around 6pm. Many stay open till 9pm from June to August. Banks generally open 9am to 5pm during the week, while a few offer evening and weekend hours. Post offices generally open between 10am and 5pm Monday to Saturday.

Police stations

To report an emergency, dial 911. If it's not an emergency, call the police on 416 808 2222. Toronto Police Service headquarters is at 40 College Street, at Bay Street. See also www.torontopolice.on.ca.

Postal services

Mailing a standard-sized letter within Canada costs 51 cents for anything up to 30 grammes. Standard letters and postcards to the US cost 89¢ up to 30 grammes, and standard letters anywhere outside Canada and the US $1.49 up to 30 grammes and $2.05 for between 30 and 50 grammes. For couriers, *see p250*.

Post offices

Canada Post
260 Adelaide Street E, at George Street, St Lawrence, M5A 1N1
(416 865 1833/www.canadapost.ca). Streetcar 504. **Open** 9am-4pm Mon-Fri; 10am-4pm Sat, Sun. **No credit cards.** **Map** p272 G7.
Toronto's first post office – and one of its last. The days of the stand-alone post office are numbered here, so check pharmacies and corner stores for post-office counters (use the website to find addresses) and stamps.
Other locations: throughout the city.

Poste restante/ general delivery

If you want to receive mail while in Toronto, but don't have a permanent address, you can have it sent to you 'care of General Delivery' to any post office with a postal code. You must retrieve it within 15 days of it being received and show at least one piece of photo ID.

Religion

Anglican
Church of the Holy Trinity
10 Trinity Square, next to Toronto Eaton Centre, Dundas Square (416 598 4521/www.holytrinitytoronto.org). Streetcar 505/subway Dundas. **Services** 12.15pm Wed; 9am, 10.30am Sun. **Map** p271/p272 F7.

Baptist
Walmer Road Baptist Church
188 Lowther Avenue, at Spadina Avenue, The Annex (416 924 1121/www.walmer.ca). Streetcar 510/subway Spadina. **Service** 11am Sun. **Map** p272 C3.

Catholic
St Michael's Cathedral
65 Bond Street, at Shuter Street, Dundas Square (416 364 0234). Streetcar 505/subway Dundas. **Services** 7am, 8.30am, 12.10pm, 5.30pm Mon-Fri; 7am, 8.30am, 12.10pm, 5pm Sat; 8am, 9am, 10.30am, noon, 5pm, 9pm Sun. **Map** p272 G7.

Jewish
Adath Israel Congregation
37 Southbourne Avenue, at Bathurst Street, North Toronto (416 635 5340/www.adathisrael.com). Bus 7/subway Wilson. **Services** usually 7am, 8pm daily; call for details.

Lutheran
Redeemer Lutheran Church

1691 Bloor Street W, at Keele Street, West End (416 766 1424). Subway Keele. **Service** 11.15am Sun.

Metropolitan
Metropolitan Community Church of Toronto
115 Simpson Avenue, at Broadview Avenue, East Side (416 406 6228/www.mcctoronto.com). Streetcar 504, 505. **Service** 9am, 11am Sun. **Map** p273 K6.
A key player in the fight for gay marriage. Sunday services draw a gay-friendly congregation.

Muslim
Madina Masjid
1015 Danforth Avenue, at Donlands Avenue, East Side (416 465 7833). Subway Donlands. **Services** Prayers five times daily; call for details.

Pentecostal
Queensway Cathedral
1536 The Queensway, at Kipling Avenue, West End (416 255 0141/www.queenswaycathedral.com). Subway Kipling then bus 44. **Services** 10.30am, 6pm Sun.

Presbyterian
Knox Presbyterian Church
630 Spadina Avenue, at Harbord Street, Harbord (416 921 8993/www.knoxtoronto.org). Bus 94/streetcar 510. **Services** 11am, 7pm Sun. **Map** p276/p272 C5.

United
Metropolitan United Church
56 Queen Street E, at Church Street, Dundas Square (416 363 0331/www.metunited.org). Streetcar 501/subway Queen. **Service** 11am Sun. **Map** p272 G7.

Safety & security

Toronto is a safe city, but exercise common sense.

● Don't walk around with valuables. Leave them in a hotel safe, and get a receipt.
● Pulling out a map on the street makes it obvious you don't know where you are.
● Most homeless people on the streets are harmless. Still, stay away from anyone who gives you a bad vibe.
● Don't carry all your cash or cards with you at one time. Travellers' cheques are accepted almost everywhere.

Directory

Smoking

The screws are tightening on smokers. A comprehensive no-smoking law has been in effect since 2004: if you want to light up, you're going outside. Heat lamps on patios keep smokers warm on winter nights.

Study

To study in Canada, foreign students need a study permit. Depending on your country of origin, a temporary visa may also be required. Applications are through your local Canadian embassy or high consulate (*see p251*).

Ryerson University

University *350 Victoria Street, at Gould Street, Dundas Square (416 979 5000/www.ryerson.ca). Streetcar 505/subway Dundas.* **Map** *p272 G6.*
Student union *RyeSac, 380 Room A62, Victoria Street, at Gould Street, Dundas Square (416 597 0723/www.ryesac.ca). Streetcar 505/subway Dundas.* **Map** *p271/p2272 G6.*
Ryerson draws on its background as a polytechnic to deliver first-rate hands-on learning in the heart of city. It is best known for its journalism, fashion and computer programmes.

University of Toronto

University *416 978 2011/ www.utoronto.ca. Streetcar 506/subway St George or Spadina.* **Student union** *Students' Administrative Council, 12 Hart House Circle, University (416 978 4911/www.sac.utoronto.ca). Subway St George.* **Map** *p274 E5.*
The closest thing Canada has to an Ivy League institution, U of T consistently ranks among the country's top three schools. It has a range of programmes, from medicine through law to Celtic studies.

York University

University *4700 Keele Street, at Steeles Avenue West, North Toronto (416 736 2100/www.yorku.ca).* **Students' union** *York Federation of Students, 336 Student Centre, North Toronto (416 736 5324/ www.yfs.ca).* Both *Subway Downsview then bus 106.*
Though the campus is remote and ugly, York is well regarded, known for its lefty women's and environmental studies programmes and business and law schools.

Telephones

Dialling & codes

Greater Toronto has three area codes: 416, 905 and 647. Generally, businesses and residences in the city have 416 numbers, while those outside the city proper (Mississauga, Richmond Hill, Markham, Pickering) have 905 numbers; 647 often applies to mobiles.

Keep in mind that as well as being a local code, 905 is also a long-distance code for southern Ontario cities such as Oshawa and Hamilton. Dialling numbers in those cities means dialling a 1 before the code and paying a long-distance charge.

The following codes are all toll-free numbers. Depending on the company or service, some numbers may not work if calling the US. You must dial 1 before the following: 800, 855, 866, 877, 888.

Making a call

All calls within Toronto must be dialled by using a ten-digit number (the first three are the area code; dial it even if you share it). To make a long-distance call within Canada or to North America, dial 1, the area code, and then the seven-digit phone number. To call overseas, dial 011, the country code, then the number (in some cases dropping the initial zero). The country code for the **UK** is 44, for **Australia** it's 61, **New Zealand** 64, **Republic of Ireland** 353 and **South Africa** 27.

Public phones

If you can find one, payphones cost 25¢ per local call. A Bell pre-paid phonecard available from most phone shops, grocery stores and pharmacies works only in Bell phones. Dial-in phonecards are your best bet for long-distance and international calls.

Operator services

Dial 0 from any phone to speak to an operator (free from payphones). Dial 00 for the international operator.

Telephone directories

To find a number, dial 411 for information from any phone. From Bell phones the service is free. Other private phone companies charge 75¢, irrespective of whether the operator finds your listing.

Mobile phones

As in the US, Canada's mobile phone (cellphone) network operates on 1900 megaHertz. This means that US travellers should be able to use their usual handset (but should check their tariffs for costs). Tri-band phones will work throughout most of North America; quad-bands tend to give some additional coverage but there is still the odd area with no coverage at all. If you have a dual-band phone or think your tri- or quad-band phone might not work, contact your service provider to find out if there is a solution (some will arrange for you to have a temporary phone while away).

If none of this works, there are three options. If you're a frequent visitor, consider setting up your own local account. A better option is to buy a pay-as-you-go phone, starting at around $125. One of the local carriers – Fido, Bell Mobility, Rogers or Telus Mobility – will be able to help you.

Alternatively, you could rent a phone via your hotel or from a private company such as **Hello, Anywhere** (416 367 4355/1-888 729 4355, www. helloanywhere.com; credit card required) or **Cell Express** (905 812 1307/1-877 626 0216, www.cell-express.com; credit card or $350-$500 deposit required), which deliver phones to your hotel for $24-$50 a week ($50-$80 a month).

Faxes

Send faxes from corner stores or copy shops (see p164).

Time

Toronto is in the Eastern Time Zone – just like New York – which is five hours behind Greenwich Mean Time. Daylight Savings begins at 2am on the second Sunday in March and ends at 2am on the first Sunday in November.

Tipping

Tipping is expected. Bar and restaurant staff have a lower minimum wage than most Canadians. Generally, tip 15 per cent on pre-tax meal bills (add the amount you'd pay in tax – it's the same percentage), and a buck or two at the bar. Hotel cleaning staff and bellhops also deserve a buck or two. Hairdressers expect tips of between ten and 20 per cent.

Toilets

Public toilets are scarce in Toronto, so use one in a restaurant or coffee shop, though note that most are reserved for customers.

Tourist information

Ontario Travel Information Centre
Atrium on Bay, 20 Dundas Street W, at Yonge Street, Dundas Square (905 274 1721/1-800 668 2746). Subway Dundas. **Open** 10am-9pm Mon-Fri; 9.30am-7pm Sat; noon-5pm Sun. **Map** p272 G6.
Tourism Toronto
Queens Quay Terminal, 207 Queens Quay W, at York Street, Financial District (416 203 2600/1-800 363 1990/www.torontotourism.com). Subway Union Station then streetcar 509, 510. **Open** 8.30am-5pm Mon-Fri. **Map** p271/p272 F9.

Visas & immigration

Residents of Britain, the US, Australia, New Zealand and Ireland do not need visas to visit Canada. For all other visitors and immigration information, see www.cic.gc.ca/english/visit/visas.html.

Weights & measures

The metric system is used in Canada.

1 centimetre = 0.394 inches
1 metre = 3.28 feet
1 sq metre = 1.196 sq yards
1 kilometre = 0.62 miles
1 kilogramme = 2.2 pounds
1 litre = 1.76 UK pints, 2.113 US pints

When to go

Climate

Toronto has one of the mildest climates in the country, thanks to the moderating effects of Lake Ontario and a southern latitude of 44° north, on par with Florence, Italy. Winter is not as bad as the rest of Canada: the city gets less snow than it used to, but visitors should bring hats and gloves as the mercury often dips below 0°C. Toronto gets plenty of sunshine year-round. Summers are hot and humid, punctuated by thunderstorms.

Public holidays

New Year's Day (1 Jan; if a Sun, then holiday is the following Mon); **Good Friday** (Mar/Apr); **Easter Monday**; **Victoria Day** (24 May if a Mon, otherwise the preceding Mon); **Canada Day** (1 July); **Simcoe Day** (1st Mon Aug); **Labour Day** (1st Mon Sept); **Thanksgiving** (2nd Mon Oct); **Christmas** (25 Dec); **Boxing Day** (26 Dec). While government offices and most banks close on Easter Monday (Mar/Apr) and Remembrance Day (11 Nov), the majority of businesses remain open.

Women

Toronto is a relatively safe city for women. Rohypnol (the 'date rape drug') has been used at bars but a new law permits patrons to take their drink with them to the bathroom. For a list of helplines, see p252.
National Action Committee on the Status of Women
234 Eglinton Avenue E, at Mount Pleasant Road, North Toronto (416 932 1718/www.nac-cca.ca). Subway Eglinton. **Open** 9am-5pm Mon-Fri.

Climate

	High (C/F)	Low (C/F)	Rainfall
Jan	-1°/30°	-7°/19°	6.1cm/1.9in
Feb	0°/32°	-6°/21°	5.1cm/1.9in
Mar	5°/41°	-2°/28°	6.6cm/2.3in
Apr	11°/51°	4°/39°	7.0cm/2.6in
May	19°/66°	10°/50°	7.3cm/2.6in
June	23°/73°	15°/59°	7.2cm/2.6in
July	26°/78°	18°/64°	6.8cm/2.8in
Aug	25°/77°	17°/62°	8.0cm/3.2in
Sept	20°/68°	13°/55°	8.3cm/2.8in
Oct	14°/57°	7°/44°	6.5cm/2.5in
Nov	7°/44°	2°/35°	7.6cm/2.6in
Dec	2°/35°	-4°/24°	7.1cm/2.4in

Directory

Further Reference

Books

Fiction

Margaret Atwood *The Tent;* *Oryx and Crake; Life Before Man; Cat's Eye; Lady Oracle; The Robber Bride; Alias Grace*
The poet laureate of modern Toronto. Atwood's *Life Before Man*, a tense love triangle, is a terrific portrait of the city in the 1970s. *The Robber Bride* dissects female rivalry, while *Cat's Eye* and *Lady Oracle* draw on middle-class life in the '40s and '50s. *Alias Grace* paints a picture of Upper Canada in colonial times.
Robertson Davies *The Fifth Business; The Rebel Angels; What's Bred in the Bone; The Manticore*
Davies adds some magic realism to his many portrayals of Toronto.
Timothy Findley *Headhunter*
Acclaimed novel updates *Heart of Darkness* and is set in Toronto.
Vincent Lam *Bloodletting & Miraculous Cures*
Short stories about young Chinese-Canadian medical students at U of T.
Anne Michaels *Fugitive Pieces*
Acclaimed novel set in World War II Poland and moves to Toronto. All about memory, loss and landscape.
Michael Ondaatje *In the Skin of a Lion*
Ondaatje morphs landmarks such as the Bloor Street Viaduct and RC Harris Filtration Plant into places of magic, depth and consequence.
Michael Redhill *Consolation*
Bridging the 19th and 20th centuries, a tale of immigration and the arrival of photography in Toronto.
Jane Urquhart *Away*
Haunting tale begins in Ireland and ends in early-days Toronto.

Non-fiction

Eric Arthur *Toronto: No Mean City*
The definitive book on Toronto's architectural history.
William Dendy *Lost Toronto*
A portrait of the Toronto lost to the wrecking ball.
Robert Fulford *Accidental City*
A personal look at the city's coming of age, by acclaimed journalist.
Sally Gibson *Inside Toronto: Urban Interiors 1880s to 1920s*
Lives led behind the lace curtains from Victorian era to the Depression.
Geoff Pevere and Greig Dymond *Mondo Canuck*
This cheeky, exhaustive tell-all puts Canuck celebs in the spotlight.
Murray Seymour *Toronto's Ravines*
Thirty-four walks in Toronto's leafy arteries.

Sean Stanwick and Jennifer Flores *Design City Toronto*
Coffee-table tome highlighting new architectural additions to the city.

Films

Ararat
(dir. Atom Egoyan, 2002)
The acclaimed director reaches back to his Armenian roots in a film-within-a-film set in Toronto.
Bon Cop, Bad Cop
(dir. Eric Canuel, 2006)
Hugely successful police comedy sends up the cultural differences between Montreal and Toronto.
Eclipse
(dir. Jeremy Podeswa, 1994)
Tale of sexual liaisons leading up to a solar eclipse.
Exotica
(dir. Atom Egoyan, 1994)
Tales of loneliness and obsession, set in a strip club.
Goin' Down the Road
(dir. Don Shebib, 1970)
Two drifters come to Yonge Street in search of a better life. A classic.
Hollywood Bollywood
(dir. Deeptha Metha, 2002)
Cheesy musical comedy celebrates Toronto's East Indian culture.
I've Heard the Mermaids Singing (dir. Patricia Rozema, 1987)
Secretary works in Toronto gallery and must deal with self-delusion.
Last Night
(dir. Don McKellar, 1998)
The apocalypse comes to Toronto. A multi-culti cast ruminates.
Lie with Me
(dir. Clément Virgo, 2005)
A young couple has a steamy affair in a suddenly sexy Toronto.
Monkey Warfare
(dir. Reginald Harkema, 2006)
Low-lifes in Parkdale comically contemplate the scene.
Niagara
(dir. Henry Hathaway, 1953)
The Falls are upstaged by Marilyn Monroe in this noirish murder tale.
Thirty-two Short Films About Glenn Gould
(dir. Francois Girard, 1993)
An innovative bio-pic about the legendary Toronto pianist.

Music

Barenaked Ladies, *Disc One: All Their Greatest Hits (2001)*
Best-of album from jokey popsters.
Broken Social Scene *You Forgot It In People* (2001)
The album that brought this Toronto indie collective to global prominence. Moody, textured, lo-fi rock.

Bruce Cockburn *Stealing Fire* (1984). Yorkville folkie goes pop.
Cowboy Junkies *The Trinity Session* (1988)
The finest album from the Timmins clan, recorded live to one mic at the city's Church of the Holy Trinity.
Death From Above (1979) *You're A Woman, I'm A Machine*
Fiery, abrasive and smart hard rock from a duo that crashed and burned.
Final Fantasy *He Poos Clouds* (2006)
Intelligent chamber pop. Won the Polaris Prize (Canada's Mercury Prize)
Glenn Gould *A Sense of Wonder* (2002)
Gould's two miraculous recordings of Bach's Goldberg Variations.
Molly Johnson *Molly Johnson* (2000)
The downtown diva channels Dinah, Janis and Billie.
Gordon Lightfoot *Songbook* (1999)
Compilation from the legendary folkie.
Martha & the Muffins *Far Away in Time* (1988).
Contains the immortal 'Echo Beach'.
Metric *Old World Underground, Where Are You Now* (2003)
Modern rock with new-wave vibe, featuring bright star Emily Haines.
Ron Sexsmith *Time Being* (2006)
Superb songs that prick at society's conscience, plus aching ballads.
Rush *Moving Pictures* (1981); *Signals* (1982); *Spirit of Radio* (2003)
Two seminal albums from legendary sci-fi rockers, plus a greatest hits.
The Tragically Hip *Up to Here* (1989)
The second album from Ontario's hugely popular rockers.
Various artists *Jazz at Massey Hall* (1953)
A legendary concert featuring Charlie Parker, Dizzy Gillespie, Art Powell, Charles Mingus and Max Roach – together for one night only.
Neil Young *After the Goldrush* (1970); *Harvest* (1972).
The living legend grew up in TO and played the Yorkville scene.

Websites

www.toronto.ca
Comprehensive guide to attractions.
www.martiniboys.com
Bar, club and restaurant reviews.
www.cbc.ca
News from public broadcaster CBC.
www.topost.ca
Archival/amateur photographs that lovingly portray the city.
www.torontolife.com
Listings/reviews from monthly mag.
www.nowtoronto.com
Listings/reviews from indie weekly.

Index

Note: page numbers in
bold indicate section(s)
giving key information
on a topic; *italics*
indicate photos.

Advertisers' Index

Place of interest and/or entertainment	▧
Railway & bus stations	▨
Parks	▧
Hospitals/universities	▧
Neighbourhood	MOSS PARK
Subway station	Ⓢ
Bus route	—75—
Streetcar route	—501—
Subway route	——

Maps

Southern Ontario

Elliot Lake

Sturgeon Falls

Sudbury

North Bay

Lake Nipissing

17

17

Killarney Provincial Park

ONTARIO

Algonquin Provincial Park

Gore Bay

69

Manitoulin Island

Georgian Bay

Huntsville

South Baymouth

Parry Sound

COTTAGE

11

Tobermory

Gravenhurst

MUSKOKA

11

Wiarton

Midland

Orillia

Lake Huron

Southampton

26

Collingwood

Barrie

Lake Simcoe

Durham

Alliston

Keswick

400

Kincardine

6

Kleinburg (p240)

404

Markham

Oshawa

21

Elora (p240)

Brampton

Scarborough

TORONTO

pp268-269

Goderich

86

St Jacobs (p240)

Guelph

Mississauga

Stratford (p241)

Kitchener

401

Burlington

Lake

St Catharines

Niagara-on-the-Lake (p237)

St Marys (p243)

Cambridge

HAMILTON

Grimsby

WINE COUNTRY

London

Brantford

403

Beamsville

Niagara Falls (p229)

Buffalo

59

24

6

3

Fort Erie

MICHIGAN

Sarnia

402

69

Petrolia

Long Point Bay

62

Dunkirk

Pontiac

94

Chatham

401

90

DETROIT

Lake Saint Clair

Windsor

86

Jamestown

Leamington

Lake Erie

Erie

Warren

Monroe

62

6

90

79

0   100 km

0   50 miles

Painesville

OHIO

Oil City

© Copyright Time Out Group 2007

Euclid

322

Lorain

Cleveland

19

80

80

Toronto Overview

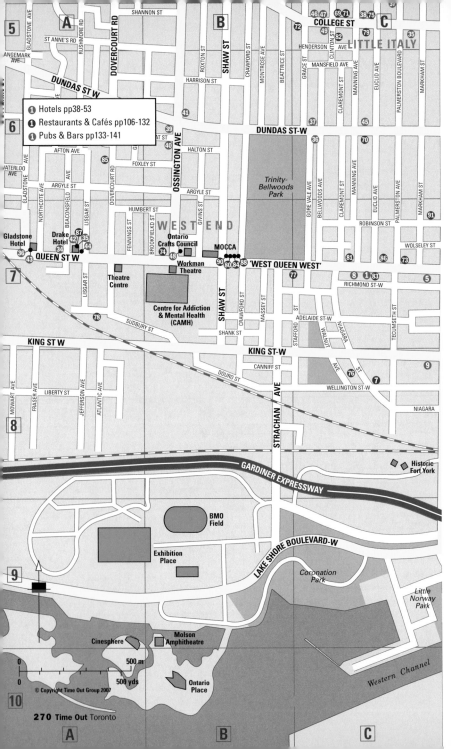

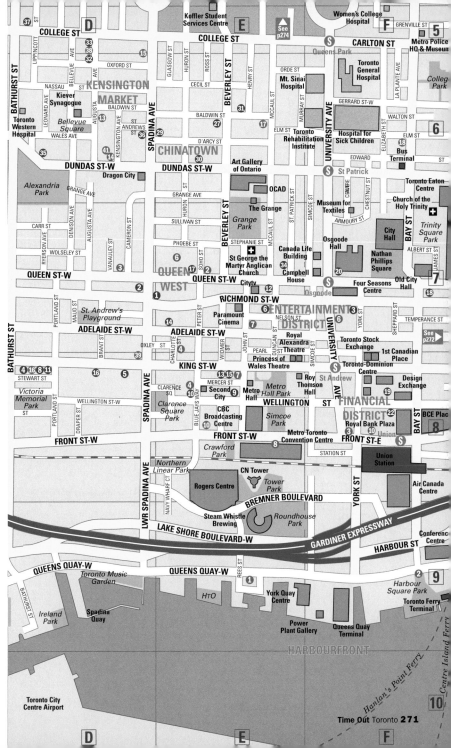

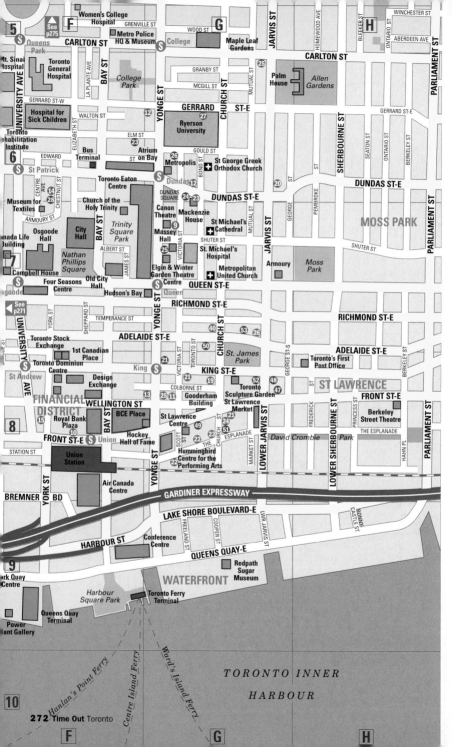

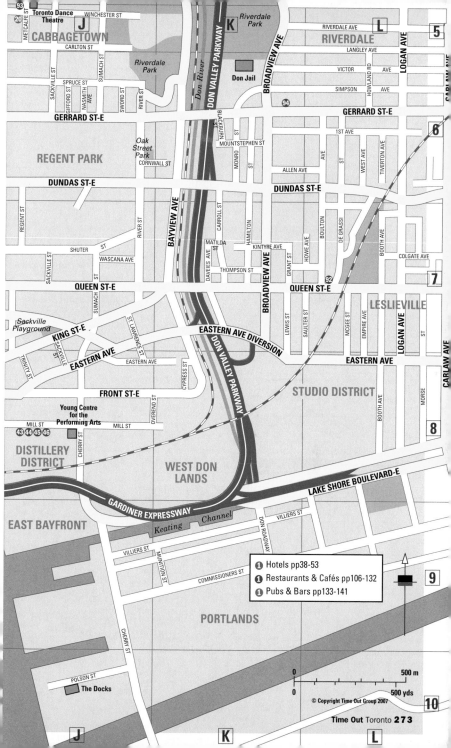

93
20

Toronto Dance
Theatre **J**

WINCHESTER ST

CABBAGETOWN

CARLTON ST

SPRUCE ST

GIFFORD ST
NASMITH AVE
SUMACH ST
SWORD ST
RIVER ST

Riverdale
Park

REGENT PARK

Oak
Street
Park

CORNWALL ST

GERRARD ST-E

DUNDAS ST-E

REGENT ST

SHUTER
ST

RIVER ST

WASCANA AVE

SACKVILLE ST

SUMACH
ST

QUEEN ST-E

Sackville
Playground

KING ST-E

EASTERN AVE

ST LAWRENCE ST
EASTERN AVE

CYPRESS ST

FRONT ST-E

OVEREND ST

Young Centre
for the
Performing Arts

43 44 45 46
CHERRY ST

MILL ST

MILL ST

**DISTILLERY
DISTRICT**

EAST BAYFRONT

GARDINER EXPRESSWAY

POLSON ST

The Docks

CHERRY ST

J

Riverdale
Park **K**

Don River
DON VALLEY PARKWAY

Don Jail

BLACKBURN
ST

MOUNTSTEPHEN ST

MONRO
ST

BAYVIEW AVE

CARROLL ST

MATILDA
ST
DAVIES ST
THOMPSON ST

HAMILTON
ST

EASTERN AVE DIVERSION

DON VALLEY PARKWAY

**WEST DON
LANDS**

Keating Channel

VILLIERS ST

VILLIERS ST

ST NICHOLAS ST
MUNITION ST

COMMISSIONERS ST

PORTLANDS

K

RIVERDALE **L**

RIVERDALE AVE

LANGLEY AVE

VICTOR
AVE

HOWLAND RD
AVE

SIMPSON
AVE

LOGAN AVE
CARLAW AVE

5

94

GERRARD ST-E

1ST AVE

AVE
ST
WEST AVE
TIVERTON AVE

6

ALLEN AVE

DUNDAS ST-E

BOULTON
DE GRASSI
BOOTH AVE

COLGATE AVE

7

KINTYRE AVE

HOWE AVE

GRANT ST

92

QUEEN ST-E

BROADVIEW AVE

LEWIS ST
SAULTER ST

MCGEE ST
EMPIRE AVE

LESLIEVILLE

LOGAN AVE
ST

EASTERN AVE

STUDIO DISTRICT

BOOTH AVE

MORSE
ST

CARLAW AVE

8

LAKE SHORE BOULEVARD-E

DON ROADWAY

9

❶	Hotels pp38-53
❶	Restaurants & Cafés pp106-132
❶	Pubs & Bars pp133-141

0   500 m

0   500 yds

© Copyright Time Out Group 2007

10

L

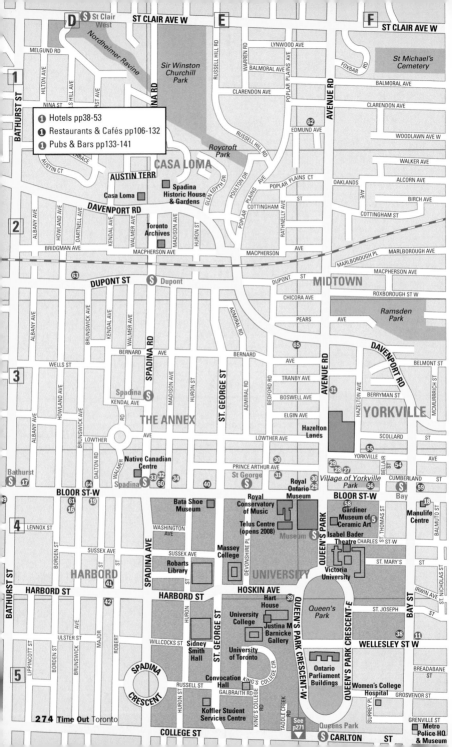

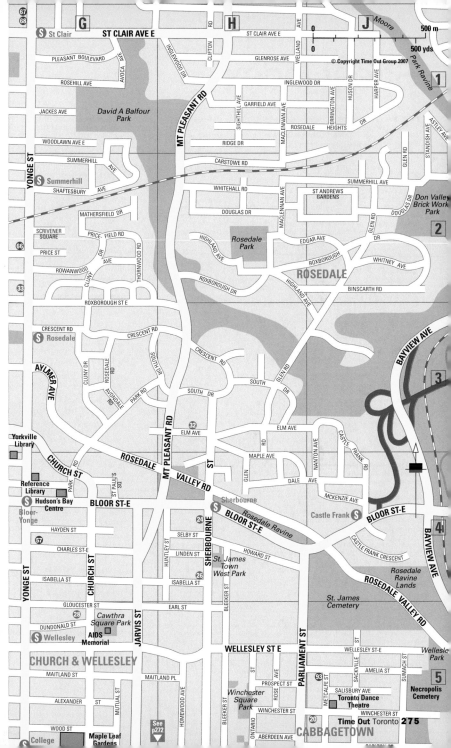

Street Index